THE QUESTION OF SOLIDARITY IN LAW AND POLITICS

What is the problem to which solidarity is invoked as a solution? How are solidarity schemes narrated? Which particular interests are pursued in its name? In this book, leading authorities in law, philosophy and political sciences respond to the solidarity question, drawing on debates on international law, international aid, collective security, joint action, market organization and neo-liberalism, international human rights across the North/South divide, African mobility, transnational labour in the digital age and populism. This volume captures the shifting nature of long-held historical assumptions on solidarity. Its twelve chapters open up for differentiated understandings of solidarity in law and politics beyond discursive cliché or ideological appropriation, bringing crises of the past into conversation with the crises of today. This book is also available as Open Access on Cambridge Core.

Eleni Karageorgiou is Senior Researcher in Public International Law. Her PhD thesis on solidarity in refugee protection has been awarded the Oscar II's stipend by Lund University. She has received funding for postdoctoral research, which led to the publication of the edited volume *Law, Solidarity and the Limits of Social Europe: Constitutional Tensions for EU Integration* (Edward Elgar, 2022).

Gregor Noll is Professor of International Law at the School of Business, Economics and Law, Gothenburg, and a guest researcher at the Swedish Defence University, Stockholm. He has written on subjects in the theory of international law, migration law, international humanitarian law and law and AI.

The Question of Solidarity in Law and Politics

Edited by

ELENI KARAGEORGIOU
Lund University

GREGOR NOLL
Gothenburg University

CAMBRIDGE
UNIVERSITY PRESS

CAMBRIDGE
UNIVERSITY PRESS

Shaftesbury Road, Cambridge CB2 8EA, United Kingdom

One Liberty Plaza, 20th Floor, New York, NY 10006, USA

477 Williamstown Road, Port Melbourne, VIC 3207, Australia

314–321, 3rd Floor, Plot 3, Splendor Forum, Jasola District Centre, New Delhi – 110025, India

103 Penang Road, #05-06/07, Visioncrest Commercial, Singapore 238467

Cambridge University Press is part of Cambridge University Press & Assessment, a department of the University of Cambridge.

We share the University's mission to contribute to society through the pursuit of education, learning and research at the highest international levels of excellence.

www.cambridge.org
Information on this title: www.cambridge.org/9781009580540

DOI: 10.1017/9781009580588

When citing this work, please include a reference to the DOI 10.1017/9781009580588

First published 2026

Cover image: AGAPE VIII by Hampe, Susanne

A catalogue record for this publication is available from the British Library

A Cataloging-in-Publication data record for this book is available from the Library of Congress

ISBN 978-1-009-58054-0 Hardback
ISBN 978-1-009-58056-4 Paperback

Contents

Notes on Contributors

Peo Hansen is Professor of Political Science at the Institute for Research on Migration, Ethnicity and Society (REMESO), Linköping University. He is the author of several books on European integration, including (with Stefan Jonsson: Bloomsbury, 2014) *Eurafrica: The Untold History of European Integration and Colonialism* and the EUSA award-winning *A Modern Migration Theory: An Alternative Economic Approach to Failed EU Policy* (Cambridge University Press, 2021).

Lisa Herzog is Professor of Political Philosophy at the Faculty of Philosophy of the University of Groningen; since 2021 she has been the Director of the Center for Philosophy, Politics and Economics. Herzog has published on the philosophical dimensions of markets, liberalism and social justice, ethics in organizations and the future of work. The current focuses of her work are workplace democracy, professional ethics and the role of knowledge in democracies.

Haris Jamil is a PhD candidate at Melbourne Law School. His PhD research examines the history of the concept of state practice in international law and its role in the making of the state. He has previously taught at the Faculty of Law, University of Delhi.

Richard Joyce is Senior Lecturer at Melbourne Law School. His research focuses on the history, theory and political economy of international law. He is the author of *Competing Sovereignties* (Routledge, 2012) and is currently leading a project funded by the Australian Research Council on 'International Law and the Challenge of Populism'.

Eleni Karageorgiou is Senior Researcher in Public International Law at the Faculty of Law at Lund University. Prior to that, she held positions at the University of Gothenburg, School of Business, Economics and Law and the Raoul Wallenberg Institute of Human Rights and Humanitarian Law. Her current research includes an investigation of the implications of EU externalization and border practices in the area of asylum, as well as a critical enquiry into the rules of international responsibility attribution.

Martti Koskenniemi is Professor Emeritus of International Law at the University of Helsinki. He is a corresponding fellow of the British Academy and a member of the American Academy of Arts and Sciences. His main publications include *From Apology to Utopia: The Structure of International Legal Argument* (Cambridge University Press, 2005), *The Gentle Civilizer of Nations: The Rise and Fall of International Law 1870–1960* (Cambridge University Press, 2001) and *To the Uttermost Parts of the Earth: Legal Imagination and International Power 1300–1870* (Cambridge University Press, 2021). His most recent publication is a joint work with Professor David Kennedy (Harvard), *Of Law and the World. Critical Conversations on Power, History and Political Economy* (Harvard University Press, 2023).

Charles Romain Mbele is Professor Emeritus of Modern and Contemporary Negro-African Philosophy at the Higher Teachers' Training College of the University of Yaoundé 1 (Cameroon). Interested in the metaphysical and political problems arising from German idealism, Marxisms and Negro-African philosophies of liberation from the mid eighteenth century to today, he develops a critical approach to new postcolonial and decolonial methodologies. He is the author of the following books: *Essay on Postcolonialism as a Code of Inequality* (CLÉ, 2010), *Pan-Africanism or Postcolonialism? The Current Struggle in Africa* (L'Harmattan, 2015), *The Theocratic Ghetto* (L'Harmattan, 2017), *System and Freedom in Modern Negro-African Philosophy* (Silex, 2018); and 'Emancipating Oneself from Merchandise', in Hadrien Buclin, Joseph Daher, Christakis Georgiou and Pierre Raboud (eds.), *Thinking about Emancipation. Capitalist Offensives and International Resistance*, preface by Jean Batou (La Dispute, 2013). Since 2014, he has been the Executive Secretary of the Kwame Nkrumah Philosophy Club. Finally, he is, on the one hand, Scientific Coordinator of the W. E. B. Du Bois Institute on Global and China-Africa Studies (Yaoundé) and, on the other hand, Coordinator for the Central Africa and Indian Ocean Region of the Pan-African Federalist Movement (PAFM-Bamako).

Frédéric Mégret is Professor of Law and holds the Hans and Tamar Oppenheimer Chair in Public International Law at McGill University's Faculty of Law. He is the co-editor with Philip Alston of *The United Nations and Human Rights: A Critical Appraisal* (Oxford University

Press, 2020); with Immi Tallgren of *The Dawn of a Discipline: International Criminal Justice and its Early Exponents* (Cambridge University Press, 2020) and, with Kevin Jon Heller, Sarah Nouwen, Jens David Ohlin and Darryl Robinson of *The Oxford Handbook of International Criminal Law* (Oxford University Press, 2020).

Patricia Mindus is Professor of Practical Philosophy at Uppsala University in Sweden, researcher at the Institute for Future Studies in Stockholm and 2023–2024 Paris Institute for Advanced Study Fellow. She directs multidisciplinary research on citizenship and migration. Her expertise is in legal and political theory. She has authored and edited a number of books including the award-winning *Cambridge Companion to Legal Positivism* (Cambridge University Press, 2021).

Eva Nanopoulos is Reader in Law at Queen Mary University of London. She is author of *The Juridification of Individual Sanctions and the Politics of EU Law* (Hart, 2020) and co-editor of *The Crisis Behind the Euro-Crisis: The Euro-Crisis as a Multi-Dimensional Systemic Crisis of the EU* (Cambridge University Press, 2019) and *Capitalist States and Marxist State Theory* (Palgrave, 2023). She is the co-director of the Queen Mary Centre of Law and Society in a Global Context and a member of the editorial collective @legalform, a forum for Marxist analysis and critique. She is currently on a Leverhulme Research Fellowship working on her new book, *A Decolonial Legal History of Sanctions*.

Gregor Noll is Professor of International Law at the School of Business, Economics and Law at Gothenburg University and held the Torsten Söderberg Research Professorate at the School of Business, Economics and Law, Gothenburg 2020–2023. Noll has written extensively on the theory of international law, on migration law, on international humanitarian law as well as on law and AI. He has developed close ties to disciplines such as political theory, the medical sciences, history and demography from an empirical foothold in legal scholarship. He is currently working on apocalyptic law, on shared responsibility and on the Stauffenberg brothers' exercise of *pouvoir constituant*.

Obiora Chinedu Okafor is the Edward B. Burling Chair in International Law and Institutions at Johns Hopkins University's School of Advanced International Studies in Washington DC, USA. He also served as the UN Independent Expert on Human Rights and International Solidarity from 2017 to 2023 and is a former chairperson of the UN Human Rights Council Advisory Committee. He has held the York Research Chair in International and Transnational Legal Studies at the Osgoode Hall Law

School of York University, Toronto, Canada, and the Gani Fawehinmi Distinguished Chair in Human Rights Law at the Nigerian Institute of Advanced Legal Studies.

Sundhya Pahuja is Melbourne Laureate Professor and Director of the Laureate Program in Global Corporations and International Law at the University of Melbourne. Her interdisciplinary work investigates the relationship between international law and inequality within and between states. She is the author of *Decolonising International Law: Development, Economic Growth and the Politics of Universality* (Cambridge University Press, 2012) and is currently involved in two Australian Research Council-funded projects – 'Global Corporations and International Law' and 'International Law and the Challenge of Populism'.

Sally J. Scholz is Professor of Philosophy at Villanova University. Her research in social and political philosophy focuses on solidarity, oppression, violence and just war theory. Her publications include the books *On de Beauvoir* (Wadsworth Publishing, 2000), *On Rousseau* (Wadsworth Publishing, 2001), *Political Solidarity* (Penn State Press, 2008) and *Feminism: A Beginner's Guide* (One World Publishing, 2010). She co-edited *Peacemaking: Lessons from the Past, Vision for the Future* (Rodopi Press, 2000), *The Contradictions of Freedom: Philosophical Essays on Simone de Beauvoir's 'Les Mandarins'* (SUNY Press, 2005) and *Philosophical Perspectives on Democracy in the 21st Century* (Springer, 2014). Scholz has served as chair of the American Philosophical Association Committee on Lectures, Publications and Research (2011–2014) and President of the North American Society for Social Philosophy (2015–2019).

Bas Schotel is Assistant Professor at the University of Amsterdam, Department of Jurisprudence. Schotel's work concentrates on legal arrangements and legal thinking that promote and hamper individual legal protection. Bas is the author of *On the Right of Exclusion: Law, Ethics and Immigration Policy* (Routledge, 2012). He also published on inter alia Frontex's operational powers, authoritarianism and administrative law, the legal history of asylum in comparison to the Dublin Regulation and EU migration deals. Recently, Bas has examined long-term pre-removal immigration detention in Europe from both a legal (*German Law Journal*, 2005) and a philosophical perspective (*European Public Law*, forthcoming).

Foreword

MARTTI KOSKENNIEMI

'*Of labour and struggle, Solidarity will rise!*' Thus opens the 'Song of Solidarity' by the Finnish left-wing vocal group *Agit-Prop* from the 1970s, the great decade of politicization, eventual over-politicization and collapse of one type of far-left student radicalism. I remember well how the marching tune sent shivers down my spine. Listening to it now, it still does. I was never a far-left activist. But, like almost everyone across the political spectrum, I was drawn to this song, like many others of its kind. Whatever may be said of far-left student activism of that era, at least the songs they sang and, outsiders suspected, the parties where those songs were sung, were far better than anyone else had to offer. And, even as one did not admire the Soviet Union or participate in solidarity tourism to Berlin 'the Capital of the DDR', one still has nostalgia for that period, not only to its musical culture but also its steadfast faith in the possibility of a better tomorrow, a tomorrow created not out of leisure and entertainment but of '*labour and struggle*'.

One of the most touching recent invocations of that period is Didier Eribon's *Returning to Reims*, where the philosopher travels from Paris to his home town after a long absence in order to deal with the aftermath of his father's death. Going through old photographs with his mother he gradually becomes acquainted with memories from his father's life – a father from whom he had been alienated as a teenager and whose attitudes and life as a worker he had detested. The family had once voted communist but had since turned into supporters of the Front National. Their racism and prejudice had now found a new home in the extreme right. With one significant exception, however. When in the 1960s and 1970s there had been a strike, as there often was, or other protest against employers, then distinctions between the 'French' on the one side and immigrants, aliens or 'Arabs' on the other, disappeared. Its place was taken, however temporarily, by the call for the unity of 'workers' against 'patrons'. Of such solidarity, the young Didier, himself a Trotskyite, had possessed no awareness. The world of *labour and struggle* that framed his family's life had seemed only repulsive. Which is why he had used his education, exceptional in his milieu, by moving to Paris so as to 'save himself' (his words) from his father's fate. Returning now, he encountered a past world of *solidarity*, of which he had never had more than a theoretical concept. [1]

Hard to say what one should think of that period – the European post-war of *labour and struggle*, the time of the *trente glorieuses*, the welfare state and flourishing social democracy. And 'communism', of course. Eribon's parents had been communists, just like the members of Agit Prop and many other seekers of solidarity, a world much misunderstood today. How does that compare with the third decade of the twenty-first century? There is enormous wealth and opportunity, but people like Eribon's parents, workers in a provincial town, would still lack access to it. And there is also anxiety and cynicism – cynicism about society, its politics, economics, its technology, cynicism about the future, even doubt if there will be one. Progress that was promised for the *labour and struggle* of the post-war period did not reach that generation's grandchildren. Instead, there is an endlessly broadening gap between those with incomprehensible amounts of wealth and those who, like Eribon's parents, survive with the barest minimum. Surveying the processes of privatization, collapsing public health and welfare services, decaying rural communities, immigration crises and environmental collapse makes one *almost* nostalgic about communism. At least today's social democracy would seem unrecognizable to post-war labour activists. Instead, the political space is penetrated by anti-democratic and exclusionary movements hostile to the ideals of emancipation that *labour and struggle* were once expected to make a reality. On the contrary, there is little confidence that the political process or the increase of scientific knowledge, once inseperable from emancipation, could uphold the common good. Might not even mentioning the common good sound like a suspect effort to exercise hegemony?

Nostalgia may be an understandable reaction to a sense of pervasive crisis, such as present media conduits offer as the appropriate characterization of the present. Is the newly found interest in 'solidarity' of which this book is an example also an exercise in nostalgia? Perhaps. Eribon's experience on his return home is likely to be familiar to many people. The post-war efforts to build the welfare state, the reassuring bedrock of the Cold War and the time when *labour and struggle* left no time to draw sharp dividing lines of 'identity' between and inside communities. Class conflict offered everyone a place and meaning. There's a reason why today's reactionary propaganda is formulated

[1] Didier Eribon, *Retour à Reims* (Paris: Fayard, 2009), especially pp. 150–153.

as 'taking *back* control'. 'Back' to where, precisely? Nobody can claim a monopoly to the use of a fighting word such as 'solidarity'. The breadth of its appeal is brought by the lightness of its substance. Perhaps we are drawn to solidarity because it carries the memory of what it was to believe that one was engaged in *labour and struggle* for a better future in common. Not that many words today speak about a shared future, even less of a future that is better *precisely because it is shared*, because it embodies a collective project of one or another kind. Might we feel drawn to 'solidarity' owing to its performative nature – the way already invoking it is to take a step or two towards the achievement of that sense of 'belonging' somewhere of which 'solidarity' speaks.

'Solidarity' is a messy word – which is not to say that it could not be subjected to the kinds of analytical, sociological, psychological, legal and other analyses of which this volume consists. Such analyses illuminate the many ambiguities in the concept. Illuminate, but never quite capture. Who seeks a definition is bound to be disappointed. Its meaning is its use. Like any fighting word, we feel 'solidarity's' power most when we use it to defend ourselves and our allies against our adversaries – the workers and 'patrons' of Eribon's narrative. To receive a grasp of the word and its power it is therefore useful to describe specific historical situations, moments of struggle, where the word has done, or could do its work. Many essays in this volume follow this path. Such descriptions have both a descriptive and a normative side – they inform us about past struggles and vest them with emotive and moral meaning. We learn both sympathy and outrage through them.

But human emotions and moral languages are fickle. Perhaps solidarity is a little like love in this regard. Or something like the *Event* in Alain Badiou's sense, breaking the monotony of daily routine, something based neither on logic nor (neo-liberal) reason but that nevertheless calls for action because the situation to which it refers somehow calls for it. [2] Perhaps it responds to the implicit appeal of the other, within or outside a religious frame. Or maybe it is just a strategic move in a struggle. As Chapter 2 suggests, it might involve taking a risk – though again, not always. As many of us 1970s students remember, it can also focus on people far away. David Featherstone gives the example of Cardiff harbour workers boycotting Italian ships during the Italo-Abyssinian War in 1935. [3] Both he and I recall the enthusiastic welcome

[2] See e.g. Alain Badiou, *Ethics: An Essay on the Understanding of Evil*, trans. Peter Hallward (London: Verso, 2001).

[3] David Featherstone, *Solidarity: Hidden Histories and Geographies of Internationalism* (New York: Bloomsbury, 2012), pp. 15–18.

given by many European countries to Chilean refugees after the Pinochet coup of 1973 – quite a striking contrast to how our countries now view the refugees from Africa or the Middle East.

Perhaps indeed there is sometimes an 'eventness' in solidarity, but not always. It may also emerge and flourish in a long, intimate relationship, the comradeship of *labour and struggle* for example. 'Solidarity of the workers'. As Eribon points out, there is usually also an element of adversity – the employer, the capitalist or perhaps the national enemy that endows the word its emotive and political power. After all, 'national solidarity' is never greater than at times of war. Solidarity also often invokes a hierarchical contrast between a dominant party and the underdog, the poor, the homeless, birthplace of the 'sympathy' that Adam Smith invoked in his early research on the character of moral sentiment. This may also be the origin of its juridical translation in welfare legislation, the bureaucratic sibling of charity. But, as Samuel Moyn, among others, has pointed out, seeking to care for the poor is surely *not enough*. [4] Solidarity is not only about the floor but also about the ceiling, the distance that law and social institutions create or maintain between those at the top and those at the bottom. And yet, merely invoking a word is insufficient. It is good to remember that a parallel gap between the rich and poor also existed in *fin-de-siècle* France at the very moment when the liberal elites of the Third Republic were propounding the ideology of 'solidarism'. [5] Ruling in the name of solidarity may express sympathy to the less well off – or it may work simply to silence them. As Chapter 4 points out, offering assistance may be an act of charity as well as an insult.

Many of the chapters within this book enquire into the relations of law and solidarity. That theme points historically to the organization of European societies in response to the rise of industrialization in the nineteenth century, the decreasing power of religion and tradition and the rise of massive urban poverty and dislocation. The liberal legislators of the period were keen to provide for a society of individual rights, especially property rights, and to make sure that the public sphere does not intervene too much in how they exercise those rights. The experiences of the French Revolution were often sufficient to persuade others not to try to legislate about solidarity, at least not in terms of someone actually enjoying a *right* to assistance (*secours publics*) as

4 Samuel Moyn, *Not Enough, Human Rights in an Unequal World* (Cambridge, MA: Harvard University Press, 2018).

5 I have discussed this in Martti Koskenniemi, *The Gentle Civilizer of Nations: The Rise and Fall of International Law 1870–1960* (New York: Cambridge University Press, 2001).

provided by the furiously socio-revolutionary Constitution of 1793. [6] It was better to separate law from morality and keep the extra-legal notion of charity alive in the sphere of personal virtue where it could be enlisted to alleviate the massive problems of liberal law. As Chapter 3 points out, it is possible to see the operation of this distinction also in the way today's human rights law distinguishes between political and social rights. Then, as now, the ruling view was that the need of assistance is both utterly indeterminate and endless so it could not be made subject to legal sanction. To think otherwise, it is assumed, would mean laying an unlimited burden on those whose rights were supposed precisely to prevent this. [7] It would be the path of socialism. There is a reason why the concept of 'solidarity' has been confined in liberal law to a certain type of contractual liability. [8]

Eventually, the classics of sociology found ways to explain why, despite the limited degree to which liberal laws could accommodate duties of solidarity, the problems of modern society still did not lead to collapse. Solidarity could be 'organic', founded on the interdependence it created between utterly different lives; *Gemeinschaft* persisted even at the end of tradition, though with changed forms. [9] Further studies of ideology, hegemony and the dialectic and cynicism of reason produced further explanations for the puzzling fact that, while revolution took place in Russia, a society least likely to having reached the Marxian tipping point, countries with much more advanced capitalist relations of production could go on re-imagining themselves as 'welfare-states'. Many of the chapters in this book quite properly rehearse aspects of this (European) story.

But many chapters also discuss solidarity as an international matter. This has been a classical aspect of the use of the concept, appearing already in Marx and Engels' *Communist Manifesto* in 1848, although today the focus has shifted to the relations between the Global North and South. The word is also invoked extensively in the context of human rights advocacy, especially in efforts to deal with the plight of refugees and migrants. If this is a 'left' form of

[6] In 1794, the mandatory provision of assistance as a 'right' was removed and replaced by the charitable idea of *bienfaisance public*.

[7] This theme is usefully developed in François Ewald, *The Birth of Solidarity: The History of the French Welfare State*, edited by Melinda Cooper (Durham, NC: Duke University Press, 2020), pp. 5–29.

[8] Karl H. Metz, 'Solidarity and History: Institutions and Conceptions of Solidarity in 19th Century Europe', in Kurt Bayertz (ed.), *Solidarity* (Dordrecht: Kluwer, 1999), pp. 192–194.

[9] The references are, of course, for 'organic solidarity', Emile Durkheim, *The Division of Labour in Society* (New York: The Free Press, 1997 [French original 1893), pp. 68–175 and for '*Gemeinschaft*', Ferdinand Tönnies, *Community and Civil Society* (Cambridge: Cambridge University Press, 2012 [German original 1887]), 22–51.

solidarity in today's international law and politics, its 'right' version surely lies in the way it can be used to isolate domestic community from whatever outside source seems to threaten its normality. Is a military alliance a system of solidarity or a system of hegemony? The distance from the call of the workers of the world to unite in the nineteenth century to today's debates about the provision of F-35 fighter planes to more or less everyone in the US sphere of influence is a graphic demonstration of the flexibility of the concept.

Despite all the conceptual, philosophical, moral and legal difficulties, 'solidarity' has much staying power and that is a good thing too. Even as it is more a platform for engagement than an algorithm with fixed results, it does keep alive hugely important themes about how to live together in a world of identity and difference. If today's greatest problems are those of inequality, both local and global, and the consequent erosion of democracy and the public services, its presence is a constant reminder that if one wants to change that situation, what is needed is *labour and struggle*.

Introduction

It Is the Best of Times; It Is the Worst of Times

ELENI KARAGEORGIOU AND GREGOR NOLL

I.1 WE KNOW IT WHEN WE SEE IT: SOLIDARITY AND STRUGGLE

When this volume was initially conceived, Ruth Maddison's exhibition titled 'it was the best of times, it was the worst of times' was on display at the Centre for Contemporary Photography in Melbourne. It included Australian solidarity posters from the 1970s and 1980s, documenting the struggles of the women's movement, gay liberation, Vietnam, nuclear, anti-fascist and other protests; the fight for equality and equal pay, the fight against discrimination, as well as the fight for fairness, acceptance and respect for all, within Australian society.

With compassion and understanding flowing together in them, the feminist photographer's pictures were seen to serve 'a testificatory function – related to *both* a person who has witnessed these events (the artist) *and* an object used as evidence (the photograph)'.[1] In the same vein, this volume's point of departure has been that, by using the language of solidarity, we – consciously or not – participate in the politics of it. Authors' testimonies on solidarity as a norm, a process, a practice, a vocabulary creating polyperspectivity – not so much in terms of what the author sees in individual cases, but in what they see directed by the actors under investigation over a span of time in history.

From the start, our intent has been to engage in a double move: to deploy history as an interpretive practice – a theory, a methodology, a philosophy – with which to engage law; and, simultaneously, to offer history as a substantive arena in which other interpretive practices from across a broader array of disciplines within the humanities and social sciences can engage with law.

[1] M. Bunyan, 'Review: "Ruth Maddison: It was the best of times, it was the worst of times" at the centre for contemporary photography, Melbourne' Art Blart, 9 April 2021, available at: https://artblart.com/2021/04/09/review-ruth-maddison-it-was-the-best-of-times-it-was-the-worst-of-times-at-the-centre-for-contemporary-photography-melbourne/ (last accessed 6 April 2023).

I.2 WHERE FROM?

Solidarity appears in international discourse as a fundamental value, incorporated into international legal norms and fostering cooperation in a world of interdependent states to address calamities and power asymmetries.[2] It is also cast as a principle of international law reflecting the unity and trust between states in achieving a common purpose by sharing benefits and responsibilities.[3] In yet another trope, solidarity figures as an ethical ideal that foregrounds the element of membership and belonging.[4] However, browsing international law textbooks, handbooks and anthologies suggests that solidarity has attracted far less scholarly attention and intellectual exploration than other core concepts such as justice, human rights and sovereignty, shaping our understanding of contemporary international law and politics. Neither has the genealogy of international solidarity been sufficiently addressed, although Martti Koskenniemi's *The Gentle Civilizer of Nations*[5] has paved the way for a wider mapping.

Recent analysis on globally significant crises and emergencies, including the question of genocide and violations being committed by the Israeli government against Palestinians,[6] the war of aggression against Ukraine and their bearing on the economy on micro and macro level, food, energy and mass migration,[7] the COVID-19 pandemic and its repercussions on global

[2] UNGA Res 193 (2004) UN doc A/RES/59/193 on the Promotion of a democratic and equitable international order, 4 lit. f. For a comprehensive analysis, see H. Krunke, H. Petersen and I. Manners (eds.), *Transnational Solidarity: Concept, Challenges and Opportunities* (Cambridge: Cambridge University Press, 2020). Also, for a fresh take on cooperative practices and questions of interdependence, see Bernard E. Harcourt, *Cooperation: A Political, Economic, and Social Theory* (New York: Columbia University Press, 2024).

[3] R. Wolfrum and C. Kojima (eds.), *Solidarity: A Structural Principle of International Law* (Heidelberg: Springer Verlag, 2010). For more recent accounts, see Cecilia M. Bailliet (ed.), *Research Handbook on International Solidarity and the Law*, Research Handbooks in International Law series (Cheltenham: Edward Elgar, 2024); Eva Kassoti and Narin Idriz (eds.), *The Principle of Solidarity: International and EU Law Perspectives* (The Hague: T. M. C. Asser Press, 2023).

[4] M. Pensky, *The Ends of Solidarity Discourse Theory in Ethics and Politics* (Albany: SUNY Press, 2008).

[5] M. Koskenniemi, *The Gentle Civilizer of Nations: The Rise and Fall of International Law 1870–1960* (Cambridge: Cambridge University Press, 2001).

[6] See ICJ, *Application of the Convention on the Prevention and Punishment of the Crime of Genocide in the Gaza Strip* (South Africa *v* Israel), 26 January 2024, followed by the ICJ's Advisory Opinion on the *Legal Consequences Arising from the Policies and Practices of Israel in the Occupied Palestinian Territory, including East Jerusalem*, 19 July 2024.

[7] AJIL Unbound by Symposium, *Ukraine and the International Order*, Volume 116/2022, 124–159.

governance,[8] the Trump administration and the rise of populism,[9] the constitutional crisis of the European Union,[10] the 2015 European refugee reception crisis,[11] the 2008 financial crisis,[12] as well as global heating and environmental challenges[13] reflect the extent to which solidarity is taken to have delivered or not. Yet, for all its merits, much of that analysis takes the concept for granted. It hardly offers any inquiry into baseline assumptions operating in law and policy debates: what is the problem that solidarity is invoked as a solution to, how are solidarity schemes narrated and which particular interests are pursued in its name?

I.3 WHERE TO?

The novelty of this book lies precisely here; in the midst of reflexive invocations of solidarity in two prominently exposed armed conflicts, and in the aftermath of a global pandemic[14] we take issue with the concept's structure, we identify critical junctures in the process of its development, including concepts it eclipsed, and map factors triggering changes in what solidarity denotes. Our engagement covers the whole spectrum of solidarity, be it as a

8 A. Peters, International Law between Covid-19 and the Next Pandemic, Max Planck Institute for Comparative Public Law & International Law (MPIL) Research Paper No. 2022-18.

9 B. Siim, A. Krasteva and A. Saarinen (eds.), *Citizens' Activism and Solidarity Movements Contending with Populism* (Basingstoke; Palgrave MacMillan, 2019).

10 X. Groussot and E. Karageorgiou, 'Solidarity and the Crisis of Values in the European Union' (2023) 6 *Nordic Journal of European Law* 29; E. Nanopoulos and F. Vergis (eds.), *The Crisis behind the Eurocrisis: The Eurocrisis as a Multidimensional Systemic Crisis of the EU* (Cambridge: Cambridge University Press, 2019). For a bottoms-up approach to solidarity and crises in Europe, see Ch. Lahusen, U. Zschache and M. Kousis (eds.), *Transnational Solidarity in Times of Crises: Citizen Organisations and Collective Learning in Europe*, Palgrave Studies in European Political Sociology (Switzerland: Palgrave Macmillan, 2021).

11 V. Stoyanova and E. Karageorgiou (eds.), *The New Asylum and Transit Countries in Europe: During and in the Aftermath of the 2015/2016 Crisis*, International Refugee Law series (Leiden: Brill, 2019); D Della Porta (ed.), *Solidarity Mobilizations in the 'Refugee Crisis' Contentious Moves* (Basingstoke: Palgrave, 2018).

12 Among others, K. Schmalenbach, S. Kirste, S. Puntscher-Riekmann, D. Wydra, K.-P. Sommermann, H. Brunkhorst, S. Scholz, M.T. Kotzur, H. Pülzl and E. Stolz (eds.), 'Transnational Solidarity: An Interdisciplinary Approach' (2014) 52 *Archiv des Völkerrechts* (Special Issue).

13 See e.g. Usha Natarajan, 'Climate Justice and the Right to Solidarity', in Cecilia M. Bailliet (ed.), *Research Handbook on International Solidarity and the Law*, Research Handbooks in International Law series (Cheltenham: Edward Elgar, 2024), pp. 241–258; S. Bogojevic and R. Rayfuse (eds.), *Environmental Rights in Europe and Beyond* (Oxford: Hart Publishing, 2018).

14 See J. Baskin and S. Pahuja, 'Never Waste a Crisis: A Practical Guide?, *Critical Legal Thinking Law and the Political*, 20 March 2020, available at https://criticallegalthinking.com/2020/03/20/never-waste-a-crisis-a-practical-guide/ (last accessed 1 June 2020).

means of short-term relief (through localism and interpersonal care), as a socio-economic redistribution scheme (state–citizen solidarity) or as a long-term arrangement in the form of internationalism (solidarity across countries). To achieve this breadth, our authors engage with solidarity as a trope in the history of ideas and reach out actively towards contemporaneous practices and applications of solidarity.[15]

The following chapters focus on the actors, norms and processes through which solidarity evolves over time, the features of the various contexts within which it operates and the actions it has been used to legitimize. We explore transformations, manifestations and trajectories of solidarity, and we hope to inspire critical engagement with routine claims about international solidarity beyond disciplinary boundaries and mainstream legal and policy debates. A diagonal reading of the following chapters suggests that there are mutual relations between the practice of solidarity, its conceptualization and its community embrace. No alterations can be made to one pole without simultaneously affecting the two other poles. Hence, we cannot distil one single conceptualization that embraces the broad variety of approaches to solidarity that are played out in the substantive chapters, and that any attempt to carve out such an approach would collapse into false universality.

The research question we pursued is straightforward in its openness: *What does it mean to pose the solidarity question today?* Beyond all analyses, solidarity remains first and foremost an event. In this book, leading authorities in law, philosophy and political sciences respond to the solidarity question, drawing on debates on international law, international aid, collective security, joint action, market organization and neoliberalism, international human rights across the North/South divide, African mobility, transnational labour in the digital age and populism. Its 12 chapters open up for differentiated understandings of solidarity in law and politics beyond discursive cliché or ideological appropriation, bringing crises of the past into conversation with the crises of today.

I.4 HOW?

The point of our volume is to capture the shifting nature of long-held historical assumptions on solidarity at a time of increasing legal, social and political urgency. Its contributors reject the celebratory language of solidarity, characteristic of the modernist period; Noll and Herzog provide non-heroic

[15] L. Herzog, 'Durkheim on Social Justice: The Argument from "Organic Solidarity"' (2018) 112 *American Political Science Review* 112.

accounts of workers' roles in their texts; Hansen offers an antidote to the romanticising of refugees, and Jamil, Joyce and Pahuja disown the consolation offered by a liberal account of solidarity. They all see their subjects at a distance and document their struggles in a daily routine. Equally, there is a rejection of cynicism; Mégret singles out instances of 'unwanted' solidarity without surrendering it outright, Karageorgiou gives the Christian intellectual history of solidarity a chance to account for itself and Okafor unfolds the South–North conflict while retaining ideational space for a solidarity beyond it. At stake is a more nuanced appreciation: not all solidarity is equally opportune and not all uses of solidarity terminology are equally valid.

In the Foreword, Martti Koskenniemi frames the question of solidarity in terms of 'labour and struggle'. Drawing on Didier Eribon's *Retour à Reims*,[16] he brings us back to the European post-war period, the time of the welfare state, social democracy and 'communism', asking 'how does that compare with the second decade of the 21st century?' He suggests that the newly found interest in solidarity may be attributed to the nostalgia it carries from post-war labour activists and the promise of a common project against sharper divisions and increased adversity – against the employer, the capitalist, the national enemy. Koskenniemi concludes that the staying power solidarity has 'is a good thing'. Today's inequalities and democratic decay make solidarity's role as a platform for engagement key, especially when rethinking of how to live together in a world of identity and difference.

In Chapter 1, Patricia Mindus draws the reader's attention to solidarity as a legal concept and its distinction from solidarity as a social practice. Her chapter documents the ubiquity of solidarity in the law and at the same time explicates their friction. She identifies historically critical understandings of solidarity in European law, including the traditional private law notion of *obligatio in solidum*, the general idea of solidarity as a cohesive force in society and the perhaps more specifically modern conception of social solidarity as generating duties on behalf of the state. In her last section, a phenomenological typology of interactions between solidaristic social practices and the law is sketched out, offering insights on the (non-exhaustive) ways in which legal scholars may relate to solidarity as social practice.

In Chapter 2, Sally Scholz focuses precisely on the question of costs of solidarity, which she formulates as a practice that involves risks. There is more to solidarity, she suggests, than merely opting to stand together for action in concert or collective action. Using an example of collective action responding to state-based treatment of migrants, Scholz shows that participants willingly

[16] D. Eribon, *Retour à Reims* (Paris: Fayard, 2009).

assume contextualized social risks across an array of commitments to solidarity. They form a loose collective, both to mitigate individual risks and burdens from communal reactions to manifest solidarity. This collective also carries its own set of risks with it. Acknowledging that the burdens of solidarity fall differently or impact other social conditions in adverse ways, Scholz offers an account of solidarity that entails a willingness to share contextualized social risk equitably. This entailment informs obligations within the solidarity relation as well as beyond it.

In a similar observatory vein, in Chapter 3, Obiora Okafor walks us through *Antinomies and Aporias in Official Human Rights Solidarity Argumentation across the Global South/North Axis*, teasing out underlying, and oftentimes opposing, assumptions about the function of the international system of rights and obligations by actors in the South and the North. Through a quasi-empirical methodology, he offers insights into the reasons why states in the Global North tend to accept and focus on binding obligations in the civil and political rights area, while demurring regarding solidarity obligations in the field of economic and social rights. In an analogous move, he tracks why states in the Global South tend to argue in favour of binding obligations with regard to economic, social and cultural rights but not nearly as much regarding civil and political rights. The chapter exposes the ironic circulation and eclipsing of these antinomies and aporias in plain sight; their relationships to state sovereignty; and their connections to global power relations as ideationally constitutive forces. In fact, it invites the reader to observe how human rights argumentation on solidarity colludes that obligations of solidarity are asymmetrical, without this being reflected in the responsibility borne by states at the international level.

From a similar vantage point of global divisions, but capitalizing on a sceptical approach, Frédéric Mégret comes to rebut the historical 'truth' that 'solidarity is a social good'; a framing often encountered with international lawyers keen to emphasize its integrative function for the international community. In Chapter 4, he explores constellations where solidarity is unwelcome and understood as both objectively and subjectively undesirable. By examining different sites of international solidarity, including the inter-state and the transnational, Mégret distinguishes between solidarity that is unwelcome on account of its effects (when solidarity actually makes things worse), on account of who it is offered by (the 'intuitu personae' of solidarity), and on account of the burden of gratitude it creates (as part of a Maussian economy of gift and counter-gift).

The African perspective expressed in Chapter 5 resonates with the question of desirable solidarity and its contingency on power relations. Charles Mbele takes international mobility as a lens for the interplay of colonialism, capitalism and ongoing injustices with solidarity. Through an empirical account of what he terms the 'Europeanization of migration', consisting of a set of formal and informal cooperation strategies that further bordering and containment as disciplining practices, he contends that solidarity has given its place to enmity. Drawing on Mbembe and others, he concludes that, within current legal structures rooted into a neoliberal thinking of dignity and rights, solidarity as a radical tool seems unreachable.

Responding to a broader debate on solidarity and the international order, Eva Nanopoulos focuses on what she terms the 'solidarity turn' in the context of collective security. In Chapter 6, she interrogates whether solidarity truly marks a break from the ideas and practices of individualism and market fundamentalism that have shaped the global neoliberal order. To determine whether solidarity is the road to salvation or merely old wine in new bottles, she reads the evolution of the principle in the law of collective security against key neoliberal writings on war, peace and global order. Nanopoulos conveys the message that solidarity does not exist outside the systems of knowledge and structures that have shaped the international legal order and, hence, offers no easy way out of the crisis. It can be re-purposed in emancipatory directions but this, she warns, requires first and foremost a re-imagination of critique.

In Chapter 7, Gregor Noll asks '*Will There Be Solidarity in Data-driven Societies?*' To what extent are the concrete historical circumstances in which solidarity emerged helping us understand contemporary preconditions of solidarity in cybernetics, AI and digitalization? To respond to this question, Noll tells the story of the transformative role solidarity played in the industrial revolution in the second half of the nineteenth century at the threshold to full-blown capitalism. Using the example of German labour conflicts and fugitive plantation slaves in seventeenth century Suriname as touchstones of solidarity and solidarity appeasement, he identifies a set of criteria for solidarity emergence which he tests on the contemporaneous context of digitalization. The issue is thereafter taken into the present: do the criteria critical for nineteenth century solidarity point to a particular ongoing or future practice of solidarity, under conditions of cybernetics, AI and digitalization? As these conditions undermine the central criterion of communal life and work, Noll denies that solidarity has a digital future.

Taking on that question, Lisa Herzog's Chapter 8 discusses *Transnational Workers' Solidarity after the Pandemic*, exploring the potentiality of digital communication that became normalized during the COVID-19 pandemic for emergent forms of transnational solidarity among those united by labour. She argues that historical forms of worker solidarity were often a combination of social and political forms of solidarity, responding to concrete local problems in concrete local settings. Through an optics of hope, Herzog provides arguments for why transnational worker solidarity is, today, needed maybe more than ever, and why they should be entitled to leverage commercial digital channels in its pursuit. Drawing on the example of digital technologies that allow not only the sharing of information, but also the connection of individuals across geographies, she concludes by postulating that workers should have a right to 'know their colleagues' along value chains.

Haris Jamil, Richard Joyce and Sundhya Pahuja's Chapter 9, on *Populism and Trans-National Solidarity*, offers an account of solidarity as the antidote to the global rise of populist nationalism. In conventional accounts, populist nationalism is placed in opposition to liberal internationalism. This conventional approach struggles to account for the role played by international law and institutions in the global rise of populist nationalism and fails to see how simple reaffirmations of liberal internationalism risk repeating and intensifying crises associated to populism. Liberal internationalism also lends itself to a thin conception of international solidarity as pertaining between states and limited to their 'co-operation'. Drawing on postcolonial critiques and Stuart Hall's conception of 'authoritarian populism', Jamil, Joyce and Pahuja explore the structural connections between populist nationalism and liberal internationalism before setting out a more radical conception of trans-border solidarity which escapes the false opposition between them. It does so by reference to the example of trans-border solidaristic action in opposition to the commercial and political activities of the Adani conglomerate.

In Chapter 10, Peo Hansen demonstrates the relevance of economic accounts in the context of refugee reception and turns the solidarity narrative on its head. Through an analysis of the basics of Modern Monetary Theory (MMT), this chapter shows that mainstream ideas on the cost of immigration builds on a flawed economic conception, one that constrains both the scope of policy options and of our thinking about migration at large. Much of it is, according to Hansen, due to the heavy imprint of the orthodox 'sound finance' doctrine on migration research and policy which assumes that central governments face a budget constraint and solvency requirement much in the same way as households, municipalities and businesses. By shifting the perspective to MMT, Hansen offers tools to modernize migration research and policy, and so establish a realistic approach to both migration and the welfare state. As macroeconomic self-interest motivates immigration to a much larger extent, appeals to solidarity are not needed to do so.

In a similar vein, Bas Schotel's Chapter 11 explores how an alternative understanding of law, as a public service, may reinforce solidarity and thus transform particular forms of economic relations. First, Schotel tracks how different solidarity conceptions relate to and can be distinguished from forms of cooperation based on neo-liberal market mechanisms. Thereafter, he focuses on the role of judges in adjudicating cases concerned with such mechanisms in a manner that promotes equality and fairness. For Schotel, elite experts, namely judges sitting on the bench of Western civil and commercial courts, may be the agents of change too, using normative legal resources to fill gaps or democratize structures, hard to address otherwise.

In the final Chapter 12, a similar invitation to rethink solidarity and its relationship with the law is extended. Eleni Karageorgiou positions the genealogy of the concept within early Christianity directing attention away from the commonly held position that it is primarily a conceptual outcome of the decolonization era. Linking the Pauline doctrine and writings of early theologians, such as Augustine, to the processes of modernity – of which notions such as international community, good neighbourliness and cooperation are a part – she traces solidarity to a Christian dynamic. This enables her to unpack the deep roots of international solidarity in international law and human rights in a messianic logic of love, sacrifice and debt. She tells a story of *agape* as a lived experience, where the conception of 'solidarity' is seen as a post-theological strategy to address human relationships in the present moment with past awareness (memory). By locating solidarity in the political philosophy of Paul and Derrida, Karageorgiou concludes that posing the solidarity question today confronts us with a 'fatal' choice between 'chronos', speaking to an eternally postponed promise, and 'kairos', which calls for a radically presentist loving politics.

If we were to cluster the contributions to this book following Madisson's optic, a triptych of observation, doubt and hope would emerge. The first step, as the chapters by Mindus, Scholz and Okafor suggest, is careful observation, followed by the labour of categorization, at times against the grain of existing solidarity conceptualizations. Observation is followed by elements of doubt that the following chapters by Mégret, Mbele, Nanopoulos and Noll, bring to the fore, namely that law harbours a rather dystopian relationship with solidarity. Doubt continues to reverberate through the contributions by Herzog, Jamil, Joyce and Pahuja, Hansen, Schotel and Karageorgiou, but theirs is an analytics of hope, stemming from solidarity's re-conceptualization and application, in digital workers' solidarity, social movements, economics, the public nature of law and, indeed, its history of ideas.

Mindful of the limitations of our own optic, in particular as regards solidarity issues which were given short shrift in this collection, as those entailed by climate change or the demographics of ageing, two remarks are due. The first is that this volume, since its conception, was meant to experiment with the solidarity lens applied to contemporary debates as a frame and as an experience; not as a theory or an interpretative device. In that sense, our aim was not to offer an exhaustive analysis of 'solidarity and . . .' issues. We hope, though, to have triggered an appetite for the readers to continue the experiment by posing the solidarity question today in relation to subjects or practices whose effects may give rise to new struggles, in one way or another, for 'solidarity'. For instance, one could ask what it would mean if the non-human and its practices were analysed through the lens of solidarity, connecting history to contemporary debates on post-humanism in law and politics.

I.5 SOLIDARITY: REOPENING THE CASE FOR CHANGE

It is the best of times; it is the worst of times: our edited volume reopens the case for solidarity at a point where the evidence for states' inability to form an international society is stark. A long history culminates and the nuances of our questions will be decisive. On what social relationships can a future justice be founded? How is it that our theology, economy and philosophy change, once they are examined through the lens of solidarity? What are the epistemic and ideological conditions of living out solidarity, what intellectual histories and histories of concrete conflicts come to a head in that concept today? Why is the law an uneasy resource in those struggles: ally and adversary in one? And what evidence has slipped from our sight over the years and must be re-exhibited?

The responses that these questions elicit on the following pages do not lend themselves to simple and straightforward judgments. But, apart from documenting their own observations, the authors of individual contributions to this volume perform themselves in their method of presenting evidence. This holds for Ruth Maddison as much as for scholarly authors engaging in the solidarity question. At the end of the day, all these modes of performance are each a suggestion of a future social, and deserve examination as such, beyond their surface depiction.

1

Solidarity and Law

Odd Bedfellows?

PATRICIA MINDUS

In Shakespeare's *The Tempest*,[1] the King of Naples' jester Trinculo, shipwrecked on a strange island, shelters from the eponymous storm under the cloak of Caliban, a malformed son of a late witch. Noticing Caliban's terrible odour, Trinculo says 'misery acquaints a man with strange bed-fellows'. Similarly, solidarity is an apparently odd bedfellow of the law. This oddity is my starting point in this chapter, and I aim to move beyond it.

Solidarity is shrouded in rhetoric in current political and legal discourses. This hampers critical reflection on how, when and why law interacts with solidaristic practices, fuelling increasing mistrust of the many merely persuasive definitions of solidarity and potentially numbing us to the motivational capital conveyed in the notion. Taking its cue from political and legal theory, this chapter argues that we ought not confuse the legal concept of solidarity with solidarity as a social practice. We must appreciate the ways in which they differ in order to conceptualize better how they are related. Such appreciation lays the ground for establishing the circumstances in which this relation is morally justifiable. More specifically, I explore solidarity as a legal concept as distinct from solidarity as a social practice, aiming to show their divergence and interplay. We can better understand the law by reflecting on how it interacts with established and emerging solidaristic practices.

I argue that solidarity and law do not blend well, and stress that solidarity is nonetheless ubiquitous in law. Historically important understandings of solidarity in law have encompassed notions as distinct as the traditional private law understanding of *obligatio in solidum*, the general idea of solidarity as a cohesive force in society, and the conception of social solidarity as generating

[1] William Shakespeare, *The Tempest*, edited by Martin Butler (London: Penguin Classics, 2015), Act 2, Scene 2, lines 14–16.

duties of behalf of the state. I then show that, despite its ubiquity, solidarity as a legal concept is under-theorized in legal science. Section 1.4 sketches a phenomenological typology of interactions between solidaristic social practice and the law: I list several types of interaction and object to one. Law may not command us to act in solidaristic ways but it may interrupt social practices of solidarity, substitute these or compensate for their failing, recognize and integrate such practices and – albeit indirectly – foster solidarity by its status-generative function.

1.1 ODD BEDFELLOWS?

Law and solidarity are, prima facie, odd bedfellows for several reasons: they differ in definitional clarity, scope, and guiding values; their conceptual pedigrees are in tension; and they involve different forms of obligations.

Firstly, common definitions of law and solidarity differ in levels of clarity. The meaning of law is more certain than the meaning of solidarity. I am not claiming that we know the *contents* of law – lawyers incessantly debate the precise meaning and limits of application of any given law – nor is there an uncontroversial theory of the *nature* of law – legal theorists make a living from this debate. However, there is consensus that 'law' refers to a kind of social practice self-described in this way, that evolved as a system of code around 3000 BC. We agree that it involves some level (and combination) of systematicity and norms of the interpretation of rules, status ascription and imposition of punishment. It is, thus, distinguishable (not separate) from other social practices like art, sport, religion, etiquette, etc. Solidarity enjoys no equivalent consensus. Solidarity can describe radically different objects: emotions, values, virtues, beliefs, social practices, obligations, attributes of certain social groups, attributes of all human societies and, of course, constitutional principles and other legal paraphernalia. Durkheim-related scholarship frequently considers whether the concept of solidarity is descriptive or prescriptive. This is telling: the very fact that there is no agreement on the central ontological matter – whether solidarity is a *social kind* determined by conventions, norms, behaviours, expectations, background circumstances, etc. – makes it different from the social kind called law.[2]

Secondly, law and solidarity have different scopes. Solidarity concerns 'life in associations and within social relationships that extend beyond relations

[2] To make my allegiances clear from the start I assume, in line with Rahel Jaeggi and Andrea Sangiovanni, for example, that solidarity is a social practice.

among intimates'.[3] Solidarity is expressed at a social meso-level and typically regards associative obligations.[4] Law is typically more all-encompassing, regulating levels stretching from the micro- (individual) to the macro- (state), including the meso-level of social interaction. That solidarity and law differ in scope is also clear for those who concede that solidarity in law, at least in its modern version that calls on the state, might stretch beyond the meso-level.

Thirdly, the practices of solidarity and law aspire to different normative values. Insofar as it aspires to realize a guiding value, law aims for justice. Solidarity goes beyond the requirements of justice: merely doing what justice requires means that you are not unjust, but it does not make you solidaristic. There are moral duties of justice, for example, those due to all human beings, but they do not characterize solidaristic action.

Fourthly, the conceptual pedigrees of law and solidarity are at least somewhat in tension. Consider the Christian tradition, a central historical source of reflection on solidarity. Here, solidarity has a relatively long history: solidarity to aid the suffering depends on identification with fellow human beings with whom we share the divinely created human condition, to whom we have obligations of aid grounded on the idea that humans are created in *imago dei*. Also, the obligation to 'love your enemy' expresses the Christian obligation to see beyond the differences between fellow humans. This tradition – to which the catholic social doctrine is central[5] – greatly emphasizes the Augustinian love of God which foregrounds the need to act in solidarity. Sometimes referred to as humanitarian solidarity,[6] this is often expressed as an essential recognition of another's dignity and personhood.[7] In this tradition, solidarity often approaches, or overlaps with, *caritas*, in opposition (again with Augustine) to *cupiditas*. In the Christian tradition, solidarity is strongly

[3] A. Sangiovanni, *Solidarity: Nature, Grounds, and Value: Andrea Sangiovanni in Dialogue* (Manchester: Manchester University Press, 2023), p. 4.

[4] Dworkin's example of associative obligations are 'the special responsibilities social practice attaches to membership in some biological or social group, like the responsibilities of family or friends or neighbors', R. Dworkin, *Law's Empire* (Cambridge, MA: Harvard University Press, 1986), p. 196.

[5] S. Stjernø, *Solidarity in Europe: The History of an Idea* (Cambridge: Cambridge University Press, 2005).

[6] R. Ter Meulen, 'Solidarity, Justice, and Recognition of the Other' (2016) 37 *Theoretical Medicine and Bioethics* 517–529, at 527. On this topic, D. Fassin, *Humanitarian Reason: A Moral History of the Present* (Berkeley: University of California Press), 2011.

[7] A. Honneth, *The Struggle for Recognition: The Moral Grammar of Social Conflicts* (Cambridge, MA: Polity Press, 1995); P. Cobben, *The Paradigm of Recognition: Freedom as Over-coming the Fear of Death* (Boston, MA: Brill, 2012); S. B. Garlington, M. E. Collins and M. R. Durham Bossaller, 'An Ethical Foundation for Social Good: Virtue, Theory and Solidarity' (2020) 30 *Research on Social Work Practice* 196–204, at 199.

connected, perhaps even originating, with love. Solidarity would also be necessary for compassion to work towards justice. Expressed through a theological framework, the claim is that solidarity would be 'love with justice' rather than 'love with charity'.[8] Solidarity here exceeds mere charity: it is a form of love. Therefore, solidarity in this tradition differs significantly from law: as shown masterfully by Remo Bodei who takes his cue from Arendt,[9] love is the fundamental opposite of law in the Augustinian tradition. Law is constriction, constraint and limitation; love its opposite. Law is marked by caducity, love is eternal. Primarily, love does not give anyone *his due*: it does not respect proportions. On the contrary, one ought to turn the other cheek. To speak with Bodei, 'love polishes law's harshness' and 'breaks through the bronze armor of the law'.[10] Having opposing historical traditions is no conclusive argument, but it contributes to the picture of the two concepts as odd bedfellows.

The fifth reason is that law and solidarity are hard to conjoin. The concepts rely on different forms of obligations, and law may not command solidaristic action. Superficially, law and solidarity both concern *actions*, at least if one takes the view that solidarity is about a particular type of practice and not, say, a mere emotion or general human virtue.[11] But it is plain that law, as Christian Thomasius (who coined the terms of this distinction) puts it, concerns 'external obligations' while solidarity may also concern 'internal obligations', that is, obligations *in foro interno*, in one's conscience, relating to *decorum* or ethical social relations. The law regulates only what modern natural lawyers claim belongs to the domain of justice (here in opposition to the domain of *decorum*, not injustice), namely the 'external actions' of the body.[12] Solidarity, by contrast, raises moral requirements of 'virtue'. We can concede that the moral requirements of solidarity are not identical to the moral requirements for human beings *qua* human beings (justice in the sense employed by moral theory, i.e. in opposition to injustice). In fact, 'humanitarian aid should be offered to human beings who suffer, no matter who they are

8 O. Ortega, 'The Gospel of Solidarity' (1994) 46 *The Ecumenical Review* 135–141, at 135.

9 H. Arendt, *Love and Saint Augustine* (first published 1929) (Chicago: University of Chicago Press, 2014).

10 R. Bodei, *Ordo Amoris. Conflitti terreni e felicità celeste* (first published 1992) (Bologna: Mulino, 2015), p. 67.

11 On the other hand, see A. Zijderveld, 'The Legal and Moral Dimensions of Solidarity' (2006) 3 *Netherlands Journal of Legal Philosophy* 306–330, at 316.

12 This pedigree of the distinction between virtue and justice was first suggested by C. Johann, *Meister in Lehrbuch des Naturrechts* (Frankfurt: Akademische Buchhandlung, 1809), who claims that distinguishing internal and external obligation allows one to distinguish natural law from positive law.

and what they are doing, whereas solidarity of solidaristic movements is expressed with respect to people ... with whom we share [political] goals.'[13] It remains undisputed that solidarity requires a form of virtuous action, namely fulfilling the moral obligation we might have as a member of some collective engaging in solidaristic action who view that collective's (or its cause's) flourishing as intrinsically linked to our own. This is, in essence, why it is ethically problematic, say, to free ride on your colleagues' collective efforts to strike against a salary cut. This places solidaristic practice squarely within the realm of *decorum* or reign of virtue.

For these reasons, law and solidarity are odd bedfellows. Surprisingly, the literature on solidarity is peppered with (often implicit) suggestions that solidarity is intimately connected to justice, such as Jürgen Habermas' claim that solidarity is *das Andere der Gerechtigkeit*, the other of justice. Surprisingly, solidarity is also a legal concept, present all over the law, even etymologically stemming from law. Yet, as a legal concept, it is extremely under-theorized. There is no reason to assume that extra-legal conceptions of solidarity would dictate the semantic boundaries of solidarity in legal sources. So, what does it mean in the law?

1.2 SOLIDARITY IN LAW

Solidarity pervades law. Consider family law. Relatives are normally expected to support each other and, in many legal systems, maintenance obligations are considered one of the main ways to materialize solidarity between ex-spouses.[14] In private law, the term commonly gives all debtors the same level of responsibility to fulfil a specific obligation. Solidarity can require that a party abstains from exercising some rights, or it can lead to certain elements of the contract being declared invalid (think of an unfair limitation of liability). It can require a judge to interpret a contract in a way that avoids a harsher outcome for the burdened party. Sometimes, it may require a party to perform an obligation that it had not expressly committed to. As known, solidarity appears in many contexts, for example, EU law, international law and beyond.

The use of solidarity as joint liability stems from Roman law where *obligatio in solidum*[15] is opposed to *obligatio pro parte*: solidarity is to give it

[13] R. Jaeggi, 'Solidarity and Indifference', in: R. Ter Meulen, W. Arts and R. Muffels (eds.), *Solidarity in Health and Social Care in Europe*, Philosophy and Medicine (Dordrecht: Springer, 2001), vol. 69, p. 291.

[14] R. Lenoir, 'La solidarité familiale: une question morale?', in S. Paugam (ed.), *Repenser La Solidarité* (Paris: Presses Universitaires de France, 2011), pp. 169–186.

[15] The typical case of cumulative joint liability was in Roman law *obligatio ex delicto*, sanctioned by private criminal actions. The culprit, having injured several people, albeit through the same

all back.[16] From the Indo-European root *sel* (i.e. that which is solid, stable and resistant), *solidum* stems from *soldo*, a fourth century BC gold coin, which 'explains why it is possible to find the root of the term solidarity in legal contexts linked to levying and payment'[17] and why it later appears in terms like 'soldier' (who would, during the middle ages, perceive *solidum* or money in exchange for military services). The Roman law idea still pervades *solidarité* in the *Encyclopédie* in 1765, and the *Code Napoléon* of 1804. In the late nineteenth century, the joint liability understanding was still widespread. Even though the modern notion of solidarity as mutual aid, assistance, cooperation, etc., had been transliterated in German already in the mid-nineteenth century, the lawyers took little notice (e.g. in the Rhineland, where the Code Napoléon was still in force until 1899, *Solidarität* concerned whether the old French penal norm, according to which accomplices were jointly liable for fines or damages, had been abolished by Prussian civil law).[18]

The solidarity we now discuss is a different, modern, invention.[19] As Sangiovanni argues, 'the language of solidarity emerges as a response to growing anxiety regarding the expansion of commercial society, large-scale industry, and the perceived collapse of traditional communities'.[20] When the normative ideal of the social contract gave way to a non-ideal 'contract society – to use Auguste Comte's, Benjamin Constant's and Herbert Spencer's terminology – the need to foster social cohesion grew, and talk of solidarity gained its modern guises. During the eighteenth century, 'gradually, the word came to be used in a broader meaning of emotionally and normatively motivated readiness for mutual support'.[21]

action, was required to pay the *poena* to each of them. See P. Bonfante, *Obbligazioni comunione e possesso, Scritti giuridici vari* (Turin: Unione Tipografico-Editrice, 1926), p. 220; E. Betti, *La struttura dell'obbligazione romana e il problema della sua genesi* (Milan: Giuffrè, 1955).

16 E. Albertario, *Corso di diritto romano, Le obbligazioni solidali* (Milan: Giuffrè, 1948), p. 11; Isnardi Parenti, *In solidum obligari, Contributo allo studio della solidarietà da atto lecito* (Naples: ESI, 2012).

17 F. Polacchini, *Doveri costituzionali e principio di solidarietà* (Bologna: Bononia University Press, 2016), p. 8.

18 RG, judgment of 30 September 1887, Az. II 126/87.

19 See H. Brunkhorst and J. Flynn, *Solidarity: From Civic Friendship to Global Legal Community* (Cambridge, MA: MIT Press, 2005).

20 A. Sangiovanni, 'How Does One Choose among Theories of Solidarity?', *Paper Presented at the Workshop 'Solidarity: We Know It When We See It'*, Gothenburg, Sweden, 25 March 2022, p. 2.

21 A. Laitinen and A. B. Pessi, 'Introduction', in A. Laitinenn and A. B. Pessi (eds.), *Solidarity: Theory and Practice* (Lanham: Lexington Books, 2015), p. XX.

By the end of the nineteenth century, solidarity was largely coextensive with the (much evanescent) value closing Robespierre's triad: Fraternity.[22] But not much is modern about this. This understanding of solidarity as grounded in membership (of a nation, guild, corporation, etc.) casts solidarity as an agent of community cohesion, the social equivalent of friendship in Aristotle or Cicero,[23] the sentimental glue without which society may not 'hold together'.[24] This idea of solidarity-as-fraternity is still pervasive in Domat's *Lois civiles*,[25] and is common in many other contexts, even beyond law.[26] Its legitimizing force is not that it protects the members, but that it protects the corporations, the societies, the organized groups. Legally speaking, this solidarity is still that of the 'brotherhood' corporations.[27]

A modern conception was on its rise, even in law: 'Between the mid-19th century and the start of the 20th century, another understanding of solidarity [in law] was gaining ground. From a primarily community-organizing principle, a new social, that is protective, meaning started to emerge.'[28] Its legitimizing force is not simply that this new solidarity would protect certain individuals from particular harms. The law has always cared for protection of vulnerable persons: protectiveness is basic in Roman legal concepts such *pietas* and *clementia*. What is new is the allocation of responsibility for this protection. Responsibility does not fall on some unprecise entity, some private

22 M. Charlot, 'Solidarité', in Ferdinand-Camille Dreyfys, Marcellin Berthelot and Hartwig Derenbourg (eds.), *La Grande encyclopédie* (Paris: Lamirault, 1885–1902), v. 30, p. 222; M.-C. Blais, *La solidarité, histoire d'une idée* (Paris: Gallimard, 2007).

23 Aristotle, *Nicomachean Ethics* (c.340 BCE) Book IX-4; Cicero, *Laelius de Amicitia* (44 BCE).

24 It is unnecessary to betray this etymology to explain how solidarity gave rise to the idea of social coercion: besides the golden coin *soldum*, 'the etymological references of the word "solidarity" leads to the latin *solere* (to be stable and whole), *solidum* (solidity, wholeness) [. . . but also] *sodalites* (friendship)': F. Giuffrè, *La solidarietà nell'ordinamento costituzionale* (Milan: Giuffré, 2002), p. 10. Author's translation.

25 See G. Alpa, 'Solidarietà', in Guido Alpa and Maurizio de Acutis e Paolo Zatti (eds.) *Casi e pareri di diritto privato: La nuova giurisprudenza civile commentate* (Padova: CEDAM, 1995), p. 368.

26 We find this view in IR theory: solidarity in the English School is presented as a pre-supposition for a well-functioning collective enforcement of international norms. See e.g. H. Bull, 'The Grotian Conception of International Society', in H. Butterfield and M. Wight (eds.) *Diplomatic Investigations* (Cambridge, MA: Harvard University Press, 1968), in which he opposes a solidarist conception of international relations in favour of a pluralist one.

27 See the use of *solidarietà* in the Italian civil code of 1942 that explains, *inter alia*, that the ban of abuse of property with *animus nocendi* (*atto emulativo*) is grounded on 'solidarity between private parties'; or art. 1, 2° co. of the Italian Law n. 563/1926, a much-quoted source of the fascist corporativist regime, on the obligation of corporations that, much like the Ancient guilds, had to protect the interests of its members *qua* members.

28 R. Cippitani, *La solidarietà giuridica tra pubblico e privato* (Perugia: Università degli studi di Perugia, 2010), p. 22. Author's translation.

law entity,[29] or to the private parties to contract as they wish.[30] It falls on a particular type of collective entity, namely, the state, called to fulfil the protection needs of individuals: the late nineteenth century idea of 'social solidarity' in its *legal* sense is to make the state responsible for protection of vulnerable individuals. This 'solidarity of the moderns'[31] – to use Peces-Barba's variation on a Bobbian theme – is, legally, that which allocates the 'obligatio' on the shoulders of the State (or some of its specific agencies).

This requires a disclaimer. A number of instances in the history of law appear at odds with this reading: familial solidarity imposes duties on family members, sometimes in nascent welfarist regimes. For example, traditional common law imposed no duty of maintenance owed by a husband to his wife or children;[32] only with the 1844 revision of the Poor Laws would it become possible for an unmarried woman to request a form of familiar solidarity from the father of her children, and married women would have to wait until 1878 for similar rights.[33] It is not that traditional forms of membership-based solidarity suddenly disappear from law, but that the birth of the 'État-providence' makes the State newly subject to obligations of social solidarity. One might venture that the innovation of the later twentieth century and early twenty-first century is to create supranational obligation-bearers: be it in the EU[34] or in

29 Think of Roman Law's *collegia funeraticia*, a private law association that provides assistance with sepulture, the medieval corporations, the late medieval and renaissance 'ospedali' and *companie del divin amore*, the confraternities, the 'misericordie', the 'schools' like San Rocco in Venice, Monti di Pietà, etcetera.

30 Cf. Alpa, 'Solidarietà', 368, who holds that the lack of negotiation and of correspectivity or reciprocity makes it the case that solidarity in law cannot be explained with reference to the form of the contract and that it is therefore better understood as 'quasi-contractual'. Also note the centrality of the notion of the 'quasi-contract', for example, in Léon Bourgeois where 'solidaristic measures' are based on an idea of society as legitimized by a tacit consent-based quasi-contract, in opposition to the modern natural law tradition of grounding public power on hypothetical individual consent.

31 Gregorio Peces-Barba Martinez, Eusebio Fernández García, Francisco Javier Ansuátegui Roig and José Manuel Rodríguez Uribes, *Historia de los Derechos fundamentales, vol. II Siglio XVII El contexto social y cultural de los derechos. Los rasgos generales de evolución* (Madrid: Editorial Dykinson, 2001), p. 211.

32 See J. Eekelaar, *Family Law and Social Policy* (London: Weindefeld and Nicolson, 1978), p. 256.

33 See V. M. Finer and O. R. McGregor, 'The History of the Obligation to Maintain' in the Finer Committee Report of the Committee on One-Parent Families Cmnd 5629, 1974, vol 2, Appendix 5, p. 100 and following, also p. 85, quoted from C. Vigneau, 'Les rapports entre solidarité familiale et solidarité sociale en droit comparé' (1999) 51 *Revue internationale de droit comparé* 51–81, at 55.

34 See e.g. F. Croci, *Solidarietà tra stati membri dell'Unione Europea e governance economic europea* (Turin: Giappichelli, 2020); D. Schiek, 'Solidarity in the Case Law of the European Court of Justice: Opportunities Missed?', in H. Krunke, H. Petersen and I. Manners (eds.),

international law.[35] Nonetheless, it is clear enough that solidarity in law, stretched beyond its narrow contractual law meaning, and adopting its modern association with social policy, social insurance, etc., is typically cast as a burden on the state, which is called to fulfil certain duties.

Remember also that these were years when the state strove to gain control of systems – traditionally left to private law groups – which care for the *beneficientia* or *caritas*. In these years the state also came to perceive those in need of 'public assistance' as a public security problem. As Foucault made his name from showing, the state comes into the realm of social policy with the aim to enhance 'ordre publique'.[36] The French movement of *solidarisme* may be said to instantiate this age quite well.[37]

The area of law highlighted by this novel form of legal solidarity is not the private law governing Ancient Roman solidarity, nor some general constitutional afflatus or public law in general, as in the traditional view of solidarity as a form of social friendship, but the newly emerging area of administrative law.[38] Administrative law was called to 'elaborate the instruments for the construction of the first systems of social insurance and other forms of protection'.[39] Recall that French administrative law purportedly stems from the 1872 *Blanco* case, a dispute on jurisdiction between private and public law. The irony of administrative law being called to realize this novel form of solidarity, so dependent on the state as the keyholder to unlock social solidarity, is that, as Denis Baranger says, 'administrative law has done extremely well without a concept of the state' and 'it was not born at the core, but in the penumbra of both private law and, to some extent, constitutional law'.[40]

Transnational Solidarity: Concept, Challenges and Opportunities (Cambridge: Cambridge University Press, 2020).

[35] See Rüdiger Wolfrum, 'Solidarity amongst States: An Emerging Structural Principle of International Law', in Pierre-Marie Dupuy, Bardo Fassbender, Malcolm N. Shaw and Karl-Peter Sommermann (eds.), *Common Calues in International Law: Essays in Honour of Christian Tomuschat* (Kehl: N. P. Engel, 2006), pp. 1087–1100,, p. 1087 et seq.

[36] M. Foucault, *Histoire de la Folie dans l'âge Classique* (Paris: Gallimard, 1972).

[37] See the (critical) outline of George Gurvitch's classic *L'idée du droit social. Notion et système du droit social. Histoire doctrinale depuis le XVIIe siècle jusqu'à la fin du XIXe siècle* (Paris: Libr. du Recueil Sirey, 1932).

[38] The term 'social law' is older and was used by, for example, Georg Beseler and Otto Gierke, but indeed it was not clear whether this *corpus* of norms was to be considered private or public. We had to wait for Hermann Roesler to talk about 'administrative social law' and for Heinrich Rosin to hold a chair in it at the University of Freiburg im Breisgau.

[39] Cippitani, *La solidarietà giuridica tra pubblico e privato*, p. 3. Author's translation.

[40] D. Baranger, 'Uncovering the Foundations of Administrative Law?', in *Foundations of Public Law* (2016) *Jus Politicum* online, available at: www.juspoliticum.com/articles/Uncovering-the-Foundations-of-Administrative-Law (last accessed 15 September 2024). See also S. Cassese, *Il diritto amministrativo: Storia e prospettive* (Paris: Giuffrè, 2010).

The 'modern' meaning of 'solidarity' originates neither with nationalist writers, nor in the social doctrine of the Catholic Church, but in the philosophical appropriation of a legal term. An early user of this 'modern' term was the proto-socialist Pierre Leroux, who declared in 1840 that 'I am the first who have borrowed the term solidarity from the jurists to be employed in philosophy ... I wanted to substitute Christian charity with human solidarity.'[41]

Yet legal science has not reflected upon solidarity as much as other basic legal notions.

1.3 AN UNDER-THEORIZED LEGAL CONCEPT

Notwithstanding its broad use in law, legal scientific theorization and analysis of solidarity as a legal concept is under-developed, even in legal scientific literature that deals with areas of law where it is commonly employed.

In legal theory – contrarily to social, moral and political theory – solidarity is hardly ever analysed. Titles by famous legal theorists that mention solidarity are often about something else.[42] Further back in history, some French-speaking legal theoreticians have gone as far as to claim that solidarity is the 'foundation of society'[43] and the source of legal norms.[44] But such bold claims have had few followers.

Anglophone legal dictionaries typically include no entry for solidarity. This includes Law's A *Dictionary of Law* (10th ed.) and Mann's *Australian Law Dictionary* (3rd ed). A search for 'social solidarity' in the Oxford University Press reference tool gives entries in dictionaries of sociology, not law. Not even the *Deutsches Rechtswörterbuch* contains an entry. Doebbler's *Dictionary of Public International Law* and Alland and Rials' *Dictionnaire de culture juridique* are exceptions, entries mostly deal with contractual matters, as is the

[41] P. Leroux, *La grève de Samarez. Poème philosophique* (Paris: Dentu, 1863), vol. 2. See also P. Leroux, *De l'Humanité, de son principe et de son avenir; où se trouve exposée la vraie définition de la religion* (Paris: Perrotin, 1840). Author's tranlation; quote taken from N. Karagiannis, 'Multiple Solidarities. Autonomy and Resistance', originally in N. Karagiannis and P. Wagner (eds.), *Varieties of World-Making: Beyond Globalization* (Liverpool: Liverpool University Press, 2007), reprinted in Swedish translation as 'Mångfaldig solidaritet. Autononomi och motstånd' (2018), 58–59 *Fronesis*, special issue 'Solidaritet' M. Wennerhag and J. Lindgren (eds.), at 109.

[42] For example, H. L. A. Hart's (1967) 'Social Solidarity and the Enforcement of Morality' 35 *University of Chicago Law Review* 1, is about using law to enforce moral beliefs.

[43] F. Gény, *Science et technique en droit privé positif* (Paris: Recueil Sirey, 1915), vol. II, p. 262.

[44] Léon Duguit, *Traité de droit constitutionnel*, 3rd ed. vol. I *La règle du droit – Le problème de l'Etat* (Paris: Ancienne Librairie Fontemoing, 1927), p. 125.

Max Planck Encyclopedia of Public International Law, with its narrow focus on just one branch of law.

The situation is not better in positive law. In public international law, for example, excepting isolated references like the Inter-American Declaration of Principles on Solidarity and Cooperation of 1936, solidarity is scarcely employed compared with, say, cooperation, collaboration, mutual support, mutual aid, etcetera. The word is absent from the United Nations Charter, to give just one example. Even when present, as in the Charter of the Organization of American States,[45] there is no definition. Despite solidarity's prevalence as a notion in Constitutions worldwide,[46] constitutional scholarship has paid little attention to it,[47] as compared to, for example, equality, fraternity, cohesion, unity and mutual assistance. A 350-year-old passage from Emer de Vattel, sometimes supposed to ground international law on the moral duty of solidarity in disasters, mentions no solidarity, but a duty to assist. *Et pour cause*, since de Vattel would have understood solidarity in Justinian's sense.

Even in EU law, where talk of solidarity has attracted much scholarly attention, 'it remains to be clarified which status the principle [of solidarity] has in EU law as well as in turn which may be its concrete normative impact'.[48] Solidarity in EU law is plurivocal. As an 'objective' of the EU[49], it is unclear whether it creates rights for individuals due to the lack of a direct effect; as a fundamental 'value' in the Nice Charter,[50] certain legal obligations for the member states may follow. This can be due to the fact that compliance of the Member States with common EU values is a fundamental requirement for the Member State to benefit from its rights under EU treatises, as the recent Budget Conditionality cases suggest.[51] But the notion also appears in

45 Eight references are made between its Preamble and the reference to the region's collective security.

46 Sangiovanni, *Solidarity*, p. 1: 'consider that 85 polities across the world refer to solidarity in key areas of their constitution, including Colombia, Romania, Albania, Algeria, Angola, Israel, Chile, Colombia, Romania, Bangladesh, Spain, Bhutan, Morocco, Cameroon, and the European Union [EU]'. See www.constituteproject.org for a searchable list of over 200 constitutions across the world. For example, Art. 2 of the Italian Constitution of 1948 prescribes the inderogable obligation of political economic and social solidarity.

47 T. H. Brandes, 'Solidarity as a Constitutional Value' (2021) 27 *Buffalo Human Rights Law Review* 59–89, at 59.

48 Croci, *Solidarietà tra stati member dell'Unione Europea*, p. 68. Author's translation.

49 TEU art 3.2. See also E. A. Marias, 'Solidarity as an Objective of the European Union and the European Community' (1994) 21 *Legal Issues of Economic Integration* 85.

50 See *inter alia* A. Grimmel and S. My Giang (eds.), *Solidarity in the European Union: A Fundamental Value in Crisis* (Cham: Springer, 2017).

51 See ECJ Cases C-156/21 and C-157/21.

legal contexts with reference to such diverse kinds of relations as hold between (a) the peoples of Europe (in the preamble of the Maastricht Treaty), (b) member states, basically amounting to sincere cooperation, (c) generations (TEU art. 3.3.2), (d) individuals,[52] (e) member states and second country nationals,[53] (f) business corporations and producers[54] and (g) the Union and overseas territories (in the preambles of the TFEU and the Maastricht Treaty). After Lisbon, solidarity was inserted *ex novo* in several articles of the treatises and appears in relation to a disparate set of policy areas, including energy policy (TFEU art. 194), anti-terrorism (TFEU art. 222), asylum, immigration and border control (TFEU art. 67 & 80), the Common Foreign and Security Policy, and so on. No wonder solidarity in EU law can mean different things, from loyalty to sincere cooperation, to something less than 'closer relations'.[55] Overarching theorization is, to my knowledge, still unavailable.

This neglect of solidarity as a legal concept leads to a hermeneutic leap of faith: it is regularly claimed that we read this absence as an 'implicit reference to the principle of solidarity', say, in the Charter of the United Nations at Article 55.[56] The insistence on solidarity in law – albeit in a widespread echoing void of theory – may partially explain the interpretative hesitations, false starts (always in Roman law where it means something else), the rhetorical pirouettes often arising from talk about solidarity in law and its confusion with allyship,[57] alliance,[58] coalition, commonality, camaraderie, partisanship, loyalty, sincere cooperation and co-ordination. Solidarity in legal settings is sometimes conflated with good faith, mutuality, reciprocity, equality

[52] C-70/95 *Sodemare*, ECLI:EU:C:1997:55 §29 and comments in F. Costamagna, *I servizi socio-sanitari nel mercato interno europeo: l'applicazione delle norme dell'Unione europea in materia di concorrenza, aiuti di stato e libera circolazione dei servizi* (Naples: Edizioni scientifiche italiane, 2011).

[53] See Title IV, *Solidarity* of the EU Charter of fundamental rights, and comments in K. Lenaerts, 'La solidarité ou Le chapitre IV de la Charte des droits fondamentaux de l'Union Européenne', in *Revue trimestrielle des droits de l'homme*, 2010, pp. 271 ff. See the case law in e.g. C-184/99 *Grzelczyk* ECLI:EU:C:2001:458, C-209/03 *Bidar* ECLI:EU:C:2005:169, C-158/07 *Förster* ECLI:EU:C:2008:630.

[54] For an overview of the case law and comments, see P. Menghozzi, 'Note sul principio di solidarietà nel diritto communitario', in *Il Diritto dell'Unione europea*, 2020, pp. 100 ss.

[55] See Croci, *Solidarietà tra stati member dell'Unione Europea*, p. 46.

[56] For such a claim, see e.g. Annaliese Aberg Scalzo, Nura Alawia and Dea Rodiqi, *International Solidarity in International Human Rights Law* (Vienna: Ludwig Boltzmann Institute of Fundamental and Human Rights, December 2021).

[57] See L. von Samson, *Allyship vs. Solidarity* (unpublished manuscript) presented at the 2021 MANCEPT workshop *The Uses of Solidarity*.

[58] R. Jaeggi, *Transforming Solidarities* (unpublished manuscript) presented at the IRCEP workshop, Milan, 2021.

and similar notions. Sometimes it appears so encompassing as to be synonymous with primacy of collective interest.[59]

Some argue that altruism would better capture what some call solidarity, at least in contractual relations.[60] I am willing to concede that this may be due to the unhappy recurrence of the 'Rosa Luxemburg conception of solidarity' that Sangiovanni outlines as being 'disposed to act in a prosocial or altruistic manner with those with whom we identify' something that would be possible to conduct by ourselves, entirely privately, in silence.[61] Solidarity is also often conflated with some (imprecise) notion of (distributive) justice according to the *brocard* that the broadest shoulders should carry the heaviest burden. As Hartzén, Iossa and Karageorgiou convincingly argued, the crisis of solidarity has even become a generalized mode of political rhetoric referring to a number of shortcomings of contemporary governance or crises.[62] Even conceding that solidarity has become a 'keyword of the contemporary political-legal vocabulary',[63] the confession is needed: 'solidarity' in law is – pace Justinian's lawyers and their contemporary contract-focused epigones – pretty vague. This might explain why lawyers' attempts to pin down the constitutional aspects of solidarity and its general legal workings eventually reach the anti-climactic conclusion that 'solidarity, in fact, before being a legal principle, is a moral and ethical value'.[64] It is always worrying when jurists are satisfied to attribute extra-legal meaning to legal terms. Similar accounts of

59 For Alain Supiot, 'toutes les institutions qui reposent sur la solidarité font . . . prévaloir l'intérêt collectif sur l'intérêt individuel': A. Supiot (ed.), *La Solidarité: Enquête sur un principe Juridique* (Paris: Odile Jacob, 2015), p. 15. Similarly, Loïc Azoulai, speaking of EU common interest, 'à coté de l'action unilatérale ou conjointe des Etats membres, audessus d'elle, se trouve une communauté d'interest et de solidarité': L. Azoulai, 'Appartenir à l'Union. Liens institutionnels et liens de confiance dans les relations entre Etat member', in Frédérique Berrod, Jörg Gerkrath, Christian Mestre, Valérie Michel, Stéphane Pierré-Caps, Robert Kovar, Denys Simon and Dominique Ritleng (eds.), *Europe(s), Droit(s), européen(s). Une passion d'universitaire. Liber amicorum l'honneur du professeur Vlad Constantinesco* (Bruxelles: Bruylant 2015), p. 32.

60 C. Leone, 'What Solidarity?' (2021) 2 *Netherlands Journal of Legal Philosophy* 239.

61 A. Sangiovanni, 'How Does One Choose among Theories of Solidarity?', *Paper presented at the Workshop 'Solidarity: We Know It When We See It'*, Gothenburg, Sweden, 25 March 2022, p. 1. Rosa Luxemburg refused as a girl to eat sugar for weeks 'in solidarity' with workers at the front who had no sugar. See also A. Sangiovanni, *Solidarity: Nature, Grounds, and Value: Andrea Sangiovanni in Dialogue* (Manchester: Manchester University Press, 2023).

62 A.-C. Hartzén, A. Iossa and E. Karageorgiou, 'Introduction', in *Law, Solidarity and the Limits of Social Europe* (Cheltenham: Edward Elgar, 2022), p. xv.

63 S. Giubboni, 'Solidarietà' (2012) 4 *Politica del Diritto* 525–554, at 525.

64 B. Bertarini, *Il principio di solidarietà tra diritto ed economia. Un nuovo ruolo dell'impresa per uno sviluppo economico inclusivo e sostenibile* (Turin: Giappichelli, 2020), p. 3. Author's translation. See also Croci, *Solidarietà tra stati member dell'Unione Europea*, p. 17: 'uno dei tratti più salienti del principio di solidarietà tra stati membri . . . [è] la discrasia – molto spesso

legal concepts like ownership, personhood or contract would strike most jurists as inadmissible. One might object that solidarity seems hard to depict fully because the concept is embodied in its actual legal instantiations, making the absence of a general definition simply an effect of solidarity's context-dependence. Although solidarity may be context-dependent, this would mean we could not say beforehand what ought to count as solidarity in law, only register *ex post facto* what has counted, reducing the action-guiding capacity that is desirable in legal concepts. Therefore, the issue is to give not a mere account of a legal term that encompasses the breadth of legal materials at hand (a challenge in itself), but a way of determining which instantiations of the concept we should accept and which we should reject as negligent uses of the legal concept, and on which grounds we should justify such rejection.

Hence, solidarity is an under-theorized legal concept. The very coupling of law and solidarity raises various questions: can solidarity be commanded? Must it be presupposed in international law? Is it a principle of international law?[65] Is solidarity a necessary complement to a rights-based concept of justice?[66] Are human rights and solidarity 'two sides of the same coin'?[67] Is it a model of federalism, somehow akin to the principle of cooperation?[68] Does familiar solidarity trump social solidarity in positive law, in many European states at least?[69] And many more. Solidarity in general is not always easy to handle, but this is *especially* true in law, where we need greater conceptual clarity given the grave consequences of erring in the dark.

The conceptual imprecision affecting solidarity in law clearly demands better theorization. Also, we should resist thinking that the concept of solidarity must obey the same semantics in law as in other settings. Legal language is known to stray quite far from ordinary language. Consider, for instance, how the term citizenship is employed in law compared with political parlance or

ravvisabile – tra l'affermazione a livello astratto della centralità di tale principio e la sua effettiva incidenza in concreto'.

65 K. Gorobets, 'Solidarity as a Practical Reason: Grounding the Authority of International Law' (2022) 69 *Netherlands International Law Review* 3.

66 Ter Meulen argues, for instance, that 'solidarity is not an alternative to a right-based concept of justice, but must be considered as a necessary complement to it' in 'Solidarity, Justice, and Recognition of the Other', p. 517.

67 M. J. Clarke, *The Vision of Catholic Social Thought: The Virtue of Solidarity and the Praxis of Human Rights* (Minneapolis: Fortress Press, 2014), p. 129.

68 E. Arban, 'Italy: The Principle of Solidarity as a Principle of Equality', in Eva Maria Belser, Thea Bächler, Sandra Egli and Lawrence Zünd (eds.), *The Principle of Equality in Diverse States* (Leiden: Brill, 2021), pp. 101–129.

69 Vigneau, 'Les rapports entre solidarité familiale et solidarité sociale en droit comparé'.

social scientific discourse.[70] For instance, solidarity between member states in the EU refers to sincere cooperation, not, say, joint action to overcome significant adversity or characterized by attitudes rooted in common identification based on a shared cause, role or condition, as with solidarity *as a social practice*. This explains the low threshold: for example, selling citizenship, regardless of how objectionable it might be, is not a behaviour of EU member states falling below the standard. When I refrain from abusing property, for example, erecting a disproportionately high party wall simply to remove light and air from my neighbour's property, I do not 'act in solidarity' with my neighbour, even though it could be said that I engage in a form of sincere cooperation. Lawyers must be aware that, while a number of conversations feature 'solidarity', we cannot presume it has a consistent meaning. We should strive to articulate why we employ the concept in the first place. As a step towards more – hopefully better – theorization of solidarity, let me sketch a phenomenology of possible relations between law and solidarity, not as a legal concept but as a social practice.

1.4 LAW AND SOLIDARITY AS BEDFELLOWS

Let us start by listing five types of interaction and investigating whether law engages in any of these in relation to the social practice of solidarity intended as joint action triggered by identification with others on the basis of, say, a shared cause, role, way of life, condition or set of experiences.

Firstly, consider the relation of rule or command. May we say that *law commands us to act in solidaristic ways*? Prima facie, this seems plausible. The law might command me to partake in social insurance schemes, to socialize risk in other ways, to materially aid my family members and others. As in Italian family law, the law might impose a sanction for not telling my partner of my infertility diagnosis or oblige me to seek to educate my children in a way to which the other parent has no objection. Law commonly imposes this kind of 'solidarity'. But, to be clear, this is not solidarity but merely a behaviour that is externally akin to solidaristic action. The very fact that, for example, the co-parent resorts to a court to impose a solidaristic framework for the education of the offspring proves the absence of commitments, intentions and attitudes typically associated with solidarity as joint action. Law imposes the obligation to mimic actions that, freely performed, appear infused by solidarity. In a nutshell, law cannot impose solidarity, only pay lip-service to it.

70 An analysis can be found in Patricia Mindus, *Hacía una teoría funcionalista de la ciudadanía* (Madrid: Marcial Pons, 2019).

As already stated, we may say that, while the law regulates external behaviour, solidarity goes further: it requires the *intention* to act in a solidaristic way. Solidarity cannot be commanded because it relies on intimate and often unarticulated personal reasons for identifying with a social group. Conceptually, as Sangiovanni explains, identification is an essential component of solidarity:[71] Solidarity requires *identification with* one another on the basis of a shared role, cause, condition or similar. I must see myself as a member of the group I am solidaristic with. It is this identification *in foro interno* that triggers the commitments, intentions and attitudes associated with solidarity as joint action. This 'attitude is *de dicto* … I identify with you on the basis of an indefinite description that we both satisfy, that defines a socially salient group, and that significantly structures our self-conception'.[72] Identification here is the kind of private and intimate matter that falls beyond the reach of the law. Law is not able to command that any particular attachment is felt. Law may impose (e.g. an obligation to recite an oath of loyalty to naturalize), but it is simply unable to command citizens to love their fatherland. Similarly, it is beyond the reach of lawmakers to rule *the foro interno* of their subjects. Law cannot make you perceive some role or condition as important for your self-conception or flourishing. The importance of the attitudinal component of *identifying with* for the practice of solidarity illustrates why solidarity and law are strange bedfellows.

But there are other ways in which we may consider this relationship: when does law intervene in a solidaristic social practice? Thus, a second way to understand the relation of the law and solidarity is to view *law as a potent tool for disrupting social practices of solidarity*.

There is a plausible sense in which members of the mafia or a terrorist cell act in solidarity, in that they believe they have reasons to identify with one another in overcoming some significant adversity (say, the police), hence engaging in cooperative reciprocal activity characteristic of solidarity. The law typically combats these forms of solidaristic actions because it does not recognize the end pursued by the mob or terrorists as being compatible with the 'order of the state': these groups act in antisocial ways.

In order to determine conditions under which the law may legitimately break down social practices of solidarity, we need to know the objectives of these practices. The

> non-instrumental value of the trusting, cooperative you-and-me reciprocal activity constitutive of solidarity is … *conditional* on the value of the ends it

[71] Sangiovanni, *Solidarity: Nature, Grounds, and Value*, p. 11 ff.
[72] Ibid.

> promotes. If the ends have no value – as we are assuming the wicked ends of the mafiosi do not – then the solidarity enacted to realize them lacks value as well. This goes for all forms of solidarity bent to wicked ends: racist groups, terrorist cells, xenophobic nationalists, and so on. While they count as forms of solidarity if all our conditions are met . . ., their solidarity has no value.[73]

The law is ill-equipped to make judgments concerning the goodness of ends, a moral-political matter. This suggests that the law may just as well disrupt solidaristic social practices that do have value in the aforementioned sense. One may imagine a community practicing solidaristic care of the land in a pre-colonial setting being disrupted by a colonial power's legal impositions to cease this activity, by imposing a market, for instance, where there were none, declaring the common land private property, spreading competition and a sense of *agon* among the former solidaristic members of the collective. Other examples include disruption of solidaristic practice among members of anarchic collectives, religious sects or masonic lodges.

The disruptive capacity of law vis-a-vis solidaristic social action can adopt many guises. Given that the recognition of the right to strike is 'one of the principal means by which workers and their associations may legitimately promote and defend their economic and social interests',[74] banning strikes would qualify as law disrupting a solidaristic practice among workers. Another example is the contemporary forms of criminalization of solidarity towards refugees that evidently disrupt solidaristic practices between citizens, non-nationals and a variety of civil society organizations.[75] Occasionally, omitting to recognize some particular existing form of solidarity may be disruptive. Consider the lack of legal recognition of *more uxorio* partnership or unmarried couples living together, which may lead to partners abandoning solidaristic patterns of behaviour they would have stuck to, had their relationship been sanctioned by law.

Thirdly, besides disrupting solidarity, the *law can substitute solidaristic practices or compensate for their failing*. Typically, only where solidarity – as non-instrumentally valuable joint action of mutual aid in the face of adversity – is lacking or deficient, does the law intervene. In this sense, law does not regard solidarity as the ensemble of dispositions of thought and behaviour that coordinates us, but such an ensemble offers the *ideal standard* against which

[73] Ibid., p. 106.

[74] ILO, 1996d, paras. 473475.

[75] See e.g. Chiara Maria Ricci, 'Criminalising Solidarity? Smugglers, Migrants and Rescuers in the Reform of the 'Facilitators' Package', in V. Mitsilegas, V. Moreno-Lax and N. Vavoula (eds.), *Securitising Asylum Flows: Deflection, Criminalisation and Challenges for Human Rights, Immigration and Asylum Law and Policy in Europe*, Volume 46 (Leiden: Brill, 2020).

the law will evaluate a given behaviour; only once we fail to meet the standard will the law be triggered. If the law holds you to a solidaristic standard (e.g. in the role of a spouse) a lack of solidaristic action will trigger legal intervention. Dissipating your salary playing poker instead of paying alimony to your ex-wife could be such a trigger in domestic family law. In such cases, the law is present only in absence of solidaristic social practice and its presence serves the purpose of *substituting or compensating for the failing of solidaristic practices*.

A fourth relation between law and solidaristic social practice is when law *integrates social practices of solidarity* (e.g. by stabilizing social expectations). The law may recognize existing forms of solidarity by noting the social existence of solidaristic relations *ex post facto*. Legal registration of trade unions may work this way. Integrating social practices of solidarity through law may operate through recognizing existing solidarities. For instance, in cases involving same sex marriage or adoption, the legal recognition of de facto solidarities stabilizes the partners', parents' and children's respective social expectations on the others' behaviour. The integration of social practices of solidarity through law may also operate through the jus-generative function of the law: the law may positivize expectations perceived to be legitimate by turning these into rights. Such a transformation of social expectations into legal rights – perhaps most emblematically in the proclamation of social and economic rights – allows the law to integrate existing forms of solidarity. Clearly, the right to healthcare or primary education does not *generate* the solidaristic action of carers. Nurses and teachers existed well before these rights were turned into law. But turning social expectations into legal rights may allow *stabilization* and possibly strengthening of such behaviour. If the law is to integrate social practices of solidarity, these must, however, already be present.

This is not so with the fifth modality of law's interaction with solidarity. Contrarily to the third and fourth type of ways in which law relates to solidaristic social practice, that do not generate new forms or stabilized forms of solidarity, the fifth modality of law's interaction with solidarity may generate new social practices of solidarity. In fact, law's status-generative function may also play a role in promoting or hindering social solidarity. The status-generative function is constituted by the use of constitutive rules in the law, and the primary way constitutive rules work in law is by defining various forms of statuses. Indirectly, law may foster (or hinder) the development of solidarity by how it designs various statuses. Take, for example, the constitutive rule in virtue of which an individual in the Third Reich was ascribed the status as Jew. The ascription of the status in itself has nothing to do with solidarity. Yet, in this particular social context, it may constitute *a ground for motivating solidaristic action*, on behalf of others towards the status-bearer, but also within the status-bearer him/herself, who hereby becomes exposed to a perspective on her own interests that he/she may previously have disregarded. Jurisprudents have, as I understand, reflected too little on this status-generative ability of law and its implication for making or breaking solidarities. In its design of legal statuses, the law enables individuals to form ways of life, experience certain things, engage in different roles; all these facts qualify as potential grounds for solidaristic practice. The status-generative function of the law may allow individuals to perceive – with greater or lesser ease – the common fate they share with fellow status-holders. Consider how the design of the citizenship status can foster or hinder solidarity with one's co-nationals. The law has an important function to play in obstructing or highlighting the common lot we share with others.

Jaeggi insists that a common lot is constructed, not given, recalling that it took a long time before the women's liberation movement could raise the 'collective consciousness' of women: 'The fact of being associated . . . has to be actualised as a willingness to identify with a certain situation (a "common lot"). . . . The "we" of the solidaristic group must first constitute itself in order to be.'[76] The law does not command attachments and willingness to identify with others, but it does shape a variety of 'we' and by designing statuses it may render identification mechanisms easier or harder. We can accept that law, in its status-ascribing function, fosters or obstructs *grounds* of solidarity, without needing to concede that law engenders solidaristic practices by command.

1.5 CONCLUSIONS

Despite its legal ubiquity, solidarity as a legal concept is under-theorized. I showed that the legal concept of solidarity diverges from solidarity as a social practice. I listed five types of relationship we find between solidaristic practice and the law and found that, although solidarity may not be commanded by law, law may still foster or hinder it. The law may: disrupt practices of solidarity; substitute and compensate for the failing of practices of solidarity; and stress or obstruct grounds for the social practice of solidarity. Being ascribed a status may constitute grounds for motivating solidaristic action. My hope is that jurists pay greater attention to solidarity in law and its relationships to solidarity as a social practice. It is valuable for our understanding of the law to reflect on how, when and why law is able to interact with already existing and emerging solidaristic practices.

[76] Jaeggi, *Transforming Solidarities*, p. 13.

2

Risking Solidarity

SALLY J. SCHOLZ

Solidarity often emerges or becomes evident in contexts where social or political relations are unequal or otherwise affected by structural injustice, in reaction to domination or in efforts to curtail dominating influences, in response to vulnerability and systemic oppression or as an immediate collective effect of times of crisis. Solidarity is a collective moral relation and *political* solidarity is "a committed unity of peoples on a range of interpersonal to social and political levels," who understand their actions for a cause as connected to those of countless others.[1] Individuals associate their efforts and well-being in the context of collective movement for social change, believing that others similarly act on a recognized interdependence with all others engaged in the collective whole. In other words, individuals choose to connect their efforts within the particular context, mediated by a cause or goal for social change, to be mutually interdependent with the actions and effort of others similarly committed to the cause. This may manifest in a concentrated endeavor or an ongoing campaign that requires multiple overlapping supportive actions.

Often characterized with expressions of "standing with" or "standing for" something – taking a stance on an issue – the core point of "standing" in solidarity is that people in solidarity need to know that there are others similarly engaged. A relationship of solidarity, however tenuous, is a unique social relation that is accompanied by risk: What sorts of risks are assumed in

An earlier version of this paper was presented for the "Meaning(s) of Solidarity" Workshop at Goethe Universität at Frankfurt am Main, Germany, November 19, 2021; and at the "Solidarity: We Know It When We See It" Workshop in Gothenburg, Sweden, March 25, 2022. Thanks to all participants for their helpful remarks.

1 Sally Scholz, *Political Solidarity* (University Park: The Pennsylvania State University Press, 2008), p. 58.

solidarity? Do all participants accept comparable or equitable risk? And what are the potential losses for those who commit to the arrangement?

Participants in solidarity willingly assume some collective risk, forming a union meant to mitigate individual risks from the larger society within which it forms, or they accrue risk together in an effort to bring about change; but solidarity also carries its own set of risks that participants accept with the belief that collective action in solidarity offers a better prospect for social change than "going it alone." Risk is part of what we undertake together. However, as I hope to show, the outwardly-facing collective risk, which is often the most common form of risk associated with movements for social change, is only one part of the risk of solidarity; understanding that helps to uncover reasons for complicating claims about equality, burden sharing, reciprocity, and shared fate in conceptualizations of or assessments of solidarity.

Importantly, the account of risk sketched in Section 2.2 assumes that solidarity is more than merely action. It is a moral relation that encourages an examination of the interconnections between situations and actions. Outwardly facing, individual and collective action in solidarity contributes to efforts to transform social conditions or situations of injustice. That outwardly-facing scrutiny also entails a personal examination of how individual actions or privileges might be contributing factors to injustice. Inwardly facing, solidarity directs actors to examine the cooperative and communicative actions among participants, to scrutinize their own participation, and to critically reflect with others on how or whether the solidary relation lives up to the values it strives to achieve in combatting injustice in the wider community.[2]

Protection and the pooling of risk, like in insurance plans, has been used to characterize the solidarity of the welfare state and even the early roots of worker solidarity in workers' mutual aid societies.[3] This *civic* solidarity at least appears to control the amount of risk any one person faces by balancing it among the associated participants. Solidarity of the welfare state tends to be described according to two aims: protection against social risk and reduction

[2] Scholz, *Political Solidarity*, pp. 71–112.

[3] E.g. David Miller, "Solidarity and its Sources," in Keith Banting and Will Kymlicka (eds.), *The Strains of Commitment: The Political Sources of Solidarity in Diverse Societies* (New York: Oxford University Press, 2017), pp. 61–79; Adam Gearey, *Justice as Welfare: Equity and Solidarity* (New York: Bloomsbury, 2012); Andrea Sangiovanni, "Solidarity in the European Union" (2013) 33 *Oxford Journal of Legal Studies* 213; Turo-Kimmo Lehtonen and Jyri Liukko, "Producing Solidarity, Inequality and Exclusion through Insurance" (2015) 21 *Res Publica* 155; Zsófia S. Ignácz, "Similarities between European and National Solidarity: An Empirical Thought Experiment about Attitudes towards Redistribution" (2021) 1 *Sozialpolitik.Ch* Article 1.3.

of social inequality.[4] In political solidarity, the pooling of or protection from risk has not been a central idea. That may be attributed to the more informal and temporary nature of political solidarity in contrast to civic solidarity or it may be because participants in political solidarity contribute to the movement in vastly different ways.[5] Regardless of the reason, I think thinking about the types of risk involved in solidarity for social change adds an important conceptual tool for understanding the uniqueness of the solidary relation. Unpacking the different facets of risk helps to reveal the distinct relations of solidarity while also suggesting paths for expanding solidarity, fostering trust, and avoiding pernicious practices of domination within the solidary relation. This approach might also contribute to understanding and assessing other forms of solidarity and thereby contribute to social scientific approaches to solidarity as well. I argue that risk in the solidary relation may be understood according to at least four facets: collective risk, personal risk, social risk, and relational risk.

In this chapter, I use two examples of political solidarity to set the stage and then present the four facets of risk evident in the relation. These four facets are not meant to exhaust the possible types of risk in the solidary relation but understanding what is at stake in each and how they might interact, I argue, reveals the importance of the willingness to share equitably contextualized social risk, attentive to the impact on personal and collective susceptibility to harm, and also acknowledging the relational risks that are taken on in solidarity relations. I am here alluding to the distinction between collective responsibility and shared responsibility. Solidarity is often affiliated with the literature on collective responsibility insofar as it indicates a relation of a collective within which positive responsibility cannot be separated. Shared responsibility, on the other hand, is usually understood as distributed. I problematize this distinction within the relation of solidarity, indicating that the risk may be both collective and shared and that the responsibility to ameliorate and alleviate risk for fellow participants is part of a process of collective rebalancing. The facets of risk might further provide a tool to augment other measures of assessing solidarity such as burden sharing. In addition, as I demonstrate, understanding the facets of risk contributes to a more nuanced conceptualization of the moral and epistemological relations of solidarity, moving beyond

4 Ignácz, "Similarities between European and National Solidarity," 4; Philip Van Parijs, "Concluding Reflections: Solidarity, Diversity, and Social Justice," in Keith Banting and Will Kymlicka (eds.), *The Strains of Commitment: The Political Sources of Solidarity in Diverse Societies* (New York: Oxford University Press, 2017), pp. 420–426.

5 Scholz, *Political Solidarity*, pp. 59–61.

approaches that present solidarity as either a symmetrical or asymmetrical relation relying on sharing of fate or deference.[6]

2.1 TWO LIVED EXAMPLES

To understand the facets of risk, it may be helpful to situate the discussion with two examples. Although the examples focus on the actions of a few, I offer them not as a way to scrutinize the behavior of some participants but rather as means of isolating and discussing facets of risk that impact others in solidarity. The first example is recounted by Chandra Russo in her qualitative exploration of solidarity along the Migrant Trail Walk.[7] The Migrant Trail Walk is an annual walk through the US–Mexico borderlands to, among other things, raise awareness to the tragedy of migrant death. Together with the "No More Deaths" movement that aids migrants by providing vital necessities like water along the border, the walk is described as both an expression of "solidarity with the migrants" and collective action in solidarity, advocating "for positive change in the borderlands." From the beginning, the Walk has included former migrants as well as students, long-time human rights activists, and people of faith; they give witness to the suffering of migrants and the vulnerabilities of those who seek to cross the border without papers, but they also aid migrants along the way, actions for which some participants have faced arrest and prosecution. The week of the walk is described by participants as "a strong witness to the commitment and passion of all involved to work for change."[8] Walkers commit to a solidary relation across ideological and motivational differences and come from diverse backgrounds, journeying as a community in solidarity, sharing stories and assisting migrants along the journey "in defiance of the borders that attempt to divide us."[9] The walk itself, in other words, is just one part of a multifaceted solidarity movement to bring social change.

As Russo explains, during one march, "a self-selected group decided to risk arrest at Border Patrol headquarters by staging a 'die-in.' … Those who organized this piece of 'guerilla theatre' believed it to be an important means

6 E.g. Sangiovanni, "Solidarity in the European Union"; and Avery Kolers, *A Moral Theory of Solidarity* (New York: Oxford University Press, 2016)

7 Chandra Russo, *Solidarity in Practice: Moral Protest and the US Security State* (Cambridge: Cambridge University Press, 2018).

8 Richard Boren et al., "The Migrant Trail: Our History," available at https://azmigranttrail.com/history-of-the-migrant-trail/ (last accessed May 10, 2023).

9 Azmigranttrail, "The Migrant Trail: Our Vision" (May 19, 2015), available at: https://azmigranttrail.com/2015/05/19/our-vision/ (last accessed May 10, 2023).

of amplifying the walk's message, dramatizing the state's violence and tragedy of migrant deaths."[10] The "die-in" proved controversial. In contrast to the "die-in" participants' aim, their act was not seen as an action in solidarity with the other walk participants or on behalf of the migrants who make the perilous journey. Not only were the Migrant Trail Walk organizers not informed of the planned performance, the media coverage of the die-in obscured the real issues that other activists on the Walk sought to highlight. Performed by white people with citizen status, the die-in also brought renewed scrutiny to areas of the border used by migrants. Although the die-in participants may have risked arrest, their actions actually heightened the risk for many migrants who make the journey unsupported by activists and without the shield of racialized citizenship. It also put the Migrant Trail Walk itself into some jeopardy and may have had negative repercussions on other migrant advocates and aid organizations that assist migrants crossing the borders.

Intuitively, I want to say that there is something wrong with the actions of actors in solidarity who, even while exposing themselves to risk, exacerbate the vulnerability and heighten the risk for other solidary actors, or perhaps worse, heighten the risk for the people on whose behalf they claim solidarity without their involvement or consent. In the example, one could cite the communicative failures in not discussing the actions with the Migrant Trail organizers, the epistemic failures in not knowing that white actors staging a die-in is racially problematic, the social and moral failures in not accurately assessing privilege in acting in a performative manner that directed attention away from the cause of ending migrant death through policy reform and directed scrutiny toward the border and those making the crossing. Each of these (and more) can be used to think through the potential problems for actors and actions in solidarity. In addition, thinking about the variety of risks involved, understanding that solidarity entails collective, personal, social, and relational risk for each participant, and thinking about how these risks are distributed might have kept the performers from acting on their plans for the die-in or transformed the action in positive ways.

In contrast, consider a participant from the first year of the Migrant Trail Walk, Daniel Strauss. Initially participating as a college student learning about migration, Strauss remained in the border region through the summer to work with the organization "No More Deaths," offering humanitarian assistance by providing water and food; Strauss returned in subsequent summers to continue volunteering. One summer, together with fellow humanitarian actor Shanti Sellz, he was arrested while transporting three migrants in need of

[10] Russo, *Solidarity in Practice*, p. 156.

medical attention. Although the case was eventually dropped, Strauss and Sellz – and many others – were criminalized for acting on humanitarian needs.[11] They risked a possible jail sentence of 15 years, impacting themselves and their families; their actions in solidarity to meet the needs of vulnerable migrants and advocate for change in the borderlands may be seen as a willingness to sacrifice and renounce privilege, the actions are also perhaps more extreme than some solidary actors are willing or able to take.

These contrasting examples bring to light the variety of risks entailed in relationships of solidarity, especially those focused on social change. Participants in solidarity engage in transformative action; they seek to transform something or some aspect of the wider social world in which they live, and, in connecting their actions with others, they understand the prospects of collective actions. Their very commitment to the cause is individually transformative as well.[12] The die-in participants took substantial personal risk in their efforts to raise awareness, a personal risk no one asked them to take that was motivated by solidarity, but their actions had an adverse impact on the collective action, the social standing of others, and the solidarity relation itself. Strauss, Sellz, and others criminalized for their solidarity, also took substantial personal risk. The impact of their actions on the collective action, the social standing of others, and the solidarity relation might be complex but is generally not immediately adverse. In both cases, the distribution of risk across a variety of different facets factors into the assessment of the solidary action.

As these examples illustrate, there are numerous risks involved in solidarity. Protection against risk may be dissected into protection against external harms (which may be collective or individual), personal harms, social harms, and relational harm. Participants accept the costs of a relationship with others in solidarity because they believe that acting collectively is necessary and that "going it alone" will not bring about the transformative change required. Solidary actors assume the costs of the relation in spite of sometimes lacking direct knowledge of the needs of and risks to other participants in solidarity. However, as the examples illustrate, the varying facets of risk affect participants differently depending on their personal situation, social status, and engagement in the collective. Awareness of the facets offers a framework for assessing individual and collective action. Actively rebalancing risk within the relation is one of the practices of trust building in solidarity.

[11] Associated Press, "Volunteers Fight Arrests for Aiding Illegals," *Deseret News* (April 2, 2006), available at: www.deseret.com/2006/4/2/19946256/volunteers-fight-arrests-for-aiding-illegals (last accessed May 10, 2023).

[12] Sally Scholz, "Persons Transformed by Political Solidarity" (2010) 8 *Appraisal* 19.

2.2 FACETS OF RISK

Political solidarity musters or collectivizes individual commitments for social change. Albeit precarious, standing with others in political solidarity aims not only to bring about social change but also to secure consociates against potential social vulnerabilities impinging on abilities in the context of the solidary relation. In other words, the collective relation will affect people differently given their social position and ability to commit to the cause. Participants expect not to be abandoned if and when the collective action gets difficult, but the expectations within solidarity extend beyond lack of abandonment. Committing to solidarity, members of the collective believe that acting together is likely to ensure a better situation, and perhaps a better outcome, than acting separately. Commitment to a cause compels solidary actors to align their individual efforts to the collective whole, knowing that others are similarly committed. Individuals contribute what they are able given their situations, including vulnerabilities as well as material and social powers. In doing so, participants accept the risk of solidarity. Risk here means the potential for harm or loss, or exposure to possible danger, precarity, or uncertainty. Although there are positive ideas associated with risk or risk taking behaviors, I want to focus on the potential negatives. The solidary relation includes not only a relation to others in solidarity, but also a relation to a larger social whole or others not or not yet aligned in solidarity, and a relation to a goal.[13] Each of these relations (and perhaps one's relation to the self) are impacted by a solidary commitment.

Each of the examples here features a collective project of border policy reform, safety for migrants, and humanitarian aid. The solidarity is both among fellow advocates, some of whom are migrants seeking a path to citizenship, and between advocates or activists and migrants. Both illustrate some participants assuming significant personal risk of arrest and punishment as they act to advance the cause of solidarity. In addition, the actions in solidarity have an impact on the social standing and relations between and among activists, many of whom are also migrants experiencing the precarious existence of life on the move.

So, while political solidarity is often conceptualized according to the (1) collective risk undertaken together, individual participants also face the (2) personal risks or potential for harm as they contribute to advancing the cause. Part of what is factored alongside the collective risk and the personal risk is the impact of solidary commitment on an individual's or group's social

[13] I unpack these relations and associated moral obligations in Scholz, *Political Solidarity* (2008).

standing, status, or power within a larger social whole, or what may be called (3) social risk. Finally, given that it is a relationship built on commitment to others similarly committed, risk-taking in political solidarity also impacts the (4) relationship of solidarity itself.

2.2.1 *Collective Risk*

The clearest and most immediate risk is associated with the project or goal of the solidary relation. The hoped-for transformation might itself involve some risk-taking in the collective action. This is clearly seen in the classic example of solidary action: workers' collective action; the unity in taking a stand for workers' rights or higher wages requires that all equally risk the possibility of loss of work and, in early workers' movements, violent retribution. Collective risk is also evident in the solidarity to which the Migrant Trail Walk gives witness. In walking together, the participants assume a collective posture against accepted social roles or norms, they find support and even safety in their collective. Whereas the workers' solidarity requires symmetrical risk taking, the Migrant Trail Walk demonstrates asymmetrical risk taking; hence at least some of the debates in studies of solidarity pertain specifically to the collective risk.

Collective action of this sort often involves accepting methods that one might not pursue on their own. That is what is meant by the outward-facing collective risk: the potential for harm in collectively responding to injustice; the risks entailed in the activism engaged for a cause. The experience of outward-facing collective risk varies depending on the form solidarity takes, the level of commitment of participants, and the external exigencies that mediate their involvement.[14] Nonetheless, the willingness to assume collective risks may be understood as a will, universally shared within solidarity, that each participant is able to contribute in a way that realizes their potential as solidary actors.

2.2.2 *Personal Risk*

In both examples, relatively socially privileged individuals engaged in personally risky action that resulted in the involvement of the police. In the case of the die-in, the activism might have important performative value in raising awareness to the phenomena of border death, whereas the case of driving migrants to a medical facility is a direct method of addressing the same issue

[14] Scholz, *Political Solidarity*, p. 60.

by seeking to prevent border death. In bringing police (and media) attention, however, both examples impact the lives of other activists, at least some of whom may not be protected by the relative social privilege enjoyed by those who engaged in personally risky action. These other activists might experience increased vulnerability because of the personally risky activism of others. The increased police scrutiny might hinder the collective efforts or damage the solidary relation as well.

Individual vulnerabilities, themselves often the result of unjust social structures like racism, sexism, citizenship status, as well as shifting circumstances within and outside the social movement, can expose solidary actors to varying levels and types of personal risk. Participation in solidarity could exacerbate the potential for harm and other costs for some members. Those who propose methods that entail greater personal risk as a means carry something like a heightened burden of proof to demonstrate that the methods or actions do not unduly burden others or exacerbate the personal vulnerability of others in such a way that their ability to participate is hindered.[15] Others may need to accept more personal costs in order to balance the collective, social, and relational costs carried by others in solidarity. This is why some accounts of solidarity point to sacrifice as an element of solidarity.

Moreover, solidarity does not necessarily entail taking personal risk, but the commitment to solidarity includes a critical assessment of the personal risks assumed by others. In other words, as a relation with others, solidarity includes some commitment to those others. Although often cast as assistance or mutuality, I am suggesting it also be understood as an assessment of the potential for harm or loss in the personal well-being of others. The solidary relation may call upon participants to help redistribute the costs and burdens of solidarity. This critical process is reflective rather than presumptive or punitive, it is open rather than arrogant. In the two examples, Strauss and Sellz of "No More Deaths" had even discussed the personal risks with their migrant passengers, noting that they could not hide them and that the passengers would be arrested if caught.[16] They had not expected to be arrested themselves for offering humanitarian aid, but they accepted that cost as part of the price of solidarity with fellow activists for humanitarianism at the border. The open, reflective process of identifying potential risks was an important part of the relation itself.

[15] Sally Scholz, "Solidarity as a Human Right" (2014) 52 *Archiv des Völkerrechts* 149.
[16] Associated Press, "Volunteers Fight Arrests for Aiding Illegals."

2.2.3 *Social Risk*

Collective action to bring about social change in solidary relations also includes *social* risks or potential for harm or damage to social relations as a result of solidarity. Social risk may be understood as the indirect adverse impact of the collective commitment of solidarity on participants' outside relations and social standing more generally. Some people may suffer the burden of unjust distribution of social risk within the solidary relation. Those who are oppressed or most affected by injustice may not be in a position to risk more than they already do to survive. Their lives, social existence, livelihoods, or other social relations may mean that they are unable to contribute much to collective struggles; those people who are privileged in relation to a particular form of oppression or injustice might risk that privilege and the security that accompanies it but are better positioned to bear the costs of the solidary struggle.[17] Navigating the effects of social risk on the lives of participants brings to light the possibilities of living differently within the solidary relation as well.

Identifying the social risk and how the burden of that commitment might fall unjustly on some members or how individual actions can violate the expectations of solidarity, is an important critical-reflective process within the relations of solidarity. The willingness to share social risk tends toward the social conditions within the solidary relation that will protect fellow participants against vulnerability while also working for the outward-facing cause. Given the context of political solidarity, challenging unjust or oppressive social conditions, the willingness to equitable share social risk implies the need for continual reevaluation of the distribution of social risk among the participants in solidarity.

On one level, we can see the impact of shared social risk in solidaristic relations as a measure of harm for redistribution: individuals who join a cause that addresses an injustice affecting some members, for instance, aim to transform those social conditions so that the latter may be full members of society; shifting some of the burdens in solidarity away from those affected members so that they can all actively engage in efforts for social change that alters the conditions of injustice. Committing to a cause in solidarity means that individual members use their power to struggle for that cause, accepting

[17] See, for example, Skye Cleary, *How to be Authentic* (New York: St. Martin's, 2022), pp. 244–45; and Iris Young, "Responsibility and Global Justice: A Social Connection Model" (2006) 23 *Social Philosophy and Policy* 105.

that one may be exposed to collective risk in the struggle but that it is better to face the struggle collectively.

In contrast to what I have been suggesting here, the sharing of risk in *civic* solidarity more closely resembles the sharing of risk in insurance plans. Indeed, civic solidarity is conceived as a means of sharing risk so that individuals will not be hindered by vulnerabilities in their exercise of civil, political, social, and economic rights. The willingness to share risk equitably in political solidarity presents some important differences. In insurance, individual participants pay their fair share into a pool so that the pool can cover a much larger sum needed for an "insurance event" should the need arise.[18] Insurance secures protection against a foreseen but unintended event. Insurance companies – or the state – act as third parties that also seek their own good. Social risk in political solidarity is not primarily aimed at protection against a harmful event. Instead, the willingness to share equitable social risk pertains to minimizing the effects of social inequality within the solidary relation. Individuals contribute what they are able given their situations, including vulnerabilities as well as material and social powers.

2.2.4 *Relational Risk*

A fourth facet of risk is the potential for harm or loss from the solidary relation itself. In some symmetrically structured solidary relations, this may be the same as collective risk, as in the case of the solidarity of workers. However, relational risk need not be reduced to collective risk even when the relationship is otherwise equal. As the other facets indicate, solidarity might include the possibility of harm or danger for some participants, while relational risk highlights the fact that the solidary relation itself might pose a hazard for some participants. The inwardly-facing or relational risks of solidarity are multiple but perhaps most evident when personal risk-taking adversely affects others in the relation, that is, when the actions of some pose a risk to the sustained collective relation and future possibilities of solidarity. According to Russo, the "die-in" posed just such a danger. Russo explains that the "die-in" "ended up having a divisive effect within the group" and obscured "the very issue these activists hoped to highlight."[19] The methods employed by some jeopardized the relation between fellow solidarity actors and the relation to the cause they all shared.

[18] Lehtonen and Liukko, "Producing Solidarity, Inequality and Exclusion through Insurance," 158.

[19] Russo, *Solidarity in Practice*, p. 156.

A mark of solidarity is that participants commitment to the cause and the relation entails a commitment to navigate through disagreement whenever possible. Disagreement about practices, methods, and expectations of solidarity bring the bonds themselves to the fore. These differences can divide solidary actors, creating the potential for conflict or contestations. Alicia Garza discusses a commitment to a process of facing disagreement, discussion, and listening that brought to light the effects of actions on individual participants and the harm to the collective bonds within the Black Lives Matter movement. They saw the need to identify the relational risk, along with the collective risk that they undertook together, and how the burden of that commitment might fall unjustly on some members, or how individual actions within the relation violate the expectations of solidarity. This internal process is important to the commitment to the cause of challenging society-wide injustice and violence, it created space and affirmed humanity of participants.[20] Garza emphasizes the connection between the commitment to a goal and the commitment to the solidary relation even while conceding the potential for harm within the relation itself. Political relations like solidarity likely also foster some interpersonal relations. Some of those will be supportive and mutually beneficial, hence the emphasis on "mutuality" found in many accounts of solidarity. But some interpersonal relations might be abusive or domineering.[21] Indeed, social movements have imploded because of the hazards of the relation usurping the focus on the cause.

Existing individual vulnerabilities may be worsened; individual particularity must be considered as the impact of the relation and the effects of actions-in-concert transform the participants, the collective, and the social whole. The solidary relation, with awareness of inward-facing risks, risks that accrue to participants within the relation itself, flexes its solidarity by readjusting to the needs of fellow actors so that single participants are not unduly harmed by the relationship or by the collective risks taken together. The potential for harm associated with the solidary relation ought to be equitable but ensuring that requires assessing the dynamic effects of the solidary relation on individuals within the relation, including personal risk and social risk, and readjusting the distribution of the burdens of the relation of solidarity when necessary. That is not to say that such solidarities will be successful at either achieving the end or goal of the cause or sustaining the praxis that marks the solidarity group. Nor does it mean that individuals will not act in ways that put others in the solidary

20 Alicia Garza, *The Purpose of Power* (New York: One World, 2020).

21 Clare Land, *Decolonizing Solidarity: Dilemmas and Directions for Supporters of Indigenous Struggles* (London: Zed Books, 2015).

relation at heightened risk. But it is to say that the commitment to solidarity involves not only the commitment to a shared cause or goal, but also active measures employed to preserve the bonds of solidarity as much as feasible. I would argue that it also means that individuals will not "go rogue" in a way that puts fellow solidary actors at heightened risk. Domination can appear when some parties abandon solidarity, potentially creating an external relation of dominance against those within the solidarity.

2.3 SUMMING UP RISK

Elsewhere I caution against inequitable distribution of social risk and connect it with other dangerous vicissitudes of the solidary relation, as when social risk is unjustifiably limited, or strategically withdrawn.[22] In these cases, relations of solidarity might heighten the danger to some, especially those participants who are vulnerable to other injustices within the social whole. Revealing how risk may be structurally maldistributed aids in unpacking the expectations of solidarity. My aim in the current discussion is merely to complicate the facets of risk in order to both show how solidarity impacts parties differently and demonstrate some of the critical powers available in assessing the balance of risk and vulnerability among solidary actors. That insight extends beyond political solidarity to other forms of solidarity as well.

The two examples presented in this chapter reveal the interplay of risks and the impact on different parties within the solidary relation. The guerilla theatre of the die-in might have been construed as brave personal risk for a cause, but it impacted the collective project in adverse ways and jeopardized the social existence of migrants seeking to cross the border. Analyzing the case understanding solidarity as "burden sharing" alone would not account for the intuition that the die-in participants violated some aspect of the relation to fellow participants. The controversy damaged the solidary relation as well and made humanitarian aid workers along the border question the commitment of the Migrant Trail Walk participants. The actions of Strauss and Sellz similarly involved personal risk for a cause and might be understood as negatively impacting the collective struggle; however, their commitment to the well-being of those with whom they act in solidarity, rather than destroying trust, demonstrated a commitment and fostered trust. They shared in the prospect of arrest that migrants face along the border, jeopardizing their own social position in the effort to protect others from the vulnerability of undocumented

[22] Sally Scholz, "Pernicious Solidarity," in Juri Viehoff and Andrea Sangiovanni (eds.), *The Virtue of Solidarity* (Oxford: Oxford University Press, 2024), pp. 194–219.

status in a scorching desert. In this case, "burden sharing" might be a valuable tool for making sense of the solidarity with migrants and fellow activists along the border, but that too seems incomplete. The burden that is shared is the personal risk of arrest, but the solidarity is also about the larger collective political action to transform border policies. Deference, which is sometimes used to conceptualize the disposition of solidary actors of privilege, also comes up short; the migrants offered to hide but Strauss and Sellz, rather than deferring to that position, indicated that they could not protect the migrants they were transporting from arrest. Their solidarity was characterized by an open willingness to share in the potential for social harm rather than to employ evasive actions that might have been aligned with the desired action of the migrants and more personally risky. Political solidarity is difficult; rather than judge whether individual actions are right or wrong in solidarity, the examples suggest it would be more productive to turn the critical examination to how the solidary relation impacts the balance of different facets of risk and fosters or impinges on trust in the relation.

Although I have focused on the facets of risk in political solidarity, other forms of solidarity similarly exhibit different, sometimes overlapping, elements of risk. Assessing solidarity – for example, social, civic, or international solidarity – using some of the complex relations of risk, moving beyond measures of shared fate or straightforward burden sharing, reveals a bit more about why solidarity is unique, how multiple expectations are combined in the relation, and why single-axis accounts of solidarity's normative obligations may not suffice.

Participants in solidarity accept the costs of a relationship with others in solidarity. They aim to reduce the potential for harm or loss experienced among fellow participants present in external relations while also mitigating risks internal to the solidarity itself. Of course, the facets of risk become most visible when they are violated, complicating the use of risk within decision making, but acknowledging the presence of risk and being aware of varying facets and distribution patterns might be useful in building trust, thereby fostering solidarity and avoiding domination within the relation.

Individuals put their power in the service of the whole rather than seeking advantage over the group or any part thereof. Creating the critical mechanisms to assess the distribution of various forms of risk within solidarity contributes to avoiding domination. The willingness to assess and share risks in the solidary relation – standing with others – means that one will not abandon the solidary group when the potential for loss emerges; and that the reflective commitment to assess the distribution of risks guides at least some actions in order to maintain the solidarity.

Movements for social change engaged in political solidarity to end injustice, oppression, or tyranny, create loosely formed solidary relations. Within this solidary collective, participants strive to enact the just relations that are absent in the situation they challenge. But domination sometimes seeps into even the most thoughtful or intentional solidarity community. Seeking to articulate a social relation that precludes domination, Jean-Jacques Rousseau eloquently asserts that "each, by giving himself to all, gives himself to no one."[23] Rousseau put equality and nondomination within the social body at the center of his body politic. The expectation is that, in committing to a social body, requiring the alienation of rights to all others in order to get them back with the full force of the community within the Rousseauian framework, no one would be unduly subject to other people or to vulnerabilities created by the organization of that structure. Complete avoidance of dominant positioning within movements for social change is likely not possible; indeed, most solidary movements or communities recognize this and factor it into the collective risk of acting together. The key is that dominant positioning – putting some actors in powerful positions over others – should not become so entrenched as to cement relations of domination and subjection, infecting the solidary relation with injustice. Equitable sharing of social and relational risk point to that readjustment to avoid domination. Looking at solidarity through the lenses of personal, collective, social risk, and relational risk reveals at least some of the transformative aspects and potential of solidarity.[24] The individual participant is transformed by the collective but also transforms the collective.

In the context of political solidarity, failure is often assessed according to whether a goal is achieved. But scrutinizing the willingness to share social risk, the impact of collective risk on individual participants, the demands of personal risk, and the potential hardships accruing because of the solidary relation could provide an alternate assessment of success. The personal and collective transformation that results reveals something about the solidary relation both in reference to the goal of solidarity (without the requirement of completeness in attaining the goal) and in reference to the solidary relation. Solidary actors expect to contribute their efforts to the collective effort. They need to know that others are similarly engaged in a relation for which and

[23] Jean-Jacques Rousseau, "On the Social Contract," in Victor Gourevitch (ed.), *The Social Contract and Other Later Political Writings* (Cambridge: Cambridge University Press, 1997), p. 50.

[24] Scholz, "Persons Transformed by Political Solidarity"; Russo, *Solidarity in Practice*, p. 130 and 138; and Meghan Clark, *The Vision of Catholic Social Thought: The Virtue of Solidarity and the Praxis of Human Rights* (Minneapolis: Fortress Press, 2014), p. 126.

within which they are willing to take risks and be transformed. They also ought to be able to trust that fellow actors in solidarity do not exploit or take advantage of the relation. Solidarity action will not protect one from repercussions of that action from those outside the solidary community, but the commitment at least implies that participants will strive to readjust the distribution of risk (of all sorts) among participants.

2.4 FOSTERING TRUST AND NAVIGATING DISAGREEMENT

Considering the facets of risk as part of the complex relations of solidarity opens the way for thinking about the development of trust in the relation. Empirical research on solidarity supports the notion that people are more likely to act if they know that others will act too; appeals to altruistic or even humanitarian claims alone will not likely generate the political response necessary for effective mobilization for social change. Bo Rothstein's study of social solidarity for civil society affirms that "forward-looking predictions" about whether fellow participants will act similarly rather than free-ride are more important for maintaining solidarity and building trust than identity, feeling, or even past commitments to social justice. Rothstein describes the "social trap": "this is [the] situation where all agents will be worse off because even if they know they would all gain from cooperation, lacking trust that the others will cooperate, they will themselves abstain from cooperation."[25] Rothstein also notes the positive impact of expectations on forward-looking action, which he thinks universal policies and institutional structures ensure in civic solidarity arrangements: "forward looking strategic thinking in the sense that *what agents do, depends on what they think the other agents are going to do*."[26] Rothstein's remarks emphasize the value of assessing the complex facets of risk and can be applied to political solidarity as well. Free riding on the collective risk is hazardous for some more than others; reciprocity of personal risks is not always desirable or feasible; and social and relational costs of solidarity for some ought to be countered with the sharing of more collective and social risk by others. Forward-looking action that stubbornly attends to the impact of the collective commitment to solidarity in and on the respective lives of participants builds trust within the relation.

[25] Bo Rothstein, "Solidarity, Diversity, and the Quality of Government," in Keith Banting and Will Kymlicka (eds.), *The Strains of Commitment: The Political Sources of Solidarity in Diverse Societies* (New York: Oxford University Press, 2017), p. 309.

[26] Rothstein, "Solidarity, Diversity, and the Quality of Government," p. 309.

Reciprocity alone does not adequately capture the dynamic interplay between situations, needs, efforts, and causes within political solidarity, although counterfactual reciprocity comes closer: "I help you now that you are in trouble because you would have helped me had I been in the same trouble, and this even if I know that this will never be the case."[27] A willingness to share equitably social risk challenges reciprocity and expands the factors of counterfactual reciprocity. Such a willingness might reasonably be viewed as a form of balancing: assessing and exchanging risks within the solidary relation and evaluating the effects of collective risk and social risk on the ability to assume relational and personal risks, for instance. So too, engaging in collective risk and demonstrating commitment through personal or social risk has a bigger impact on the relation of solidarity among members than identity with or immersing oneself in the situations of oppression.[28] Concrete practices that engender trust, such as openly assessing risk and the distribution of social risk as well as collective risk, contribute to maintaining the cooperative bond of solidarity. Actors in solidarity have to be able to see that their "standing together" has a forward-looking goal, and they need to believe that others are similarly thinking both laterally toward them in the solidary relation and forward toward that which they can achieve together.

These are complex demands that distinguish solidarity as a relation from mere collective action or identity group affiliation. Solidary actors adopt a mode of thinking that considers the direct connections between action and injustice in their social criticism of existing society, but that also considers the forward-looking possibilities of something different which is lived in the relations with similarly committed others in solidarity. Equitable sharing of social risk allows an individual to assume or accept this complex, even burdensome, mode of thinking and being because of the belief that other solidary actors are similarly engaged.

Solidary groups do not need to seek consensus (and formal procedures of decision-making are relatively rare in loosely formed social movements). But the investment in an alternative solidary community focused on ameliorating injustice or seeking not to recreate injustice in the solidary relation itself implies that working together in spite of disagreement and through disagreement is better for our individual and collective well-being than otherwise. I would distinguish two basic forms of conflict within solidarity. The first is a pernicious form that shifts burdens unduly onto some participants as when relations of domination infect the solidary group. The second is a productive

[27] Van Parijs, "Concluding Reflections," p. 421.
[28] Land, *Decolonizing Solidarity*, p. 149.

form of disagreement or conflict that opens space for the praxis of solidarity to continue to transform. In other words, the need to assess the distribution of various forms of risk within solidary relations means that concrete practices of attending to others (listening, observing lived realities, and seeking historical understanding, to name just a few) become important elements of the solidary relation and an individual's solidary disposition. Cleary captures this well in describing acting in solidarity: "Actions always take place amidst a haze of ambiguity and risk, so we have to do what we can to become aware of the paradoxes of action, to look for alternate points of view, to listen to people who disagree, to stay open to changing our minds when we discover we've made mistakes, but to leap in and act anyway."[29] Disagreement about method, especially when those methods heighten risk for some participants, demands work to maintain the solidary relation, even while continuing to address the cause for social change that unites participants. As Garza emphasizes, practices of repair demonstrate the challenge of conflict and the possibilities that emerge when conflict becomes an accepted element of solidary relation insofar as it helps participants reflect on, discuss, and perhaps recommit to the social.

2.5 CONCLUSION

The relation between solidary participants and the goal, and the relation among solidary participants, are analytically or conceptually distinguishable; however, within the work of solidarity, they are lived together. Individual actors commit to a shared goal and act toward that goal, understanding their actions in solidarity as actions-in-concert with all other participants. For the individual, the goal might inform the agency insofar as it sets the agenda for decision-making. For the group, the lived experience of agency in solidarity works toward the shared goal. Agency and goal unite in the relation of solidarity itself. That is the crucial point: solidarity is distinct from merely collective action because a relationship, however tenuous, is maintained beyond a given action or even a given set of actions. A workers' union, not merely a collective action of striking, evinces a relation of solidarity. The strike demonstrates an opportunity or moment for intense critical reflection when social risk is perhaps most evident and the willingness to share social risk equitably is most needed. Notice that this is slightly different than the notion of "mutual advantage" which is often used within discussions of solidarity. Rather than thinking through what advantage we can all share, we shift to

[29] Cleary, *How to be Authentic*, p. 248.

think about how the distribution of risks – collective, personal, social, and relational –affects consociates.

One objection to the account sketched here is that the emphasis on assessing risk and considering the vulnerability of others at least implies a conscious choice open to negotiation and deliberation. In response, I would argue that the willingness to accept and share social risk in solidarity, like the assumption of risk in other moral relations, surely is sometimes consciously chosen, but participants also sometimes find themselves assuming social risk without their consideration of the choice. Just as one can be swept up in friendships or loving relations – or perhaps a better analogy is being swept into a situation of rescue, realizing that one is committed to the relation without choosing it, one may be swept up in solidarity. The commitment is lived or experienced. The appearance of a voluntary choice to engage in solidarity is found especially in asymmetrical solidarity relations, where powerful actors join with those who suffer oppression or injustice in a shared commitment to a cause. But, in other relations, risk emerges with the collective commitment wherein individual actors are motivated by a number of diverse compulsions.

In a related vein, it might be suggested that the focus on risk reduces solidarity to an interpersonal relationship or even an individual disposition. On the contrary, as I have sketched the facets of risk here, the solidarity is a moral relation entailing networks of relations between and among participants, the goal of solidarity, and outside others. Understanding solidarity as a moral relation in this manner does not invite the critique that the self-interest of human beings makes solidarity impossible because of the reluctance to tie one's lot to that of others. Centering social risk, the willingness to share and the equitable distribution of risk, shifts the question about self-interest. Self-interest becomes an aspect of risk factored into the social risk of solidarity. This does not, of course, mitigate the powerful incentives to act in self-interested ways outside of solidarity. But it does allow us to begin thinking about solidarity as consistent with, rather than opposed to, self-interest.

Focusing on the risk of relationships within political solidarity, and the prospect of fostering such relations in expansive movements for social change, offers another way to think about solidarity in addition to the action-in-concert to accomplish a cause for social change. Assessing risk guides praxis, avoids domination, and establishes trust. Risking solidarity – willingly accepting to share equitably risk related to working collectively for a cause or goal – not only transforms the individual and the group, solidarity transforms politics. Acting in solidarity creates new communities or new collective imaginaries that redefine social and political relations, offering new and creative accounts of what constitutes membership or participation, while also navigating or negotiating conceptions of legitimate expectations of solidaristic others.[30] In doing so, the risk of solidarity is disruptive and destabilizing; it recreates politics anew, risking stability in favor of a participatory self-critical relation that dares to provide a new model of how to engage together across differences while also critically constituting or reconstituting the ties that bind. Willingness to share equitably collective, personal, social, and relational risk in particular contexts is at the heart of solidarity.

[30] Maurice Stierl, "A Sea of Struggle: Activist Border Interventions in the Mediterranean Sea," in Ilker Ataç, Kim Rygiel, and Maurice Stierl (eds.), *The Contentious Politics of Refugee and Migrant Protest and Solidarity Movements* (New York: Routledge, 2017), pp. 47–48; Russo, *Solidarity in Practice*, p. 146; and Peter Hall, "The Political Sources of Social Solidarity," in Keith Banting and Will Kymlicka (eds.), *The Strains of Commitment: The Political Sources of Solidarity in Diverse Societies* (New York: Oxford University Press, 2017), p. 214.

3

Antinomies and Aporias in Official Human Rights Solidarity Argumentation across the Global South/North Axis

OBIORA CHINEDU OKAFOR

3.1 INTRODUCTION

3.1.1 *Conceptual Framework*

Utilizing a quasi-empirical methodology, this chapter teases out and reflects on certain antinomies and aporias that tend to characterize the broad sets of international human rights solidarity argumentation that emanate from each of the Global North and Global South. The chapter focuses on the broad tendencies within each of these bodies of argumentation regarding the appropriateness or otherwise of the imposition of international legal *obligations* on states to express international solidarity to victims of human rights violations and deprivations around the world. The targeted Global North/Global South bodies of argumentation tend to focus chiefly on who is *obligated* to extend such international human rights solidarity, to whom, and in what ways.

The concern here is not just with the mere fact of the existence of significant antinomies and aporias within each of the Global North's and Global South's broad sets of international human rights solidarity argumentation. It is also with the rather ironic circulation and eclipsing of these antinomies and aporias in plain sight; their relationships to state sovereignty argumentation; and their connections to global power relations as ideationally constitutive forces. In the last respect, the key question is what the relative

The author would like to thank Jeff Baek, Okechukwu Effoduh, David Chang-Dae Hyung, and Shea Wilcox for their excellent research assistance. He is also grateful to the editors of this volume and Prof. Anu Bradford of Columbia Law School; Prof. Carlos Vazquez of Georgetown Law School; and Prof. Md. Rizwanul Islam of North-South University, Bangladesh, for facilitating the presentation of earlier drafts of this chapter to scholarly audiences at their various universities.

roles of values/norms in international human rights solidarity argumentation are, vis-à-vis global power relations. All of these issues raise the key question of the extent to which global power asymmetries, significantly more than human rights ideals, continue to condition when, how, and in relation to what or whom, scholars and practitioners ask the solidarity question today, including in relation to UN (human rights) bodies.

To illustrate, the kind of more specific sub questions that drive this enquiry include, for example, why the so-called responsibility to protect (or R2P) as a hard law obligation (not its soft law or "charity based" form) is not much more widely viewed in either UN or Global North official human rights discourse as extending either at all, or nearly as much, to economic and social rights deprivation and protection in much poorer countries.[1] Why does legally binding R2P, at least as a concept and discourse, appear to focus near exclusively, if not totally, on civil and political rights deprivation and protection in the same much poorer countries?[2] Why, for example, have the ostensibly protective impulses and logics undergirding legally binding R2P not yet been extended to any significant degree to the area of access to COVID-19 vaccines in most of the world? With notable exceptions, Global South countries tend to stand firmly in favor of ensuring that the two positions outlined here are "righted," while Global North countries have not tended to be nearly as enthusiastic.

On the other hand, why do the very same Global South countries who tend to strongly endorse binding international human rights solidarity obligations on the global level in favor of the advancement of economic and social rights within their territories also tend to oppose binding obligations or authority in favor of Global North states to intervene (not necessarily forcibly) to help protect against egregious violations of civil and political rights in those same places. Significant exceptions do, of course, exist in this regard, including in the case of intra-African interventions in such cases by African regional bodies.[3]

To what extent can the answers to these kinds of questions, and the positions taken in relation to them across the Global North/South axis, be

[1] This is apparent from the texts of the relevant paragraphs in the *UN World Summit Outcome Document* of 2005, which focuses almost entirely on genocide, ethnic cleansing, war crimes, and crimes against humanity (all which, admittedly, can have a more minor economic and social rights deprivation aspect). See A/RES/60/1, paras 138–139.

[2] Ibid.

[3] See Christina Powell, *The African Union's Emerging Peace and Security Regime: Opportunities and Challenges for Delivering on the Responsibility to Protect: The African Union and the Responsibility to Protect* (Pretoria: Institute for Security Studies, 2005), p. 11.

chiefly attributed to the immanent and/or social power of human rights norms and values? One does not have to be an international relations "realist" to see that there seems to be a lot more at play in the kinds of arguments favored by states on both sides of the Global North/South axis than simply strong beliefs in, or adherence to, international human rights ideas, values, and norms.

To be clear, however, the point of this chapter is not to argue in favor of either the Global North or South positions on such questions at hand, but to demonstrate and critically reflect on the nature and implications of the antinomies and aporias that appear to be present in each of the targeted Global North/South bodies of discourse (concerning the obligatoriness of expressing international human rights solidarity in specific contexts).

3.1.2 *Methodology*

A quasi-empirical approach is adopted in order to grapple with the chapter's key concerns in a more concrete way. The overarching question that is raised in this introductory section is systematically investigated through a survey, and analyses, of the specific sample slices of international human rights argumentation described in this chapter. In order to ensure the feasibility of the research that animates the chapter, its focus is limited to an investigation of *official* (i.e. state-made) international human rights solidarity argumentation, within specific UN bodies. Thus, the bodies of such argumentation that are analyzed here are limited to statements made, and votes taken, within the UN General Assembly (UNGA), Security Council (UNSC), and Human Rights Council (UNHRC). The purposive selection of the UN itself and these specific UN bodies as the primary sites within which to analyze the targeted type of argumentation was suggested by the very nature of that argumentation.

The investigation of these UNGA, UNSC, and UNHRC statements and votes focused, in turn, on relevant statements made and positions taken by a purposively selected, but broadly representative, sample of key states and regional bodies from each of the Global North and South. The selection of a state as "key" was a function of its relative power and influence within its geopolitical region (though, due to space constraints, not all key countries could be included). In the end, whatever its policy choices, each selected state tends to typify countries identified as either belonging to the Global North or the Global South. The purposive nature of this sample, and the aforementioned inbuilt "controls," were deemed appropriate, given the well-established historical trend, as recorded in the relevant literature (discussed throughout this chapter). The tenor of this literature suggests that there was little to no reasonable expectation that a different slate would yield a different result.

These purposively selected countries and regional bodies are as follows: Global North states/regional bodies – the United States, the United Kingdom, France, Russia, and the European Union; and Global South states/regional bodies – India, Nigeria, Brazil, the African Union, and China.

Regarding the inclusion of China in the Global South, it should be noted that, although that state is now, in many respects, economically, politically, and militarily powerful and influential enough to be characterized as a Global North state, its continued subordination to the United States in some respects (such as in UN politics and in regard to being mostly at the receiving end of the US/China economic sanction "war"),[4] and its enduring close alignment with the Global South group at the UN,[5] leaves its location in the typology employed here at least open to serious debate. However, given the vastly dominant orientation toward the Global South of its historical and current UN praxis, it is treated here as – on balance – a Global South state.[6] In any case, as Karin Mickelson has taught us, countries ultimately self-identify (or not) as part of the Global South.[7]

Regarding the UNGA, extensive searches of key and related proxy terms and expressions (such as international solidarity, responsibility to protect, intervention, humanitarian intervention, military intervention, sanctions, and Chapter VII) were conducted. Four hundred meeting records were read.

There were 64 meetings in which relevant issues were discussed. During those meetings, the United States made a total of 19 statements in the debates and votes at these sampled meetings, the United Kingdom made 6, France 7, Russia 18, the European Union 11, China 18, India 10, Nigeria 8, Brazil 8, and the African Union made none. It should be noted here that the fact that certain selected states or international organizations sometimes did not make any statement or vote does not raise any significant methodological issue. For example, survey participants sometimes abstain.

Regarding the UNSC, the focus was also on official statements and votes in that body. In phase one of this research, hundreds of meeting records (from the 5615th meeting on January 11, 2007 to the 8950th meeting on January 19,

4 See Jeremy Feltman, *China's Expanding Influence at the UN: And How the United States Should React* (Washington DC: Brookings Institution, 2020), pp. 1–3; and Anthony Tellez, "Here Are All the U.S. Sanctions against China," *Forbes Magazine*, February 8, 2023, available at: www.forbes.com/sites/anthonytellez/2023/02/08/here-are-all-the-us-sanctions-against-china/?sh=2c88001715b4 (last accessed September 15, 2024).

5 The Group of 77 at the United Nations, available at: www.g77.org (last accessed September 15, 2024).

6 Ibid.

7 See Karin Mickelson, "*Rhetoric and Rage*: Third World Voices in International Legal Discourse" (1998) 16 *Wisconsin International Law Journal* 353.

2022) were surveyed looking for similar key words and expressions as were focused on in the research into UNGA debates. One hundred and three meetings met the criteria. During these meetings, the United States made 33 statements in the debates/votes at these sampled meetings, the United Kingdom made 25, France 37, Russia 36, the European Union 2, China 23, India 7, Nigeria 6, Brazil 10, and the African Union 2. In phase two of this aspect of the research, all UNSC debates that had human rights on their agenda were searched. There were about ten records that fit this description. Only four of those meetings debated to a significant extent any of the issues related to the current research. During this sub-set of meetings, the United States made 1 statement in those four meetings, the United Kingdom made 2, France 2, Russia 4, the European Union none, China 2, India 1, Nigeria none, Brazil none, and the African Union none.

Regarding the search of the records of UNHRC meetings, the focus of the survey was mainly on the votes taken in that body on the international legal obligations of states to aid in the realization of economic and social rights around the world. Six recent UNHRC resolutions that were adopted by recorded votes were analyzed closely to assess the voting records on these issues of the eight purposively sampled states and regional bodies already identified. These six UNHRC resolutions were adopted between July 2020 and April 2022. Although this is a shorter historical period than was focused upon in our search of meeting records of the UNSC and UNGA, there is ample evidence in the literature to suggest that the observed voting pattern of these states was not significantly different on the questions at issue in this chapter in the two decades before the period July 2020.[8]

In the end, the body of evidence thus collected was analyzed against the conceptual framework outlined here for the extent to which it supports or troubles the content and orientation of that frame.

3.1.3 *Limitations of the Research*

Since the focus of the research on which this chapter is based was on official human rights solidarity argumentation within the UN, the chapter does not necessarily account for the tendencies within and orientation of other types of international human rights solidarity argumentation (as for e.g. those made by civil society groups). What is more, the chapter does not incorporate data from debates and votes in other UN rights organs or specialized agencies. Secondly, the focus of this chapter is on international human rights solidarity argumentation at the global level, and not on similar kinds of argumentation at various

[8] See Simon Hug, "Dealing with Human Rights in International Organizations" (2016) 21 *Journal of Human Rights* 15.

regional levels (e.g. at the African Union, European Union, Commonwealth, Association of Southeast Asian Nations, or Organization of American States).

It should be noted, however, that none of these limitations is fatal to the argument developed in this chapter. This is because the evidence canvassed is from the proceedings of the UN's three major, and arguably most important, organs. In any case, the preexisting literature strongly suggests that the positions taken in these three UN organs by the purposive sample of states that are focused on in this chapter tends to represent both the positions they have taken in other fora and the behavior of similarly situated or peer states.[9]

3.1.4 *Definitions*

The key terms and expressions that animate and frame the discussion in this chapter require definition. Regarding the concept of *international human rights solidarity*, I adopt the latest version of the definitions offered by successive UN Independent Experts appointed by the UN Human Rights Council to study it and its implications in and for international law and relations. According to these experts, this expression denotes: "The expression of a spirit of unity among individuals, peoples, States and international organizations, encompassing the union of interests, purposes and actions and the recognition of different needs and rights to achieve common goals."[10]

As it is used in this chapter, the term *antinomy* simply refers to "logical contradictions."[11] This definition is preferred despite the availability of more complex definitions within various academic disciplines. As used here, the term *aporia* is defined as an irresolvable internal contradiction or logical disjunction in an argument or set of arguments. I do, however, retain a hint (only a hint) within my usage of the term aporia of its quality of serving as a kind of "creative force," or at least, as "possibly creative,"[12] reflecting the Socratic use of aporia as a way to bring to light a need for further investigation.[13]

9 For example, see Anne Orford, "Muscular Humanitarianism" (1999) 10 *European Journal of International Law* 679–711, at 680; and Berta Hernández-Truyol, "Human Rights, Globalization, and Culture," in Berta Hernández-Truyol (ed.), *Moral Imperialism: A Critical Anthology* (New York: New York University Press, 2002), pp. 355–356.

10 See the *Draft UN Declaration on the Right to International Solidarity* (2017), and the *Revised UN Draft Declaration on the Right to International Solidarity* (2023).

11 See Moshe Farjoun, Wendy Smith, Ann Langley, & Haridimus Tsoukas (eds.), *Dualities, Dialectics, and Paradoxes in Organizational Life* (Oxford: Oxford University Press, 2018), p. 141.

12 See Valiur Rahaman, *Interpretations; Essays in Literary Theory* (Jaipur: RBSA Publishers, 2011).

13 Vasilis Politis, *The Structure of Enquiry in Plato's Early Dialogues* (Cambridge: Cambridge University Press, 2015), p. 93.

And so, of course, even within the antinomies and aporias that are observed, some emancipatory potential may be evident. For, as Upendra Baxi has taught us, have not even human rights discourses and praxis themselves *always* accommodated *both* politics of emancipation and politics of domination – and has it not done so in every single epoch and at one and the same time?[14]

The concept of *power* that is deployed in this chapter is largely Weberian. And so, it primarily denotes "the probability of forcing one's will on the behavior of others."[15] This conception of power is, however, modified by Foucault's crucial and well-known caveat that power is relational.[16] As used here, the term *interest* refers to "something that improves [or is perceived as likely to improve] one's position with respect to either of these is in his interest."[17]

The concept of *norms* that is preferred here refers to authoritative standards for assessing conduct (as opposed to denoting a pattern of accepted behavior).[18] Connected, but different from "norms," the term *values* is used here as denoting "what is deemed good, such as when we say that knowledge or justice are values, which ought to be promoted. Talk about values is also often talk about ideals that guide one's actions."[19]

3.2 ON THE ANTINOMIES AND APORIAS THAT CHARACTERIZE OFFICIAL HUMAN RIGHTS SOLIDARITY ARGUMENTATION ACROSS THE GLOBAL SOUTH/NORTH AXIS

3.2.1 *The Tendency to Antinomy and Aporia in Official Global North International Human Rights Solidarity Argumentation*

3.2.1.1 The Character of the Broad Set of Arguments that Tend to be Made by Global North States

THEIR BROAD POSITION ON A BINDING INTERNATIONAL CIVIL AND POLITICAL RIGHTS SOLIDARITY OBLIGATION The studied UNSC debates

[14] See Upendra Baxi, *The Future of Human Rights* (Delhi: Oxford University Press, 2006), p. 11.
[15] See Catherine Brennan, *Max Weber on Power and Social Stratification: An Interpretation and Critique* (Milton Park: Taylor & Francis, 2018), p. 72.
[16] See Michel Foucault, "The Subject and Power" (1982) 8(4) *Critical Inquiry* 777–795, at 777–788.
[17] See Theodore M. Benditt, "The Concept of Interest in Political Theory" (1975) 3 *Political Theory* 245–258, at 256.
[18] But see Cristina Bicchieri, *The Grammar of Society: The Nature and Dynamics of Social Norms* (Cambridge: Cambridge University Press, 2006).
[19] See Christine Tappolet & Mauro Rossi, "What Is Value? Where Does It Come From? A Philosophical Perspective," in Tobias Brosch & David Sander (eds.), *Handbook of Value: Perspectives from Economics, Neuroscience, Philosophy, Psychology and Sociology* (Oxford: Oxford University Press, 2015), pp 3–22, p. 4.

and votes reveal certain dominant patterns in the official international human rights solidarity argumentation of the sample of Global North states/regional bodies that are focused on in this chapter. These Global North states and regional groups (namely the United States, the United Kingdom, France, and the EU) tended to affirm the existence of a binding international civil and political rights solidarity obligation and also strongly support the imposition of sanctions or of intervention, at the very least by the UNSC, ostensibly in order to protect civil and political (CP) rights around the world. Thus, despite their consistent opposition to the UNHRC's appointment of a UN Independent Expert on Human Rights and International Solidarity,[20] as is well known, Global North states in the UNSC have tended to strongly support the expression of international solidarity in aid of the protection of CP rights the world over, and have usually done so on the basis of their view that this kind of praxis is both authorized by, and required under, international law.[21]

A few examples from the records of these UNSC debates and votes will suffice to illustrate these interconnected points. First, in the debate during UNSC meeting No. 8945 on the "Situation in Mali," the United States strongly supported intervention to protect lives, property, and freedom of movement in that Global South country, stating that MINUSMA (the UN intervention force there) "needs, following the Secretary-General's proposal, an increase to its troop ceiling. That will help protect civilians in central Mali with more quick-reaction forces and air assets." Despite its opposition to the use of the UNSC's Chapter VII authority in dealing with the situation in that particular area, the US delegation supported MINUSMA during UNSC meetings Nos. 8809, 8273, and 8794. The United States also supported external interventions of one type or other to protect civilians during UNSC meetings Nos. 8859 and 8290 on "Sudan and South Sudan." The positions taken by France and the United Kingdom during the sampled UNSC meetings fit into the same mold. In all of these cases, the tenor of the records of the meetings also show that:

(a) the United States, France, and the United Kingdom supported *a binding legal obligation* on states (and certainly on members of the UNSC) to

[20] For example, see the recent vote recorded at the 50th Session of the UNHRC on Resolution A/HRC/L.9 on July 7, 2022.

[21] Some prominent academics have also lent support to this broad argument. See Laurence Boisson d'Charzounes, "Responsibility to Protect: Reflecting Solidarity," in Rüdiger Wolfrum & Chie Kojima (eds.), *Solidarity: A Structural Principle of International Law* (Berlin: Springer, 2010), pp. 94–95; and Harold Koh, "Humanitarian Intervention: Time for Better Law" (2017) 111 *American Journal of International Law Unbound* 287.

express a type of international solidarity by intervening in suitable situations around the world in aid of the protection of certain human rights;
(b) these Global North states appeared to be acting in conformity with the conception of the responsibility to protect (R2P) that is outlined in the text of the relevant paragraphs of the UN Summit Outcome document; and
(c) the human rights interventions that these states supported were almost entirely aimed at protecting CP rights, such as the rights to life, freedom of movement, and property.

To be sure, there were in very few cases some mention (especially by France) of the extension by Global North states of humanitarian aid to the populations of the countries in which the interventions at issue were being undertaken, but these were references to charitable gestures rather than to the implementation of a binding international legal obligation to express international solidarity. Overall, the dominant pattern revealed here is very much in line with the historical behavior of these particular states, and of Global North states in general.[22]

It should be noted, however, that Russia (which – though largely non-Western in alignment – can only be reasonably characterized as a Global North state) tended to buck this trend. In the UNSC meetings canvassed, Russia almost always rejected the imposition of sanctions or of intervention as a means of protecting CP rights in other countries. Russia has also not tended to see the imposition of such sanctions as an action that is required by international law.[23]

It is also noteworthy that the sampled UNGA debates and votes (as are described in Section 3.1) showed similar trends to those reported with regard to the debates and votes in the UNSC. For instance, France mostly supported military intervention and sanctions in aid of the protection of CP rights in other lands. As might be expected from the preceding discussion, Russia mostly rejected the imposition of such sanctions/interventions, arguing that they tend to threaten international peace and security.[24]

THEIR BROAD POSITION ON A BINDING INTERNATIONAL ECONOMIC AND SOCIAL RIGHTS SOLIDARITY OBLIGATION Despite the strength of the commitment of the sampled Global North states to implementing an international

[22] See Anne Orford, *Reading Humanitarian Intervention* (Cambridge: Cambridge University Press, 2003), p. 158; and Hernández-Truyol, "Human Rights, Globalization, and Culture," 355–356.
[23] For example, see UNSC, 77th year: 8944th meeting, Monday, January 10, 2022.
[24] For example, see UNGA, 75th session, 5th Committee, 8th meeting, Wednesday, December 30, 2020.

legal obligation on states (read powerful states) to express international solidarity to victims of CP rights violations around the world, there is little evidence in the studied UN debates and votes of significant Global North state support for a binding international legal obligation to express international solidarity to poorer states in aid of the fuller realization of economic and social (ES) rights in those countries. Indeed, there is explicit evidence in the records of the UNHRC that these Global North states tend to strongly oppose the existence of a *binding* international legal obligation on states to aid in the realization of ES rights beyond their national frontiers.[25]

In addition to the tenor of this evidence from the records of the proceedings of the UNHRC, it is significant in the current respect that, during the negotiations for the adoption of the Optional Protocol to the International Covenant on Economic, Social and Cultural Rights (OP ICESCR), almost all Global North states involved argued that international cooperation and assistance (a key component of the international human rights solidarity obligation) was merely a moral rather than an international legal obligation under the International Covenant on Economic, Social and Cultural Rights (ICESCR), while Global South states argued the opposite.[26] It is pertinent to note that this position contrasts with the view of the authoritative interpreter of the ICESCR, the UN Committee on Economic, Social and Cultural Rights.[27] This committee has emphasized that it is "particularly incumbent on states parties and other actors *in a position to assist*" (i.e. almost always Global North states) to provide international assistance and cooperation, especially economic and technical, to enable developing countries to fulfil their "core and other obligations" under the Covenant.[28]

And, further, the overwhelming orientation of the evidence gleaned from the targeted UNHRC proceedings indicates that these same Global North states are extremely reluctant to agree to, or endorse the implementation of any UNHRC mandated, or even strongly hortatory, measures designed to implement international ES rights solidarity obligations in a robust way. For example, following debate in the UNHRC on Resolution A/HRC/RES/49/15 ("effects of foreign debt and other related international financial obligations of states on the full enjoyment of all human rights, particularly economic, social and cultural rights"), adopted March 31, 2022, all EU states (France included) and the United States voted against its adoption. Among other

[25] For example, see A/HRC/RES/50/8, July 19, 2022.
[26] See E/CN.4/2006/47, paras 77–86.
[27] Committee on Economic, Social and Cultural Rights, General Comment No. 14 (2000), paras 43–45.
[28] Ibid.

things, this resolution "reiterates the call on industrialized countries [i.e. the Global North] to implement the enhanced programme of debt relief without further delay and to agree to cancel all the official bilateral debt of those countries covered by the programme in return for their making demonstrable commitments to poverty reduction," so as to enhance poverty reduction in the Global South. While there were other reasons offered by these Global North states for their opposition to the adoption of this resolution,[29] logically, the fact that this text called upon them to begin implementing a robust debt relief program of a kind that they have largely failed to do for decades was most likely one of those reasons.

A very similar story unfolded in regard to the otherwise successful votes on the adoption of the following UNHRC resolution: A/HRC/RES/49/19 ("promoting and protecting economic, social and cultural rights within the context of addressing inequalities in the recovery from the COVID-10 pandemic"), adopted April 1, 2022, which "stresses that it is essential to scale up international cooperation to support developing and least-developed countries and those in marginalized and vulnerable situations who are disproportionately bearing the socio-economic impacts of the pandemic ... as part of the global response and recovery efforts based on unity, solidarity, multilateral cooperation and the principle of leaving no one behind." This was also the case with A/HRC/RES/47/11 ("the contribution of development to the enjoyment of all human rights"), adopted July 12, 2021, which "calls upon Member States and the United Nations system, including its funds and programmes and specialized agencies, in accordance with their mandates, to continue to mobilize resources to carry out development cooperation and to assist States, particularly developing and the least developed countries, upon their request, in promoting sustainable development."

The Global North opposition and resistance to the imposition of any kind of international legal mandate on them to express international solidarity in aid of the realization of ES rights in poorer countries (including even soft international legal obligations) has perhaps been at its strongest in regard to the enunciation and implementation of the duty to cooperate in aid of the fuller realization by various peoples in the Global South of their right to development.[30] For example, EU states voted against UNHRC resolution A/

[29] For the reasons long offered by most Global North states, and a strong rebuttal, see A/HRC/25/50, March 27, 2014.

[30] For example, see "Why a Convention on the Right to Development?" (July 3, 2019), available at: www.cetim.ch/why-a-convention-on-the-right-to-development/ (last accessed September 24, 2024).

HRC/RES/48/8 ("promotion of a democratic and equitable international order"), adopted October 8, 2021, which – among other things – emphasized

> (c) the right of every human person and all peoples to development; ... (e) The right to an international economic order based on equal participation in the decision-making process, interdependence, mutual interest, solidarity and cooperation among all States; ... (m) The promotion of equitable access to benefits from the international distribution of wealth through enhanced international cooperation, in particular in international economic, commercial and financial relations.

A very similar voting pattern was observed in relation to UNHRC resolutions A/HRC/RES/48/10 ("the right to development"), adopted October 8, 2021, which emphasized "the need to strive for greater acceptance, operationalization and realization of the right to development at the international level while urging all Member States to undertake at the national level the necessary policy formulation and to institute the measures required for the implementation of the right to development as an integral part of all human rights and fundamental freedoms."

The same kind of story played out with regard to UNHRC resolution A/HRC/RES/44/18 ("enhancement of international cooperation in the field of human rights"), adopted July 17, 2020, which "urges States to take, upon request by affected Member States, the measures necessary to enhance bilateral, regional and international cooperation aimed at addressing the adverse impact of consecutive and compounded global crises, such as ... financial and economic crises ... on the full enjoyment of human rights."

It is telling, for the purposes of the argument being made, that this pattern of opposition and resistance on the part of the Global North to legally binding duties on states that are in a position to do so, to positively express international economic and social rights solidarity toward much poorer states, has remained so, despite the fact that, at most, only a handful of states (such as the United States) continue to explicitly deny the status of economic and social rights as human rights.

3.2.1.2 The Antinomies and Aporias within this Broad Set of Global North Arguments

An analysis of the largely opposing approach(es) to international solidarity that has been adopted by these sample Global North states in their UNSC, UNGA, and UNHRC praxis, depending quite significantly on whether it is CP or ES rights that are engaged, suggests that their broad body of international human rights solidarity argumentation is marked by antinomy and aporia.

If, by antinomy, we mean a contradiction or a paradox, then there is certainly a significant conceptual contradiction or paradox in accepting (as almost all of these Global North states do, save the United States) that ES rights are human rights that are indivisible from, inextricably tied to, and interdependent with CP rights;[31] arguing strongly in favor of an international legal obligation to express international human rights solidarity when CP rights have been or are likely to be breached; and then rejecting a similar obligation in the face of ongoing or potential ES rights breaches.

What, however, is the creative potential, if any, and howsoever mild, of this aporia? Could it be that highlighting it more could trouble Global North officialdom's narratives and self-images enough to produce a measure of change in the opposing direction, toward the greater acceptance of binding international ES rights solidarity obligations and therefore in favor of significantly greater enjoyment of the fruits of international ES solidarity praxis around the world? This may well be so, but it should be noted that faith and even hope in this possibility may not account as fully as it ought to for the materiality and persistence of the power/interest calculus that has contributed appreciably to the generation of this aporia in the first place.[32]

3.2.2 *The Tendency to Antinomy and Aporia in Official Global South International Human Rights Solidarity Argumentation*

3.2.2.1 The Broad Character of the Arguments that Tend to be Made by Global South States

THEIR BROAD POSITION ON A BINDING INTERNATIONAL CIVIL AND POLITICAL RIGHTS SOLIDARITY OBLIGATION The sampled UNSC debates and votes described in Section 3.1 indicate certain key patterns. A few examples will suffice to illustrate the dominant tendency to hesitation and ambivalence (and certainly not robust support) of Global South states toward the implementation (even by the UNSC) of a binding international CP rights solidarity obligation. First of all, China has – at best – been largely lukewarm toward the (robust) implementation of such an obligation and has, thus,

[31] See the *Vienna Declaration and Program of Action*, June 25, 1993, to which all the sample Global North states subscribed.

[32] For the difference between faith and hope in international law, see Karin Mickelson, "Hope in a TWAIL Register" (2020) 1 *Third World Approaches to International Law Review* 14.

tended to view international sanctions and interventions to protect such human rights as the right to life, property, and freedom of movement with a significant degree of suspicion or hesitation. It expressed this position for instance in the debates on the following situations: UNSC meeting 8945 on Mali (during which it exhorted fellow UNSC member states to listen to Mali's point of view); meeting 8859 on South Sudan (where it called on the UNSC to heed the AU's call to lift sanctions on that country); meeting 8710 on Libya (during which it urged the council to rather enforce the arms embargo on Libya instead of authorizing a military intervention in that country); meeting 8468 on Darfur (where it called on the council to primarily focus on strengthening Sudan's internal state capacity and to lift the sanctions it imposed on that country); and meeting 8288 on Mali (during which it urged the international community to support the people of Mali in making their own decisions).

India tended to remain quite wary of international (read Global North) intervention in the affairs of other states ostensibly to protect CP rights (read Global South states), as it has almost always been throughout its history.[33] For example, in UNSC meeting 8906, it urged the much greater use of the less forceful process and authority in chapter 6 of the UN Charter, rather than what it saw as too ready a resort to chapter 7 of that constitutional document. In meeting 7019, it argued that the protection of civilians during armed conflict was primarily a national responsibility and that international intervention to do so should not be resorted to too readily.

Brazil tended to argue that the imposition of sanctions or of interventions ought to be utilized as a last resort – reflecting a regional historical tendency to be generally wary of Global North intervention allegedly in aid of CP rights in the Global South.[34] For example, in UNSC meeting 7247, on the maintenance of international peace and security, it warned against coercive (not necessarily military) interventions to protect (mainly) CP rights and argued that: "it is necessary to abandon the reflex of resorting to coercive measures as the very first option. Unilateral sanctions, for example, corrode the credibility of the international order, frequently harm the civilian population and have demonstrably revealed themselves to be inadequate in changing behaviour."

The sampled UNGA debates/votes showed similar trends. For example, during the UNGA debate held in October 2015 on its Agenda item 84,

[33] See Yeshi Choedon, "India on Humanitarian Intervention and Responsibility to Protect: Shifting Nuances" (2017) 73 *India Quarterly* 430.

[34] See Margaret Keck & Karthryn Sikkink, *Activists beyond Borders: Advocacy Networks in International Politics* (Ithaca, NY: Cornell University Press, 1998), pp. 84–85.

Nigeria's argument reflected the dominant tendency among Global South states. It argued that:

> The imposition of unilateral sanctions [including in aid of the protection of CP rights] runs counter to sovereign equality and international law. Imposition of sanctions on any sovereign State should always be in conformity with the provisions of the Charter. It was noteworthy that almost all existing sanctions targeted developing countries belonging to the African Union, the Group of 77 and China and the Non-Aligned Movement. Sanctions should be applied only as a last resort, after exhaustion of all other peaceful means of dispute settlement ... The frequency of the resort to sanctions should be reduced, their scope narrowed and their duration shortened to avoid prolonged damage to the interests of targeted States and their populations.

It is of course true that Global South states do, at times, support or fail to strongly object to international intervention in aid of the protection of CP rights, especially in situations where there have been egregious violations of those rights over some period. And this is well reflected in the record of the UNSC and UNGA meetings studies. Nevertheless, the overall point being made here, regarding the dominant tendency of these states to be suspicious or hesitant about both binding obligations on states (read more powerful states) to express international CP rights solidarity and the expression of such solidarity toward them, remains valid.

THEIR BROAD POSITION ON A BINDING INTERNATIONAL ECONOMIC AND SOCIAL RIGHTS SOLIDARITY OBLIGATION Despite the historical reluctance of most Global South states to strongly embrace the notion that international law requires, or even authorizes, states to positively express international solidarity to victims of CP rights violations around the world (especially in a unilateral, robust or coercive manner), the studied UN debates and votes strongly demonstrate robust and near total Global South state support for the binding international legal obligation on all states that are able to do so (usually Global North states) to positively express international economic and social rights solidarity to poorer states.[35]

This dates back to, at least, the early 1960s, in which the then newly postcolonial Global South argued for the prioritization of "collective" ES rights over "individual" CP rights.[36]

[35] For example, see their already discussed strong support for the UNHRC resolution on foreign debt.

[36] See Hernández-Truyol, "Human Rights, Globalization, and Culture."

What is more, as we have already seen, unlike their Global North counterparts, these Global South states adopted a similar position during the negotiations for the adoption of the OP ICESCR, arguing – in effect – that, under the ICESCR, the expression of international ES rights solidarity was *not* merely a moral obligation on all states, but was also a binding international legal obligation.[37]

Secondly, unlike almost all the Global North states, Global South states tend to very strongly support the implementation of UNHRC mandated measures on states, or strong exhortations by that body on them, to implement robust international ES rights solidarity obligations. This is clear from the affirmative votes by Global South states in favor of all the following already discussed resolutions: A/HRC/RES/49/15; A/HRC/RES/49/19; A/HRC/RES/47/11; A/HRC/RES/48/8; A/HRC/RES/48/10; and A/HRC/RES/44/18. It should be noted, however, that Brazil (under Jair Bolsonaro's presidency) was the only Global South state that either abstained or voted against any of these resolutions.

Global South support for an international legal mandate on all states that are in a position to do so to positively express international ES rights solidarity toward poorer countries does perhaps climb to its apex in relation to the duty on all states to cooperate toward the fuller realization of the right to development.[38] For example, all Global South states (save Brazil under Bolsanaro, which abstained in each case) voted in favor of the following UNHRC resolutions that seek to implement this right in fuller measure: A/HRC/RES/48/8; A/HRC/RES/48/10; and A/HRC/RES/44/18.

3.2.2.2 The Antinomies and Aporias within this Broad Set of Global South Arguments

The foregoing analysis of the behavior of our sample Global South states within three major UN bodies suggests that their broad approach(es) to international human rights solidarity also varies to a significant degree, depending on whether it is CP or ES rights that are at issue. This does suggest that their broad body of international human rights solidarity argumentation is also marked by antinomy and aporia, though in a flipped, and certainly different, kind of way. The antinomy and aporia that is thus revealed in this Global South state case appears to be in a reverse relationship to the antinomy

[37] See E/CN.4/2006/47, paras 77–86.

[38] See Bonny Ibhawoh, "The Right to Development: The Politics and Polemics of Power and Resistance" (2011) 33 *Human Rights Quarterly* 76–104, at 95.

and aporia that marks Global North international human rights solidarity argumentation.

There is certainly a paradox in accepting (as almost all of these Global South states do) that CP rights are human rights that are indivisible from, inextricably tied to, and interdependent on, ES rights;[39] arguing strongly in favor of an international legal obligation to express international human rights solidarity when ES rights (including the right to development) have been or are likely to be breached; and then so often rejecting or hesitating about the existence or robust implementation of a similar obligation in the face of ongoing or potential CP rights breaches.

What is more, there is also – to a significant degree – an aporia (seen as a basically irresolvable logical disjunction) within the broad set of Global South argumentation on international human rights solidarity that has just been outlined and analyzed. For, how can one easily resolve an internal contradiction that stems from arguing in favor of an international legal obligation to express international solidarity in aid of the protection abroad of one category of human rights (i.e. ES rights), while so often arguing against the existence of a similarly robust international legal obligation to assist in the realization of another type of human rights (i.e. CP rights), when one has already acknowledged that these CP rights are inseparable/indivisible from ES rights?

The possible creative potential, if any and howsoever mild, of this aporia in Global South state international human rights solidarity argumentation, would appear to be akin – in some ways – to that outlined already in connection with the discussion on the aporia in the dominant Global North state argumentation on this topic. First, highlighting this aporia even more than it already has been help trouble Global South officialdom's narratives and self-images enough to produce a measure of change in the opposing direction, at least toward even greater discursive acceptance by these states of binding international CP rights solidarity. This could over time enure in favor of significantly greater benefits from such international CP solidarity praxis – if with all the serious caveats that must be entered regarding the ways in which global power dynamics can deeply complicate and render that possibility undesirable to a large extent.

3.3 RECOVERING THE POWER/INTEREST, NORMS/VALUES NEXUS

In my view, the foregoing discussion has at least two conceptual implications. The first relates to the relationship between international human rights

[39] See Vienna Declaration and Program of Action.

solidarity argumentation and its state sovereignty counterparts. The second concern is entailed but not necessarily limited by the first. It is with regard to the necessity for a more accurate calibration of the power/interest, norms/value nexus in international human rights solidarity argumentation. This is necessary given the circulation in plain sight of explicit or implied representations of that conceptual nexus that do not bear as accurate a relationship to the actually existing one as they ought to.

3.3.1 *International Human Rights Solidarity Argumentation and its State Sovereignty Counterparts*

It seems that one of the things going for the targeted sets of Global South bodies of international human rights solidarity argumentation is that their orientations on either side of this axis tend to map onto the orientations of state sovereignty argumentation. Global North states appear to make arguments that they view as protective of their state sovereignty and interest (understood as freedom of action). This is evident in their position against binding international ES rights solidarity obligations that would mandate them to part with a significant amount of resources, with considerably less wiggle room to deploy such resources to gain influence, but in favor of binding international CP rights obligations which tend to advance their power and influence over the governance of Global South states.

Global South states essentially act similarly. They appear to make international human rights solidarity arguments that they view as protective of their state sovereignty and interests. This is the case with their tendency to argue against binding international CP rights solidarity obligations that significantly constrain the control their governing elites have over their own societies, while embracing binding international ES rights solidarity obligations that would mandate a flow of much needed resources to them without such resource flows tending to diminish their freedom of action by being tied to the even closer alignment of these Global South states with Global North interests and priorities.

And so, similar forces seem to be at play across both sides of the Global North/South axis, if with different consequences. And, with notable exceptions, such as in China's case, similarly situated countries (historically, socio economically and political power wise) tend to make similar arguments about both international human rights solidarity and state sovereignty. And so, the former kind of argumentation implicates the latter, and vice versa. All this in turn also seems significantly more related to the character and potency of global power relations than to the immanent or social force of human rights values/norms themselves.

Another way to put this is that, from the discussion in Section 3.2, official international human rights solidarity argumentation across the Global North/South axis seems to be significantly *more* about political and socio-economic struggles regarding the assertion, diminishment, or denial of state sovereignty than it has been about the advancement of human rights values and norms themselves. Norms tend to become more displaced or shifted further to the margins when either side is convinced that its enjoyment of freedom of action is at risk. Too often, this has produced flips and flops in positions taken in both international human rights and state sovereignty argumentation, depending on the specific values/norms at issue and their perceived implications for the freedom of action of the Global North or South states that are engaged. And so, as it turns out, by observing these flips and flops in international human rights solidarity argumentation, we may be able to demonstrate that state sovereignty is definitely not *passé* or as diminished as many would like to think![40] As well, by observing the flips and flops in state sovereignty (as freedom of action) argumentation within international human rights solidarity debates, we may be able to show that international human rights solidarity (even in its hard law forms) will remain with us in some form(s) for a long time yet. This is because both geo-political blocs that debate international human rights solidarity favor it in one form or the other. And so, either way, solidarity will continue to be affirmed. Perhaps, these realizations should lead us to *calibrate better* our understandings of the relative roles played by global power and norms/values in international human rights solidarity argumentation and the relationship between power/interest and norms/values in such argumentation.

However, it should be noted that the goal here is not to exemplify IR realism – at least not uncritically. In fact, as I have argued extensively elsewhere,[41] its near counterpoint in international relations theory, social constructivism,[42] is a stronger set of ideas for understanding much international law and relations praxis. The point remains, nevertheless, that the power/interest and norms/values nexus needs to be better calibrated. For, as Anghie has taught us, claims of international (human rights) solidarity have had a very long history and career of being driven by, and projecting/

[40] See Antony Anghie, "Rethinking Sovereignty in International Law" (2009) 5 *Annual Review of Law and Social Science* 291–310, at 292.

[41] See Obiora Chinedu Okafor, *The African Human Rights System, Activist Forces and International Institutions* (Cambridge: Cambridge University Press, 2007).

[42] For instance, see Alexander Wendt, "Constructing International Politics" (1995) 20 *International Security* 71.

facilitating, Global North/South advantage and domination.[43] As this chapter has shown, the projection of, or resistance to, power has been central in both the Global North's and South's international human rights solidarity praxis. The extent to which this kind of domination/resistance dynamic continues to be at play in contemporary international human rights solidarity argumentation, and its exact nature, should therefore be an important subject of scholarly enquiry.

3.3.2 *Recovering the Power/Interest, Norms/Values Nexus*

Also, as already hinted at in the foregoing discussion regarding the international human rights solidarity/sovereignty argumentation connections, the evidence analyzed in Section 3.2 strongly indicates that, much more than values and norms, the nature of global power relations appear to play *much more* of a role in shaping or calibrating positions taken on international human rights solidarity on either side of this Global North/South geopolitical axis than is readily admitted by the relevant states. Yet this reality tends to be elided in official pro-international human rights solidarity (including pro-democracy and pro-humanitarianism) discourse. Even well-meaning academics are too often not free of blame in this regard.

It is therefore important for critical internationalists to continue to expose and recover more fully the actually existing calibration of the nexus between power/interest and norms/values in international human rights solidarity argumentation. It is key that the relationship between these two sets of factors is more accurately depicted toward a better understanding of the character of official international human rights argumentation (and indeed praxis).

A better understanding of this specific power/interest and norms/values nexus will have important implications for our (re)understandings of official international human rights argumentation: how these bodies of argumentation come to be constituted; by whom?; how certain versions of that discourse become dominant; how we come to "know" who the "good actors" who show international human rights solidarity are and are not; and how we come to "know" who the "bad actors" who do not express international human rights solidarity are and are not.

It should also be noted that, although the role of values in international human rights solidarity remains significant, detailed analysis of this is beyond the scope of this chapter.

43 See Antony Anghie, *Imperialism, Sovereignty and the Making of International Law* (Cambridge: Cambridge University Press, 2005).

3.4 CONCLUSION

This chapter utilizes a quasi-empirical methodology to demonstrate and reflect upon the character of official (state-made) international human rights solidarity argumentation across the Global North/South axis and its socio-economic and political contingency. It first maps the antinomies and aporias in each of these bodies of international human rights solidarity argumentation (their respective flips and flops) as the issues at hand and the foci of the debates change from civil and political (CP) rights to economic and social (ES) rights, and vice versa. It thereafter shows how these flips and flops in the official international human rights solidarity argumentation of Global North and South states map closely onto their state sovereignty (as freedom of action) argumentation/positions. The chapter also argues that this phenomenon is *more* closely linked to the nature and orientation of global power/interest relations than to the immanent force of, or belief in, human rights norms/values by states across this divide. Such beliefs are, of course, important. The point is that they are not nearly as determinative as seems to be too often suggested. Lastly, the chapter also argues that a better calibration and understanding of the power/interest and norms/values nexus in official international human rights solidarity argumentation across the Global North/South axis will have certain important constitutive implications for understanding of that discourse itself and its related praxis.

It should be noted, however, that the chapter does not make a simple argument regarding the ways in which states project global power in pursuit of their perceived interests. Instead, it demonstrates how their projection of global power in pursuit of their interests has produced antinomies and aporias in their official international human rights solidarity argumentation, and its deeper implications for our very conception of who and what "good" international human rights solidarity actors are or are not.

These points provide important insight into how to respond to the overarching question that this volume tackles: how to talk about solidarity today. They illuminate for us the extent to which global power asymmetries, significantly more than human rights ideals, continue to condition when, how, and in relation to what/who, scholars and practitioners ask the international solidarity question today, including in relation to UN (human rights) bodies.

4

Unwelcome Solidarity

FRÉDÉRIC MÉGRET

4.1 INTRODUCTION

Solidarity is generally emphasized as a social good and may well often be. International lawyers, in particular, have frequently invoked it as a kind of precarious keystone in the international legal edifice.[1] International lawyers, in particular, have a strong *a priori* in favor of solidarity as synonymous with greater international community integration. The main concern is with a lack of sufficient solidarity rather than its excess. In that, international lawyers tend to merely reproduce truisms about the interdependence of nations that are part of the core ideological baggage of the discipline. That discourse, moreover, has tended to be a byproduct of international legal thinking rather than one grounded in the praxis of international relations. This is a pity because attention to the *practice* of solidarity deserves better than platitudes.

Rather than focus on solidarity as a necessarily positive value, then, I propose to explore the history, nature, and politics of what I describe as "unwelcome solidarity" understood as solidarity that is conceived by its purported recipients as somehow undesirable. I seek, in particular, to identify what might be problematic about some forms of solidarity, and the sort of implicit claims about self, identity, and dignity that are made in the process of rejecting solidarity.

Note to begin with that we have no reason to think that the solidarity of states is necessarily an unmitigated good simply because it is internationally minded. In fact, internationalist solidarity as such is at best a second order

[1] Rüdiger Wolfrum and Chie Kojima (eds.), *Solidarity: A Structural Principle of International Law* (Heidelberg: Springer, 2010).

value, compared to what it is harnessed to. Operation Condor, for example, was set up by the Southern Cone countries to share the burden of repressing liberals and leftists, leading to abduction, torture, and execution.[2] The solidarity of human rights violators at the Human Rights Council, including horse trading of candidates and mutual back scratching, is often seen as problematic. The solidarity of thieves, such as it may be, is not much of a solidarity. The line between liberal and illiberal internationalisms (in addition to the sheer vagueness of those terms) is a fluid and thin one.[3]

Indeed, solidarity might evidence more *a priori* positive inclinations and still be problematic. Consider, for example, the effort, limited and halting as it may be, by European states to better spread the "burden" of hosting refugees.[4] On one, inter-state level, it is only fair that states should equally assume their responsibilities on some basis other than their proximity to Mediterranean shores; but, seen from an individual asylum seeker perspective, one may see such agreements as merely part of complex technologies to deny one's agency.[5] "Better solidarity" might become synonymous with states refusing to share their burden on account of some more or less pretextual complaint about how it is distributively allocated.

By the same token, simply because some states consider that certain forms of solidarity are unwelcome does not necessarily make it justifiably so. There will also be refusals of solidarity that betray, under some accounts, problematic policies. Consider, for example, the refusal by the Myanmar junta to accept foreign, particularly Western aid, after the tsunami, arguably prolonging the suffering of its population. Rejecting solidarity might only reflect a form of misplaced pride in the circumstances,[6] or maybe a tyrannical inclination.[7] Even Japan's polite rejection of aid after the Kobe earthquake was described as excessively rigid and technocratic, in light of the needs of its population.[8]

2 Joan Patrice McSherry, "Operation Condor and Transnational State Violence against Exiles" (2019) 36 *Journal of Global South Studies* 368.

3 Philippa Hetherington and Glenda Sluga, "Liberal and Illiberal Internationalisms" (2020) 31 *Journal of World History* 1.

4 See Chapter 10, by Hansen.

5 Marcia Vera Espinoza, "The Limits and Opportunities of Regional Solidarity: Exploring Refugee Resettlement in Brazil and Chile" (2018) 9 *Global Policy* 85.

6 Charlotte Dany, "Failed Cooperation in Times of Natural Disasters: Explaining the Rejection of Humanitarian Aid" (2020) 20 *International Relations of the Asia-Pacific* 193.

7 "Venezuela: UN Agency Warns of Humanitarian 'Catastrophe'," *DW*, March 3, 2018, available at: https://p.dw.com/p/2uDQU (last accessed August 15, 2022).

8 Nicholas Kristof, "Sticking to the Rules – A Special Report; Japan Reluctant to Accept Help from Abroad for Quake Victims," *The New York Times*, February 5, 1995, available at: www.nytimes.com/1995/02/05/world/sticking-rules-special-report-japan-reluctant-accept-help-abroad-for-quake.html (last accessed August 15, 2022).

Without going as far as to suggest that there is an obligation to accept genuine solidarity, the moral value of solidarity also lies in the ability of purported recipients to graciously receive it. In war settings, refusing humanitarian assistance or access may be in violation of international humanitarian obligations. Syria's refusal of aid designed to rescue 200 000 civilians in Ghouta is one such instance.[9]

What constitutes unwelcome solidarity, then, needs to be conceived in terms of some underlying normative theory or at least understanding of why or when solidarity might or might not be welcome. Take one recent example from the corporate world. New Balance is a famous brand of trainer shoes. In 2016, its founder hinted to the *Wall Street Journal* that he thought Trump might be a step in the "right direction" for America given the Republican party's opposition to the Trans-Pacific Partnership (TPP), which New Balance also opposed. Following that somewhat offhand statement, the *Daily Stormer*, a Neo-Nazi site, endorsed the shoes as "the official shoes of white people," urging its readers to buy them.[10] New Balance then had to go out of its way to reject that support. The "solidarity" expressed by the *Daily Stormer* with New Balance was not meant to embarrass the company (which in ordinary circumstances would surely like to receive free endorsements), but it was nonetheless deeply unwelcome.

Real world manifestations of solidarity may be both welcome and unwelcome in different proportions. The focus on the unwelcome kind is not meant as a general diatribe against solidarity as much as it is based on the intuition that we often sharpen the trenchancy of concepts by examining their opposites. This will provide an opportunity to examine both the dynamics of excessive solicitousness and the politics of not wanting to be helped. I will focus on a variety of concrete examples. The general intuition is that, even as the discourse of solidarity becomes justifiably more widespread, we have reason to be wary of uncritical appeals to it.

This chapter adopts quite a capacious understanding of international solidarity, that goes beyond the inter-state. This is as an acknowledgment that the sites of international solidarity have long been diversified and encompass much solidarity that is transnational – by certain peoples with other peoples,

[9] "Syria: Denial of Care and Food for Civilians in Eastern Ghouta Must Stop – UN Experts," *OHCHR*, November 10, 2017, available at: www.ohchr.org/en/press-releases/2017/11/syria-denial-care-and-food-civilians-eastern-ghouta-must-stop-un-experts (last accessed August 15, 2022).

[10] Kim Bhasin, "New Balance Created Its PR Crisis. Neo-Nazis Aren't Helping," *Bloomberg*, November 15, 2016, available at: www.bloomberg.com/news/articles/2016-11-15/new-balance-created-its-pr-crisis-neo-nazis-aren-t-helping (last accessed August 15, 2022).

rather than necessarily only or necessarily involving sovereigns. It is also as a recognition that some of the more elaborate and provocative debates on solidarity have occurred well beyond the confines of international law, in the broader realm of transnational social relations marked not by legal obligations but by identity, affect and exchange,[11] what Bertrand Badie recently described as inter-societal relations.[12] Nonetheless, the chapter does keep as its central focus the international order as a unique site of solidarity, one occurring specifically between often incommensurable and irreducible entities that it seeks to transcend in ways that also sometimes expose its limitation.

How, then, might one conceptualize "unwelcome solidarity" in terms of the politics of international relations and how is it mediated by international law? Solidarity operates on the margins of such relations, as part of a "politics of emotion" of what is otherwise characterized by distrust or, at best, rational cooperation. This is why manifestations of solidarity have always been somewhat of a mystery for observers of international politics. On one level, unwelcome solidarity might just be fake and, therefore, hypocritical. We have little patience for solidarity posturing that does not involve an actual cost, gift, or concession. Solidarity is cheap and can be seen as part of an economy of "virtue signaling."[13] There is, then, much discussion of the politics of half, fake, or misguided solidarity.

The more interesting question for this chapter's purposes, however, is whether solidarity might be justifiably unwelcome even when it is in good faith or independently of whether it is in good faith or not. For example, it has been argued that solidarity and the "centering of Western subjects"[14] may help reconduct problematic tropes (notably femonationalist or homonationalist) about the civilizational superiority of those professing solidarity.[15] Solidarity with victims can be a thin disguise for imperialist ventures as in some cases of humanitarian intervention.[16] Rather than questioning the motivations of those who profess solidarity, then, I want to discuss how

[11] Avery Kolers, *A Moral Theory of Solidarity* (Oxford: Oxford University Press, 2016).

[12] Bertrand Badie, *Inter-socialités: Le monde n'est plus géopolitique* (Paris: CNRS éditions, 2020).

[13] See Chapter 2, by Scholz.

[14] Niamh Ní Mhaoileoin, "The Ironic Gay Spectator: The Impacts of Centring Western Subjects in International LGBT Rights Campaigns" (2019) 22 *Sexualities* 148.

[15] Egbert Alejandro Martina, "Wanted for Love, But Not Here: The Travelling Rights of African LGBT Activists," *Critical Legal Thinking*, August 12, 2013, available at: https://criticallegalthinking.com/2013/08/12/wanted-for-love-but-not-here-the-travelling-rights-of-african-lgbt-activists/ (last accessed May 15, 2023).

[16] Ayça Çubukçu, "The Responsibility to Protect: Libya and the Problem of Transnational Solidarity" (2013) 12 *Journal of Human Rights* 40.

solidarity may be unwelcome regardless of its motivations and even, perhaps particularly, when it is sincere.

Specifically, the chapter highlights three ways in which solidarity might be unwelcome: because it makes things worse; because it comes from the wrong source; or because it unduly obliges its recipient. The three are not incompatible but their problematic character increases from the most superficial to the most fundamental.

4.2 "WITH FRIENDS LIKE THAT": WHEN SOLIDARITY MAKES THINGS WORSE

On a first, pragmatic, and instrumental level, solidarity might simply complicate the situation of those who are its intended beneficiaries. The Japanese case for refusing aid after Kobe, for example, was that many Western medicines sent to the country were dosed inadequately. Often well-meaning aid will face obstacles simply because it is redundant with the resources of the receiving country and requires significant administrative resources in times of crisis to simply manage. Evidently, solidarity should not make things worse, and states are justified in limiting its incidence when it does.

More problematically, solidarity may displace local leadership, crowding out home grown political movements by showering them with solicitude, or substituting to their own language of emancipation one elaborated elsewhere and for different circumstances. Hence, Lina Alsaafin points out how the West's praising of non-violent tactics in Palestine also tends to displace Palestinian self-determination, including when it comes to means.[17] In that context, Richard Falk has even acknowledged occasionally himself "being unwittingly paternalistic, if not complicit with an unhealthy 'tyranny of the stranger'."[18] Similarly, Emi Koyama has expressed concern about US activist claims of being the "voice of the voiceless" when a loud community of LGBT activists exists in Uganda.[19]

Even when solidarity is broadly felt to be going in the right direction, the particular means used may be denounced as ultimately not helping local

[17] Linah Alsaafin, "How Obsession with Nonviolence Harms the Palestinian Cause," *The Electronic Intifada*, July 10, 2012, available at: https://electronicintifada.net/content/how-obsession-nonviolence-harms-palestinian-cause/11482 (last accessed March 1, 2024).

[18] Richard Falk, "Pros and Cons of Western Palestinian Solidarity," *Al Jazeera*, July 18, 2012, available at: www.aljazeera.com/opinions/2012/7/18/pros-and-cons-of-western-palestinian-solidarity (last accessed May 15, 2023).

[19] Emi Koyama, "The Uganda Controversy: Solidarity vs. Imperialism in LGBT Organizing" (2010) 25 *Tikkun* 59.

constituencies. For example, it has been pointed out that sanctions against Iran in the wake of the 2022 wave of protests "have less in common with liberal solidarity and more in common with siege starvation tactics as old as war," essentially asphyxiating the economy and harming local populations.[20] Concern has also been expressed that calls for sanctions to punish Uganda's LGBT policies "could lead to the collapse of social order in a country like Uganda, endangering many more lives of LGBT Ugandans than the legislation itself would."[21] Perverse effects abound in this context, and cannot be redeemed merely by pointing to loose good intentions.

Moreover, even when transnational solidarity is genuine and otherwise potentially helpful, its very existence may make it easy for a regime to portray groups as foreign manipulated (along with the possibility that, of course, they occasionally *are*). This vulnerability to the accusation that one is a "foreign stooge" may then designate one for further repression. The US State Department, for example, has long supported pro-democracy groups in and outside Iran, notably by training them abroad. This "solidarity" with those fighting against the Iranian regime has frequently been denounced by Iranian authorities as part of an effort to cause "anarchy and domestic unrest" in ways that have caused "increased public anger and hatred against America,"[22] in ways that at least problematize its overall usefulness to the very actors it is supposed to support. Similarly, Yoweri Museveni of Uganda has accused civil society organizations of being "internal saboteurs, acting on behalf of foreign interests."[23] President Putin has long made the claim that "foreign hands" are involved in protests and opposition to the central pillar of his dictatorship,[24] as has President Lukashenko of Byelorussia.[25] Indeed, governments themselves may be vulnerable to the accusation that they are merely tools of foreign

20 Roman Cabay, "Responding to Iran: Sanctions Are Not Solidarity," *The Organization for World Peace*, October 12, 2022, available at: https://theowp.org/responding-to-iran-sanctions-are-not-solidarity/ (last accessed May 15, 2023).

21 Koyama, "The Uganda Controversy," 59.

22 Bill Samii, "Iran: Tehran Opposes U.S. Pro-Democracy Initiatives," *Radio Free Europe/Radio Liberty*, April 22, 2005, available at: www.rferl.org/a/1058600.html (last accessed July 29, 2022).

23 "Under Siege Museveni Seeks Support on Oil Law, Aid Cuts," *The East African*, December 15, 2012, available at: www.theeastafrican.co.ke/tea/news/east-africa/under-siege-museveni-seeks-support-on-oil-law-aid-cuts–1313810 (last accessed July 29, 2022).

24 Ellen Barry, "Putin Aide Says Foreign Hands Are behind Protests," *The New York Times*, February 3, 2012, available at: www.nytimes.com/2012/02/04/world/europe/putin-aide-promises-significant-changes-in-russian-political-system.html (last accessed July 29, 2022).

25 Maria Tysiachniouk, Svetlana Tulaeva, and Laura Henry, "Civil Society under the Law 'On Foreign Agents': NGO Strategies and Network Transformation" (2018) 70 *Europe–Asia Studies* 615.

powers as a result of the conspicuous "solidarity" of allies. This was the case of the last Shah of Iran, who quite incautiously blamed the British and the Americans for decisions he had himself taken, leaving his own prestige and credibility seriously weakened.[26] Such accusations have resurfaced frequently in the case of Afghanistan, Iraq, and others, where being seen as being on the receiving end of solidarity can in fact weaken rather than strengthen governments.

It matters little in this context whether claims about the nefarious dimensions of solidarity are true. The point is that foreign solidarity can be a mixed blessing for dissidents in particular, creating acute dilemmas and possibly the need to dissociate themselves from those in solidarity with them. One Russian law (itself inspired by an older, similar US law), for example, requires anyone who receives "support" from or is under "influence" from outside Russia to register and declare themselves as "foreign agents." Effectively, NGOs are asked to "out" themselves as externally compromised merely as a result of being recipients of foreign solidarity. The law has been repeatedly expanded to cover not just organizations engaged in "political activity" but also those receiving any amount of foreign funding toward publication. Some, such as Russia's Committee against Torture or Dynasty Foundation (a major science and education fund), have dissolved themselves rather than operate under the law. In other words, they have stood by the notion that their willingness to be the beneficiaries of Western solidarity should not lead to their being sanctioned at home, but at the cost of their very existence: the victims, in a sense, of solidarity with them.

Of course, in terms of principles, the case for solidarity being unwelcome merely because it upsets authoritarian states can be a relatively weak one. On some level, the direct responsibility for banning NGOs and marginalizing dissidents is clearly the home state's, not that of their foreign funders; but at the very least states or constituencies who profess solidarity with others should be wary of how it might make those they claim to support appear. The question is nonetheless why certain forms of solidarity might be justifiably unwelcome above and beyond states' more or less opportunistic motives for criticizing them. Indeed, the problem is made acute by the fact that, although the Kremlin's paranoia about civil society with or without foreign links is well known for example, it is not as if some Western NGOs do not, indeed, participate in the projection of forms of soft power and possibly more. Solidarity must also be seen in light of a long tradition of practices of foreign

[26] Fakhreddin Azimi, *The Quest for Democracy in Iran: A Century of Struggle against Authoritarian Rule* (Cambridge, MA: Harvard University Press, 2009), p. 276.

interference that are no less real simply because they can also be opportunistically exaggerated.

4.3 "YES, JUST NOT FROM YOU": THE *INTUITU PERSONAE* OF SOLIDARITY

A second way in which solidarity might be understood to be unwelcome, then, is when emanating from the "wrong" source. This goes against the cosmopolitan idea that all solidarities are equal and that solidarity is all the more welcome that it comes from a position of abstract disinterestedness. Quite what that space of cosmopolitan impartiality would be and how it may be occupied is perennially unclear (there is always some pre-existing pattern of relations that directs solidarity in some direction rather than others, otherwise solidarity is both random and bland). More importantly, solidarity often seems to be justifiably based on a range of affinities that do not so much belie its universalist impulse as they ground it in the reality of ongoing social relations.[27] But this means that, if there is to be a solidarity based on affinities, then there must also be forms of solidarity that miss the mark precisely because they are not based on such affinities. Here the problem is not so much that the solidarity might be *de facto* unhelpful but that the particular political relationality it suggests is problematic.

One can conceive of a number of such forms of unwelcome solidarity in the international realm. A typical case is provided by unwelcome offers in the context of humanitarian catastrophes. For example, Israel made offers of humanitarian assistance to Lebanon after the Beirut blast, or to Iraq and Iran after earthquakes there, as did China to Taiwan after an earthquake. The "receiving" states in these cases nonetheless expressed ambivalence or declined on the basis that this particular solidarity was suspicious, coming as it did from a perceived enemy.[28] More recently, the citizens of Kherson are said to have refused humanitarian aid from occupying Russian troops.[29] The

[27] Joshua Hobbs and James Souter, "Asylum, Affinity, and Cosmopolitan Solidarity with Refugees" (2020) 51 *Journal of Social Philosophy* 543.

[28] "Iran–Iraq Earthquake: Israeli Offers of Help to Victims 'Turned down'," *The Independent*, November 15, 2017, available at: www.independent.co.uk/news/world/middle-east/iran-iraq-eathquake-latest-updates-israeli-offers-help-turned-down-benjamin-netanyahu-victims-aid-a8056076.html (last accessed May 16, 2023).

[29] Oleksandr Korniyenko [@OlekKorn], "Citizens of #Kherson Refused Humanitarian Aid from the Occupiers. The Occupiers' Trucks Went Back. I Call on International Humanitarian Organizations to Help with a Green Corridor to #Ukraine! @RedCrossUkraine @RedCrossEU #StopPutinNOW," March 4, 2022, available at: https://x.com/OlekKorn/status/1499750168954036227 (last accessed September 18, 2024).

problem is not that Israeli humanitarian aid in Iran or Russian aid in Ukraine is objectively problematic (as in Section 4.2), but that the recipient of solidarity objects to its source as such and the sort of political effect it is being put to.

The point here is merely that there is an element of *intuitu personae* involved in solidarity: that we do not value all solidarity equally and may indeed have reasons to reject some of its expressions based on who it comes from. Agents are not simply generally in want of abstract solidarity; they are, if anything, open to receiving solidarity from particular constituencies as opposed to others. Some manifestations of solidarity may seem as if they have merely as their goal a distraction from one's own participation in oppression and a sort of free riding on the struggles of others.[30] Solidarity with a people one has otherwise contributed to impoverish or alienate will sound hollow. Even in the context of diasporas, support from certain groups may appear inimical to struggles fought at home. For example, there has been criticism of nationalist and imperial Iranian groups showing up at protests to support the women's movement in Iran as essentially substituting their own patriarchal and regressive policies to those of other groups.[31]

More ontologically, solidarity aspires to express a kind of horizontal equality to the "other" which may be performatively problematic. It seems to say "we are in this together." It is, on the one hand, the opposite of solicitousness, pity, paternalism, or of a merely humanitarian attitude. So, to accept solidarity – that is, to accept that one is the object of someone else's solidarity – is to accept that one is indeed in some crucial respect in unison with those who profess their solidarity toward oneself. By contrast, solidarity may feel misplaced when it comes from an enemy, or a dominant party that cannot be expected to feel what one is going through or, worse, that displaces one's own agency under the guise of expressing sympathy with one's plight or seeks to affirm a form of superiority.

Unwelcome solidarity of that kind, then, is a solidarity that, in its more or less wholesome embrace, seeks to artificially or arbitrarily dissolve the distinction between "us" and "them." It is obnoxious because it hints at – it affirms, in fact – a commonality of fate that may not, in fact, exist, or only exists artificially through the gesture of solidarity that seeks to construct it (at least, it is precisely the question whether one wants to be the recipient of solidarity by

30 Orly Noy, "If Israelis Want to Support the Women of Iran, Start with Palestinians," +972 *Magazine*, October 13, 2022, available at: www.972mag.com/edition/iran-women-protests-palestinians/ (last accessed May 16, 2023).

31 Ian Parker, "Iran Demonstration in Manchester: Disruption and Solidarity," *Anti-Capitalist Resistance*, September 25, 2022, available at: https://anticapitalistresistance.org/iran-demonstration-in-manchester-disruption-and-solidarity/ (last accessed May 15, 2023).

this "other"). Rather than affirming a common reciprocal bond between equals, then, it may merely reinstate the bondage of a master–slave relationship. To refuse this kind of solidarity, then, is the truly emancipatory gesture because it calls the bluff on the equal value of all forms of solidarity and the wholesomeness of that particular embrace.

Paradoxically, this may particularly be the case of a certain type of bland universalist solidarity of the sort loosely associated with cosmopolitanism and international law, that is, a solidarity that is crushing in its hegemony because of its lack of any particular *intuitu personae*. Consider, for example, the recurrence of appeals to a radical commonality of fate expressed in the "Nous sommes tous américains" (after 9/11), "Je suis Charlie," "We are all Palestinians," or "We are all Ukrainians." Such slogans "express empathy, outrage, and horror by subsuming ourselves in victims' identities."[32] They may, as such, be both appealing in their radicality but also invasive, effectively displacing the identity of the victim or claiming some kind of absolution from the harms suffered by others, sometimes in part through "our" fault. They may highlight the construction of a particular privilege – the privilege to even be in a position of solidarity – and the normative significance, on the other hand, of the ability to refuse solidarity as a form of amalgamation.

Consider, *ad absurdum*, what our reaction would be to "We are all black" for example or "We are all women" as a reaction to the BLM and MeToo movements, respectively, expressed by non-black persons and men. Even if well-intended, as responses to the legacies of slavery or misogyny, these would arguably not remotely pass as a form of (welcome) solidarity. They would immediately be taken down as a form of hegemonic appropriation by those who cannot possibly fully inhabit what it means to be a victim in this context. The problem is not with solidarity in itself, but a radically abstract solidarity that erases all sense of difference. In a sense, those claiming solidarity are implicitly claiming a symbolic "out" from what is, problematically, their lot. This is partly because their solidarity *inter se* has historically been the problem: one cannot easily undo that in-group solidarity by rhetorically manifesting an out-group one. Paradoxically, victim groups may need the dominant "in their place," as expressing at least some kind of notional in-group solidary responsibility for what they stand for.

The point, then, is not so much that such statements are facile, but that they can provide an all-too-convenient escape hatch from what "we" actually are by

[32] Amanda Hess, "#IAm: The Default Mode of Showing Solidarity in the Hashtag Era," *Slate*, January 9, 2015, available at: https://slate.com/news-and-politics/2015/01/jesuischarlie-the-default-mode-of-showing-solidarity-in-the-hashtag-age.html (last accessed May 15, 2023).

violently erasing the distinction between giver and recipient of solidarity. To live out one's solidarity with victims may be a way to not confront one's complicity with their oppression, or at least the considerable differences in vulnerability to harm even in the process of "solidarizing." Hence, it has been argued that, in the foreign Palestine activist community, the "equalization of American and Palestinian suffering" leads to a situation where "expressions of responsibility are trumped, effaced, and metamorphosed in such a way as to obstruct the very politics for which solidarity was offered in the first place,"[33] leaving those engaged in solidarity strangely "off the hook."[34] As argued by Sophia Stamatopoulou-Robbins, "American citizens, whose government is the most vehemently and uncritically supportive of Israeli policies, are thus extracted from their own political contexts; that is, they are detached from the taxes, votes, and purchases that structure their complicity to the injustices they observe."[35] Similarly, prominent European women cutting their hair in solidarity with Iranian women has been decried as unhelpful to the extent that these same women have previously stayed mum when it comes to their own countries' prohibition of the Islamic veil.[36]

On some level, the excess of solidarity might constitute a form of "passing," a type of solidarity that usurps not only the agency but the very identity of those it professes to support. One extreme case is Rachel Dolezal, the white woman who infamously passed as black whilst being specifically involved in the politics of black resistance as president of the NAACP in Spokane, Washington.[37] Hers was, therefore, an appropriation not only of blackness but specifically of black victimhood. Sally Munt, speaking of the omnipresence of the *argumentum ad misericordiam* in the media, hints that she "can well imagine how a shamed young personality yearning to connect might have had trouble with the entitlement of white privilege, and fly toward the

33 Sophia Stamatopoulou-Robbins, "The Joys and Dangers of Solidarity in Palestine: Prosthetic Engagement in an Age of Reparations" (2008) 8 *CR: The New Centennial Review* 111–160, at 127.

34 Ibid., 128.

35 Ibid., 134.

36 Nadeine Asbali, "White Actresses Cutting Inches off Their Hair Isn't the Solidarity Iran's Women Need," *Metro*, October 12, 2022, available at: https://metro.co.uk/2022/10/12/white-actresses-cutting-their-hair-isnt-the-solidarity-irans-women-need-17535386/ (last accessed May 15, 2023).

37 Justin Moyer, "'Are You an African American?' Why an NAACP Official Isn't Saying," *The Washington Post*, June 12, 2015, available at: www.washingtonpost.com/news/morning-mix/wp/2015/06/12/spokane-naacp-president-rachel-dolezal-may-be-white/ (last accessed September 18, 2024).

phantasmic glow of black solidarity."[38] After all, "Vicarious observation of, or participation in, rituals of trauma or loss can give a frisson of excitement . . . ."[39] Notwithstanding, Dolezal was widely excoriated for pushing notions of solidarity so far as to operate a kind of perverted substitution of victimhood.[40]

This connects to debates that have emerged in South Africa over the legacy of Steve Biko and his understanding of blackness as a category of political conscience rather than a biological reality. Expounding on some of the ambiguities of Biko's categorizations, Xolela Mangcu has argued that, just as blacks can "pass" as whites, the converse was true in South Africa where "black" came to encompass at least non-whites participating in the black struggle.[41] Responding to that piece, Keolebogile Mbebe has countered that "because white people cannot experience the alienation that non-white people do, they cannot attain Black Consciousness and, thus, cannot be Politically Black."[42] In particular, whites in solidarity with blacks cannot experience either the material or mental components of discrimination: their solidarity is useful, but it cannot fundamentally erase differences of experience. This suggests limits to a sort of solidarity that does not know its place and which, in its exuberance, almost displaces the very possibility of solidarity.

Thus, in the terms of Steve Biko, "no white person can escape being part of the oppressor camp,"[43] and "total identification with an oppressed group in a system that forces one group to enjoy privilege and to live on the sweat of another, is impossible."[44] That ontology simply cannot be renounced, and solidarity that ignores it is mere kitsch. For Howarth, white allyship that identifies as black deprives the black consciousness movement of "a clear racial frontier around which oppositional identity could be forged."[45]

In turn, this connects to a significant literature on the promise and pitfalls of "allyship" in social movements. The old labor workers' idea that "an injury to one is an injury to all," has been reappraised in light of particularly US social

38 Sally Munt, "Argumentum Ad Misericordiam: The Cultural Politics of Victim Media" (2017) 17 *Feminist Media Studies* 866–883, at 876.

39 Ibid.

40 Alisha Gaines, *Black for a Day: White Fantasies of Race and Empathy* (Chapel Hill: The University of North Carolina Press, 2017).

41 Xolela Mangcu, "Whites Can Be Black," *City Press*, July 5, 2015, available at: www.news24.com/citypress/voices/whites-can-be-blacks-20150703 (accessed September 9, 2016).

42 Keolebogile Mbebe, "Whites Cannot Be Black: A Bikoist Challenge to Professor Xolela Mangcu" (2018) 65 *Theoria: A Journal of Social and Political Theory* 24–47, at 25.

43 Steve Biko, *I Write What I Like: A Selection of His Writings* (London: Heinemann, 1987), p. 23.

44 Ibid., p. 66.

45 David Howarth, "Complexities of Identity/Difference: Black Consciousness Ideology in South Africa" (1997) 2 *Journal of Political Ideologies* 51–78, at 67.

and racial struggles and the anxiety that white solidarity will result in white centering, thus problematically reinscribing racial domination.[46] In one extreme scenario, as outlined by Scott Morgensen, the contrite settler subject becomes the inheritor of indigeneity.[47] Amidst criticism of the "ally industrial complex," one indigenous activist deplores the inability or unwillingness to follow through with the ultimate consequences of one's allyship:

> The ally establishment co-opts decolonization as a banner to fly at its unending anti-oppression gala. What is not understood is that decolonization is a threat to the very existence of settler "allies." No matter how liberated you are, if you are still occupying indigenous lands you are still a colonizer.[48]

Returning to international relations and law, then, "solidarity" may be unwelcome because it comes from a constituency that one does not wish to receive solidarity from, either because of its perceived hostility (solidarity is hypocritical) or because of its sheer impossibility (solidarity is in bad faith) or because it destroys a meaningful distinction between recipient and giver (solidarity dissolves its conditions of possibility).

On a first level, one may perceive expressions of solidarity as claiming an equality that is simply not there, whose implicit assertion does violence to the actual inequality that undergirds it and that is used, in fact, to cynically raise the profile of the provider of solidarity at the expense of the receiver. Hence, the Israeli government reportedly jumped to the conclusion that Iran and Iraq had refused its offer of humanitarian assistance after the earthquake that shook both countries. As such, those countries were said to have shown "their true face" (even though a subsequent Haaretz investigation suggested the offer had, in fact, never been received).[49] Consider the following statement by Netanyahu as an example of a kind of "solidarity" that thrives on cosmopolitan abstractions to, effectively, make a political point about national superiority:

46 Mia McKenzie, "No More 'Allies'," *BGD*, October 1, 2013, available at: www.bgdblog.org/2013/09/no-more-allies/ (last accessed August 15, 2022); Andrea Smith, "Unsettling the Privilege of Self-Reflexivity," in France Winddance Twine and Bradley Gardener (eds.), *Geographies of Privilege* (New York: Routledge, 2013).

47 Scott Lauria Morgensen, "The Biopolitics of Settler Colonialism: Right Here, Right Now" (2011) 1 *Settler Colonial Studies* 52.

48 "Accomplices Not Allies: Abolishing the Ally Industrial Complex," Ind*igenous Action*, May 4, 2014, available at: www.indigenousaction.org/accomplices-not-allies-abolishing-the-ally-industrial-complex/ (last accessed August 15, 2022).

49 Uri Blau, "Israel Claimed Iran Refused Its Offer for Humanitarian Aid. Red Cross Says Otherwise," *Haaretz*, November 16, 2017, available at: www.haaretz.com/israel-news/2017-11-16/ty-article/.premium/israel-claimed-iran-refused-its-aid-offer-red-cross-says-otherwise/0000017f-e925-dc7e-adff-f9ad36f90000 (last accessed August 6, 2022).

> I've said many times that we have no quarrel with the people of Iran. Our quarrel is only with the tyrannical regime that holds them hostage and threatens our destruction. *But our humanity is greater than their hatred. Israel continues to be a light unto the nations and this is what I am proud of. And all of you can be proud of Israel's morals, and Israel's might.*[50]

What one witnesses here is, then, in all likelihood an effort to disparage the Iranian and Iraqi regimes under the guise of bringing assistance to their populations – a sort of cosmopolitan anti-politics that feigns to not understand why, given conditions of enmity between parties, grandiose but vacuous professions of solidarity might be unwelcome. The offer may even have been made in the sure knowledge that it would be rejected. Of course, it remains possible that offers of aid (as in South Korea's offers of humanitarian aid to North Korea or Israel's more successful offer to Turkey) are also a first salvo in a policy of *détente*, but the point is that the offeror of solidarity in such a scenario "wins" either way by getting to frame the relationship: either solidarity is accepted and the generosity of the donor is recognized; or solidarity is somehow imposed and the distinctness of the recipient is denied; or solidarity is rejected and the receiver can be blamed.

Paradoxically, the more abstract and universalist the solidarity, the more it incurs the suspicion of artificiality, whereas a solidarity grounded in the idiosyncratic affinities of amity and kinship may at least lay a better claim to genuineness. For example, the "universalist" solidarity with the Venezuelan victims of Maduro supposedly at stake in the inter-state (Argentina, Canada, Colombia, Chile, Paraguay, and Peru) referral of Venezuela to the ICC is suspicious because it is difficult to disentangle from the anti-Bolivarian politics of the Lima group. The dominant narrative of solidarity in international law is often too committed to this particular universalist narrative – *erga omnes* obligations somehow pushing states to intervene on behalf of others for seemingly no other reason than protecting the core values of the system – to provide a compelling account of what solidarity actually stands for. Having failed to provide a convincing case of why solidarity would not be welcome, it will fail to provide an understanding of circumstances where it would.

The critique of "allyship" in the activist realm may, moreover, provide a powerful prism to criticize international solidarity posturing that is simultaneously wholly complicit in what it denounces. Consider, for example, development aid or climate mitigation understood as forms of Western "solidarity" with the Global South. What this solidarity framing eludes is the extent to

[50] Ibid. (emphasis added).

which the West is merely remedying manifestations of its own ongoing privilege as well as continuing age-old patterns of domination.[51] This suspicion touches even states, such as the Nordic countries, that have a more distant historical relationship to colonization but whose claim to "exceptionalism" rooted in solidarity with the third World and "well-meaning whiteness" is belied by their complicity in post-colonial continuities.[52] It has led calls for challenging the "anti-politics of humanitarianism" in the Palestinian context, as a solidarity that casts Israeli occupation as a mere externality under the guise of supporting Palestinian development.[53] In the worst case, solidarity becomes a sort of gaslighting, all the more likely to be voiced that it is, at heart, an empty promise.

4.4 "THANKS, BUT NO THANKS": ON BURDENS OF GRATITUDE

The argument for unwelcome solidarity taken from the fact that it contradicts an underlying *intuitu personae* in at least some cases still leaves a large field of possibilities for welcome solidarity. Why might solidarity, even when it does not emanate from the "wrong" party, still be, in some sense, unwelcome? Or, relatedly, how one might further understand and even justify a refusal of solidarity that might objectively benefit one's people merely on the grounds that it comes from the wrong party? One lead is here that the problem of solidarity is not (or not just) its source, but its fundamental mode of operation, specifically the fact that solidarity is not as generous or, strictly speaking, "free" as it seems.

Marcel Mauss's theory of the potlatch has long underscored the centrality of an economy of giving to social solidarity. In particular, Mauss emphasized that the gift is never entirely free (even though it is disinterested), but that it conditions a series of reciprocal exchanges. The gift engages the honor of the receiver, obliging him to reciprocate, sooner or later (the mechanisms of the don/contre-don). The logic of the gift, then, is said to structure relations in between the models of the interest-driven market and what might be forms of pure altruism. The "essence of the gift," it has been said, "[is] that it [is] not a

[51] Michael Mikulewicz, "The Discursive Politics of Adaptation to Climate Change" (2020) 110 *Annals of the American Association of Geographers* 1807.

[52] Lene Bull Christiansen and Ashleigh Harris, "The Danish African: Wolle Kirk, Whiteness and Colonial Complicity" (2013) 11 *KULT-Postkolonial Temaserie* 45; Suvi Keskinen, Salla Tuori, Sara Irni and Diane Mulinari (eds.), *Complying with Colonialism: Gender, Race and Ethnicity in the Nordic Region* (New York: Routledge, 2016).

[53] Linda Tabar, "Disrupting Development, Reclaiming Solidarity: The Anti-Politics of Humanitarianism" (2016) 45 *Journal of Palestine Studies* 16.

gift."[54] To the extent that the gift is interested, it is in creating and sustaining a relation between donor and receiver in the form of a social bond.

In Maussian anthropology, the solidarity of the gift is primarily understood as a positive function, something that unites societies over time beyond interest calculation. But, lurking beneath the theory, is also a hint of solidarity's dark side. Solidarity, as a form of gift that obliges those who receive it, may be socially awkward, especially when the gift cannot be reciprocated. One is effectively made into the donor's debtor, obliged by their "noblesse oblige." The non-reciprocated or non-reciprocable gift, then, may be a way of exercising power over the receiver in a context where "the impoverishment of the ability to reciprocate impinges on the nature of receiving and impedes the relationship of mutuality that The Gift seeks to foster."[55] Indeed, "Charity is still wounding for him who has accepted it, and the whole tendency of our morality is to strive to do away with the unconscious and injurious patronage of the rich almsgiver. The invitation must be returned, just as 'courtesies' must."[56]

As Mauss put it, then, "To give is to show one's superiority, to be more, or to be higher in rank, magister. To accept without giving in return, or without giving more back, is to become client and servant, to become small, to fall lower (minister)."[57]

Moreover, we have no reason to think that the donor does not know this and that the gift does not come with the more or less deliberate "strings attached" of faux-solidarity, a solidarity proffered only to symbolically humiliate the receiver and enhance the prestige of the donor. But the point is that, even if the donor does not know this, the donor's "gift" of solidarity obliges: the theory is not a theory of the agency of giving but of the socially structuring role of the gift. Thus, it is that the political economy of the gift can be understood, among other things, as central to the constitution of colonization and the creation of bonds of loyalty between ruler and subject.[58]

Amidst a resurgence of interest in Mauss's ideas when it comes to international relations[59] arguably paved by Mauss's own interest in

[54] Jacques Godbout and Alain Caille, *The World of the Gift* (Montreal: McGill-Queen's University Press, 1998), p. 92.

[55] Robert Kowalski, "The Gift: Marcel Mauss and International Aid" (2011) 27 *Journal of Comparative Social Welfare* 189–205, at 195.

[56] Marcel Mauss, *The Gift: The Form and Reason for Exchange in Archaic Societies* (London: Routledge, 2002), pp. 83–84.

[57] Ibid., p. 95.

[58] Harry Liebersohn, *The Return of the Gift: European History of a Global Idea* (Cambridge: Cambridge University Press, 2010).

[59] Grégoire Mallard, *Gift Exchange: The Transnational History of a Political Idea* (Cambridge: Cambridge University Press, 2019).

internationalism,[60] the idea of the inter-temporal rough reciprocity of the gift as a basis of international social life aligns neatly with ideas about international law that have sought to shun both the narrow instrumentalism of interest-driven theories and the normativism of the natural law tradition. As if, perhaps, habitual compliance with international law had less to do with the legally binding character of norms than the way in which they structure, over time, processes of giving and counter-giving.

Certainly, ideas about giving and solidarity raise questions about the nature of international society and the extent to which it can sustain conditions of "generalized reciprocity" over time; that is, paradoxically, conditions under which the underlying demand for reciprocity can be temporarily suspended or diffused (i.e. in that one is not constantly asking for an immediate quid pro quo to any donation). In that respect, Maussian thinking invites us to move beyond the contractual framework of international law to emphasize the role of solidarity in the constitution of international society, not just as bilateral exchange but as sustaining a veritable global economy of multilateralism.[61]

Moreover, Mauss's ideas can also help explain the sort of gift-giving "above and beyond" the mere solidarity of international law, a formal solidarity of obligation often relying on moribund expressions of will rather than the actualization of empathy that is at the heart of the French sociologist's theory. There is no doubt that gift giving above and beyond legal obligations can provide a sometimes-tenuous basis for ongoing social bonds, even in conditions of adversariousness. For example, it has been contended that the humanitarian aid given by Israel to Syrians in the Al-Qunaytirah region between 2012 and 2018 had created openings for "friendly" relationships.[62] Similarly, Volker Heins and Christine Unrau have brought attention to the importance of the kind of transnational solidarity expressed by ordinary Germans making "gifts" to refugees.[63] In such cases, fragile bridges can be built between communities.

Having said that, the question for our purposes is how unilateral offers of gift might be specifically *un*welcome on Maussian grounds. Even though Maussian theory can provide keys to understand the sustenance of

60 Frédéric Ramel, "Marcel Mauss et l'étude des relations internationales: un héritage oublié" (2004) 36 *Sociologie et sociétés* 227.

61 Frédéric Ramel, "How to Understand International Society Differently: Mauss and the Chains of Reciprocity" (2018) 14 *Journal of International Political Theory* 165.

62 Beata Paragi, "Israeli Cross-Border Assistance to Syrians: Creating Bonds by Giving?" (2021) 28 *Mediterranean Politics* 250.

63 Volker Heins and Christine Unrau, "Refugees Welcome: Arrival Gifts, Reciprocity, and the Integration of Forced Migrants" (2018) 14 *Journal of International Political Theory* 223.

international order despite the profoundly agonistic nature of the system,[64] it can also occasionally shed light on how the politics of solidarity might also turn out to be a politics of subjugation. It is particularly in the context of international aid assistance that the idea of the gift has been put to work, including to show some of the gift's ambiguities.[65] Indeed, the fraught, tense operation of the international system suggests a situation in which obligations of reciprocating cannot be put off for very long, notwithstanding the seeming gratuity of solidarity.

Unrequited giving, in particular, has long been identified as a potential key to deeply asymmetric relationships despite or even because of its very liberality. Georges Bataille, for example, argued that the Marshall Plan was a form of gigantic potlatch in which the United States sacrificed national resources in order to increase their prestige in Europe and humiliate the Soviet Union.[66] This left the receiver, Europe, strangely out of the picture, something that Wilton Dillon, an American anthropologist, sought to correct by highlighting the consequences of "downward giving" on Europe, notably in terms of expectations of very real "gratitude, affection, anti-Communist votes, and permission to build military installations and station troops."[67] Dillon accounted for the fact that the Marshall Plan resulted in "hostility toward their protector-benefactors" and anti-Americanism rather than gratefulness based on the inability of the French to pay back the gifts and thus assert their standing as equals.[68]

It also resulted in a quixotic quest for counter-gifts and a pursuit of restored French grandeur, as visible in the Suez adventure or the search for nuclear weapons as a form of "psychological release" from the tyranny of giving back.[69] Indeed, the sting of the gift is felt with all the more intensity that it coincides in some cases with brusque reversals in fortune. This was the case of Western Europe after the Second World War. It was also evident in "the

64 John Oates and Eric Grynaviski, "Reciprocity, Hierarchy, and Obligation in World Politics: From Kula to Potlatch" (2018) 14 *Journal of International Political Theory* 145.

65 Volker M Heins, Christine Unrau and Kristine Avram, "Gift-Giving and Reciprocity in Global Society: Introducing Marcel Mauss in International Studies" (2018) 14 *Journal of International Political Theory* 126; Alex Enachioaie, "Aid as Gift: International Aid between Theory and Practice," Undergraduate Dissertation, University of Kent, June 1, 2014, available at: www.academia.edu/9270716/Aid_as_gift_International_aid_between_theory_and_practice (last accessed August 6, 2022); Kowalski, "Marcel Mauss and International Aid."

66 Georges Bataille, *La Part Maudite: Précédé de la Notion de Dépense* (Paris: Editions de Minuit, 1967).

67 Wilton Dillon, *Gifts and Nations: The Obligation to Give, Receive and Repay* (New York: Routledge, 2017), p. 76.

68 Ibid., p. 78.

69 Ibid.

sudden status of [post-Soviet] societies in the 1990s as recipients of Western aid [and] thus a profound reversal of their self-image as aid givers."[70] To be a "provider" and to become a "receiver" of solidarity crystallizes the adaptability of the fluxes of solidarity, but it also highlights the risk of brusque *déclassement* (loss of status).

This suggests that, even in international relations there is always more at stake in solidarity than merely "giving aid." There is, in fact, no such thing as a free lunch. Solidarity also potentially obliges and those who cannot repay their debt are thereby easily if discreetly subjugated: giving is/as a form of power. This idea is visible, then, in a variety of facets of international life. After the Cold War, the United States had certain expectations that it would get a share of the pie of reconstruction in Eastern Europe, just as both the United States and the Soviet Union had earlier had huge expectations about the gratitude they were owed for liberating Europe. Similarly, President George W. Bush is said to have been obsessed by the need for Iraqi leaders to strongly express their gratitude to the United States for "liberating" the country.[71] This has surfaced most dramatically and recently in diplomatic outbursts urging Ukraine to more demonstratively – if nothing else, at this still early stage – express its gratitude to the West for aiding it in its fight against Russia.[72] No doubt the powers that be will come knocking in due course and demand their symbolic due: liberation from Russia will not come at zero cost in terms of independence and ongoing burdens of gratitude, a fact that Ukrainian leaders may belatedly become aware of,[73] even as some argue that it is the West that increasingly has a huge debt of gratitude to Ukraine.[74]

Development assistance has also been analyzed as a classic form of unreciprocated giving. The crucial insight for Tomohisa Hattori, for example, emphasizing the primarily "symbolic" power of the gift, is that "the wide

70 Thomas Carothers, "Western Civil-Society Aid to Eastern Europe and the Former Soviet Union," *Carnegie Endowment for International Peace*, September 1, 1999, available at: https://carnegieendowment.org/1999/09/01/western-civil-society-aid-to-eastern-europe-and-former-soviet-union-pub-145 (last accessed August 6, 2022).

71 Fred Kaplan, "Why Is Bush so Obsessed with Ungrateful Foreigners?," *Slate*, March 13, 2007, available at: https://slate.com/news-and-politics/2007/03/why-is-bush-so-obsessed-with-ungrateful-foreigners.html (last accessed August 15, 2023).

72 Lara Jakes, "'We're Not Amazon': Britain's Defense Minister Says Ukrainian Officials Should Show More Gratitude," *The New York Times*, July 12, 2023, available at: www.nytimes.com/2023/07/12/world/europe/uk-ukraine-ben-wallace.html (last accessed August 15, 2023).

73 Luke Harding, "'Thank You, Ben Wallace!' Ukraine Bemused and Irritated by UK's Call for Gratitude," *The Observer*, July 15, 2023, available at: www.theguardian.com/world/2023/jul/15/ben-wallace-defence-secretary-ukraine-gratitude (last accessed August 15, 2023).

74 Timothy Snyder, "Gratitude to Ukraine," *Thinking about...*, December 11, 2022, available at: https://snyder.substack.com/p/gratitude-to-ukraine (last accessed August 15, 2023).

ranging policy objectives attached to foreign aid are secondary to a more basic role of affirming the social relation in which they are extended (which, in this case, describes an underlying condition of inequality)."[75] But that relationship is not one between equals, since it constructs, in the words of Didier Fassin, "those for whom the gift cannot imply a counter-gift, since it is assumed that they can only receive" as "the indebted of the world."[76]

Drawing on Bourdieu, Hattori further conceptualizes foreign aid as "symbolic domination, or a practice that signals and euphemizes social hierarchies."[77] Specifically, "giving" transforms the donor's "status in the relationship from the dominant to the generous." Therefore:

> In accepting such a gift (i.e. one that cannot be reciprocated), a recipient acquiesces in the social order that produced it: in other words, he or she becomes grateful. It is this active complicity on the part of the recipient that gives the practice of unreciprocated giving its social power ... what begins as a simple euphemization of a social hierarchy can become an active misrecognition over time, eventually naturalizing the material inequality between donor and recipient as the normal order of things.[78]

One can detect traces of this, for example, in the context of China's COVID vaccine diplomacy and the kind of burdens that this liberality has (was meant to?) engendered.[79]

The logic of the gift, then, helps understand why states may be ambivalent vis-à-vis ostentatious displays of solidarity, even when these might otherwise be useful or not emanate from the presumptively wrong party. It is not just that receivers are not interested in the kind of ongoing relationship that the gift signifies, it is also that they fear being put in a relationship of subjugation by a solidarity that cannot be reciprocated, except with gratefulness and subservience. Of course, giving back is always a possibility and may sometimes involve merely notional giving, but the obligation is always there and ends up sustaining a relationship of domination and subservience.[80]

75 Tomohisa Hattori, "Reconceptualizing Foreign Aid" (2001) 8 *Review of International Political Economy* 633–660, at 639.

76 Didier Fassin, "Humanitarianism as a Politics of Life" (2007) 19 *Public Culture* 499–520, at 512.

77 Hattori, "Reconceptualizing Foreign Aid," 639.

78 Ibid., 640.

79 "The Guardian View on the Politics of Generosity: Gifts with Price Tags," *The Guardian*, April 8, 2020, available at: www.theguardian.com/commentisfree/2020/apr/08/the-guardian-view-on-the-politics-of-generosity-gifts-with-price-tags (last accessed August 6, 2022).

80 Beáta Paragi, "Contemporary Gifts: Solidarity, Compassion, Equality, Sacrifice, and Reciprocity from an NGO Perspective" (2017) 58 *Current Anthropology* 317.

4.5 CONCLUSION: SOLIDARITY AND THE CHALLENGE OF RECIPROCITY

This chapter has sought to stress the salience of the politics of being on the receiving end of solidarity. Where international lawyers have been mostly interested in solidarity as a cohesive agglutinant for the international community at large, it has sought to transcend such abstractions to highlight the praxis of solidarity, drawing on a range of illustrations extending beyond international law. In the process, the chapter has sought to shed light on one particular dimension of the praxis of solidarity, namely the extent to which it may well be unwelcome. Against a perspective focused traditionally on the "supply side" of solidarity, it has insisted on taking seriously the actual "demand" for solidarity. And, contra traditional realism's suspicion that solidarity is just make-believe, it has foregrounded a wariness with solidarity's all-too-real actual operation against the background of problematic post-colonial and racialized assumptions.[81]

In short, the chapter suggests we should be mindful of how invocations of and appeals to solidarity construct both the provider and the recipient of solidarity as part of ongoing social ties. Solidarity does not as much emerge from unproblematic bonds as it seeks to construct them, raising questions about who decides on the perimeters of communities of solidarity. This is particularly the case of international solidarity as something that emerges well beyond the confines of polities understood as the "normal" locus of social solidarity. One should be wary of international lawyers' tendency to posit solidarity as "already there" and inherent to the international system rather than something that is constantly being constructed and deconstructed (solidarity and un-solidarity). Instead, the chapter has brought attention to "imaginaries of solidarity" or "non-solidarity" activated by social actors themselves.

One thing that the chapter might be seen as underscoring is the importance of willingness to have other parties be in solidarity with oneself. To be invited "into" solidarity may be an important dimension of what makes solidarity worthwhile. For example, Ukrainians have left no doubt that they very much expect international solidarity against Russia. The International Solidarity Movement was founded at the insistence of Palestinian activists themselves who sought foreigners to bear witness to what was happening under occupation. There may also be certain obligations of gracefulness in being the recipient of solidarity, to the extent that this solidarity is not ill-meaning or

[81] Nina Glick Schiller and Andrew Irving (eds.), *Whose Cosmopolitanism?: Critical Perspectives, Relationalities and Discontents* (New York: Berghahn Books, 2014).

problematic in some of the ways illustrated in the chapter. For example, the "courage [of some Syrians] to accept Israeli gifts"[82] has been praised as permitting a thin bond to emerge between Israelis and Syrians, in otherwise highly fraught geopolitical circumstances.

By the same token, the chapter suggests caution about legislating duties of solidarity under international law or human rights. This is not merely because an obligation of solidarity trivializes what the performance of solidarity entails; it is also because one should be wary, on the receiving end, of international actors feeling as if they ought to be recipients of solidarity in all cases. To have no choice but to accept whatever solidarity is coming and at what price is an extreme form of dispossession of self. An obligation to be the passive recipient of solidarity would be, paradoxically, the exact opposite of what solidarity entails: the ability to be mutually in solidarity with the other as a recognition of a commonality of fate and a willingness to assume the obligations (including of reciprocal giving) that come with it.

Moreover, positing the absolute value of solidarity could detract from the obligation of those "giving" to critically examine their own giving *élan*, and how it might be a source of awkwardness in social relations (including through solidarity that is much less of an ostentatious performance and that makes space for reciprocity). In that respect, the chapter was also a contribution to how a politics of allyship might become more of a politics of comradeship, instead of one focusing on one's own "downward" duty to the less well off.[83] It raises the question of how "we 'in solidarity' might extract ourselves from that cozy, comfortable feeling of solidarity with the 'victims'" by "rearticulating our relationship to the 'perpetrators' while at the same time avoiding self-sainthood."[84]

The emphasis on "unwelcome solidarity," then, sheds light indirectly on what might be welcome forms of solidarity. Against the relative heavy-handedness of state-to-state solidarity and its sometimes-problematic politics, one way of viewing welcome solidarity might be as that solidarity that transcends borders and expresses radical forms of brother/sister-hood with others facing similar plights. The intimate domain of the inter-personal may be one in which solidarities express themselves in the rawest fashion, without the corrupting leverage of international relations or the reductionist language of international law.[85] However, neither civil society nor public opinions can be

82 Paragi, "Israeli Cross-Border Assistance to Syrians," 251.
83 Jodi Dean, *Comrade: An Essay on Political Belonging* (London: Verso, 2019).
84 Stamatopoulou-Robbins, "Joys and Dangers of Solidarity in Palestine," 114.
85 Patrick Hayden and Natasha Saunders, "Solidarity at the Margins: Arendt, Refugees, and the Inclusive Politics of World-Making," in Kei Hiruta (ed.), *Arendt on Freedom, Liberation, and Revolution* (Cham: Palgrave Macmillan, 2019), pp. 171–199.

expected to be free of the dilemmas that structure all solidarity, including the challenge of remedying obvious asymmetries.[86]

Finally, the chapter has brought attention to the need to think of ways in which solidarity might or might not be made to be reciprocal. The value of the gift as an anthropological conceit that might be extended to international relations at large is its flexibility and adaptability. Counter-giving is never about a strict quid-pro-quo, the sort of formal symmetry that only a rather sterile modernist mindset can envisage under international law. It allows for creativity, even cheekiness and irony in the act of subversive counter-giving, as when President Chavez of Venezuela sent oil to poor Americans to heat themselves in the Winter.[87] But it is counter-giving nonetheless, a way of providing opportunities in a relationship that do not excessively burden one party with the curse of always being on the receiving end of the other's liberality.

[86] Hjalmar Bang Carlsen, Nicole Doerr, and Jonas Toubøl, "Inequality in Interaction: Equalising the Helper–Recipient Relationship in the Refugee Solidarity Movement" (2022) 33 *VOLUNTAS: International Journal of Voluntary and Nonprofit Organizations* 59.

[87] Rebekah Kebede, "Venezuela Brings Free Heating Oil to Poor in NY," *Reuters*, December 14, 2007, available at: www.reuters.com/article/citgo-energy-bronx-assistance-idUSN1425588920071214 (last accessed August 15, 2022).

5

On Migration

An African Perspective

CHARLES ROMAIN MBELE

5.1 INTRODUCTION

Migration and the right of peoples to regulate mobility remain at the centre of ethical, political and philosophical controversies throughout the modern world. Traces of this can be found in the writings of Kant, Arendt, Rawls, Rancière, Agamben, Baumann, Derrida, Mbembe and others. What is now clearly apparent is that the context of generalized free trade is shattering and destroying the idea of solidarity that comes from Christian *caritas*. In an empirical and concrete approach, we make reference to the ethics of solidarity that formally shapes the 'new partnership' between Europe and Africa: both parties reaffirm their commitment to enhancing cooperation and dialogue on migration and mobility, 'in a spirit of shared responsibility, solidarity, reciprocity, mutual respect and accountability'.[1] Our argument emphasizes above all that the Europeanization of the migration issue as it relates to Africa finds its limit in the contractualization of mobility with the 'readmission' or 'repatriation' of African immigrants being prescribed. A pessimistic vision, therefore, concludes that the current world order, characterized by power relations, maintains 'illusions of solidarity',[2] in particular because of the flows of

To the St. Bernard Church Strikers in 1996.

1 Council of the European Union, *Partnership Agreement between the European Union and Its Member States, of the one part, and the Members of the Organisation of the African, Carribean and the Pacific States, on the other part*, Interinstitutional File 2021/0145 (NLE) (Brussels: 19 July 2023), article 2 para 1, (hereinafter *New Partnership Agreement*), available at: https://data.consilium.europa.eu/doc/document/ST-8372-2023-REV-1/en/pdf (last accessed 14 September 2023).

2 É. Njoh-Mouéllè, *Mondialisation, rapports de forces et illusions de solidarité. Essais philosophiques et politiques* (Yaoundé: Presses de l'UCAC, 2016).

capitalism that brutally exclude by means of the 'camp-form' or the 'border-form'. From then on, on an Arendtian basis, many think that the abstract human representation – that of the human being as such – is limited in the case of stateless persons, emigrants, undocumented immigrants, refugees, displaced persons, 'deportees', blocked at borders or parked in 'camps' and 'detention centres' in train stations, ports, airport basements, motorway service areas and so on. For men to whom only

> their belonging to humanity 'in its pure state' remains, one could have thought that they fall precisely under the defence of human rights . . . of this instance which declares the humanity of man inalienable, imprescriptible, inherent in his 'nature' and 'prior' to his social, political, legal attributes . . . The mere fact of belonging to 'humanity' in no way guaranteed them the right to have rights. The loss of national rights, the loss of citizenship, the absence of protection from a government . . . all this leads to [their] superfluity . . . Far from considering that the 'substance' of humanity remains, while its 'accidents' have disappeared, the world has seen nothing sacred in the abstract nudity of the human being.[3]

With the strengthening of neoliberal globalization born after the fall of the Berlin Wall, we have seen, not more solidarity, but the erection of more walls, ramparts, electric fences, at the same time as 'enmity' winning hearts and no real rapprochement between peoples. Thus, the West closes its borders, while designating Africans as enemies or threats. Despite the successive partnership agreements between the European Union and the Organisation of African, Caribbean and Pacific States (OACPS), Africans are abandoned to die in the desert, at sea or enslaved in Libya. African migration movements towards Europe and inside Africa are thus characterized by a general fabric of inhuman and tragic violence, because the figure of the insolvent and unprofitable immigrant is criminalized and subjected to brutal legal and police repression. This point of view, stemming from an 'anthropology of the good for nothing' ('*anthropologie du bon à rien*') – according to a phrase used by Bernard Ogilvie – shows that this structural violence can no longer only give rise to a call for care, concern, attention and benevolence. The new relations between capital and labour show that it is not a question here of vulnerabilities or transitory suffering, but of power relations linked to the structure of the universal market with the constitution of what has received various names in the history of modern thought: '*Pöbel*' (Hegel), '*Lumpenproletariat*' (Marx) and 'human superfluity' (Arendt). It is, therefore, a question of putting in place

3 M. Revault d'Allones, *Le Dépérissement de la politique. Généalogie d'un lieu commun* (Paris: Aubier, coll. 'Alto', 1999), p. 276.

the thought of a restructuring and an egalitarian rebalancing of power relations in the world – far from the sole exchange value. Such a thought will be based on the one hand on a solidarity activity as we have seen in places such as Sangatte, Calais, Lampedusa and Lesbos. It will also be based on the fact that immigrants are also actors who construct the teleology of a more fraternal humanity because they weave solidarities at the start and with those they meet. Our postulation is, therefore, the following: we must oppose the unspoken on migration and mobility, namely the phobia of fraternity and solidarity through the retrograde affirmation of the community of soil, of blood, of the hierarchization of men and societies. We must affirm a concrete utopia of equality, by means of which men and women would be more united and more hospitable.

5.2 MIGRATION: AN ANCIENT PHILOSOPHICAL QUESTION

In the spirit of Montaigne, preoccupied by the 'cannibals', Kant thinks in his *Project of Perpetual Peace* that the earth is round and, therefore, intended for all, and calls for the right to hospitality and the movement of people. But, since this transcendent moment of universal thought, a greater feeling of solidarity has not developed, an exit from national or individual egoisms, to aim for the adoption of modes of collective regulation on a planetary scale of the challenges that humanity faces. The attitude towards the question of migration, on the contrary, allows us to doubt it. A requirement for a reorientation of thought is all the more necessary since, in *The Law of Peoples*, John Rawls,[4] theorist of the idea of justice, is against the Kantian law of a cosmopolitan law (*Weltbürgerrecht*). The global *alt-right* speaks less prudishly in terms of invasion and of the 'Great Replacement'.

Regarding Africa, a historical approach shows that the issue of migration first entered the media, political and theoretical discourse of current Africa in the early 1980s with the expulsions of African immigrants from Nigeria and Gabon, countries then facing the first throes of an economic crisis where the end of the welfare state was in the works. It then became more radical in the 1990s with extreme material scarcity caused by the passive insertion of the subcontinent into neoliberal globalization with structural adjustment policies. By sterilizing the African political scene with its hegemonic alternative (*Adjust or Perish*), free trade brings the question of autochthony into common discourse with terms such as *Ivorianness*, *Congoleseness*, *Gaboneseness*, *Zambianness*, the opposition of natives and non-natives, the 'hygienic'

[4] John Rawls, *Le Droit des gens* [1993], traduit de l'américain et avant-propo de B. Guillaume, commentaire de Stanley Hoffmann (Paris: Esprit, coll. "Bibliothèque 10/18", 1999).

opposition between real men and cockroaches (*inyenzi*), 'dubious citizenship', the idea of 'true or false Anglophones', the requirement of a 'certificate of nationality' issued by the police or the courts to access the computerized or biometric identity card, and so on. Cynical demagogues used the constitution of electoral lists to bring the question of electoral fraud to the forefront. The use of unregistered immigrants was then denounced.[5] The theme of autochthony takes on a new idiosyncratic accent here because of a neoliberal globalization that sees the return of societies of status and rent. But the question of autochthony is not, however, new in the history of humanity. Indeed, confronted with greater powers in terms of knowledge, wealth and demography, the Greek city in crisis questioned its identity, its roots. Greece then developed categories and statuses to distinguish Greeks from non-Greeks, foreigners and stateless persons, citizens from non-citizens. The law of Pericles in 451 or 450 BCE even prohibited marriage between certain categories, with the risk that their children would be declared bastards (*nothoi*) – with a double consequence, namely their exclusion from the list of citizens and the reduction of their inheritance rights.[6]

5.3 INDIGENOUS CITIZENSHIP AND THE QUESTION OF FOREIGNERS ACCORDING TO PLATO

The issue of indigenous citizenship autochthony is that of Plato's *Menexenus*. This dialogue was much in demand as such at the end of the last century by the European far right. According to Socrates, the role of the funeral eulogy was to 'celebrate the city in every way and … those who died in war and … the whole line of ancestors who preceded us and ourselves …'.[7] The eulogy praises the origin of the Greeks, noble by birth, because

> their ancestors were not of foreign origin and that, therefore, their descendants were not immigrants in the country whose ancestors had come from elsewhere, but natives, who lived and dwelt in their real homeland and who were not nourished by a stepmother, but by the maternal earth in which they lived, and that today, after their death, they rest in their own earth, the one who gave birth to them, nourished them and received them into her bosom.[8]

5 On these questions, P. Geshiere, *The Perils of Belonging. Autochtony, Citizenship, and Exclusion in Africa & Europe* (Chicago: The University of Chigago Press, 2009).

6 M. I. Finley, *Mythe, mémoire et histoire* (Paris: Flammarion, 1981), p. 78.

7 Platon, *Ménexène, Œuvres complètes*, sous la direction de Luc Brisson (Paris: Flammarion, 2008), p. 234a.

8 Ibid., p. 237b.

The Greeks, says Plato in *Timaeus* (23e) and *Critias* (109c–110b), are like Erichtonus, born of the earth like Hephaestus. Until *Republic* (III 414cd; IX 575d), the legend of the natives (*autochtones*) remains linked to a civic theme: this noble lie allows the creation of a citizenship of affiliation and, therefore, of exclusion. The occurrence of the term 'foreigner' in *Crito* was already inseparable from that of the citizen. In the remembrance of the statutes, it is a question of evoking the insecurity of the exile, deprived of freedom and risking slavery. In a prosopopoeia, the laws demonstrate to Socrates that the condition of citizen, slave of his city in the city is still preferable to that of the exile, this other figure of the fugitive slave abroad. It is a civic lesson linked to autochthony and sedentariness: Socrates is a sedentary person, unlike the sophists, foreigners, itinerants, nomads and specialists in travel. As in *Menexenus* (237b–238a), citizens must be taught the belief in autochthony, so that they experience feelings of filial piety for their motherland.

The theme of autochthony remains, however, an identity and historical reconstruction. Indeed, the country inhabited at that time by the Greeks was initially that of the Pelagians. Plato also returns from a reflexive and heuristic point of view to this distinction between citizens and foreigners with the Egyptian journey and the discovery of the other, physically and metaphysically. From *Gorgias* onwards, the figure of the anonymous Stranger becomes recurrent in Platonic dialogue: he constitutes the substitute for Socrates and henceforth leads the game of *logoï*. The haunting presence of the Stranger as Plato's spokesman – the Stranger of Elea, the Athenian Stranger, Timaeus of Locri, Diotima of Mantinea or simply Socrates, a stranger in his own city according to Phaedrus – seems to signify the privilege of exotic reason, which always directs the mind towards another world. Plato's philosophy of otherness makes him relativize the swelling of the similar and the same of ethnocentrism which refuses the other and the different. Plato now establishes against Parmenides the reality of non-being to which the dignity of the other is entrusted. Being explodes into a plurality of genres: being, movement, rest, the same and the other and their mutual relations. In *Politics* (262a–263a), Plato rejects as a prejudice the division of humanity into Greeks and Barbarians if it is not based on a theory of generic man. This stands in contrast to Aristotle, who developed the theory of climates to justify the exclusion and servitude of certain peoples. Against established norms, the question of foreigners is posed by Plato as a problematic question. As it is no longer possible to think of the same without the other, the question of the foreigner or the other becomes an eminent philosophical question.[9]

[9] H. Joly, *Études platoniciennes. La question des étrangers* (Paris: Vrin, 1991), pp. 12–90.

If the reconstruction of identity shows the historical and temporal relativity of the idea of autochthony, it nevertheless exists from a cultural point of view. Indeed, men who violently conquer a country invest in it anthropologically – by 'cosmizing' it, Mircéa Eliade showed in his works:

> A symbol of the pre-formal, the Dragon is considered the true 'master of the place', the native par excellence, against whom the conquerors must fight before occupying a territory and organizing it (i.e. 'forming' it, 'cosmizing' it). A certain number of myths and legends, narrating the struggle of a hero who came from abroad and the Dragon, absolute master of a country, express the conflict between the natives – or the representatives of the old order of things – and the victorious invaders who end up founding a new order (new State, new dynasty, new social organization ... The victory against the native Dragon expresses the victory against the representatives of a previous situation, homologous to 'Chaos'. By conquering the country, one 'creates' it again, since one gives it a new 'form'.[10]

The creation of a new *kòsmos*, a new world order, takes up a recurring cosmogonic theme in the history of the founding of cities. The enterprise of 'cosmization' rids the earth of the indigenous monster (dragon, sphinx, cyclops, harpies, daughters of Lemnos) and makes it suitable for human habitation. Thus, in the *Enuma Elish* of Akkad, the process of transforming chaos into cosmos, the creation of a new citizenship, is done in the struggle of the young Marduk against Tiamat, a figure of the indigenous symbolizing chaos, the embryo of the world, the abortion of being. More precisely, Tiamat is the ophidian monster that the young hero massacres. From that moment on, the cosmogonic myth engenders the classical opposition in Semitic and Indo-European mythologies between mortals and immortals, gods and men. Stories of this nature later formed the matrix of Hesiod's myth of races, where autochthony suggests a transfer of sovereignty. The Hesiodic myth of races thus opposes a divine race in which *dikè* reigns, a world of titans, giants and dragons characterized by *hubris*. These two antithetical worlds thus violently oppose each other from an ethnic, moral and political point of view. The Batutsi cosmogony of Rwanda goes in the same direction when it tells of the cosmization of Central Africa – an embryonic universe – by a hero who came from abroad.[11] In the Greek case, this perspective is inflected by the Eleusinian mysteries that announce a new world where the man to whom

[10] M. Eliade, 'Structure et fonction du mythe', in Serge Sauneron and Jean Yoyotte (eds.), *La Naissance du monde* (Paris: Seuil, coll. 'Sources orientales', 1959), p. 485.

[11] E. Gasarabwe, *La Geste Rwanda* (Paris: UGE, coll. '10/18', 1978), pp. 34–38.

they are addressed is without 'acceptance of borders'.[12] For the Eleusinian mysteries this comes from initiation or a demanding educational process. And, for the later Plato, this emotional link to the earth can be relativized by what makes man, namely education, and its reverse face, the relativity of things. It is the Eleusinian and Platonic perspective that will be deployed in a manifest way in the cosmopolitan law to which Rawls opposes himself.

5.4 KANT'S THEORY OF THE LAW OF MIGRATION

The question of immigration accesses the concept with modernity, following the global expansion of humanity of European origin to enrich itself through trade and conquest. Kant is the one who best expresses, in his *To Perpetual Peace* (1795), the need for a reception without hostility of immigrants, trade being incompatible with war. Cosmopolitical law implies conditions of universal hospitality which concretely means the freedom of movement of people:

> We are speaking not of philanthropy, but of law. Therefore hospitality [good neighbourliness] means the right of a foreigner not to be treated with hostility when he arrives upon the soil of another. The native may reject the foreigner if it can be done without his perishing, but as long as he stays peacefully, he must not treat him hostilely. It is not the right of becoming a permanent [*Gastrecht*] which the foreigner may request, for a special beneficial treaty would be required to make him a fellow inhabitant [*Hausgenosse*] for a certain period. But it is the right to visit [*Besuchsrecht*] which belongs to all men – the right belonging to all men to offer their society on account of the common possession of the surface of the earth. Since it is a globe, they cannot disperse infinitely, but tolerate each other. No man has a greater fundamental right to occupy a particular spot than any other.[13]

Two limitations emerge, however, from Kantian thought on this subject. First, Kant's fundamental goal is to justify the commercial expansion of Europeans by giving them the possibility of a circulation of people and goods among other peoples. Then, starting from a contractualist definition of the State, he poses the right of visit as an essential device of the right to hospitality. Such a device does not account for the permanent installation of the visitor as a possible conclusion of the free circulation. Kant could not think of it at the

[12] L. Gernet, *Anthropologie de la Grèce antique* (Paris: Flammarion, 1982), p. 16.

[13] Immanuel Kant, 'To Eternal Peace' [1795], in Carl J. Friedrich (ed.), *Basic Writings of Kant*, with an Introduction by Allen W. Wood (New York: The Modern Library, 2001), pp. 443–476, at pp. 448–449.

time he thought about, but the reality of permanent installation will, centuries later, lead the Western extreme right to the fantasy of the foreign body generally posed as being impure, in such a way that the danger is then both the immigrant and the migrant who are engaged in mobility. But, since the Kantian perspective remains firmly anti-colonialist, we must go further and observe his demand for a universal city composed of nation-states outside the state of nature. By recognizing themselves as citizens of the world, they guarantee their co-existence in contrast to an international law regulated by the right to war. Kant makes cosmopolitan law something inherent to citizenship. And the citizen of the world must deploy his potentialities through an educational process that abolishes egoism and establishes the awareness of a right of humanity as a universal norm that restricts the sovereignty of nation-states.

5.5 STATELESSNESS AND THE RESURGENCE OF AN ORGANICIST PHILOSOPHY

But, with the power acquired by European nations, *Realpolitik* theses emerge with the resurgence of an organicist philosophy of the Herderian, Fichtean and Hegelian type. This values the power of a community or a State against the Kantian cosmopolitan right to emigrate and to universal hospitality or the need for social and economic rights on a global scale. For example, Kant mentions the right to subsistence at the national and international level in the case of the Eskimos in the 'First Supplement' of *To Perpetual Peace*.[14] The Kantian cosmopolitan right was about making the right to immigration expand trade between peoples through 'gentle commerce' according to a word from Montesquieu. In fact, beyond the desire to justify European commercial expansion, trade as a vehicle for the progress of humanity towards perpetual peace is taken by Kant in the sense of interaction and circulation. Today, in this spirit, Habermas, in many of his writings, justifies the right to immigration by considering the point of view of immigrants and the historical background that allowed Europe to enrich itself and develop. The Habermasian position is more or less a response to John Rawls's work *The Law of Peoples* (1993). Rawls opposes the principle stated by Kant of a cosmopolitan law implying conditions of a universal hospitality which concretely means the freedom of movement of people. Rawls bluntly believes that disordered countries must be prevented by means of 'just war' from

[14] E. Kant, "To Eternal Peace" [1795], trans. C. J. Friedrich, *Basic Writings of Kant*, edited and with an introduction by A. W. Wood (New York: The Modern Library, 2001).

transferring their excess populations to Western countries. Rawls developed political realism at a time when the question of immigration is once again becoming central to political philosophy. The same causes producing the same effects (the need to flourish, to respond to the call of the open sea, to have new experiences, to find jobs, to enrich oneself, to trade) and, as in past centuries that experienced European immigration, the world has been witnessing an intensification of African, Latin American, Arab, Asian and Eastern European immigration since the decade when Rawls wrote *The Law of Peoples*. But Rawls analyses its political, socio-economic and spiritual issues in a culturalist way. Appearing with the end of the Cold War, Rawls's *The Law of Peoples* appears as one of the speculative manifestos of the Western conception of politics and international relations: here, the guiding principles that prevail are charity (aid or assistance) and indifference. In reality they hide the right of the strongest, the recourse to just war, violent interference in the affairs of other peoples, the fight against immigration from the global South. It is not a question – following the 'principle of difference' in his *Theory of Justice* – of defining a fairer and more egalitarian redistributive structure at the international level. But, under the logic of power, an organicist *Realpolitik* is opposed to the non-Western world in the name of the priority defence of the interests of Western peoples, in particular human rights. Rawls, therefore, resorts to the opposition between democracy and authoritarian oligarchy, between 'rich and well-ordered societies' and 'disordered' and 'poor' societies. Because the wealth of opulent societies resides in their political and cultural traditions, their knowledge and human capital as well as their capacity for economic and political organization, Rawls rejects any claim to a liberal principle of distributive justice on an international scale. In his eyes, economic injustice results less from the poor distribution of wealth than from factors of internal justice in poor countries: oppressive governments, corrupt elites and decomposed political cultures, unreasonable and oppressive religions towards women, overpopulation.[15] Rawls interprets the capitalist economy in a culturalist way by blaming the 'losers' in the areas of its collapse for their problems, their archaic cultural models being incompatible with the market: poor people exist in the global South because of their culture and their unreasonable, corrupt and despotic political systems (in the sense of Montesquieu). In light of this reading of the international economic system, Rawls admits for the North 'the legitimate right of a people to restrict

[15] J. Rawls, *Le Droit des gens* [1993], traduit de l'américain et avant-propos de Guillarme, *Commentaire* par S. Hoffmann (Paris : Esprit, coll. 'Bibliothèque 10/18', 1996), pp. 103–104.

immigration'.[16] But he nevertheless demands the right to emigrate to the South without reciprocity, on the grounds that poverty does not concern the North, which should not be subject to obligations of international justice. He asserts peremptorily that a poor state cannot 'compensate for its irresponsibility in maintaining its territory and conserving its natural resources by engaging in ... migration to the territory of another people without their consent'.[17]

Rawls does not revisit Kantian cosmopolitan law by chance nearly 200 years after the publication of *To Perpetual Peace*. His aim is to refocus it on the right to migration within the sovereign framework of a few nation-states. For him, it is a question of restricting as much as possible the utopia of a right to global citizenship. From that moment on, in fact, the global refugee and immigrant crisis – the result of historical violence linked to wars, socially brutal economic policies and often abusive restrictions on emigration – argues for the expansion of Kantian cosmopolitan law based on 'the original community of the surface of the earth'. Rawls opposes such an orientation. He, therefore, limits the debate to human rights, examined from an 'ideal theory' opposing 'liberal societies' and 'hierarchical societies'. However, such a perspective is little concerned with the contradiction that arises between the conflicts caused by the promotion of human rights and the interests of Western nationals beyond borders. Stanley Hoffmann[18] has observed that, in US–Japanese trade relations, between the United States and France in foreign policy and security, Canadian and Spanish fishing practices, democratic states defend first and foremost 'state interests' of a geopolitical nature; this can be seen in French interventions in black Africa, as well as in the support given by the Americans or the French to different repressive regimes. He thought that Rawls ends up with 'a code of conduct that is too thin and too conservative, especially in a world in which interdependence empties sovereignty of the best part of its substance'; Rawls also resorts to vague principles of formation and regulation of possible associations between democratic societies, or the 'norms of equity' concerning trade and cooperation agreements.[19]

We can also observe the use of Kant himself against the Kantian theory of the right of migration. An argument from the Kantian point of view is put forward against radical cosmopolitan law and in favour of control of immigration and the reception of immigrants and refugees by the nation-states of the civilisational area extending from the *Rio Grande* to the *Oder-Neisse*. This

16 Ibid., p. 69, note 1.
17 Ibid., p. 69.
18 S. Hoffmann, 'Commentaire', in: John Rawls, *Le Droit des gens* [1993], *op. cit.*, pp. 126–127.
19 Ibid., p. 125 *sq*.

argument concerns the importance of public debate in Kantian republicanism. Thus, D. Weinstock considers that

> the reliability of the Idea of the social contract … the basis of the legitimacy of all legislation in the ideal Kantian Republic, depends … on the existence in the political society to which it applies of a sphere of free public debate. Now such a sphere of exchange of ideas and opinions depends, among other things, on the State being able to control the number of newcomers as members of its political society and on being able to impose certain conditions of membership on the persons it admits.

From this, a conclusion is drawn: 'the principle of a sphere of free public debate' gives right and strength to the Western capacity to control immigration both in terms of the number of immigrants received and the conditions that any Western state will be entitled to impose on them.[20]

As Platonic analyses of foreigners suggest, autochthony was criticized in antiquity and later on by Kant, who affirms the common possession of the earth and the right of all to move freely. Against this conception, the power of European states in modernity has made the doctrine of the right of the strongest triumph with the conquest of America and the Berlin Conference from November 1884 to February 1885. Reinforced, on the one hand, by the economic crisis in the late 1970s and, on the other hand, by neoliberal policies, this tradition, centred on European interests, has imposed itself on continents that can be appropriated by particular or collective powers such as the European Union, with free oceans for circulation and trade, the external enemy (*justus hostis*) outside the border suspending the guarantees of the Westphalian international legal order and leading to the legalization of unequal rules. In Section 5.6, we shall see that, despite the reaffirmation of the principle to 'address migration in a spirit of solidarity … in full respect of international law, including international human rights law',[21] power is expressed in the treaties that regulate the asymmetrical relations between Europe and Africa in general, and on migration and mobility in particular.

5.6 THE 'READMISSION CLAUSE' OR COOPERATION BEYOND THE LAW

Openness and closure: this is the antinomy at the heart of the organicist philosophy that has emerged since the 2000s from the cooperation and

[20] D. Weinstock, 'Vers une théorie kantienne du droit de migration', in P. Laberge, G. Lafrance, and D. Dumas (dir.), *L'Année 1795-Kant. Essai sur la paix* (Paris: Vrin, 1997), p. 227.

[21] Title VI Migration and Mobility, article 73, New Partnership Agreement.

partnership agreements signed in Cotonou, as well as those currently being ratified since 15 November 2023 in Samoa between the Europe of 'common values' and the countries of Africa, the Caribbean and the Pacific. The contradiction is based on one fact: Europe demands that the economic life of the countries of origin of immigrants be opened up to world trade, but subsidises its industry and agriculture, with the consequence of destroying the lives of young rural people and fishermen; it barricades itself against migratory flows from Africa. With the establishment of neoliberal globalization, the closing of European borders to Africans takes on the form of a delusional obsession aimed at contractualizing the statelessness, deportation and undesirability of African immigrants. The paradox is that the partnership philosophy between Europe and Africa promotes in principle, and in an ideal way, privileged relations around equality, dialogue, friendship, reciprocity and solidarity. Where one would have believed that certain situations depend as much on these principles as on politics and not on the market, we observe that, structurally, a double contradiction is linked to African immigration: the desire to integrate into the 'global economy' by the *Treaty of Maastricht* in 1992 and the closure of the right to migration or freedom of movement, because the objective is to fix Africans in the subcontinent where they can be exploited. Faced with workers who are no longer integrated by capital, excluded or thrown away, Europe assumes an ethical contradiction between an incantatory rhetoric on the promotion of human rights and the inclusion of the statelessness of many Africans as a priority axis of cooperation. A reminder of the facts and data is necessary to try to understand this situation. In its Title XVII, Article 130 u–y, the *Treaty of Maastricht* sets the political and human framework for development cooperation, namely consolidating democracy and the rule of law, respect for human rights and fundamental freedoms. In the same treaty, the principle of 'zero immigration' is defined, as the European basis for 'controlling migratory flows'. Since immigration and asylum now fall under Community competences (this will still be the case with the EU *Pact on Migration and Asylum* adopted on 10 April 2024), it was within the Tampere Community framework of October 1999 that European heads of state and government asked the European Union to include a 'repatriation' or 'readmission clause' in agreements with African, Caribbean and Pacific (ACP) countries. The problem is that this 'readmission clause' is in conflict with Article 13 of the *Universal Declaration of Human Rights*, which guarantees the right of everyone to leave any country, including their own. From this point of view, illegal emigration becomes a concept that contravenes this fundamental rule of international law.

But, in the name of 'solidarity development', the 'readmission clause' stipulates that 'each ACP State will accept the return and admit its nationals illegally present on the territory of an EU State while scrupulously respecting the rules of international law'. To put it into practice, the Schengen countries have negotiated with certain countries so that they constitute themselves as a first circle surrounded by a 'sanitary cordon' made up of candidates for membership of the European Union, Mediterranean countries, the countries of the former USSR, Turkey, North African countries such as Libya, Algeria and especially today Tunisia which abandon African immigrants in the desert or in the sea at Ceuta and Mellila, turning the *Mare Nostrum* of imperial Rome into the sea of the dead. These countries receive economic aid if they control transits, clandestine immigration channels or accept the outsourcing of immigrant management (as Rwanda did under Rishi Sunak's UK premiership). With regard to scrupulous respect for the rules of international law, Switzerland became in the 2000s the laboratory for the policy of 'readmission' of stateless persons. It rejects illegal immigrants in Africa, because, for it, 'all Africans are Ivorians', according to *Courrier international* (n° 486, 24 February 2000) and *La Lettre du continent* (n° 345, 27 January 2000). Without being a member of the EU, Switzerland aims to be integrated into its European environment, by trying to control migratory pressure through the model of three concentric circles: the inner circle includes the member states of the European Economic Community and the Free Trade Association where there is free movement of people; the middle circle assumes flexible control of immigration for the recruitment of a skilled workforce (United States, Canada and the countries of Central and Eastern Europe); the outer circle includes all states that do not respect human rights and neither European culture in the broad sense nor the same living conditions as the Swiss. In the last circle are the African 'deportees' – according to a terminology used in Switzerland. Having often benefitted from a residence permit as 'highly qualified specialists' or being genuine rejected asylum seekers, these 'undesirables' (whether they are Guineans, Liberians, Sierra Leoneans or Jamaicans) are turned back without a legal basis, entrusted for 500 French francs to an Ivorian lawyer, responsible for finding their 'country of origin' on the basis of their appearance or morphological characteristics. The 'clause of readmission' of *heimatlos* by any ACP country has a similar operation to the model of 'deportees' in Switzerland.

Beyond the formal contradictions with international law, the 'clause of repatriation' or 'readmission' has a double content: it hypocritically instrumentalizes the phraseology of human rights; it is discriminatory and racist compared to the concrete decisions of Europe. First, Europe's anti-migratory fantasy towards Africans lacks coherence at a time when young Europeans are emigrating all over the world in search of new experiences and jobs that they cannot find in their home countries. Second, Europe is far from closing itself off to all immigration. The Old Continent selects 'qualified' immigration, imposing the predominance of its strategic, commercial interests, its 'democratic values' and civilization, not to mention the unspoken things loudly expressed by the extreme right (invasion, 'Great Replacement', change of people or modification of the demographic composition). This openness has been paid for at the price of asylum policy, with Germany having opened itself massively, selectively and temporarily to the skills of the *Ausländer* (IT specialists from the East and the Orient, welcoming millions of Syrians), for the benefit of her labour market policy. In France, in July 1998, there was the discreet dissemination of a circular for the granting of a residence permit to computer scientists, in the spirit of welcoming artists and researchers. In 2022, Europe welcomed eight million Ukrainians without a single cry about the 'Great Replacement' or recourse to the principle of 'remigration' thought up by Vlams Belang.[22]

5.7 THE FIGHT AGAINST IMMIGRATION, THE PROMOTION OF INHOSPITALITY AND THE REJECTION OF SOLIDARITY

In terms of education, the *Edufrance* programme formalized a few decades ago the approach of 'chosen', 'qualified' and 'cultural' immigration, with the adoption of the 'merit-based system of immigration'. Establishing a commercial approach based on the Anglo-Saxon entrepreneurial model, this structure worked to implement a new policy of international relations in higher education. By opening up to the 'global training market', it set a few guidelines: no longer giving priority to students from the Maghreb and black Africa, considered too poor; approaching the best students from emerging countries (China, India, Mexico, Argentina, Venezuela, Japan, Canada) which are major exporters of highly skilled young people and future elites. By smoothing out the finicky and discriminatory measures for welcoming

[22] On the the difference in treatment in Europe between Ukrainians and other refugees, see R. Bueno Lacy and H. Van Houtum, 'Europe's Selective Dehumanisation: The Revival of Geographical Determinism as Rationalisation to Justify the Preferential Protection of Ukrainian Refugees in the EU', in S. Carrera and M. Ineli-Ciger (eds.), *EU Responses to the Large-scale Refugee Displacement from Ukraine: An Analysis on the Temporary Protection Directive and Its Implications for the Future EU Asylum Policy* (Florence: European University Institute, 2023), pp. 446–498. Our remarks do not overlook the great precariousness experienced by certain groups of the Ukrainian population with the ongoing war.

the rich regions of the world, we have witnessed a new avatar of the logic of class – or race? – at the international level. With this differentiation, the university partnership has become normative and anthropologically qualifying. Black Africa in particular is integrated into the principle of the Other, the foreigner, even the strange who does not inspire confidence, frightens, threatens. Otherness having become a source of hostility, aid appears as a tool of stigmatization that calls for 'inhospitality', rejection and suspicion of immigrants, far from any moral priority of solidarity.

With the conventions between the European Union and the Organization of African, Caribbean and Pacific States, the Europeanization of the migration issue was achieved in a concrete way by forceps, far from the ethical idea of solidarity on which these organizations are based. Political concerns took precedence over economic issues under the corset of a macro-economic orthodoxy of adjustment to the structure of neoliberal globalization contrary to the 'spirit of Lomé': 'Generally speaking, with regard to the Bretton Woods institutions, many programs or concepts . . . and the "messages" are sometimes opposed: adjustment slows investment, while the Union had long-term development as its objective, the European Union wanted a partnership while adjustment is an asymmetrical negotiation, the European Union had a regional approach, while structural adjustment programs are national'.[23] These contradictions of the 'new partnership' are closely linked to the question of the 'readmission clause' which empties economic solidarity of any moral content. Since the 1980s, it has essentially been a question of fixing Africans in place, of sending them back or of parking Africans in national reserves or warehouses allowing them to benefit from external aid, because the 'Empire' is keen to drive back 'the new barbarians': 'The North/South opposition resurrects this ideology of inequality, of asymmetry . . . There is no doubt that . . . the South is now entrusted with the role of the new barbarians facing a supposedly reunified, imperial North, the repository of the universal values of liberal and democratic civilization'.[24] It is therefore a question of setting up a *limes* that separates the two worlds in a sort of 'global apartheid': 'Protecting the civilization of the North . . . by the violent abandonment of the South, identified with barbarism', by containing 'the masses of the South' by creating 'buffer states' along the *limes* that monitor it.[25] It is a double violence: a process of barbarization of the periphery and a policy of closure and exclusion

[23] Y. Dauge, *Le Nouveau partenariat UE-ACP: changer de méthode* (Paris: Assemblée nationale, 1999), p. 21.

[24] J. C. Rufin, *L'Empire et les nouveaux barbares* (Paris: Latès, 1991), p. 23 *sq*.

[25] Ibid., p. 29.

of the 'Empire'. A nodal centre of the new partnership between Europe and Africa with the supposed loss of Africa's geostrategic interest and the emergence of dangers and new needs for cooperation in the East, immigration is part of a defensive and negative ideology of Europe with regard to Africa: 'Development aid [is useful] in the fight against immigration'.[26] Rufin summed up this general problem in terms of the fear of 'submersion' or 'invasion': 'The only real passion that the South unleashes throughout Europe [is] the fear of immigration'.[27] In such a conceptual framework, where it is necessary to 'prevent political and social dangers', 'cooperation becomes a tool at the service of the North: it is the instrument of the stability of the South despite development or without it'.[28] The language used in official EU documents on the new Partnership Framework confirms Rufin's assertions: 'The special relationships that Member States may have with third countries, reflecting political, historic and cultural ties fostered through decades of contacts, should also be exploited to the full for the benefit of EU'.[29]

5.8 CLOSING EXIT OPTIONS IN MIGRATION

Migratory flows are only the visible face of invasions and military interventions (such as that of the West in Libya), proxy wars, mythological rivalries, ideological conflicts, historical violence, material scarcity experienced by a large part of humanity and climatic disasters. This explains the massive

> geographic mobility of Africans ... The quest for a nest egg to 'get on their feet', and in particular to take a wife, the attraction of the city and its wealth, the curiosity of travel and the boredom of life in the bush, drought ..., the structural necessity of the capitalist economy explain to a large extent the regularity of the migratory phenomenon.[30]

The migratory dynamic shows that the adjustment to the structure of neoliberal globalization is experienced in a painful way by hundreds of millions of Africans. Thrown onto the roads of migration and forced displacement, many fleeing adjustment perish from poverty, die under bullets during 'food riots', from cold under the wings of airplanes, drown at sea, die of starvation in the desert, end up as slaves or end up in 'detention centres' or 'waiting zones' in

26 Ibid., p. 43.
27 Ibid., p. 176.
28 Ibid., p. 129.
29 COM (2016) 385 final, Brussels, 7 June 2016.
30 J.-F. Bayart, *L'État en Afrique. La politique du ventre* (Paris: Fayard, coll. 'L'espace du politique', 1989), p. 314.

Europe. This is because the management of European citizenship is now exclusive to third parties, in particular 'immigrants' who have been settled on European soil for a long time. In *Nous, citoyens d'Europe? Les frontières, l'État, le peuple*, Étienne Balibar was able to put forward the idea of a 'hidden apartheid'. 'Extra-community' foreigners, in this case Africans south of the Sahara, have been considered 'undesirable' since the end of the 1990s, that is to say precisely at the time when the practical effects of the austerity policies imposed by Europe began to be felt and forced Africans into imaginary or physical exile from their world. Also, with a view to establishing total capitalist productivity, theorists have thought about the *exit* of African societies from the metaphysical era of incompleteness, from the Void to the hegemonic Fullness of classes linked to capital. The concrete objective is to block any *exit option*, any evasion or any exit from political domination, economic exploitation and social exclusion. The main idea was to counteract the flight from economic exploitation in migration: '… escape is still a strategy that constitutes the production of politics and social relations … "Flight" has not disappeared, it has remained as a major mode of historicity south of the Sahara, it persists in undermining civic space, in constraining the process of accumulation of power and wealth and in making predation easier than exploitation'.[31]

This is the basis of the Cotonou (2000–2020) and Samoa (November 2023) agreements. Europe, which conceptualizes immigration laws around 'migration and mobility' or 'migration and asylum', wants to 'block and push back' immigrants, sort or collect those who meet the needs of the capitalist system, lock up and push back those who pass through, or else distance and subcontract or outsource migration control to third countries such as Tunisia and Rwanda. To hide the violence of these processes, an irenic ideological discourse was born on the cosmopolitan mix and 'multiple ancestries' around mobility, hybridity, fluidity, mixing and wandering. The political and anthropological critique of this mixed vision suspects the desire to render invisible the violence of a differentiation and fragmentation of the workforce. In reality, it is the conceptualization of an indefinite extension of the market without resistance from a human, political or union totality that would oppose it. This hides the violence of the market order, of the 'commodity form', under the guise of a fluctuating, destructured and deterritorialized generic human identity.[32] The ideological discourse on diversity and crossbreeding does not hide the desire to create a class identity divided between those who exploit and

[31] Ibid., p. 315.

[32] A. Jappe and R. Kurz, *Les Habits neufs de l'Empire. Remarques sur Negri, Hardt et Rufin* (Paris: Léo Scherer, coll. 'Lignes', 2003), p. 43.

those who are exploited. This ideological discourse is contemporary with the strengthening within Africa and on a global scale – thanks to the process of primitive accumulation of capital – of a class power with as corollaries an ethnicization and a racialization of anti-systemic revolts. André Tosel also criticized the thesis of the 'indeterminacy of the mixed-race multitude':

> This indeterminacy is reproduced when the heterogeneity of the multitude seems to be taken into account as a nomadic and mixed-race multitude formed by populations resulting from immigration. Empire rightly defends the right to move, to cross borders, but it erects it as an ontological actuality without taking the measure of the capitalist modes of segmentation and differentiation which are in fact processes of racialization and ethnicization of the international workforce and which, at the same time, constitute an immense obstacle to collective action. More than the exaltation of the generic power of the multitude, it would be useful to analyze the new forms of division of the human species, leading to the concentration of freedom and security in a transnational ruling class that is becoming ever more indifferent to the fate of the rest of humanity, ever more exempt from any responsibility towards all those it exploits and condemns to live in existential illiberty and insecurity. How can we re-politicize men doomed to ghettoization and impolitic and self-destructive violence? How can we also raise the question of the necessary alliances between the latter and the other classes with immediate non-converging interests?[33]

In Africa, this process, induced by adjustment, takes forms or inclinations aimed at an identity constitutionalization with the discourse of autochthony with the ideology of 'I was there before'. Which means I am entitled to more protection and benefits.

5.9 MBEMBE AND THE LIMITS OF CARE, BENEVOLENCE AND PHILANTHROPY IN THE FACE OF A SANCTUARIZED EUROPE

Achille Mbembe has developed, in a trilogy consisting of *Politics of Enmity*, *Brutalism* and *The Earthly Community*, a new ideology on migration around *care*, by calling for benevolence, solicitude, attention, vulnerability and suffering. The relationship and morality of *care* aim to repair both people and the environment. Mbembe now insists on the need for 'a symbiotic fusion of life and mobility': moving like life imply crossing 'lines and barriers', that is to say, in other words, that moving or the capacity to move without brakes

[33] A. Tosel, 'Obsolescence ou actualité du concept d'impérialisme', in Jacques Bidet (dir.), *Guerre impériale, guerre sociale* (Paris: PUF, coll. 'Actuel Marx Confrontation', 2005), p. 87.

across the world is an essential dimension of being human and, for some people, vital conditions of survival are involved. He also regrets a fact: while displacement involves 'the entire body', it turns out that the body parts of some are made available to others, are 'bioavailable' – for example, through egg donation. It is, therefore, a question of redefining and reconfiguring the relations of social exchange where the body becomes 'a privileged site for the extraction of surplus value', life being thereby calculated and recomposed, because part of its organs or fluids are mobilized for the safeguarding of the lives of others than oneself. The consequence of the shift from fusion to a bifurcation between life and bodies is that all bodies are no longer supposed to shelter the same life and the same breath: they are *discount bodies*, at the limits of life, the life they shelter being uninsurable because of a relationship of radical inequivalence with insured bodies: at the heart of contemporary migration and work policies are processes consisting of emptying certain bodies of all value and dignity, assigning them to marginal places on different scales of insurability and uninsurability. It is about slowing down the dynamics of interactions between them, creating distance, breaking the relational chains within the social body to institute new models of individualization. Restrictions on freedom of movement are no longer only the work of powerful states; they are at work on a global scale. By deepening the asymmetries of space and time between different categories of humanity, they fuel the ghettoization of entire parts of the world:

> [They aim to 'confine' the undesirable] in incoherent temporalities and spatializations, to the point of giving these populations the illusion of living territorially separated. Moreover . . . these restrictions are based even more on ideas of repressive selection of the species. Only those who potentially generate value count as life and can be authorized to come and go. In this context, borders are designed to materialize the principle of dissimilarity rather than that of affinity. Obstacles to the free movement of people therefore serve as partitions between different varieties of the human species . . .. Bodies are increasingly divided between those who count and the others, between those who can move and those who cannot or must not, or only under the strictest conditions. Bodies prohibited from crossing the border are not insured. They must be hunted down, captured, put aside.[34]

Mbembe highlights a double issue. First, there is a psychic issue: in fragmented spaces, stretched temporalities and endless expectations, humans oscillate between invisibility, waiting and erasure, with absolute surveillance

[34] A. Mbembe, *La Communauté terrestre* (Paris: La Découverte, 2023), pp. 136–138.

implying a policy of 'cleaning' at the heart of a transition towards a new system of automation. Second, there is a democratic issue: the contradiction at the heart of the liberal order is found in the tension between freedom and security, order and movement; it is doubled by making a safe society no longer free because of the obsession with controlling appearances, namely 'who is who, who lives where, with whom, and since when, who does what, who comes from where, who goes where, when, how, why'? Migrants and refugees pay the price of 'a society of security'.[35] The question: what to do with those whose existence no longer seems necessary to our reproduction, those who are 'useless' or 'disposable' – those whose existence is perceived as a physical or biological threat to our own lives, namely those whose movements of exodus and migration can destabilize the still productive and profitable areas? The answers to this dilemma have consisted in 'territorially excluding all bodies deemed unassimilable, unwanted, illegal, dispensable or superfluous' as was the case

> in the early stage of the modern colonial and genocidal era ... with the American natives herded into reservations, the prison islands of Guyana, the penal colonies in Australia or the camps and bantustans in South Africa. In later models of colonial occupation, the control of vulnerable, undesirable, surplus or racialized populations is exercised through ... confinement and modulated blockade. In principle, a blockade prohibits, prevents or limits access to a confined territory ... effectively transforms it into a prison territory ... in which the undesirable or illegal are governed in the abdication of all responsibility for their lives and living conditions.[36]

Added to this at the beginning of the twenty-first century were wars against flows, mobility and circulation that target both individual bodies and entire sections of a humanity deemed worthless. All this stems, says Mbembe, 'from borderization, decided and implemented in the name of freedom and security ... Wars against mobility focus on bodies at a time when national affiliations are used as weapons. Since the right to belong is reserved only for some, the temptation to brutalize others without incurring legal consequences extends in some cases to the organized underworld, the police and the bureaucracy',[37] with the dream of national, ethnic, racial or religious purity.

Faced with the epistemic disorientation caused by major political, economic, climatic, technological and imaginary shifts, Mbembe proposes other theoretical imaginations and uses the archives that Édouard Glissant called

[35] Ibid., p. 139.
[36] Ibid., p. 140.
[37] Ibid., p. 141.

the *Tout-monde*, because he wants to get out of the archives of a single province of the Earth.[38] His goal is to combine the time of human societies with geological and climatic time, the time of plants and animals, microbes, bacteria and viruses, the biosphere and the thermosphere, the oceans, orbital space, the time of all forms of life. From then on, the *Tout-monde* refers to three distinctive features: a total break with any form of self-closure, whether it takes the form of a territorial, national, ethno-racial or religious enclosure; an opposition to the authoritarian universalization of the colonial enterprise of conquest; an *exit* from the ignorance desired for our own limits.[39] It is also part of the horizon of 'anticolonial and post-Eurocentric thoughts',[40] in the South and throughout the world. Because postcolonial and decolonial thoughts would deal with entanglements, passages and bridges, multiple genealogies and sinuous and interconnected lines against lines of occupation, walls and prisons to be built of late Eurocentrism.[41] To calls for closure, secession, withdrawal and enclosure, Mbembe therefore proposes care and reparation[42]. He makes them the basis of truth and justice to reconnect with faith in the future, for an anticipation of catastrophe against a backdrop of anxiety and panic. He is thinking in particular of the global alt-right which anticipates, against minority and immigration activists, the end of the white race, besieged and threatened with extermination. It, therefore, creates on the one hand the fantasy of enclosure and its corollary, eradicating and extirpating violence with a desire for brutality, especially towards the losers, the weakest and most vulnerable, and on the other hand the fantasy of extinction and replacement.[43]

5.10 HOW TO RECONNECT WITH A FUTURE OF SOLIDARITY

We believe that this philosophy, on migration as on everything else, is limited to a moral negation of politics, especially international politics. Our situation results from a concentration of capital in a few hands with the dizzying downgrading of the majority that turns against the most miserable, a class of superfluous people against whom there is a certain call for more brutality. Beyond the repression of migration, beyond the idea of a generic mixed-race or migrant humanity and of the *Tout-monde*, we propose the course of a

38 Ibid., p. 155.
39 Ibid., pp. 182–183.
40 Ibid., p. 184.
41 Ibid.
42 Ibid., p. 7, p. 5.
43 Ibid., pp. 185–186.

pandemocracy by means of a generalized material power resulting from the universalization of the industrial revolution. The equality of power that can result from the mastery and universalization of the principles of the industrial mode of production by our peoples still immersed in the agro-pastoral mode of production has a first-rate ethical–political issue. The gap with the capitalist centres that control industrial civilization in fact pushes the latter to choose the right immigrant, to reject the one who is not useful, to expel the undesirables. When industrial civilization will become universal, when the peoples who today provide the strongest contingents of a rejected migration and mobility have got their hands on the principle of modern power, a relative equality will be established in the world. It is at that moment that people will be able to satisfy their needs for health, work, food and accomplishment within their countries. With the same level of power, people will then be able to negotiate the question of migration as the most powerful peoples do today. When the industrial revolution has spread to the peoples of the Periphery, the principle of equality will probably be dominant in the world. 'The workers of the Centre [of the world]', to use the old terminology referring to the opposition between the developed world and the under-developed world, will cease to identify with the capitalists of the Western countries who pose as the place of passage of their prosperity, of their protection, while designating the peoples of the South as enemies. With the predominance of equality in the relations between men both within societies and between peoples, the forms of organization in general will become more in conformity with the deep nature of human beings which is fundamentally the same. The peoples will then be able to truly negotiate in all equality to know how to resolve the question of the circulation of the labour force and the hospitality of men and women throughout the world.

From this, some conclusions emerge. With the 'right to readmission' of African immigrants, the idea of solidarity at the heart of the partnership philosophy between Africa and Europe is emptied of all content, especially since it draws unspoken racist words towards Africans cast as culturally unassimilable and civilizational incompatible and incommensurable, based on a new racist discourse that puts cultural difference before biological sameness. Then, the resulting economic austerity hinders the mutual recognition of human dignity. Nowhere, under liberal democracy after 1989, have we seen more united people become 'more human': social suffering, economic wars, terror of minorities, unleashing racism and xenophobia tear apart the so-called democratic West as well as the rest of the world. Derrida also noted two wounds of the 'new world order'. First, there is 'the massive exclusion of homeless citizens from any participation in the democratic life of states, the expulsion or deportation of so many exiles, stateless persons and immigrants from a so-called national territory that already announce a new experience of borders and national and civil identity'.[44] This situation due to 'external debt and other related mechanisms [that] starve or drive to despair a large part of humanity'[45] results in an ontology that makes 'the stable and presentable determination of a locality (the *topos* of territory, soil, city, body in general) an identity of anguish and panic that takes archaic forms. Then there is a second plague of our world economy: 'Interethnic wars ... are multiplying, guided by fantasy and an archaic concept, by a primitive conceptual fantasy of the community, the nation-state, sovereignty, borders, soil and blood'.[46] These phenomena are general. Thus, Africa, under structural adjustment for more than three decades, is prey to a rise in xenophobia, just like Europe, America and the rest of the world. Certainly, the logic of exclusion against African immigrants is less based on racial differentiation than on ethnic arguments – even if racial differentiation is asserting itself in the consciences of the Maghreb, notably in Tunisia where there is now fear of a change in the demographic composition. Xenophobic rejections take extreme forms here, the paroxysmal forms being the Rwandan genocide, 'a poisoned fruit of structural adjustment'.[47] There is also the enslavement of African migrants in Libya, a result of historic and geopolitical violence. In such a context, 'the African immigrant is thus a perfect scapegoat. He is often the first to be associated with barbarity and crime. As in ancient Greece, where the foreigner had no right to be there and where Plato recommended 'the exposure of delinquents ... at the border of the country'. In sub-Saharan Africa, the foreigner is expelled manu militari, or even lynched. His death sentence, in a religious and ritual or expeditious and popular sense, is all the more easily approved by the community as it makes it possible to avoid vendettas within the community.[48] Urgently, the migration issue calls more than ever for the acceleration of the inter-African movement of people and goods and for the abolition of visas within Africa. While waiting for the restructuring of a world order that brings more peace, making 'the right of citizenship' on the 'surface of the earth' requires the democratization of borders, the object of the struggles for conditions of migration and asylum in solidarity.

[44] J. Derrida, *Spectres de Marx* (Paris: Galilée, 1993), p. 135.

[45] Ibid., p. 136.

[46] Ibid., p. 137.

[47] M. Chossudovsky, 'Les fruits empoisonnés de l'ajustement structurel' (1994) *Le Monde diplomatique*, 2 November.

[48] M.-A. Perouse de Montclos, 'Des boucs émissaires parfaits: l'Afrique rejette ses propres immigrés' (1999), *Le Monde diplomatique*, December.

6

Neoliberalism, Solidarity and the Law of Collective Security

EVA NANOPOULOS

6.1 INTRODUCTION

Solidarity seems on course to becoming for our age what human rights were for the end of the Cold War. The literature on solidarity has grown dramatically in the last few years in both international relations and international law. And the language of solidarity appears in an increasing number of legal documents and statements, most notably the UN Draft Declaration on the right to solidarity (thereafter 'the Draft Declaration'),[1] which defines solidarity as 'the expression of a spirit of unity among individuals, peoples, States and international organizations, encompassing the union of interests, purposes and actions and the recognition of different needs and rights to achieve common goals'.

That solidarity has acquired such purchase in international legal discourse and practice is not surprising. The solidarity turn, on the one hand, could be seen as the expression of, and attempt to respond to, our 'new age of catastrophe',[2] an epoch characterized by a deepening crisis of global capitalism with unprecedented geopolitical, economic, political and biological dimensions. Indeed, the draft declaration explicitly foregrounds the role of solidarity 'in preventing and overcoming global challenges such as health emergencies, environmental degradation, climate change, armed conflict [and] forced

[1] For the latest version, see Human Rights Council, Revised Draft Declaration on Human Rights and International Solidarity A/HRC/53/32.

[2] Alex Callinicos, *The New Age of Catastrophe* (Cambridge: Polity, 2023).

migration'.[3] And, as the editors remind us in their Introduction, solidarity has generally tended to accompany moments of crisis.

On the other hand, the solidarity turn could also be seen as symptomatic of the more specific crisis of the international legal order and the age of human rights. Solidarity may be conceived as a human right in documents like the draft declaration, but its articulation on the surface differs from the hegemonic understanding of human rights that has characterized the last three decades in at least two ways. Its collective dimension, which is implicit in its call to unity and contrasts with the individualism of rights. And its welfarist connotations, which is implicit in its emphasis on common goals and contrasts with the market-friendly orientation of contemporary human rights.[4] Tellingly, the right to solidarity in the draft declaration is more reminiscent of the language of 'third generation' rights, which, for as long are they were mobilized by the 'third world', were ironically viewed as mere (utopian) aspirations rather than legally binding or enforceable rights.

But if solidarity is called upon to address the many challenges of our 'age of catastrophe', to what extent is its deployment in international law and international legal discourse truly divorced from the ideas and practices that have characterized the neoliberal age which has shaped the international legal order over the last three decades and arguably led to an aggravation of the very crises solidarity is now called upon to tackle? Is international legal solidarity the road to salvation and redemption or is the 'age of solidarity' just old wine in a new bottle, with the neoliberal logic prolonged into the future under a different name?

To answer these questions, the chapter explores the connections between solidarity and neoliberalism using the example of collective security (CS). Although there is no mention of solidarity in the UN Charter, several scholars read the document as expressing the principle's 'highest degree of c onstitutionalization' in international law.[5] On a general level, this constitutio nalization is associated with the commitment members have undertaken to assist the UN (art.2(5) UN Charter (UNC)) and to 'take joint and separate action in co-operation with the Organization for the achievement of the purposes set forth in Article 55' (Article 56 UNC), which sets out the

3 Revised Draft Declaration (n 1) preamble.

4 Jessica Whyte, *The Morals of the Market: Human Rights and the Rise of Neoliberalism* (London: Verso, 2019).

5 Karel Wellens, 'Revisiting Solidarity as a (Re-) Emerging Constitutional Principle: Some Further Reflections', in Rüdiger Wolfrum and Chie Kojima (eds.), *Solidarity: A Structural Principle of International Law* (Heidelberg: Springer, 2010), pp. 3–54, p. 4. For an argument that sees solidarity as the weakest element of UN law on peace and security, see Hanspeter Neuhold, 'Common Security: The Litmus Test of International Solidarity', in Rüdiger Wolfrum and Chie Kojima (eds.), *Solidarity: A Structural Principle of International Law* (Heidelberg: Springer, 2010), pp. 193–223.

conditions for the creation of 'stability and well-being which are necessary for peaceful and friendly relations among nations', namely economic and social progress and development, international cooperation and solutions and respect for human rights. But constitutionalization is also more specifically associated with the UN system of collective security (CS) in the form of the obligation to give effect to Resolutions of the UN Security Council (UNSC) designed to restore international peace and security (Article 25 UNC). Some scholars disagree with the characterization of CS as a form of solidarity, arguing that solidarity is characterized by 'spontaneity',[6] not a legal duty of the kind that defines the system of CS. Yet, legalization does not in itself seem to be a bar to solidarity. Historically, legal codification has been seen as one of the ways in which the normative basis of social solidarity could be articulated.[7] And instruments like the Draft Declaration show that legalization, indeed c onstitutionalization, is key to how solidarity is today conceived at the international level. For many scholars, finally, CS influenced 'the emergence of a variety of other manifestations of solidarity in international law',[8] making it a potentially illuminative case study for assessing its prospects and limitations.

That those connections have never been explored is not surprising. Neoliberal thought was explicitly developed as a critique of, and in opposition to, the practices and politics that are commonly associated with solidarity, including equality, welfarism, collectivism and socialism. As such, any notion of 'neoliberal solidarity' could on the surface appear like a contradiction in terms. In addition, neoliberalism was long approached as a theory of economics, rather than international politics. To use the field of CS to investigate the neoliberal influences on the international law and practice of solidarity would seem to be not only a contradiction, but an outright aberration.

And yet: failing to investigate the role of neoliberalism in shaping the solidarity of CS would be a mistake. As we will see, neoliberal theory did address questions about war and peace. Indeed, one of the key debates neoliberals were engaged in was precisely about the role of the market in international politics and the relationship between the market, war and peace. Some of them also wrote explicitly about the first iteration of an institutional

6 Danio Campanelli, 'The Principle of Solidarity', in *Max Planck Encyclopaedia of Public International Law* (Oxford: Oxford University Press, 2011), paras 11–13.

7 Kostia Gorobets, 'Solidarity as a Practical Reason: Grounding Authority of International Law' (2022) 69 *Netherlands International Law Review* 3, at 5–11.

8 Themis Tzimas, 'Solidarity as a Principle of International Law: Its Application in Consensual Intervention' (2019) 6 *Groningen Journal of International Law: International Legal Reform* 333, at 337.

CS introduced by the Covenant of the League of Nations.[9] And, equally importantly, key neoliberal thinkers were directly involved in, and presumably influenced, the establishment and functioning of the League of Nations, the first legal instrument to have introduced a system of CS. One of them is Walter Lippman, a chief advisor to President Woodrow Wilson, who helped draft, and penned the authoritative interpretation of, Wilson's famous 'fourteen points', a set of principles designed to inform peace negotiations after World War I. Lippman's book *The Good Society* formed the basis of a colloquium organized in Paris in 1938 where the term 'neoliberalism' was first coined and which is widely seen as the precursor of the Mont Pellerin Society (MPS) founded by Hayek in 1947. Another is William E. Rappard. A founding member of the MPS, Rappard was a Swiss delegate to the Paris Peace Conference of 1919 and went on to hold several positions in the League, including as the director of its Mandates Division. He also produced extensive writings about the League, the UN, and broader questions of international peace and security, in which he expressively conceived of CS as an expression of international solidarity.[10] From a broader institutional perspective, finally, recent research[11] suggests that the International Institute of Intellectual Cooperation (IIIC), a consultative body of the League of Nations, played a key role in the emergence of neoliberalism 'as an intellectual and political project'.[12]

To explore the connections between neoliberalism and solidarity in the law of CS, Section 6.2 first places neoliberal views on international peace and security in the wider context of neoliberal theory, epistemology and ontology. Section 6.3 turns more specifically to the neoliberal vision of CS, even though few neoliberals used the term. Section 6.4 examines to what extent these neoliberal ideas were reflected in the emergence and evolution of solidarity in the international law of CS. Section 6.5 turns to the implications of my analysis for our approach to, and indeed critique of, solidarity in CS. My argument is: (a) that neoliberals made the institutionalization of the market order the only means of securing peace; (b) that they envisaged CS

9 For an overview of his writings, see William E. Rappard, 'Vues Rétrospectives sur la Société des Nations' (1967) 71 *Collected Courses of The Hague Academy of International Law: Recueil des Cours* 194.

10 e.g. William E. Rappard, *The Quest for Peace since the World War* (Cambridge, MA: Harvard University Press, 1940).

11 Hagen Schulz-Forberg, 'Embedded Early Neoliberalism: Transnational Origins of the Agenda of Liberalism Reconsidered', in Philip Mirowski, Dieter Plehwe and Quinn Slobodian (eds.), *Nine Lives of Neoliberalism* (Brooklyn, NY: Verso, 2020), p. 177.

12 Jurgen Reinhoudt and Serge Audier, *The Walter Lippmann Colloquium: The Birth of Neo-Liberalism* (Cham: Palgrave, 2018), p. 18.

as a system of international policing designed to spread and secure the international market; (c) that this neoliberal vision of CS played a role in shaping the duty of solidarity in the international law of CS; and (d) that existing critiques, as they presently stand, do not provide us with sufficient tools to challenge neoliberal (market) solidarity. The conclusion, on that basis, sounds a note of warning to the enthusiasm that has surrounded the adoption of solidarity in international legal discourse and practice and calls for a renewed engagement with its ideological and material underpinnings.

6.2 THE NEOLIBERAL PEACE OF CATALLAXY: PEACE AS INSTITUTIONAL MARKET ORDER

Neoliberal views about international order, war, peace and, crucially, CS must be seen in the context of their broader social, political and legal theory. The neoliberal movement includes several 'schools of thought' with contrasting views. But abstraction made of the differences between different schools or individual neoliberal thinkers, neoliberalism as a whole largely developed as an attempt to save and reinvent liberalism in the face of what neoliberals saw as a crisis of the liberal order and the threat of communism. As a result, neoliberalism can helpfully be defined by its opposition to two currents: socialism and classic laissez-faire liberalism, what has been referred to as the 'dual attack' or 'dual argument'.[13]

Contrary to socialism, neoliberals re-centred the role of the markets in maintaining social order, rejecting efforts to create 'artificial economic bonds of solidarity' through planning. Given the pluralism characterising modern 'open societies' and the inherent limits of human knowledge, for them, agreement over purposes and the processing of information to achieve them was simply impossible and could only result in conflict or totalitarianism. Instead, social harmony and co-existence could only be achieved through the market, where different preferences and interests interact spontaneously to produce outcomes that satisfy a greater range of needs and 'enhance for all the prospects of achieving their respective purposes'.[14] By coordinating the actions of individuals and groups with different ends, 'cattalaxy' – the abstract 'order brought about by the mutual adjustment of many individuals economies in a

[13] Ola Innset, *Reinventing Liberalism: The Politics, Philosophy and Economics of Early Neoliberalism (1920–1947)* (Cham: Springer, 2021).

[14] Friedrich Hayek, *Law Legislation and Liberty: New Statement of the Liberal Principles of Justice and Political Economy* (London: Routledge, 2012), p. 110.

market'[15] – would transform enemies into friends and, hence, secure lasting peace.

Contrary to their nineteenth century liberal counterparts, however, neoliberals did not believe in the inherent stability[16] or self-regulation of markets (i.e. that the peace of cattalaxy would arise spontaneously and that the market order could function autonomously). They rejected both the assumption that economic reason inhered in individuals and that society was characterized by a natural harmony of interests. Instead, the (formal and substantive) preconditions for a market order had to be established and continuously secured. Tellingly, alternatives to the term 'neoliberalism' have included 'constructor liberalism' and 'positive liberalism', highlighting its more interventionist dimension.[17]

Formally, such conditions included a 'strong state'[18] – there could be no liberal society founded on free enterprise and competition without government – as well as a strong legal apparatus, which scholars often highlight to denote the affinities between neoliberalism and ordoliberalism. Their theory of the state and of law differed, however, from their socialist counterparts. The state's role was not to intervene *in*, but to police the conditions *of*, the market. And, contrary to regulatory law, the law should not prescribe concrete ends but consist of abstract rules of conduct that direct the actions of individual actors.

These rules were not, however, devoid of substance. As Whyte's brilliant study of neoliberal human rights shows, they also had a moral dimension. The market, for neoliberals, pre-supposed the adoption of a 'common ethical code', 'a set of individualistic, commercial values' geared towards 'the pursuit of self-interest above the development of common purposes' which Hayek would call the 'morals of the market'[19] and Mises the 'market civilisation'.[20] Hence, the policing function of the state and law extended to securing those moral and, as we shall see, cultural pre-suppositions.

Their critique of socialism and classical liberalism, moreover, was not merely theoretical. As Innset highlights, Hayek 'made the alleged impossibility of socialism into a question of epistemology, one of how knowledge is arrived

15 Ibid., p. 109.

16 Philip Mirowski, Dieter Plehwe and Quinn Slobodian (eds.), *Nine Lives of Neoliberalism* (Brooklyn, NY: Verso, 2020), p. 14.

17 Reinhoudt and Audier, *The Walter Lippmann Colloquium*, p. 18.

18 e.g. Werner Bonefield, 'Freedom and the Strong State: On German Ordoliberalism' (2012) 17 *New Political Economy* 633.

19 Whyte, *The Morals of the Market*, p.11.

20 Ibid., pp. 54–60.

at in a modern, intertwined world'. This position, Innset further stressed, entailed nothing short of a 'whole new way of seeing markets' as 'mediators of modernity' rather than mere 'sites of commerce and exchanges'.[21] And it also had an ontological dimension. Given that individual freedom could only be secured *through* the market, contrary to classical liberalism, neoliberalism granted ontological primacy, and thus sovereignty, to the market, rather than the individual or the people.[22]

Together, these had important practical ramifications. One is the infamous maxim 'there is no alternative', though not only as a political agenda, but as an epistemological truth. For neoliberals, the market is not only a superior, but the only possible, form of knowledge; that is to say, markets alone, to the exclusion of humans, are capable of the act of knowing. The other is the necessary subordination and adjustment of the whole of society, including its individual units, to the imperatives of the market order and the division of labour.

These theoretical, epistemological and ontological pre-suppositions about the superiority of the market also fed into their views about international peace and security. For neoliberals, the principles of international order should be developed out of and, with some adjustments, by analogy to the principles of the domestic order. Again, this placed them against both Marxist and classic liberal theory. Contrary to Marxists, capitalism was not the source of, but the solution to, war and conflict. Peace, therefore, could be achieved not by the abolition but by the universalization of the market order. Contrary to classical international liberalism's understanding of the pacifying function of the market,[23] however, a spirit of commerce and free trade could not arise naturally from increased inter-dependence. Instead, the pre-conditions for the international market had to be established, which, in the international context, entailed the universalization of the market civilization (i.e. the law and morals of the market).

Again, the neoliberal position on war and peace had deeper roots and implications. Epistemologically, it was based not only on the pacifying function of the market, but also a methodological objection to what Popper called 'historicism'[24] (i.e. the assumption that one can make historical predictions).

[21] Innset, *Reinventing Liberalism*, p. 34. On epistemology, see also Martin Beddeleem, 'Recoding Liberalism: Philosophy and Sociology of Science against Planning', in Philip Mirowski, Dieter Plehwe and Quinn Slobodian (eds.), *Nine Lives of Neoliberalism* (Brooklyn, NY: Verso, 2020).

[22] Whyte, *The Morals of the Market*, p. 23.

[23] We see this in Montesquieu conception as 'doux commerce' as well as later theories of liberal peace and/or capitalist peace.

[24] Karl R. Popper, *The Poverty of Historicism* (Boston: Beacon Press, 1957).

Given the limited character of human knowledge, seeking to establish peace by identifying and eliminating the causes of war was not only unscientific or unreasonable but so impossible as to be absurd.[25] There is no alternative to the spontaneous peace of catallaxy. Ontologically, the sovereignty of the market applied to states as much as individuals and pre-supposed not only formal limitations on national sovereignty, but also a more substantive subsumption of statehood to the market logic. 'What we envisage', Röpke explained, is 'not a national order which is an end in itself and which in the event of conflict sacrifices the international order but one whose line of conduct is fixed upon the principles of international order and whose whole social organization is fundamentally directed towards building up and supporting it'.[26]

6.3 THE NEOLIBERAL SOLIDARITY OF CS: POLICING THE INTERNATIONAL MARKET ORDER

These premises and overall vision shaped neoliberal views of CS. In his conclusion to his 1940 *The Quest for Peace*, Rappard explained that lasting peace is possible between separate political units only in one of four hypotheses: (1) if there is no contact between them; (2) if they cooperate freely and fraternally; (3) if they are all subject to the supreme rule of one of them; and (4) if they all accept a common law to which they consent to sacrifice a share of their independence. Each corresponded to four types of peace: an undesirable peace of autarky; a fragile peace of cooperation, which prevailed under the League of Nations; an objectionable peace of subordination; and a stable, long-standing, 'organised peace'.[27] For Rappard, the latter would be 'to the international community what order is to a national community: the result of certain habits, certain principles, certain institutions, certain procedures and sanctions, which are intended to prevent the outbreak of violence'. Short of a world federation it would at least entail 'a state of international relations based on the legal organization of the world of nations'.[28]

Not all neoliberals shared Rappard's optimism about the prospects of achieving the peace of catallaxy through a formalized system of CS, or international institutions and laws more broadly. Such was Mise's position, who generally clung on to old free market ideals:

[25] Karl R. Popper, *The Open Society and Its Enemies* (Princeton: Princeton University Press, 2020), ft 3, pp. 608–610.

[26] Wilhelm Röpke, *International Order and Economic Integration* (Dordrecht, Holland: D. Reidel Publishing 1959), p. 19.

[27] Rappard, *The Quest for Peace*, p. 498.

[28] Ibid., p. 9.

> What is needed to make peace durable is neither international treaties and covenants nor international tribunals and organizations like the defunct League of Nations or its successor, the United Nations. If the principle of the market economy is universally accepted, such makeshifts are unnecessary; if it is not accepted, they are futile. Durable peace can only be the outgrowth of a change in ideologies.[29]

Rappard himself, moreover, acknowledged not only the limitations of existing CS arrangements but the unlikely prospects of a world government with a proper world police.

Following World War II, things began to change. The establishment of the MPS in 1947 was driven as much by ideological affinities as by a feeling of deep alarm about the deepening crisis of liberalism and the broader crisis of civilization that it had led to as well as a sense of urgency to 'rework' liberal tenets to fit modern conditions. 'Over large stretches of the Earth's surface', the founding statement of the MPS opened, 'the essential conditions of human dignity and freedom have already disappeared'. And, since that 'international crisis [was] only one part of the general crisis of society today', according to Röpke, it could only be overcome by similar solutions (i.e. the establishment of a market order), to which neoliberals now had to urgently attend.[30]

In this context of dread and moral panic, support for an 'international framework of law and order' backed 'by solid sanctions'[31] and a strong international police that would learn from the League's mistake grew. As early as 1945, Popper warned against the (utopian) belief that the laws and morals of the market order could ever be fully universalized. The 'propaganda for ending *all* wars is self-defeating. We must end international anarchy, and be ready to go to war against any international crime',[32] he insisted. Subsequently, neoliberal thinkers agreed. 'The apparatus of modern war is so formidable, the cost of its maintenance so onerous, the dangers of actual conflict are so great, that we cannot afford to rely on spontaneous goodwill', Robbins concluded in his 1969 investigation of the economic causes of war.[33]

[29] Ludwig Mises, *Human Action: A Treatise on Economics* (Auburn, Alabama: Ludwig von Mises Institute, 1998), p. 682.

[30] Röpke, *International Order*, p. 69.

[31] Lionel Robbins, *The Economic Causes of War* (New York: Howard Fertig, 1969), p. 105. The legal element of international ordering was central to the Geneva School. See Quinn Slobodian, *Globalists: The End of Empire and the Birth of Neoliberalism* (Cambridge, MA: Harvard University Press, 2018).

[32] Popper, *The Open Society and Its Enemies*, p. 606.

[33] Robbins, *The Economic Causes of War*, p. 104.

As Slobodian documents,[34] moreover, anxieties about international order increased with decolonization and the emergence of an increasingly militant third world seeking a new international economic order that clashed with the neoliberal vision, rooted as it was in the permanent sovereignty over natural resources and global economic redistribution. Röpke offers perhaps one of the most chilling articulations of the neoliberal mindset at that time:

> What can all these things avail, what can the finest plans for an international order avail if the soul of each individual is disordered, if the political, economic and social structure of the individual nations does not fulfil the pre-requisites for an international order, in short, if the moral, intellectual, political, economic and social disorder in our society is not righted throughout its entire structure, beginning with the individual, and including the family, our fellow-workers, the local community and the whole nation? ... What can be expected from international conferences and conventions under such circumstances? ... Is there not a chance of [them] only developing into new sources of dissension instead of harmony for the nations as long as the latter are not sound within, and before their ethical and mental state, as well as their political and economic constitutions, have become mature enough for a far-sighted and generous universalism?[35]

This new consensus never resulted in a comprehensive theory of international policing. But several neoliberals made suggestions about its characteristics, partly drawing an analogy with the policing function of the 'strong' neoliberal state (for a summary of some of its key characteristics, see Table 6.1). First, to restate the obvious, the aim of neoliberal policing is the pursuit of peace, not in the negative sense of the absence of military violence but in the more positive sense of establishing and securing the legal and moral presuppositions of international order (i.e. the international market civilization). This means neoliberal policing is broader than both wars against aggressors and law enforcement. Second, waging war on crime means intervening not only in cases of aggression or of armed conflict between states, but against all criminals, that is, enemies of the (open market) society, which include states and individuals alike. Thirdly, its beneficiaries were primarily non-state (economic) actors rather than states. Fourthly, temporally, neoliberal policing should be proactive rather than reactive, positive rather than negative. This meant an emphasis on crime prevention, including the 'emergence of those policies which are eventually responsible for conflict'.[36] But also, to quote

[34] Slobodian, *Globalists*.
[35] Röpke, *International Order*, p. 13.
[36] Robbins, *The Economic Causes of War*, p. 105.

from Hayek, a focus on the 'wholesale transformation' of the 'societies and ways of life' of non-liberal societies. Spatially, finally, international policing should be universal, that is, it should cover all territories and societies.

The practical consequences are far-reaching. Given the epistemological primacy of the market, in the face of hostility and resistance to market civilization, there is no alternative but destruction or elimination. Such cases, Popper argued in a statement that bears a chilling resemblance to the treatment of Iraq after the Gulf War, would justify the international community taking control of an aggressors' resources, prevent its re-armament and administer it as an international territory, never to be returned. The ontological primacy of the market, on the other hand, meant such cases raised no conflict with state sovereignty or individual freedom. For Popper, a crucial difference remains between 'civil and international peace' and hence between domestic and international policing. The function of the state is to protect 'its units or atoms' (i.e. citizens). But, given the state is not a 'natural unit', the same cannot apply to international organizations, which should therefore aim to protect not their constitutive entities, namely states, but individuals within states. Breaking the 'political and military power' of aggressors, Popper stressed, in no way undermined the interests of individual citizens who could still engage in legitimate economic activities.[37]

Only Rappard explicitly envisaged the legal basis of international policing as a form of 'international solidarity'. But to the extent that solidarity constitutes the legal expression of the system of policing, as it does in the actual CS, then we could summarize the above by saying that neoliberal solidarity involves a legalized obligation upon the 'open' international society to expand and secure, by whatever means, the legal, institutional and moral pre-conditions that alone can produce peace and that therefore prevail over any notion of popular or national sovereignty. Neoliberal solidarity is not an act of common political will for a concrete purpose. It is an institutionalized duty to collectively, blindly and wholly commit to whatever action is needed to secure the universalization of the market civilization.

6.4 SOLIDARITY IN THE LAW OF COLLECTIVE SECURITY: TOWARDS A NEOLIBERAL UTOPIA?

6.4.1 *The League Model: Planting the Neoliberal Seeds?*

To what extent has this neoliberal vision shaped the emergence and development of CS as a form of international solidarity? The system of CS was first

[37] Popper, *The Open Society and Its Enemies*, ft 7, pp. 606–607.

introduced by the Covenant of the League of Nations. Under Article 10, all League members undertook to 'respect and preserve as against external aggression the territorial integrity and existing political independence of all Members of the League'. 'Should any Member of the League resort to war in disregard' of the Covenant, Article 16 continued, 'it shall ipso facto be deemed to have committed an act of war against all other Members of the League' and be met with economic sanctions, backed by force if necessary.

The duty of solidarity was from the outset influenced by proto-neoliberal ideas. Many saw the system of CS as marking the beginning of a new world order,[38] which broke with nineteenth century liberalism. Rappard, moreover, explicitly associated his vision of an organized peace with Wilsonian idealism, the seeds of which, he claimed, had been planted with the creation of the League and the 'principles of active solidarity' enshrined in Articles 10 and 16.[39]

In line with neoliberal prescriptions, with the introduction of CS, the problem of war and international peace indeed became a problem of law and order.[40] The duty of active solidarity marked the first time that sovereignty – then largely an attribute of colonial powers – was limited in pursuit of the higher end of international peace and security based on a common moral condemnation of war as instrument of international politics. It was also the first time that commitment took the form of a legal obligation superseding other international commitments and enforceable against any of its members. From that perspective, the duty of solidarity provided the basis of an embryonic form of international policing, similar to the policing of domestic crime, changing the nature of war from a private institution between belligerents to a public war against an 'internal enemy' and bringing an end to the principle of neutrality.

At the same time, the duty still bore the imprint of the 'old world order'.[41] The duty's object was the pursuit of negative peace, that is, the absence of war – internal law and order, including colonial wars, remained under state jurisdiction. The duty's targets and beneficiaries were States rather than individuals – solidarity was designed to protect the territorial integrity and political independence of its members from aggression by another State. Legally, the duty was 'imperfect' in the sense that states were free to determine whether an act of war had been committed. Temporally, solidarity was

38 See, e.g. Östen Undén, 'The Philosophy of Collective Security' (1955) 25 *Nordic Journal of International Law* 3.

39 Rappard, 'Vues Rétrospectives sur la Société des Nations', p. 211.

40 Alexander Orakhelashvili, *Collective Security* (Oxford: Oxford University Press, 2011), p. 1.

41 William E. Rappard, 'Why Peace Failed' (1940) 210 *The Annals of the American Academy of Political and Social Science* 1.

negative: collective action was meant to deter aggression.[42] Spatially, its reach was limited: the US, notoriously, refused to join the League, and colonized and semi-colonized territories were altogether excluded from its purview. Epistemologically, the system was based on the idea that violence could be prevented and, ontologically, it was grounded in the superiority of the state and the political (as opposed to the international market, and the economic sphere). In that sense, the duty of solidarity was closer to a system of collective self-defence based on the common interest of League members to avert war, than the normative expression of a truly international system for policing crime.[43]

For neoliberals, the limited nature of solidarity signed the League's death warrant. For Robbins, the League made the 'weaknesses of a mere association of sovereign states' and the 'possibility of a harmony of interests between them ... painful evident' and warned that the 'realisation of the principles of liberalism in the international sphere' would not succeed 'so long as CS is driven merely by the idea of common interest and the futility of violence'. Similarly, Rappard was adamant that the League failed because of the prioritization of sovereignty over international solidarity,[44] as well as its European, rather than 'universal' character,[45] which both weakened and limited the powers of the world's policeman.

6.4.2 *The Charter Model: Two Steps Forward, One Step Back?*

Following the demise of the League of Nations and the outbreak of World War II, the duty of solidarity re-emerged in the post-World War II order through a range of obligations states have undertaken under the UN Charter. Central to the duty is the member states' conferral, in Article 24, of primary responsibility for the maintenance of international peace and security to the UNSC and their commitment under Article 25 to abide by its decisions. Its substantive and operational scope are then defined in Articles 39, 41 and 42, which give the UNSC the power to 'determine the existence of any threat to the peace, breach of the peace, or act of aggression' and to 'decide what measures shall be taken in accordance with Articles 41 and 42, to maintain or restore international peace and security'.

42 See, e.g. Nicholas Mulder, *The Economic Weapon: The Rise of Sanctions as a Tool of Modern War* (New Haven: Yale University Press, 2022).

43 Ronald St. J. Macdonald, 'Solidarity in the Practice and Discourse of Public International Law' (1996) 8 *Pace International Law Review* 259.

44 Rappard, *The Quest for Peace*, p. 175.

45 Rappard, 'Vues Rétrospectives sur la Société des Nations', p. 143.

The Charter model of solidarity stood in a no less ambivalent relationship to neoliberal ideas than its predecessor. Many scholars described the UN as a structure set up by the Great Powers to maintain order and the UNSC as a 'police officer' set up to pursue 'international police action'. Linguistically, there was a marked shift in vernacular, from the language of 'war' and 'aggression' to the language of peace and order.[46] Formally, the duty of solidarity in Article 25 no longer depended on state discretion, but was to be activated by a centralized quasi-executive authority whose decisions states were bound to follow. Its targets were not only aggressors, but peace-breakers (i.e. 'enemies of the peace'). Temporarily, the duty acquired a more proactive dimension, triggering solidarity-based action in the face of not only aggression but also threats to the peace. And spatially, too, its scope expanded in that it applied to almost all sovereign entities.

But, if these brought CS closer to the neoliberal idea of international policing, the system of the UN Charter was still premised on the ontological superiority of the state. Internal order remained the preserve of states. Under Article 2(7), the UNSC could not intervene in matters which are essentially within the domestic jurisdiction of states. And the maintenance of international order was not universal in the sense of applicable to all UN members. Instead, in line with Churchill's vision of the World's 'Four Policemen', international police power was placed in the hands of powerful states, which, by means of the veto, both immunized themselves from police actions and held the ultimate say over the scope of international policing. As we shall see, Rappard was extremely critical of the veto and the UN system of CS.

6.4.3 *The Post-Cold War Model: Building Neoliberal Peace?*

Few of the early neoliberals lived to see and assess the many changes that the system of CS underwent after the end of the Cold War. But it is more than plausible they would have viewed them positively. The formal architecture of CS remained the same, including the veto, which hence limited the territorial reach of international policing. But new socio-economic and geopolitical conditions enabled a far-more expansive reading and more frequent exercise of the powers of the UNSC bringing the law and practice of CS much closer to the neoliberal idea of international policing.

[46] David Kennedy, 'The International Human Rights Regime: Still Part of the Problem', in Rob Dickinson, Elena Katselli, Collin Murray and Ole W. Pedersen (eds.), *Examining Critical Perspective on Human Rights* (Cambridge: Cambridge University Press, 2012), p. 29.

The aim of CS shifted decisively to the realization of a 'positive peace'. Many identified it with liberal peace, that is, the promotion of liberal values and institutions. The UNSC now intervened primarily in response to internal conflict or instability. Temporarily, the CS shifted from 'a culture of reaction, to a culture of prevention'.[47] Punitive sanctions or peacekeeping operations were now supplemented by a variety of far more forward-looking instruments, from peace-building missions to the international administration of territories. And, finally, with formal decolonization, the territorial reach of policing expanded to cover the entire world.

The affinities with neoliberal thought deepened following the war on terror. The aims of CS now build on a 'new security consensus' characterized by a comprehensive approach to collective security and rooted in the 'inextricable link of security, economic development and human freedom'.[48] Its scope expanded to include not only threats to the peace, but all threats to 'human security' independent of their impact on state security. As a result, non-state actors were included as both targets and beneficiaries of CS. Temporarily, its coordinates shifted yet further, embracing a pre-emptive risk-based approach that required not only action based on risk or suspicion, but regulatory, quasi-legislative initiatives binding on all. Spatially, CS intruded in spaces from which it was previously excluded, running deep into the governance of the state and the lives of its population. It became increasingly polarized along friend–enemy lines, requiring not only the transformation and disciplining but also elimination of the enemies of security.

This new system also had epistemological and ontological implications, even if these are not always explicitly articulated. Epistemologically, the system shifted away from the romantic ideal that war and violence could be prevented towards a more pragmatic and forceful commitment to the everyday administration and containment of crime. Ontologically, the focus shifted decisively away from the state and state sovereignty. The state was now seen to have only an instrumental, rather than intrinsic value. And sovereignty was redefined away from the Westphalian model of 'sovereignty as autonomy' epitomized by the principle of non-intervention towards a model of 'sovereignty as responsibility' where sovereignty was conditioned upon the states' ability and willingness to secure the livelihood of its subjects.

[47] See Kofi Annan, Press Release SC/6759, 29 November 1999.

[48] For a useful overview of the conceptual shift involved, see Anne Marie Slaughter, 'Security, Solidarity, and Sovereignty: The Grand Themes of UN Reform' (2005) 99 *The American Journal of International Law* 619.

TABLE 6.1 *Characteristics of solidarity*

Solidarity	Neoliberal	League	Charter	Post-Cold War	Twenty-first century
Objective	market civilization	absence of war	negative peace	positive peace	comprehensive security
Status	legal	legal	legal	legal	legal
Character	instrumental	instrumental	instrumental	instrumental	instrumental
Targets	enemies of the (market) order	aggressor states	peace-breaking states	enemies of peace	enemies of security
Beneficiaries	humanity	states	states	states	humanity
Temporality	proactive	negative (deterrence)	preventative	pre-emptive	proactive
Spatiality	universal	imperial	partial	international	universal

6.5 CHALLENGING NEOLIBERAL SOLIDARITY

6.5.1 *Critiques of Solidarity in the Law of CS*

6.5.1.1 Realist Critiques: Between Unfulfilled Promise and Unrealizable Utopia

Why does this excavation of the neoliberal underpinnings of the solidarity embedded in CS matter? There is no shortage of critiques of the system of CS and, at least implicitly, of the duty of solidarity that underpins it. One strand, which we could call 'realist' without implying that its proponents necessarily subscribe to a realist theory of international relations, incorporates realist insights into classic liberal idealistic and/or legalistic understandings of CS,[49] bringing attention to how politics, power and sovereignty limit the possibilities of realizing the solidarity of CS. Such limits include the de facto dominance of powerful states, particularly the United States, who successfully co-opt the system of CS to pursue their interests. They also include the 'legalized hegemony'[50] embedded in the veto of the permanent members of the UNSC, as a result of which solidarity is subject to the solidarity between the great powers, alongside the agreement of members of the UNSC. Historically, these limits are associated with the 'dark periods' of the UN when solidarity proved impossible because the UNSC was either paralysed or side-lined, most notably during the Cold War. Geographically, they have carved out 'non-solidarity' zones, spaces, people or issues that are either immune to, or do not benefit from, the effects of solidarity, depending on whether the emphasis is on solidarity as a disciplining or protective tool.

Building on Koskenniemi's broader approach to international law as a system oscillating between apology and utopia,[51] Danchin, for example, sees CS being caught in an oscillation between a balance of power model (apology) and a world government model (utopia).[52] In the specific context of the UN Charter, this oscillation manifests itself in the various mechanisms

[49] See, e.g. Nigel D. White, 'On the Brink of Lawlessness: The State of Collective Security Law' (2002) 13 *Indiana International & Comparative Law Review* 237.

[50] Gerry Simpson, *Great Powers and Outlaw States* (New York: Cambridge University Press, 2004).

[51] Martti Koskenniemi, *From Apology to Utopia: The Structure of International Legal Argument* (Cambridge: Cambridge University Press, 1989).

[52] Peter G. Danchin, 'Things Fall Apart: The Concept of Collective Security in International Law', in Peter G. Danchin and Horst Fischer (eds.), *United Nations Reform and the New Collective Security* (Cambridge: Cambridge University Press, 2010).

designed, on the one hand, to preserve state freedom and autonomy (e.g. the principle of equality of states; the right to self-defence; the principle of non-intervention in domestic affairs) and on the other, to restrain state power (e.g. the prohibition on the use of force; the UNSC's primary responsibility to protect international peace and security; and the duty of solidarity itself), resulting in a paradoxical 'hybrid collective security system', an 'order without government'.[53]

From this perspective, notwithstanding its legalization in the UN system of CS solidarity is at best an unfulfilled promise, and at worse an unrealizable utopia, that will remain caught in the politics of the international legal order.[54] The latter may explain why solidarity in the context of CS does not feature prominently in recent studies which see it as a principle designed to move the international legal order away from its 'outdated' focus on 'promoting the self-interest of States' to one 'that pursues common (community) interests and attempts to find solutions to problems affecting all humankind'.[55] The former is why international policing has had nothing to contribute to two of the most deadly wars of our present: Russia's war on Ukraine and Israel's war on the Palestinian people.

6.5.1.2 Critical Approaches: From Differentiation to Domination

Critical scholars have gone further, highlighting the illiberal or neo-colonial dimensions of international law and, hence, CS. Examples of the illiberal critique include Buchan's distinction between an international community of liberal states and the broader international society[56] or Simpson's distinction between Charter liberalism and liberal anti-pluralism.[57] Both distinctions are

[53] Ibid., p. 42. He borrows this term from Inis L. Claude, Jr., 'Comment on "An Autopsy of Collective Security"' (Winter 1975–1976) 90 *Political Science Quarterly* 715–717.

[54] This critique is also implicit in Neuhold, 'Common Security'.

[55] Eva Kassoti and Narin Idriz (eds.), *The Principle of Solidarity: International and EU Law Perspectives* (The Hague: TMC Asser Press Springer, 2023), p. 4.

[56] Russell Buchan, *International Law and the Construction of the Liberal Peace* (Oxford: Hart Publishing, 2013).

[57] Gerry Simpson, 'Two Liberalisms' (2001) 12 *European Journal of International Law* 537. Simpson also uses the terms 'neoliberalism' or 'new liberalism' to describe what he calls 'liberal anti-liberalism'. However, his understanding of neoliberalism as liberal anti-pluralism differs from neoliberalism in the sense of the body of work produced by the neoliberal thought collective. Both share a premise of hierarchization, but they significantly differ in terms of its justification and scope. Neoliberalism as liberal anti-pluralism places the ontological focus on the individual and classified states based on their adherence to certain rights or norms. Neoliberals ascribe ontological priority to the market and hierarchize both individuals and states based on their aptitude to the market.

deployed to frame changes to international law and highlight how, after the Cold War, sovereignty was re-defined to pre-suppose liberal democratic government, turning CS into a means to enforce liberal norms against non-liberal states. Examples of the neo-colonial critique include Anghie's framing of the UN global war on terror as a continuation of the colonial distinction between 'civilized' and 'non-civilized' societies[58] and Orford's work on the responsibility to protect.[59] These approaches cast the shift to sovereignty as responsibility as a new form of neo-colonialism.

For these scholars, solidarity is, at best, discriminatory (i.e. based on double-standards) and, at worst, a tool of neo-colonial domination. Its targets are primarily countries of the global south, various 'rogue' or 'failed' states and other disobedient actors. For the illiberal critique, this is because of the consolidation of liberal hegemony. For the neo-colonial critique, this is because of solidarity's colonial antecedents. Indeed, as has been remarked, in the nineteenth century the concept of solidarity was used as 'a justification for colonial domination' when 'responsibility of states to one another became the "civilizing mission" of European states in their quest for colonial control over the population of other states'.[60]

6.5.2 *Limitations*

However insightful these critiques are, their neglect of the neoliberal underpinnings of the solidarity of CS may lead them to reproduce the neoliberal status quo. Without engagement with the ideological and political content of solidarity, realist arguments risk promoting the legalization of neoliberal solidarity. Neoliberals were very critical of the veto power and more generally of the politicization of international law: their project, if anything, was precisely about limiting, if not erasing, politics from the operation of the international order. This included limiting democratic influences and the power of newly emerging post-colonial states, but also hegemonic capture. Rappard, for example, condemned the Charter for creating 'two distinct sets of rights and duties'[61] and effectively placing the P5 'above the law'. This, he claimed, had no precedent in either international law or domestic law and had created an

58 Antony Anghie, *Imperialism, Sovereignty, and the Making of International Law* (Cambridge: Cambridge University Press, 2005).

59 Anne Orford, *International Authority and the Responsibility to Protect* (Cambridge: Cambridge University Press, 2011).

60 Macdonald, 'Solidarity in the Practice and Discourse of Public International Law', 261.

61 William E. Rappard, 'The United Nations from a European Point of View' (1946) 55 *The Yale Law Journal* 1036, at 1041.

'international aristocracy of the powerful ... endowed with almost unlimited authority over the underprivileged masses' and 'impunity in case of violation of their pacific covenants'.[62] Far from the expression of the collective will of an international community, the duty of solidarity was in reality subordinated to, and hence but the normative manifestation of, the will and interests of the P5. This fitted into his broader condemnation of a 'peace of subordination' based on the supreme rule of one over the whole, which he associated with the Pax Romana or the Franco–British hegemony of the 1920 and 1930s[63] and which could be extended to the post-Cold War Pax Americana. Might may take precedence over right in times of war, he explained, but 'in the long run, peace can be maintained only by the subordination of might to right'.[64] The realistic critique, in other words, is far from incompatible with neoliberal solidarity.

Without engagement with neoliberal ideology, on the other hand, the critical project might fail to challenge the specific ways in which exclusion, discrimination and neo-colonial forms of domination work themselves through the (neoliberal) duty of solidarity today.

Market civilization pre-supposes universal formal inclusion, and, to that extent, universal legal subjecthood and formal equality between states. In its utopic iteration, the neoliberal project indeed consists of the universalization of the laws and morals of the market. Although they were no anti-imperialists,[65] many were critical of the old colonial order. As we saw, Rappard disparaged the UN Charter for violating the principle of sovereign equality. And he viewed the mandate system as a medium for integration and assimilation, not for permanent control over mandate territories. Even Mises, the most open proponent of racial hierarchy, deplored the prevalence of the militarist-imperialist principle, which interprets human society as 'forcible repression of some of its members by others' rather than the 'friendly division of labour' and the 'development of trade' that underpins the 'peaceful principle'.[66] As such, formally, neoliberal solidarity was not meant to be applied in a discriminatory or neo-colonial fashion.

But the realization of market civilization does not preclude hierarchy and domination. In fact, it presupposes both. As we also saw, neoliberal support for

62 William E. Rappard, 'The United Nations as Viewed from Geneva' (1946) 40 *American Political Science Review* 545, at 548–549.

63 Rappard, *The Quest for Peace*, pp. 498–499.

64 Rappard, 'The United Nations from a European Point of View', 1042.

65 Susan Pedersen, *The Guardians: The League of Nations and the Crisis of Empire* (Oxford: Oxford University Press, 2015).

66 Ludwig Mises, *Socialism: An Economic and Sociological Analysis*, trans by J. Kahane (New Haven: Yale University Press, 1962), p. 302.

a strong international policeman to the enemies of the open societies was rooted in two assumptions. The first is that the market civilization would not spread spontaneously but had to be enforced. Forceful intervention in non-liberal states is therefore inherent in the neoliberal understanding of peace. The second is that, even with strong enforcement mechanisms, the spread of the laws and institutions of the market (i.e. of liberal states and institutions) can never be fully realized. This assumption may have been partly based on empirical observations. Many individuals and states did not embrace liberal ideas, indeed one of the dominant ideologies of the time, socialism, openly disparaged them. But it also came to be based on deeper presuppositions. Overtly or not, for neoliberals, not all individuals and societies display an equal aptitude to the market, which is shaped not only by ideological posture, but cultural, racial and gendered traits. Recent work has shown that none other than Hayek separated 'mankind into a civilised and an uncivilised part'.[67] At first, this was premised on the distinction between liberal and illiberal societies, which he acknowledged had to be subject to different rules. But, gradually, Hayek not only came to associate (market) civilization exclusively with Western liberal values but also to see non-Western liberal societies as inherently aggressive.[68]

From that perspective, there is no contradiction between liberalism and liberal anti-pluralism: under its neoliberal reincarnation, liberalism presupposes anti-pluralism, that is, the unequal application of norms of international law such as the principle of non-intervention and the suppression, by whatever means, of non-liberal societies. Neither is there a contradiction between an international community of liberal states and the broader international society of states: states can only exist as independent equals if they abide by liberal values; there can be no international society of states outside the international community of liberal states. Nor, finally, is there a contradiction between the market civilization and neo-colonialism: peace depends on inequality and domination. This, moreover, is no ideological preference or material fact: it is the natural order of things. Epistemologically, there is no alternative to tackle violence than legalizing the discriminatory and neo-colonial solidarity of the market. And ontologically, such solidarity is 'naturalized': both individual legal subjecthood and sovereignty can only exist if they align with the rules of the market civilization.

More generally, existing critiques of CS and international law may underestimate the deeper ideological work and struggle required to re-direct

[67] Jorg Spieker, 'F. A. Hayek and the Reinvention of Liberal Internationalism' (2014) 36 *The International History Review* 919, at 920.

[68] Ibid.

solidarity towards the achievement of more emancipatory objectives. The UN draft declaration on the right to solidarity speaks of solidarity as a universal spirit of unity purposively mobilized to direct common action to tackle the many challenges of our age of catastrophe. But, under a neoliberal paradigm, this is pure fantasy. Only the international market is capable of integrating 'all mankind into a single society' and hence solidarity is not a 'spirit of unity' but an existential universal duty to abide by market rules. And any 'method of creating solidarity' through the identification of common ends would be to revert to the social and political model of 'closed' societies, that is, a sign of tribalism and backwardness.[69]

6.6 CONCLUSION

I began this chapter by raising two questions: is solidarity immune to the neoliberal ideology and practices that have characterized the last three decades and does the 'solidarity turn' offer a promising way forward in terms of tackling the many crises that characterize our 'age of catastrophe'? My answer is a qualified no. The example of CS certainly shows that no idea or practice, solidarity included, is inherently 'good' or exists outside the systems of knowledge and structures that have shaped the international legal order. Reaching out to 'solidarity' as a principle or normative ideal is no magic way out of the crisis. This does not mean there is no scope for re-purposing solidarity in emancipatory directions that break with the market logic traversing international laws and institutions. But to do so, I warned, may require a renewal of the project of critique.

Here I focused on illustrating the need for greater engagement with neoliberal thought in our understanding of solidarity in international law and discourse. However, an emphasis on ideas, as the present chapter offered, is not enough. The possibilities and limits of international solidarity do not reside only in the matrix of assumptions and ideas that shape international law but in its material basis, specifically in the material basis of (neoliberal) capital accumulation. Racialized, gendered and cultural hierarchies, market competition and extractivism might have deepened in the neoliberal age, but these remain an expression of the logic of division, competition and extraction underpinning a system defined by the valorization of capital. Only by also attending to this capitalist basis of international law can we hope for progressive solutions to the current crisis and, ironically, this may partly require not a global commitment to unity and common action, but many solidarities that aim to challenge and disrupt the 'natural' status quo.

69 Hayek, *Law Legislation and Liberty*, p. 149.

7

Will there be Solidarity in Data-Driven Societies?

GREGOR NOLL

7.1 INTRODUCTION

Solidarity is but another word for an early phase in the genesis of a political community. What an emergent community is about to have in common is contingent on technology. At the present juncture, the solidarity question resonates with digitalization and AI. Is solidarity possible in societies characterized by the exchange of data, under conditions of digitalization and AI? If not, why not? These are the questions I pursue in this chapter.

In pursuit of an answer, I will draw on two historical cases of two paradigmatically solidaristic communities, one situated in mines and factories of the European mainland, the other in plantations of European colonies. While the first is inconceivable without steam power, the second was driven by slavery and, later, by systems of indentured labour. In digitalization and AI, data is a central driver. As expressions of industrialism broadly understood, all three cases – mines and factories, plantations and data-driven societies – were brought about by surges in technological innovation and their capitalist implementation. In the case of plantation slavery, the ability to occupy lands, pursue monoculture and to ship Europeans, slaves and agricultural products across vast maritime expanses are components of an industry no less complex than setting up large-scale mining operations or, for that matter, search

I am indebted to Dr. Daniel Steuer, to commentators and participants of the Gothenburg Workshop "Solidarity: We know it when we see it" on 25 March 2022 for helpful comments and critique.

engines.[1] I intend to tease out commonalities and differences between the two historical cases with the help of four heuristic elements: (1) communal living of labourers entailed by the industrialization of a new technology (steam powered mining and foundries and slavery-powered plantation agriculture, respectively), (2) under-regulation of the industry and its labour relations, (3) the emergence of resistant proto-law amongst labourers and (4) the response of repressive-appeasing law by owners and the state. Eventually, these four elements allow me to extract two necessary attributes of solidarity: the sharing of a *physical place* by labourers forming a community in solidarity, and the situation of that place *on the inside* of a politics of exploitation, rather than beyond it. These attributes allow me to consider whether solidarity is possible in data societies.

The first historical case tracks German coal and steel workers' resistance to exploitation during the industrial revolution in the second half of the nineteenth century and at the beginning of the twentieth century (Section 7.2). Not only was this period formative for the conceptual history of solidarity, at the threshold to full-blown industrial capitalism, solidarity arguably played a politically transformative role. My second historical case explores community formation by the Maroon, a group of fugitive plantation slaves in eighteenth-century Suriname (Section 7.3). Plantations have been cast as 'factories in the field'[2], inviting us to consider plantation slavery and steam-powered mining and manufacturing as two aspects of the same phenomenon: capitalist industrialism. That instantiation of colonial solidarity is not only prior to European industrial labour solidarity, but also arguably more radical: as we will see, the Maroon opted out of capitalism.

In Section 7.4, I explore whether the four structural elements critical for eighteenth and nineteenth century solidarity may assist us to understand the prospects for solidarity in data-driven societies. I conclude that cybernetics, digitalization and AI undercut the preconditions for solidarity, as they eradicate the sharing of a physical place on the inside of exploitation politics. In Section 7.5, I raise the issue of who is the agent of solidarity in a coda to this chapter.

1 With Lewis Mumford, both cases could be described as megamachines, integrating human and technological resources in one and the same organization. Lewis Mumford, *The Myth of the Machine. Technics and Human Development* (New York: Harcourt, 1967).

2 See e.g. Kenneth Stampp, *The Peculiar Institution: Slavery in the Ante-Bellum South* (New York: Vintage Books, 1956), p. 42 for one of the early uses of the term 'factories in the field' to denote plantations. For a current overview of research on the link between plantation slavery and industrial capitalism, see Maxine Berg and Pat Hudson, *Slavery, Capitalism and the Industrial Revolution* (Cambridge: Polity, 2023).

7.2 A SOLIDARITY MOMENT IN THE STEAM ECONOMY: WORKERS IN GERMAN COAL AND STEEL INDUSTRIES

A reading trail connects AI and digitalization with the 'social question' of nineteenth-century industrialism. Once AI and digitalization have awakened your interest in cybernetics, you search for its sources, moving backward from the standard accounts of 1940s wartime applications to calculate the trajectory of anti-aircraft fires to late nineteenth century advances in mathematical modelling of complex processes,[3] ever-important to insurers of complex industrial risks, which, in turn, raises the question why insurance had attained such a prominent role, moving you to consider whether the nineteenth century cluster of industrialism, revolutionary threat, changes in liability law and the advent of welfare law is a kind of playbook we need to study carefully in order to understand the contours of what is happening in the relation of AI and digitalization to law.

Let me briefly introduce how this cluster came about. In nineteenth-century Germany, industrialism swept workers into novel forms of communal living and conditions of labour that were part of the industrial revolution and, due to their novelty and scale, largely beyond regulation. Workers reacted to these changes by associating in a way usually labelled as workers' solidarity. These associations brought about a strong sense of intra-group obligation that we could describe as a private proto-law. The legality of their actions was challenged from the start, with employers denouncing the novel phenomenon of strikes as illegal and systematically shunning deliberations with worker committees.[4] Once owners and the government realized that worker associations, the unions germinating from them, and socialism were not going to go away, they reacted by combining repression with welfare-related entitlement. Socialism was formally outlawed, and an appeasing legislative package was adopted, prescribing strict liability for certain categories of industrial accidents,

[3] Vilém Flusser suggested that the invention of computing is retraceable to the advent of differential calculus in late nineteenth century mathematics. Vilém Flusser, *Schreiben für Publizieren. Text, Ton + Hypertext* (1992), emulated version, available at: https://sites.rhizome.org/flusserPEB/ (last accessed 5 August 2024). See also Vilém Flusser, *Von der Freiheit der Migranten. Einsprüche Gegen den Nationalismus* (Berlin: Bollmann, 1994), pp. 127–129.

[4] In the comprehensive 1889 strikes affecting all German coal pits areas, the first response by the *Bergbaulicher Verein*, an owners' association in the Ruhr area, of 12 May 1889, was to state that the strike took place on '*ungesetzlichem Boden*', i.e. without a legal base. Lorenz Pieper, 'Der Ausstand vom Jahre 1889' (1905) *Aufsätze über den Streik der Bergabeiter im Ruhrgebiet, Schriften der Gesellschaft für Soziale Reform* Heft 5 des II. Bandes, 367–386, at 369. Given the novelty of mass strikes, it is hard to assess whether that claim is correct in the under-regulated situation obtaining before the German lawgiver began to regulate industrial labour relations.

obligatory accident, health and pension insurances and providing welfare benefits for workers and their families, albeit on a rather limited scale. During the time of the normatively under-regulated emergence of industrialism, the proto-law of solidaristic workers' associations had provoked the creation of new state law in response – a state law drawing inspiration from solidaristic demands as much as confronting them. Let us look at the individual elements of this jurisgenetic structure. They are industrialized communal living, under-regulation, solidaristic proto-law and, finally, repressive-appeasing state law.

First, there is the element of industrialized communal living. Generally, nineteenth century coal and steel industries in Germany concentrated workers in industrial barracks-like housing around factories and mines with miserable working conditions. The uniformity of housing and work, with workers of the same profession and the same workplace living together in the same space was a precondition of worker self-organization and German socialism.[5] Fascinatingly, this housing was *part* of industrial technology, meaning that, with industrial housing, technology and its owners *created* the very conditions that just might have led to a revolutionary change of ownership of the means of production in nineteenth-century Germany. During the second half of the nineteenth century, the coal and steel industry established new operations in rural areas unfit to absorb the great number of workers needed. In this phase of expansion, the uniformity of housing and work was an important factor in attracting and retaining workers, with a person's labour contract often being linked to the rental contract for a flat in a housing project owned by the employer, giving employers 'the means to control the life and political behaviour of workers beyond the workplace'.[6] Such workers lived and worked in a normatively very dense environment in which the employers' politics manifested itself around the clock.

The absence of pertinent regulation by law or contract is the second element in the structure I propose. Employers enjoyed the benefits of a regulatory landscape where old rules had been scrapped without new ones having emerged yet. There was a decade-long inter-regnum of under-regulation. The 1865 Prussian Mining Act did away with numerous legal rules and claims, and abolished the principle that all mining is under the ultimate direction of the state (the *Direktionsprinzip*).[7] Just at the time when

5 I am indebted to Lisa Herzog for vividly pointing this out to me. See also Section 8.2 of Herzog's chapter, arguing that many paradigmatic forms of solidarity, especially in the history of the labour movement, were characterized by a *combination* of social and political solidarity.

6 Lutz Niethammer, 'Wie wohnten Arbeiter im Kaiserreich?' (1976) 16 *Archiv für Sozialgeschichte* 61–134, at 77.

7 Franz-Josef Brüggemeier, *Grubengold: Das Zeitalter der Kohle von 1750 bis heute* (München: C. H. Beck, 2018), pp. 140–141.

novel technology that had led to a sizeable expansion of coal production in the United Kingdom and elsewhere was imported into the Ruhr area, the state withdrew as a regulator. What is more, the law was slow and late in addressing workplace health and safety issues.[8] The minimalist public law approach taken after 1870, as detailed at the end of the current section, reflected this tardiness of regulation. Neither was there any leeway for individual workers to negotiate workplace safety aspects into their individual employment contracts, or, for that matter, any other condition of employment. On the contrary: industrial labour lived off the standardization of its processes.

Third, technology and social reorganization of industrial labour led to the self-organization of those subjected to technology in their labour. What is of interest to us here, is that common actions based on solidarity first emerged in the context of these forms of self-organization, that is, before – or outside the context of – the institutional forms of social democracy. At times, such actions could take contractual expressions. I use the term 'proto-law' for these relations resulting from workers entering into association and putting themselves at risk of dismissal or repression in order to bring about a better regulation of working conditions. All this would be at local level and within a short timeframe, by contrast to the medium- to long-term timeframe of social democracy and its national aspiration.

How are we to imagine this proto-law that emerged from the self-organization of workers threatened with immiseration by work accidents or dismissal? Locally, union-like associations emerged and sought to cartelize the negotiating power of single workers faced with owner demands on extended working hours or on the imposition of dismal and dangerous working conditions. Such associations followed the delineation of professions or task specializations in the industry in question.[9] To avoid being prohibited under the 1878 Socialist Law (*Sozialistengesetz*), these associations made a point of not self-identifying as unions.[10] The proto-law made by worker associates could take the form of private oral contracts to associate. One case in 1907 illustrates the response of Ruhr coal workers to the introduction of a markedly authoritarian management system (the Stinnes system, named after German

[8] The Prussian Industrial Code of 17 January 1845 offered no effective norms on the protection of workers' health. Arne Andersen, 'Arbeiterschutz in Deutschland im 19. und frühen 20. Jahrhundert' (1991) 31 *Archiv für Sozialgeschichte* 61-82, at 64.

[9] This was part of a wider pattern: 'It was . . . craftsmen who were the first to collectively rebel against capitalist working conditions in Europe. When these revolts began to spread to the industrial workforce, the first worker associations were founded, and strikes took place.' Axel Honneth, *The Working Sovereign: Labour and Democractic Citizenship*, trans by Daniel Steuer (Cambridge: Polity, 2024), p. 77.

[10] Jürgen Kuczynski, *Die Geschichte des Alltags des deutschen Volkes, Band 4, 1871–1918* (Köln: Pahl-Rugenstein, 1982), p. 276.

industrialist Hugo Stinnes, 1870–1924). Faced with the incipient repression of their local and limited attempt at organizing, a group of pit foremen drew up a written agreement, adding a financial penalty to be paid by those breaking the ranks of the newly formed local organization: 'I oblige myself to remain faithful to the organization. Should I leave it, I will pay 10 Mark as penitence [*Reuegeld*].'[11] The dimension of trust among fellow workmen is moulded into a legal commitment, and a minimalist institution – 'the organization' – is created along the way. On the other side of the equation, the affected industry owner pressed workers to sign contracts committing them not to associate and to agree to their own dismissal, should they break that contract.[12] All in all, what flourished during these times dominated by state *laissez-faire* and *laissez-souffrir* was a private law of sorts, formally frail and politically portentous.[13]

As the example of self-organizing pit foremen suggests, particular professional categories among the newly mobilized, urbanized and co-housed workers were the source of resistance to industrial transformation. Just as technology could call forth forms of housing facilitating the control of workers, the same technology boosted collectivism within professions and ultimately produced the bearers of a solidaristic resistance in Germany. This is not without historical irony: exert a certain form of pressure on workers, and the structures generated by technology and capitalism start to turn against owners and directors.

When the German government devised counter-laws during the 1870s and 1880s, they were carefully tailored to thwart as much as to appease resistance from these groups, bringing us to the fourth and last element of my structure (repressive-appeasing law). We should imagine this as a massive public law intervention into the laissez-faire of German industrial markets, in part tangibly onerous for industry owners. The adoption of the Socialist Law in 1878 is the best-known attempt at large-scale repression of workers' self-organization.[14] Remaining in force until 1890, it prohibited socialist, social democratic

[11] Quoted in Ibid., p. 273. Author's translation.

[12] Quoted in Ibid., p. 274.

[13] I refrain from an exploration of organized German Social Democracy as a formalization of worker solidarity here. Scholars of the German labour movement have debated at length whether and to what extent German Social Democracy represented workers' interests or became a centre of domination of its own. For an overview, see Dieter Langewiesche, 'The Impact of the German Labour Movement on Workers' Culture' (1987) 59 *Journal of Modern History* 506–523, at 508–509.

[14] Gesetz gegen die gemeingefährlichen Bestrebungen der Sozialdemokratie [Law against the publicly endangering aspirations of social democracy], 21 October 1878 (RGBl. S. 351) (original version, later amended).

and communist associations, gatherings and publications. The Socialist Law gave a powerful tool to law enforcement authorities and courts to disrupt self-organization at local, regional and national level. Before it came into force, workers' protests were simply dispelled by police or military. Now, the law had entered the fray, legalizing the use of law enforcement resources even in situations where self-organization had not grown into full-blown protests yet.

As a primary measure of appeasement, the introduction of strict liability for certain industries by the Bismarck government[15] softened the effects of workplace accidents to a degree and greatly stimulated the emergence of appropriate private insurance solutions for industry owners. The significance of this legislation must not be underestimated: The question of workplace accidents figured very prominently in German debates at the time, as industrialized labour had exposed workers to novel, aggravated dangers. In particular, young mining workers' conditions of work entailed extreme morbidity and mortality rates.[16] Liability for such accidents was hard to attribute to owners under traditional forms of culpa models. The introduction of strict liability was carefully tailored to fit specific industries,[17] namely those in which self-organizing workers figure prominently. By way of example, the building industry objectively exposed its workers to considerable dangers at work, yet it was not included in strict liability legislation. By way of example, building workers were not housed communally as miners or steel workers, and would need to muster much greater resources to compensate for that lack of proximity. With the establishment of strict liability, the lawmaker acted strategically, seeking to drain out self-organization where it cropped up.

To the introduction of strict liability for certain industries, the gradual introduction of welfare-style worker insurance was added, with social insurance introduced in 1883 and health insurance introduced in 1884. However, welfare provision through these laws was kept at a minimum level and financed to an important part by workers' contributions. The outspoken objective of these legal changes was to avert revolution, and they came in tandem with a robustly enforced legal repression of social democracy.

[15] An excellent overview is in Regina Ogorek, *Untersuchungen zur Entwicklung der Gefährungshaftung im 19. Jahrhundert* (Köln und Wien: Böhlau, 1975). See also Franz Josef Brüggemeier, 'Eine Kränkung des Rechtsgefühls? Soziale Frage, Umweltprobleme und Verursacherprinzip im 19. Jahrhundert' (1994) 15 *Archiv für Sozialgeschichte* 106.

[16] Michael Martin, 'Allgegenwärtiger Tod. Arbeitsbedingungen und Mortalität im Ruhr-Bergbau bis zum Ersten Weltkrieg' (2009) 34 *Historical Social Research/Historische Sozialforschung* 154.

[17] In 1848, the Prussian Supreme Tribunal assumed workers to have freely agreed to face the risks of industrial work. For a discussion of the judgment, see Brüggemeier, 'Eine Kränkung des Rechtsgefühls', pp. 112–113.

An analytically significant moment occurred when appeasement policies targeted the housing conditions of workers, addressing head-on the crammed communal living conditions that made workers organize themselves. Industry owners had taken initiatives at building worker settlement already back in the mid-nineteenth century, many of which stacked workers in high-occupancy buildings close to the industry. But, in the last decades of that century, a turn in workers housing took place. From then onwards, many leading industries opted for spreading out workers in settlements whose quasi-rural apparition was supposed to evoke a sense of *Heimat*, or homeland, among its inhabitants.[18] Houses are machines for living in, as Le Corbusier later famously wrote; in this case, they were designed as machines for living one's love to the homeland – instead of living solidarity with worker-neighbours.

In the course of this shift, workers' housing initiatives by Friedrich Krupp's armament works turned away from the pre-1870s densely occupied multi-level tenements towards the cottage community of *Altenhof* (1892–1907) and the *Margarethenhöhe* (1909–1918) garden settlements. Also, as part of its wider labour policies, the German government promoted the development of new working-class housing in the periphery of large cities such as Berlin or Hamburg. Drawing on debates in German social-democratic publications of the late nineteenth century, Philipp Reick suggested that 'organized labor opposed decentralization not only based on economic and socio-cultural reasons. Rather, workers opposed decentralization also because at least until the end of the century, central neighborhoods provided the movement with crucial spaces for collective action and political participation'.[19] This turn from a type of industry-appended housing that fostered the emergence of class solidarity to one that was meant to promote workers' belonging to the nation corroborates that state and industry owners understood very well which preconditions were required for solidarity and resistance.

The process of repression and appeasement by the German government and affected industrial owners did not do away with the original tensions that germinated in local labour conflicts of the nineteenth century. Rather, these tensions survived into the new century, with revolutionary escalation remaining limited to the Weimar period of the 1920s. It was National Socialism that largely neutralized the political solidarity of workers during the Third Reich when, notwithstanding harsh working conditions and

[18] Cedric Bolz, 'Constructing "Heimat" in the Ruhr Valley: Krupp Housing and the Search for the Ideal German Home 1914–1931' (2011) 34 *German Studies Review* 17.

[19] Phillipp Reick, 'Desire or Displacement? Working-Class Notions of Urban Belonging in Late-Nineteenth-Century Germany' (2019) 45 *Journal of Urban History* 1193–1211, at 1211.

deteriorating labour conditions, only a limited number of strikes occurred.[20] Ultimately, deindustrialization and the slow demise of coal power eliminated the political agency of mining and steel workers in contemporary Germany.[21]

So, in all, what did steam power do to law in the case of the German industrial revolution? It brought about a structure where technological reorganization of production tips over into workers' self-organization in solidarity, which engenders legal counter-organization by response. The communal life of workers in a joint physical place turns out to be the tipping factor. The agglomeration of housing and work brought opportunities for close horizontal encounters among German workers in the same industry operation and the same professional sub-groups. This suggests that geographical proximity alone is not enough. A necessary requirement for jurisgenetic solidarity is the availability of a common physical space, providing a parliament of sorts, where compromises can be trashed out and positional unity manufactured. All this is done with the purpose of bringing about normative stability: a *lex inter partes* brought about by private contracts.

7.3 A SOLIDARITY MOMENT IN PLANTATION SLAVERY: MAROON COMMUNITIES IN SURINAME

In his *Diarium Surinamicum*, the botanist Daniel Rolander, a student of Carl von Linné, documented his 1755 research journey to the Dutch colony of Suriname.[22] Minute descriptions of plants and animals dominate, but often Rolander comments on the life of slaves, and on the cruelty colonists inflicted on them. Several entries relate to fugitive plantation slaves who settled in remote upriver locations, from which they raided Whites travelling outside their settlements and White settler plantations.[23] In certain of those passages, Rolander uses the term 'black rebels' and recorded that Dutch-language settlers referred to them as 'weck-loopers' – literally those who run away. The groups of fugitives from slavery is today referred to as Maroons, and Maroon societies formed in different locations across the Caribbean. They represented a formidable challenge to White settler colonialism, whose

[20] Günter Morsch, 'Streik im "Dritten Reich"' (1988) 36 *Vierteljahrshefte für Zeitgeschichte* 649.

[21] See Lutz Raphael, *Jenseits von Kohle und Stahl. Eine Gesellschaftsgeschichte Westeuropas nach dem Boom* (Berlin: Suhrkamp, 2021).

[22] Rolander's long unpublished journal was translated by a team led by James Dobreff from the original Latin to English and published in Volume 3, Book 3 of *The Linnaeus Apostles: Global Science & Adventure* (London & Whitby: IK Foundation & Company, 2008), pp. 1217–1570 [hereafter *Rolander's Journal*].

[23] *Rolander's Journal*, entry of 27 December, p. 1485.

occasional attempts to exterminate the Maroons by military means remained unsuccessful, and ultimately gave way to the conclusion of peace treaties between settlers and groups of Maroons.

In his entry of 13 January 1756, Rolander reasons at length on the conflict between Whites and slavery fugitives. On that day, at crossroads in Paramaribo, the colony's capital, a herald publicly proclaimed a decision of the senate:

> to send out a military expedition against the enemy blacks in the next few days. Besides the injuries suffered at the hands of the blacks, the motivation for this expedition is the unsuccessful outcome of the previous expedition, … That victory had given the black slaves confidence, with the result that the respect, fear and obedience which they owed to their masters, had begun to diminish. They were beyond thinking about the recuperation of their liberty; they now dared to even talk about it in some places. The security of the whites demanded a quick stop to these swelling problems. People claimed the best way to put an end to it was for an army to completely wipe out the black enemy.[24]

In the same entry, Rolander concludes that '[t]he blacks are too many for being subjugated by the white inhabitants or by a thousand soldiers sent from Holland'.[25] He adds that 'the black slaves would not have conceived their implacable hatred of the whites, or rebelled or even thought of undertaking such daring deeds, if they had been treated with less harshness – to say nothing of cruelty'.[26] Rolander then suggests that 'mildness and chastisement' would have been a more effective system, as slaves treated in that manner testified to him elsewhere that they were content, and that they would not have been better off in Africa.[27]

Suriname's European colonization had been a plurinational effort from the outset. As Karwan Fatah-Black's work details, it remained a heterogeneous affair throughout the early modern period. The first expeditions to the Guiana coast in the early seventeenth century were, he argues, 'based on shared business interests rather than being strictly French, Dutch, Irish or English undertakings'.[28] It makes sense to read Surinamese plantation slavery as

24 *Rolander's Journal*, entry of 13 January, pp. 1508–1509.

25 Ibid, p. 1509. Arends suggests that 23 666 African slaves were living in Suriname by 1740, based on head tax records, and that the 'estimated number of permanent run-away slaves' between 1702–1749 was 1 396. Jacques Arends, *Language and Slavery: A Social and Linguistic History of the Surinamese Creoles* (Amsterdam: John Benjamins Publishing Company, 2017), pp. 153 and 159.

26 *Rolander's Journal*, entry of 13 January, p. 1509.

27 Ibid.

28 Karwan Fatah-Black, *White Lies and Black Markets: Evading Metropolitan Authority in Colonial Suriname, 1650–1800* (Leiden: Brill, 2015), p. 16.

cropping up from industrialization and globalization rather than being an outflow of nation-statism. It illustrates the reach of private ownership in the colonial context that plantation owners in Dutch Suriname organized their own armed protection and covered the expenses for the military protection of their premises organized by the Dutch governor.[29] These entrepreneurs of an industry based on human labour met a permissive regulatory environment that often limited itself to lending sovereign legitimacy to colonial appropriation. In the context of British colonialism, Philip Stern has shown the Company to be no mere merchant, but a form of early modern, colonial state and sovereign, laying the foundations for the British Empire in India.[30]

Today, there are six established Maroon groups in Suriname, and one of the two largest are the Samaraka Maroons.[31] As societies driven by oral tradition, the Maroon did not produce documents reflecting the proto-law on which these six communities rest, but their sociogenesis can be tracked through the proxy of language. A comprehensive overview of creolists' efforts to determine when Samarakan creole formed is in Jacques Arends' 2017 monograph, arguing that an earlier belief of a relatively short formative period from 1690 to 1712 lacked empirical foundation.[32] Overall, as André Pakosie writes,

> Around the middle of the 18th century several consolidated Maroon groups emerged in different parts of Suriname's interior. Until the year of abolition (1863), slaves escaped in great numbers from Suriname's plantations. Many were caught; others, unable to survive in the harsh conditions of the tropical forest, returned to the world of slavery. Hundreds of refugees, however, managed to keep themselves alive; they settled on the upper reaches of rivers, and sought protection from their pursuers by withdrawing behind rapids and waterfalls, and many miles of almost impenetrable rain forest. When small bands of fugitive slaves coalesced to form larger groups, the *Loweman* as these Maroons called themselves, they began to pose a military threat to the plantation colony.[33]

German industrial workers traded the existential risk of inhuman work conditions for another one: that of being sacked wholesale for associating with each

[29] Sylvia W. de Groot, 'The Boni Maroon War 1765–1793, Surinam and French Guyana' (1975) 18 *Boletín de Estudios Latinoamericanos y del Caribe* 30–48, at 37.

[30] Philip Stern, *The Company-state: Corporate Sovereignty and the Early Modern Foundation of the British Empire in India* (New York: Oxford University Press, 2011).

[31] Different spellings of the names of Maroon groups are used in original sources and the research literature.

[32] Arends, *Language and Slavery*, pp. 35–99.

[33] André R. M. Pakosie, 'Maroon Leadership and the Surinamese State' (1996) 37–38 *Journal of Legal Pluralism & Unofficial Law* 263–277, at 264.

other and losing the sole source of individual or family subsistence. By escaping, fugitives from plantation slavery in Suriname also traded the considerable risks of being a slave[34] against another type of existential risk: being exposed to a hostile nature without secure provision of food and shelter, and being targeted for punishment or subjected to attempts at military annihilation by settler armies.[35] That apart, the very project of transitioning from a haphazardly configured group of escaped slaves into a functioning society of escapees could fail miserably. What if the act of escaping produced a dangerous life in solitude and intergroup strife rather than a relatively secure one within the mutuality of an emerging society? German industrial workers were recruited from different classes and areas, but in all cases a basic socialization had been achieved to a large degree at a point prior to recruitment. For plantation escapees, basic socialization was a labour yet to be done, illustrated by the emergence of a group-specific Maroon creole, integrating elements from African and colonial languages.[36] Abduction into slavery took place from different West African communities. Therefore, escapees could not necessarily fall back on earlier group identities. They had to build communities anew, forming what has been termed a socioterritorial movement.[37] The point of solidarity was exactly that: becoming *Loweman*, becoming Maroon.

There is another commonality, one that initially seems paradoxical. Without the German mining and steel industry, there was no worker solidarity. And, without the industry of plantations, no communities of solidarity among its slaves and escapees. What interests me is that nodal point where techno-social reorganization (in plantation slavery and the Second Industrial

[34] 'The Political Council did not consider the existing forms of punishment of runaway slaves (torture and, beginning in 1721, the death penalty) sufficiently dramatic: a new one was added which consisted in the severing of the Achilles tendons of the violator.' de Groot, 'Boni Maroon War', 38.

[35] Rolander documents how the crania of recaptured fugitive slaves were put on public display along riverbanks to illustrate the gravity of punishment awaiting those fleeing captivity. 'On the river-banks we saw in several places human skulls affixed to upright, wooden stakes. … It is the custom for black slaves who laid violent hand on themselves, or were caught having secret communications with the rebels or disloyal runaways … to suffer this kind of punishment.' *Rolander's Journal*, entry of 5 August, p. 1322.

[36] Van't Klooster et al. were able to show that Saramaccan Maroons used their ethnobotanical knowledge and native languages to name the flora in their new environment, with 39% of Saramaccan plant names being traceable to African origins. Charlotte I. E. A. Van't Klooster, Vinije Haabo, Margot van den Berg, Piet Stoffelen, and Tinde R. Van Andel, 'African Elements in Saramaccan Maroon Plant Names in Suriname' (2022) 100 *Botany* 141.

[37] The term 'socioterritorial movement' was suggested by Zavala Guillen to analyse processes within a Maroon-descendant community in Northern Columbia. Ana Laura Zavala Guillen, 'Maroon Socioterritorial Movements' (2022) 112 *Annals of the American Association of Geographers* 1123.

Revolution in Germany) tipped over into self-organization and solidarity (for Maroons and for German industrial workers, respectively). The slaves, as much as German industrial workers, were put out of the reach of existing regulation by the massive techno-social changes wrought by industrialization and globalization. Ironically, by forcing both groups into communal living arrangements, industrialists and plantation owners provided an indispensable condition for sparking political resistance. This holds, all differences notwithstanding.[38] The factor behind violent repression turned out to be the factor behind emancipatory solidarity.

Solidarity among German industrial workers expressed itself and was conditioned by what we might call associative agreements. These ranged from promises in informal settings to formal associations with statutes and financial contributions. I have labelled them as proto-law, filling an emergent space of solidarity with norms and rudimentary institutions. In the case of the Maroons, we lack sufficient sources to explore analogous proto-law within Maroon groups and, beyond the formation of Maroon creole, its linguistic carrier. We only know that inter-escapee solidarity was sufficient for a form of sociogenesis into several Maroon groups taking place, providing them with institutional structures and leadership hierarchies. These allowed the Maroon groups of Suriname to become parties to bilateral peace treaties with the Dutch colonial administration. Such treaties were concluded with three established Maroon groups: the Ndjuka (1760), the Saamaraka (1762) and the Matawai (1767).[39] They enabled the Maroon parties to adapt their life to peaceful conditions and to move to, or extend their power into, more prosperous areas. This came at a price, though. Of particular interest to me are clauses to the effect that the Maroon parties were to deliver all later runaway slaves to the slave masters.[40] This reformist move would, in effect, exclude future generations of fugitives, thwart an expansion of Maroon sociogenesis

38 For plantation slaves, the force of industrialization manifested itself in violent abduction and cruel forms of punishment which German workers were not subjected to. For the latter, the force of industrialization manifested itself in threats to the livelihood of their families and themselves.

39 Pakosie, 'Maroon Leadership', 265.

40 The Saramaka Peace Treaty concluded between the Saramaka Maroons and the Dutch colonial government on 19 September 1762 features a clause obliging the Maroon to return fugitives from slavery to the Dutch authorities in paragraph 4: 'They [the Saramaka Maroon] should return all the Blacks who have escaped or run away from the Whites since the Auka Maroons came to them with Willie … The treasurer shall pay them fifty guilders in Surinamese money … And all the runaway Blacks they return, the Governor or the Court shall be permitted to do anything they like with them …' [English translation from the Sranan original by Jaques Arends, in Arends, *Language and Slavery*, p. 331.]

and make the Maroon project sterile in the transformation of industrializing and globalizing politics. The Maroon agreed not to enter into negotiations with other groups, such as Amerindians, without permission of the colonial power, effectively depriving them of their capability to run their own foreign policy, as Pakosi notes.[41] The colonial power had effectively succeeded in making a repressive and appeasing state law that would curb the revolutionary potential of active solidarity – as German welfare laws did in conjunction with the prohibition of socialist association.

In all, the peace treaties were inducing no less than a form of counter-solidarity. This counter-solidarity was sufficiently effective to stop alliances between the established Maroon groups and the Boni Maroon, a relatively new group likely to have emerged during the first half of the eighteenth century.[42] As Dutch public records from the relevant period suggest, the Ndjuka Maroons assisted the Dutch in tracking down and fighting the Boni Maroon group.[43] The alliance projected in the treaties functioned in practice. It effectively introduced a rift between Maroon groups, with the binding power of a common past as forcibly displaced African fugitives proving insufficient to engender solidarity across these groups.[44]

The Maroons leveraged solidarity to establish a functioning social, political and legal community, with the element of communal life and work being decisive. Today, the six established Maroon groups 'remain distinct tribal entities whose autonomous political status finds support in eighteenth- and nineteenth-century peace treaties and in historical relations between the coastal government centre in Paramaribo and the leaders of the different tribes'.[45] This autonomy brings Aonghas St-Hilaire to draw the conclusion that, at least prior to the 1940s, the Surinamese Maroon formed a 'world system' of their own, as a minuscule alternative to the only other world system on offer: capitalism.[46] While there might be a seductive appeal in this special

41 Pakosie, 'Maroon Leadership', 266. In the Saramaka Peace Treaty, this obligation is laid down in paragraph 12: 'Never should they become allies with anybody, not with the Mapana Maroons or Auka Maroons, to do bad things to any White or to help them in any way to do bad things to the Whites.' Arends, *Language and Slavery*, p. 335.

42 For an extensive recapitulation of the Boni Maroon war based on Dutch records, see de Groot, 'Boni Maroon War'.

43 Ibid.

44 However, it is not clear exactly where the limits of countersolidarity was. Arends points out that 'Maroon groups, including the Saramaka, were continuously being supplemented by new arrivals, a process which continued even after the conclusion of peace treaties in the 1760s . . .'. Arends does not identify a source for his claim. Arends, *Language and Slavery*, pp. 98–99.

45 Aonghas St-Hilaire, 'Global Incorporation and Cultural Survival: The Surinamese Maroons at the Margins of the World-System' (2000) 4 *Journal of World-Systems Research* 101–131, at 102.

46 Ibid., 104.

status, its price tag is isolation and the inability to extend the reach of the Maroon political project.

While German workers remained within a system of labour exploitation and exercised solidarity on its inside, the Maroon left the plantations and placed their exercise of solidarity on the outside of the system of exploitation that had brought them together. While the German workers' remaining on the inside eventually resulted in Social Democracy and a long history of repetitive solidarity practices that grew together with the industries providing its base, the Maroon's outsider status disallowed solidarity to grow in tandem with the technology that brought it about and relinquished the Maroon to the status of external collaborators to colonial exploiters. I conclude that the sharing of a physical place by exploited labourers is a critical factor for the forming of a community in solidarity, yet that place needs to be on the inside of a politics of exploitation, if solidarity is to endure.

7.4 A SOLIDARITY MOMENT IN DATA SOCIETIES?

The case of the Maroon suggests that the juris-generative pattern behind the term 'solidarity' is not particular to production in certain European industrial centres and to the interaction between European industry workers, industrialists and states. The point of comparing the metropolitan case of Germany industry worker solidarity with the colonial case of Maroon solidarity was to test whether the four identified elements (industrialized communal living, public under-regulation of labour in revolutionized production in conjunction with resistant proto-law and repressive-appeasing state law) helps us to think about solidarity under conditions of AI and digitalization.

It can be argued without too much difficulty that we are indeed in a state of public under-regulation today, obtaining from an appropriation of social resources by digital entrepreneurs. Structurally, this situation is comparable to the one permitting British and Dutch slave traders and plantation owners to exploit a normative environment infamously framed as *terra nullius*.[47] To be

[47] The doctrine of terra nullius is associated with British attempts to extend imperial rule over the sea to imperial rule over other continents, famously articulated in John Donne's 1622 *terra nullius* conceptualization, extending to cases where 'the [original, GN] inhabitants doe not in some measure fill the Land, so as the Land may bring foorth her increase for the vse of men: for as a man does not become proprietarie of the Sea, because hee hath two or three Boats fishing in it; so neyther does a man become Lord of a maine Continent, because hee hath two or three Cottages in the Skirts thereof'. John Donne, 'A Sermon vpon the Eight Verse of the First Chapter of the Acts of the Apostles. Preached To the Honourable Company of the Virginia Plantation, 13th of Novemb. 1622, by Ionne Donne Deane of Saint Pauls' (1624) *STC* 922.21, at 26. For an account of the terra nullius doctrine in British colonial expansion, see Patricia

sure, ascribing the quality of *terra nullius* to plantation colonies did not imply that the public lawmaker of the British empire should engage in the regulation of newly appropriated territories. Rather, private interests setting up and operating plantations were laying down their own norms as they went along. The massive collection of data by private companies assisted by the United States[48] and China today resonates to quite a degree with the acquisition of colonial resources by private companies in the heyday of plantation colonialism.[49] So does the fact that 'frontier AI' is largely subject to self-regulation by the industry itself.[50] When EU regulators stray too far into the *terra nullius* appropriated by digital entrepreneurs, technological monarchs threaten to sanction the EU by withdrawing technology from its jurisdiction.[51]

However, it appears that under-regulation is the only straightforward commonality that links plantation slavery and the industrial revolution with AI and digitalization. At face value, it is hard to identify forms of communal living in AI and digitalization coeval with the upheaval and reorganization of human life and work that is characteristic for plantation slavery and the industrial revolution. Both pushed or forced human labourers into an amalgam of

Springborg, 'Hobbes, Donne and the Virginia Company: Terra Nullius and "The Bulimia of Dominium"' (2015) 36 *History of Political Thought* 113.

48 Brännström and others argue that '[t]he global free flow of data is an intrinsic aspect of informational capitalism. Assuming a constitutive, but not commanding role for law in informational capitalism, we conclude that the US attempt at ensuring free flow for its informational corporations is neither an entirely contingent nor a necessary outcome. It is a product of legal imagination.' In the politics of data flows, it is notable that attempts by the Global South to shape a solidaristic system based on informational sovereignty has so far been met by the countersolidarity of Western actors insisting on the primacy of IP law. Leila Brännström, Markus Gunneflo, Gregor Noll and Amin Parsa, 'Legal Imagination and the US Project of Globalising the Free Flow of Data' (2023) 39 *AI & Society*, available at: https://doi.org/10.1007/s00146-023-01732-y (last accessed 20 August 2024), quotation taken from the abstract.

49 See, e.g. Stern, *The Company-state*. A more recent example of public–private role divisions in colonization are the erstwhile German 'protectorates' in the Pacific, which were dominated by trading companies during their initial phase at the end of the nineteenth century, until the catastrophic consequences of the private model brought the German government to assert itself at the turn to the twentieth century. See Hermann J. Hiery, *Fa'a Siamani: Germany in Micronesia, New Guinea and Samoa 1884–1914* (Wiesbaden, Germany: Harrassowitz Verlag, 2020).

50 Cristina Criddle and Madhumita Murgia, 'Tech Alliance in AI Sandards Push to Fill "Gap" in Regulation', *Financial Times*, 25 October 2023, available at: www.ft.com/content/32e2b696-4677-4ba8-a93f-59927e1af2a2 (last accessed 14 September 2024).

51 George Hammond and Scott Chipolina, 'Sam Altman's Vision for AI Puts Him on Collision Course with Regulators', *Financial Times*, 25 July 2023, available at: www.ft.com/content/1d1cb2b3-391c-4dc8-ba5b-fedd379b7fb0 (last accessed 14 September 2024).

communal living and working conditions, which turned out to be a critical enabler of solidarity.[52]

In the European power struggles since the advent of industrialization, the question of which level of integration between life and work is required for political self-organization is, I would argue, central. To corroborate that, let us revert to German workers' solidarity and consider the point at which conflicts on industrial work and industrial politics came to a head. During the 1918–1920 German revolutions, worker and soldier councils grabbed power locally and regionally – in all instances, power was lost as fast as it had been won. Worker and soldier councils offered themself as a logical culmination of the solidarity structures brought forth by working and living communally. Harry Graf Kessler, a German intellectual, reports a private discussion in the immediate aftermath of the short-lived Munich council revolution of April 1919 in his diary:

> Cassirer, who arrived from Munich yesterday, reported about the council revolution. ... Discussion with Breitscheid and Cassirer about the council system deep into the night. My justification for the council constitution: an enterprise can be represented because it is a communal form of life [*Lebensgemeinschaft*], whereas an electoral ward is not a communal form of life; district-based elections are paper elections in which voters lack the requisite information to judge the elected. ... Cassirer denied that communal forms of life emerge in today's factories. On the contrary, machines would turn humans into isolated atoms.[53]

Janus-like, the machinic character of industrialism toggles between enabling, and subsequently destroying, worker solidarity, with the degree of communality it permits in both living and working being a decisive factor. Here, the technological, the social and the political play out as facets of one and the same phenomenon. Exactly how technology and accumulation articulate the communality of life and work determines the extent of solidarity. This is an important lesson to be learned from European industrialism, even though Cassirer and other pessimists of the 1920s were proven wrong: workers were still capable to stage extensive strikes in Western Europe during the Cold War, which suggests that the machine did not fully render humans into isolated atoms.

[52] Other authors believe that digital platforms are providing a sufficient basis for the emergence of solidarity today. See, e.g. Chapter 8, by Herzog.

[53] Harry Graf Kessler, *Aus den Tagebüchern 1918–1937* (München: Deutscher Taschenbuch-Verlag, 1965), p. 81 [translation by Daniel Steuer and the author]. In the quote, Kessler's interlocutor is Paul Cassirer, a Berlin art dealer.

Compared to the machines of the 1920s, the machine of AI and digitalization is capable of dismantling communal work and life to a different order of magnitude. Digitalization is capable of disintegrating the experience of human communality even where humans share a joint physical space. AI delivers a specific contribution to that process, breaking down, as it does, human life and work into fragmented behaviours, subjected to tracking, probabilistic prediction and partial automation. 'Big data does subjects differently', as Marie Petersmann and Dimitrii Van Den Meersche point out, making them fluid and relational.[54] This fluidity may work against solidarity. Evidence from Kazakh digital platform couriers and Filipino online entrepreneurs corroborate that the degree of communality in their work and life is insufficient to engender resistance arising from the solidarity of protolegal contracting.[55] By contrast, where digital workers share the same workplace, unionization is attempted, as 2023 reporting on Meta content moderators in Nairobi shows: Filtering some of the internet's most horrific content with an average handling time of 55 seconds per task, moderators developed signs of trauma, founded a union and took their employer to court for subjection to digital sweatshop conditions.[56] The 2016 strike of London Deliveroo riders, known as the 'first strike of the platform economy', also suggests the centrality of a common physical workplace for the emergence of solidarity, even if it is as extensive as a large city.[57]

54 Marie Petersmann and Dimitrii Van Den Meerssche, 'On Phantom Publics, Clusters, and Collectives: Be(com)ing Subject in Algorithmic Times' (2023) 39 *AI & Society* 107–124, at 110.

55 Drawing on qualitative field research in Kazakhstan in 2016 and 2021, Sabina Insebayeva and Serik Beyssembayev studied labour conditions and resistance action by platform couriers, noting the occurrence of strikes, but also workers' limited leverage to change the system, concluding that 'it is too early to discuss the formation of a labour community' (at 76). Sabina Insebayeva and Serik Beyssembayev, 'Digital Platform Employment in Kazakhstan: Can New Technologies Solve Old Problems in the Labor Market?' (2023) 103 *International Labor and Working-Class History* 62. In their research on how digital workers in a Global South context experience precarity, Soriano and Cabañes observe that the main venue for exchange among Filipino online entrepreneurs are Facebook groups, that remain unable to 'enact ... substantial pressure upon platforms to address oppressive conditions'. Cheryll Ruth R. Soriano and Jason Vincent A. Cabañes, 'Entrepreneurial Solidarities: Social Media Collectives and Filipino Digital Platform Workers' (2020) 6 *Social Media + Society* 1–11, at 9.

56 David Pilling and Madhumita Murgia, '"You Can't Unsee It": The Content Moderators Taking on Facebook', *Financial Times*, 18 May 2023, www.ft.com/content/afeb56f2-9ba5-4103-890d-91291aea4caa (last accessed 16 September 2024).

57 While Deliveroo subdivided the city of London into different zones, its London riders overcame these divisions and gathered for a six-day wildcat strike in front of the London head office of the company, arranging impromptu mass meetings. Jamie Woodcock and Callum Cant, 'Platform Worker Organising at Deliveroo in the UK: From Wildcat Strikes to Building Power' (2022) 25 *Journal of Labor and Society* 220. For an overview of delivery platforms and

The question driving this chapter is whether solidarity is possible in societies characterized by the exchange of data, under conditions of digitalization and AI. The early evidence we have on solidarity in data societies confirms the centrality of communal life and work in a shared physical space. Much will depend on which data societies develop, but it is safe to say that digital technologies provide ample opportunity for a counter solidarity politics of *divide et impera*.

7.5 CODA: WHO IS THE AGENT OF SOLIDARITY?

Reviewing mainly French solidarism literature as it presented itself at the outset of the twentieth century, Célestin Bouglé identified original sin as the common base of conceptualizations of solidarity.[58] Within Christianity, the fall is an experience common to all mankind by virtue of being the progeny of Adam and Eve. It gives solidarity its conceptual contours through a negative referent: the *absence* of community with god enacted in the eviction from paradise. This is a version of solidarity that maximizes inclusion: solidarity is but the experience of absent community with the divine, communalized across mankind as a whole.[59]In this reading, every human is an agent of solidarity.

The universal aspiration of cybernetics and digital technologies maximizes inclusion in a similar way. Cybernetics imply that capitalism expands through an unprecedented level of abstraction (as argued by Timothy Erik Ström[60]). And, as almost everyone utilizes a digital platform and generates data, everyone seems to be a data worker, or, in Varoufakis' more polemical terminology, a 'cloud serf': 'The true revolution cloud capital has inflicted on humanity is the conversion of billions of us into willing cloud serfs volunteering to labour for nothing to reproduce cloud capital for the benefit of its owners'.[61] For us all as cloud serfs, Varoufakis considers modes of resistance that are characterized by low risk-taking on the individual level, such as consumer boycotts of a particular platform provider, such as Amazon. He sets this off from the high-

organizing migrant workers in London and Berlin, see Oğuz Alyanak, Callum Cant, Tatiana López Ayala, Adam Badger and Mark Graham, 'Platform Work, Exploitation, and Migrant Worker Resistance: Evidence from Berlin and London' (2023) 34 *The Economic and Labour Relations Review* 667.

58 Célestin Bouglé, *Le Solidarisme* (Paris: Libraries-Editeurs, 1907), p. 13, crediting Joseph de Maîstre's political theology as a base for relating solidarity to original sin.

59 Chapter 12, by Karageorgiou, offers a reading of solidarity through the Christian tradition of agape, pivoting on the community with the divine.

60 Timothy Erik Ström, 'Capital and Cybernetics' (2022) 135 *New Left Review* 22.

61 Yanis Varoufakis, *Technofeudalism. What Killed Capitalism* (New York: Vintage, 2023), p. 79.

risk strategies of earlier industry workers engaging in strikes that put their livelihood on the line.[62] This seems to underplay the difficulties of effectively organizing such actions on a politically significant scale and over a politically significant period of time.

Other contemporary writers are no less affected by the lure of extending the group of solidarity agents conceptually. In their 2018 study on digital solidarity, Horan Lee and Ronald Staples first make existing solidarity conceptions more capacious to then capture solidarity phenomena in digital work life with it.[63] While this keeps solidarity in the game at the verbal level, it ends up in mere stipulation, with a perennial promise of political potential – but actual political impotence. If everybody is potentially an agent of solidarity, the difficulty moves instead to the question of what exactly it is that we need to do 'in solidarity' to change an exploitative techno-economic system.

I have gone in a reductive direction and sought out a minimalist conception of solidarity as a trigger point for resistance. The factor of communal life and work proved to be pivotal in the tracking of protolegal solidarity.[64] The advantage of a minimalist solidarity concept is that it keeps close to historical transformations of plantation and industry capitalism. Thereby, it remains sensitive to the question whether capitalism is approaching the end of its road in cybernetic technology, or whether we are just in for another round of abstraction, and another round for solidarity. Epochal framing is but an aspect of methodological framing. If we assume that capitalism prevails beyond the changes wrought by cybernetics (and, as it were, the heritage of industrial emissions), then it is only solidarity in this known form that has come to the end of the road. However, it might also be the epoch of capitalism itself that has come to the end of the road, once the reformative safety valve of solidarity is no longer accessible.

62 Ibid., p. 179. The dimension of risk in solidarity is explored in Chapter 2, by Scholz.

63 Horan Lee and Ronald Staples, 'Digitale Solidarität Unter Arbeitnehmer*innen' (2018) 25 *Industrielle Beziehungen/The German Journal of Industrial Relations* 495.

64 In his attempt to liberate the study of solidarity from its European 'trade union fetishism', Atzeni suggests that we consider the formation of collectives instead: 'This methodological shift would help to recover a truly multidisciplinary lens in studies of collective labour and to incorporate, for instance, the contributions made, particularly, by the Marxist social movements studies tradition to illustrate the different, non-trade union dynamics of working-class organization, or the human geography perspectives taking account of territoriality in the shaping of collective organization. This shift would force researchers going beyond the study of the organization per se to actively document how labour processes, geography of production, gender, race, and ethnic differences and dominant patterns of governance impact upon collective labour identities' [References omitted]. Maurizio Atzeni, 'Workers' Organizations and the Fetishism of the Trade Union Form: Toward New Pathways for Research on the Labour Movement?' (2021) 18 *Globalizations* 1349.

8

Transnational Worker Solidarity after the Pandemic

LISA HERZOG

8.1 INTRODUCTION

"Solidarity" is often evoked as the modern heir of "fraternity," and described as a necessary complement to freedom and equality. A sense of belonging, and a willingness to stand up for each other, is needed to counterbalance the centrifugal forces of equal freedom. Solidarity is needed for fighting for the rights of those whose freedom is not yet quite equal. But who can be solidaristic with whom? And how can solidarity be more than an abstract slogan, and lead to real action and social change? In this chapter, I ask these questions regarding solidarity among workers, and in particular among workers who are part of global value chains.[1] Historically, worker solidarity has been crucial for improving the legal status and the material conditions of members of the working class. Such improvements are also urgently needed in today's world. I will argue that recent changes in technological possibilities, digital habits, and working conditions have opened up new opportunities,

I wrote this chapter as a researcher situated in the Global North, mostly familiar with forms of solidarity that exist in Europe. I cannot claim to have full insight into the perspectives and challenges of individuals situated in the Global South. I am deeply grateful to those from whom I have learned more about the situation of workers in the Global South, especially Neera Chandhoke and Flávia Máximo. I would also like to thank Ranyta Yusran for her very valuable comments and reading tips, especially about worker solidarity in the Global South, at the workshop in Gothenburg in August 2022. I also thank the other participants for their comments and questions.

[1] I assume that there will continue to be global value chains, even though they might be reconfigured given the current geopolitical challenges, with some production processes being nationally reintegrated.

especially for what I call "solidarity along value chains," as a sub-form of transnational worker solidarity.

In the face of the global economy we live in, one might wonder why we do not see more signs of "transnational worker solidarity" or "labor transnationalism." It does, after all, have a long history, both in the Global North and in the Global South, with examples of solidarity actions ranging from support for anti-colonial movements to anti-fascist struggles.[2] Dockworkers and seafarers often played a particularly important role in such activities. For example, in a famous solidarity strike in the 1940s, Australian, Chinese, and Indian maritime workers in Australian ports boycotted ships transporting cargo and weapons to Dutch colonizers in solidarity with the Indonesian struggle for independence from Dutch colonial rule.[3] A particularly interesting case is the "Industrial Workers of the World," a radical syndicalist union association which, since its founding in 1905, had an internationalist and anti-racist outlook, working frequently with immigrant workers and also organizing across borders.[4] In recent years, unions have tried to grasp the opportunities of online communication for sharing information and campaigning between countries.[5] Sociological analyses of historical cases in the Global North can be found mostly in "Global Labour Studies," which grew out of the earlier approach of "New International Labour Studies."[6]

However, as Katherine Nastovski argues, "the conceptualization of labour transnationalism within scholarship remains ambiguous and imprecise in its

[2] See e.g. David Featherston, *Solidarity: Hidden Histories and Geographies of Internationalism* (London: Zed Books, 2012). On the history of the International Trade Union Committee of Negro Workers, see Holger Weiss, *Framing a Radical African Atlantic* (Leiden: Brill, 2014); on transnational collaboration between unions within Europe, see Katarzyna Gajewska, *Transnational Labour Solidarity: Mechanisms of Commitment to Cooperation within the European Trade Union Movement* (London: Routledge, 2009).

[3] Heather Goodall, *Beyond Borders: Indians, Australians and the Indonesian Revolution, 1939 to 1950* (Amsterdam: Amsterdam University Press, 2018), especially chapter 6.

[4] Peter Cole, David Struthers, and Kenyon Zimmer (eds.), *Wobblies of the World: A Global History of the IWW* (London: Pluto Press 2017) or Verity Burgmann, *Revolutionary Industrial Unionism: The Industrial Workers of the World in Australia* (Cambridge: Cambridge University Press, 1995).

[5] See e.g. Thorsten Geelan and Andy Hodder, "Enhancing Transnational Labour Solidarity: The Unfulfilled Promise of the Internet and Social Media" (2017) 48 *Industrial Relations Journal* 345, on "Union Solidarity International," an example I discuss in Section 8.3.

[6] Katherine Nastovski, "Transnational Labour Solidarity and the Question of Agency: A Social Dialectical Approach to the Field" *Labor History*, online first, 1. See also Susanne Pernicka, Vera Glassner, Nele Dittmar, and Adam Mrozowicki, "When Does Solidarity End? Transnational Labour Cooperation during and after the Crisis: The GM/Opel Case Revisited" (2017) 38 *Economic and Industrial Democracy* 375 for an overview of different approaches.

use."[7] Drawing on philosophical literature on solidarity can throw new light on this question. I use the conceptual framework developed by Sally Scholz in order to reflect on transnational worker solidarity. I am interested in forms of worker solidarity that lead not merely to vague expressions of sympathy, but to active engagement (in whatever concrete form it can take in a given context). For, as one union leader put it, "The idea of international solidarity, as good as it sounds, means nothing unless you can develop specific actions."[8] Therefore, I start by looking at the social conditions that contributed to worker solidarity being such a powerful force in certain historical periods, and ask whether they can teach us anything for the present situation. I argue that historical forms of labor solidarity often brought together what Sally Scholz calls "social" and "political" solidarity: solidarity based on shared features and belonging, and solidarity oriented towards shared goals.[9] The globalization of many value chains has undermined the conditions for this overlap.

But the extensive use of digital technologies for connecting people, which was widely practiced during the pandemic lockdowns in many countries in 2020–2021, opens up new opportunities in this regard, especially for solidarity along value chains where workers might already be digitally connected.

In Section 8.2, I use Scholz's distinction between different types of solidarity to argue that historical cases of successful worker solidarity could often combine social and political forms of solidarity. I also draw on some economic and psychological considerations that help explain how worker organizations could bring about solidaristic *action*. I then discuss why, despite various reasons for pessimism, transnational worker solidarity remains highly relevant for today. I discuss the opportunities of digital technologies that allow individuals not only to share information, but also to connect across geographies, potentially leading to a renewal of the kind of overlap between social and political solidarity that had historically been so powerful. But, often, these opportunities cannot be developed because of legal obstacles (e.g. companies blocking contacts). Therefore, I conclude by postulating that workers should have a right to "know their colleagues," such that those who already work together as a matter of fact, but are separated geographically, can connect in ways that can, potentially, lead to strong forms of solidarity.

7 Nastovski, "Transnational Labour Solidarity and the Question of Agency," 2; her own aim is to develop a critical approach on the basis of theories from economic geography.

8 Phillip Jennings, general secretary of the International Federation of Commercial, Clerical and Technical Employees, quoted in Andrew Herod, "The Practice of International Labor Solidarity and the Geography of the Global Economy" (1995) 71 *Economic Geography* 341.

9 Sally Scholz, *Political Solidarity* (University Park: Penn State University Press, 2008), esp. chapters I–III.

8.2 HISTORICAL WORKER SOLIDARITY: SOCIAL AND POLITICAL

"Solidarity" contains the Latin stem *solidus*, which means "strong" or "solid." At the core of the concept, there is the idea that certain individuals have strong bonds among each other that make them aware of shared interests or shared goals. But the term gets used in widely varying ways: from the historical use of "working class solidarity," to its use in Catholic social doctrine or liberation theology, to online petitions that claim to be "in solidarity with" a certain cause. There have been many attempts to provide classifications of types or dimensions of solidarity, in both the social sciences and philosophy. I here draw on Sally Scholz's distinction between social, civic, and political solidarity (but civic solidarity will not play a major role in my argument), which builds on previous conceptualizations and provides a useful framework.

All concepts of solidarity, Scholz argues, assume that solidarity "mediate[s] between the community and the individual,"[10] consists of a "form of unity" between people,[11] and "entails positive moral obligations."[12] *Social* solidarity can be described as "a measure of interdependence among individuals within a group"; in other words, here it is group membership that matters.[13] *Civic* solidarity describes membership in a civic organization – typically a state – in which certain institutions ensure that every member has access to the minimum provisions that are needed for civic participation.[14] The paradigmatic form of this type of solidarity is the welfare state; solidarity is here implemented in clear institutional structures with ensuing rights and duties for individuals. *Political* solidarity, lastly, focuses on a "mutually shared vision," a goal that individuals want to achieve together, typically in opposition to some common enemy or opponent.[15] This opens up the possibility of engagement by groups who are not themselves the victims of the injustices or forms of oppression in question, although, for their solidarity to be genuine, they must fulfil certain conditions, for example that they acknowledge the epistemological and moral privilege of the victims of oppression.[16] Finally, Scholz also points out that there are sometimes uses of the term "solidarity" that are "parasitic" on genuine forms, which lack important elements of the latter and are used as

[10] Ibid., p. 18.
[11] Ibid., p. 19, see also p. 43.
[12] Ibid., p. 19.
[13] Ibid., p. 21.
[14] Ibid., p. 29.
[15] Ibid., p. 34.
[16] Ibid., chapter V, esp. pp. 165–172.

rhetorical devices, in cases in which it would be more appropriate to use other terms, such as "sympathy."[17]

As emphasized in Section 8.1, I am mostly interested in forms of solidarity that involve active engagement – "strong" forms of solidarity, in Scholz's terminology.[18] In what follows, I argue that many paradigmatic forms of solidarity, especially in the history of the labor movement, were characterized by a *combination* of social and political solidarity, and that this fact probably contributed to their success, a claim that I undergird by arguments from psychology and social theory. Of course, this does not mean that solidarity would have been an *automatic* result of these relatively favorable circumstances. Solidarity still had to be enacted by individuals who took on leadership roles, and whose contributions I certainly do not want to belittle. But if, following E. P. Thompson and others, one understands class as not a "thing" but something that is "happening," one needs to pay attention to how these processes were situated "within everyday life and social relations."[19]

A stylized picture of the historical circumstances in which workers in Europe and North America, in the nineteenth and early twentieth century, lived and work, looks roughly like this. Individuals worked together, physically, in direct contact with each other.[20] In many occupations (e.g. in mining) they *had* to rely on each other, for their own physical safety and in order to get the job done. In addition, they often also lived together: before the era of mass transportation, individuals had to live in walking distance from their workplaces. Worker settlements would therefore often spring up in the direct neighborhoods of mines or factories, and, while the living conditions were often gruesome, they also brought people closely together and created shared interests (e.g. in relation to local public goods).

Ken Loach's movie *Jimmy's Hall* provides a sense of these historical conditions (of course with some artistic license but based on historical facts). In this movie, communist Jimmy Gralton returns to his native village in Ireland after having spent 10 years in the United States. He brings with him "modern," democratic ideas that the local authorities (the mayor, the factory owner, the priest) abhor. Jimmy hears from young people in the neighborhood that they

[17] Ibid., pp. 46–48.

[18] Ibid., p. 14.

[19] Nastovski, "Transnational Labour Solidarity and the Question of Agency," p. 7.

[20] Even earlier forms of labor solidarity can, arguably, be found in the European guilds; however, they also had many exclusionary effects. See e.g., Anthony Black, *Guilds and Civil Society in European Political Thought from the Twelfth Century to the Present* (Ithaca, NY: Cornell University Press, 1984) or Sheilagh Olive, *The European Guilds: An Economic Analysis* (Princeton, NJ: Princeton University Press, 2019).

need a space for gatherings: for entertainment but also for educational and artistic activities. To respond to this need, he establishes a local center, "Jimmy's Hall," that quickly becomes popular and buzzes with activities. But the conservative resistance grows and one night, the hall is burned down; Jimmy Gralton gets deported back to the United States.

Another historical account, from an urban context, can be found in Sara Horwitz's narrative about her family's involvement in New York unionism in the early twentieth century.[21] Horwitz portrays the close-knit communities of immigrant garment workers, and describes how early unionists, such as her grandfather, fought for better responses to the workers' needs, such as access to health care and better housing. The activism often ran in families, and Horowitz – a successful organizer of New York freelancers – credits her own family background for her understanding of strategies of organizing.

Using the lens of Scholz's framework, we can see how, in these historical cases, social and political solidarity overlapped to a great extent. Workers were members of the same communities, based on shared working experiences, everyday geography, and sometimes shared immigration backgrounds. Often, sheer necessity probably forced individuals to help each other out when it came to everyday needs. In addition, there were clear shared goals, in the sense of political solidarity, and also shared enemies: often local employers but also local authorities, as in the case of *Jimmy's Hall*. This situation was a contingent consequence of the state of technology and work organization: the presence of factories in which workers would find employment, but the absence of cheap means of transportation, which meant that they had to live close to their workplaces. And, of course, this kind of closeness can also bring conflicts, for example, over local resources. But, overall, it is likely that it created situations in which individuals had far more to gain than to lose by joining forces.

This overlap of social and political solidarity, under conditions of geographical and social closeness, led to a number of psychological and practical conditions that facilitated active forms of political solidarity. A first factor is *trust*: high levels of familiarity offer the breeding ground for relationships of trust among individuals, and these in turn make it more likely that they are willing to take risks, or pay a price, for furthering each other's interests.[22] A second factor is epistemic *salience*: if people live and work close to each

[21] Sara Horowitz, *Mutualism: Building the Next Economy from the Ground up* (New York: Random House, 2021), chapters 1–2.

[22] On the philosophical dimensions on trust, see e.g. the chapters in Judith Simon (ed.), *The Routledge Handbook of Trust and Philosophy* (London: Routledge, 2020).

other, each other's well-being and interests will be obvious for them, and they get reminded of them every day. Being indifferent to the fate of a co-worker, say in a case of chronic sickness, is psychologically far less likely if this co-worker is someone one runs into on a daily basis. Of course, this may not be *sufficient* to understand one's common fate and the common membership in a "class." And yet, the ground on which the seeds of class consciousness can fall, to put it metaphorically, seems relatively fertile, epistemically speaking.[23]

An undergirding explanation from social theory is that – putting it into economic jargon – the *transaction costs* for solidaristic action are low, in at least two senses. First, the transaction costs for gathering information about people's grievances were low because it was easy to speak to each other, or to directly see which problems someone suffered under. The risk of misinformation and misunderstandings that many contemporary attempts of "global solidarity" run – that those who want to "show solidarity" actually do not quite know what the other side needs and wants – was unlikely to be relevant in such circumstances. Second, the transaction costs for organizing were also low, in the sense that word of mouth could travel quickly and that it was obvious where to meet if one wanted to join forces.[24] For the latter issue, the concept of "focal point" is a good starting point. Thomas Schelling has introduced this concept for describing points of coordination that different parties would know about, without even having to explicitly communicate about them – such as when a meeting "in New York" would be assumed to be at the central station at 12 o'clock.[25] Workers living and working together in close-knit communities would very easily find "focal points" for joint action. They would, after all, face up to very similar obstacles, created by the same opponents, often the company they worked for. Of course, workers' struggles were also embedded in international networks, as the case of *Jimmy's Hall* also shows, with the protagonist bringing ideas from the United States to Ireland. Another famous example was Frederick Douglas touring in Ireland and Great Britain in the 1840s to campaign for an end to slavery.[26] And yet, the overlap

[23] See also Charles Heckscher and John McCarthy, "Transient Solidarities: Commitment and Collective Action in Post-Industrial Societies" (2014) 52 *British Journal of Industrial Relations* 627–657, at 630.

[24] Of course, as the example of *Jimmy's Hall* – with the need for a public venue – shows, there were not necessarily good meeting facilities for, for example, longer discussions. But there were shared and known public spaces in which individuals could communicate with one another, without the need for any further medium of communication.

[25] Thomas C. Schelling, *The Strategy of Conflict* (Cambridge, MA: Harvard University Press, 1960).

[26] David Featherston, *Solidarity: Hidden Histories and Geographies of Internationalism* (London: Zed Books, 2012), p. 1.

of social and political forms of solidarity, and the practical advantages it brought, arguably contributed to the successes that the workers' movement made in the late nineteenth and early twentieth century.[27]

Today, the "working class" is much more scattered, along many dimensions: geographically, in terms of the legal situations that individuals face, and also in terms of lifestyles and mentalities.[28] At least this follows if one assumes that a precariously employed adjunct professor in the United States, an Indian "clickworker" for Amazon Mechanical Turk,[29] and a cleaner in Europe are all members of the "working class." In what follows, I will not discuss the various ideological and political changes that challenge the very meaning of "working class" today. Instead, I will focus on the problem of geographical spread among people who would, in other historical periods, have been direct colleagues. I am interested in the potentials of new technologies and the experiences of their use during the pandemic for connecting such individuals. Before, however, I want to briefly justify why one should think that the idea and practice of "worker solidarity" can still be relevant today.

8.3 WHY WORKER SOLIDARITY IS STILL NEEDED TODAY

Among empirical researchers, there are voices of both optimism and pessimism about the potentials for transnational worker solidarity.[30] Nobody, however, denies the great obstacles it faces. Why then, should one return to that old idea? Even if worker solidarity had been part of the answer to many social questions in the past, why think that it can still be part of the answer today? The converging point of different answers, I take it, is that in a globalized economy, the responses of workers need to be globalized as well.[31] Supply chains span the globe, with raw materials and products going through the hands of workers on different continents. Workers may even have the same

[27] I emphasize these behavioral, practical factors precisely in order to avoid problematic forms of essentialism around the notion of solidarity (see Featherstone, *Solidarity*, chapter 1, for a discussion).

[28] Heckscher and McCarthy, "Transient Solidarities," 634–635.

[29] Mary L. Gray and Siddharth Suri, *Ghost Work: How to Stop Silicon Valley from Building a New Global Underclass* (Boston: Houghton Mifflin Harcourt, 2019).

[30] Ronald Munck, "Workers of the World Unite (At Last)," *Great Transition Initiative* (April 2019), available at: www.greattransition.org/publication/workers-of-the-world-unite (last accessed September 19, 2024) and the other contributions that comment on his piece offer a good overview, with a preponderance of optimistic voices.

[31] See e.g. James Atleson, "The Voyage of the Neptune Jade: The Perils and Promises of Transnational Labor Solidarity" (2004) 85 *Buffalo Law Review* 87; or Katherine Nastovski, "Transnational Labour Solidarity as Transformative Practice: Reframing the Role of Labour Transnationalism" (2021) 12 *Global Labour Journal* 113–130, at 115.

employer, with the same logos and brand names travelling with the products. As one unionist put it, concerning relations between workers in the United States and Mexico: "If the companies are international now, we the workers must also be international. We are facing the same one – Driscoll's."[32]

I take it that these global webs of collaboration, created by the supply chains for specific products and services, provide structures around which transnational solidarity could, in principle, crystallize. Of course, there is also talk of "global solidarity" in a much broader and general sense, which is often meant to reach those most in need of support. But without any shared experiences, or reasons for why to be solidaristic with *this* rather than *that* group, it can be difficult to build networks that support strong forms of action, that is, actual protests or sympathy strikes, which require the willingness to accept certain risks.[33] Without such commonalities, today's globalized workforce is in the same situation that Simone de Beauvoir had described with regard to women, in contrast to workers: in closer proximity with their oppressors (employers and patriarchic men, respectively) than with each other.[34] For de Beauvoir, this was one of the reasons for why women by and large did not show a lot of solidarity with each other. Global capitalism, it could be said, provides the perfect "divide and conquer" strategy vis-à-vis workers, by spreading them out into different countries, with different lifestyles and worldviews, making invisible to them what they have in common and who their common opponents are.

And yet, in a kind of paradoxical dialectic, this same global capitalism also brings workers together. Of course, it does not bring all workers together – instead, it creates what Andrew Herod describes as "new geographies" in which, for example, "tech-savvy workers in plants across GM's corporate structure can easily make direct linkages with one another, sometimes even bypassing their national office altogether."[35] The very juxtaposition of "the local" versus "the global" – with the image of the latter being somehow on a "higher" scale than the former – gets upset in the complex networks of twenty-

32 Quoted in David Bacon, Rosa Luxemburg Stiftung, and Institute for Transnational Social Change, "'Your Liberation Is Linked to Ours' International Labor Solidarity Campaigns," *UCLA IRLE Reports* (2015), p. 21.

33 See Chapter 2, by Sally Scholz.

34 Simone de Beauvoir, *The Second Sex*, trans. C. Borde and S. Malovancy-Chevallier (New York: Vintage Books, 2009 [1949]), pp. 28–29. I thank Sally Scholz for pointing this parallel out to me.

35 Andrew Herod, "Contribution to GTI Roundtable 'Planetizing the Labor Movement'," *Great Transition Initiative* (April 2019), available at: www.greattransition.org/roundtable/workers-world-andrew-herod (last accessed September 19, 2024); see similarly Featherstone, *Solidarity*, pp. 52–56.

first-century production processes.[36] The same holds for the pressure points at which influence can be exercised: strikes by a handful of workers as neuralgic points in a corporation's logistics, for example, can have a massive influence on its global processes, whereas forms of protest in less strategically crucial places may not exert any pressure.

It is the potential of this kind of "solidarity along value chains" that I am interested in. It partly overlaps with *union*-based forms of transnational solidarity but is not necessarily identical. To provide a point of contrast, consider the case of "Union Solidarity International," a UK-based organization founded in 2010 to tap the potentials of the internet for union solidarity, as analyzed by Torsten Geelan and Andy Hodder.[37] It attempted to reach audiences across national borders, but not so much within specific value chains or within the same companies, facing the same problems. Its ultimate aim was to get people to become activists on the ground, in their specific situations.[38] While interesting in many ways, this approach is different from what I have in mind, which would focus on value chains in which individuals are *already* connected. Moreover – and this is a point to which I come back in Section 8.4 – this approach was mostly about sharing information, not so much about allowing people to directly interact and build connections.

Why could it be a promising strategy to focus on value chains? My suggestion is that they create spaces of common identity and common concern which, up to a point, can recreate the kind of overlap of social and political solidarity that many historical cases of working-class solidarity instantiated. Émile Durkheim famously argued that, in processes of divided labor, the meaning of an individual's work can only become visible if one takes into account the broader value chain. As he wrote:

> The division of labor supposes that the worker, far from remaining bent over his task, does not lose sight of those cooperating with him, but acts upon them and is acted upon by them. He is not, therefore, a machine who repeats movements the sense of which he does not perceive, but he knows that they are tending in a certain direction, toward a goal that he can conceive more or less distinctly. He feels that he is of some use …, his actions have goals beyond themselves … Thenceforth, however specialized … his activity may be, … he knows that his activity has a meaning.[39]

36 Ibid.

37 Geelan and Hodder, "Enhancing Transnational Labour Solidarity."

38 Ibid., p. 352.

39 Émile Durkheim, *The Division of Labor in Society*, trans by W. D. Halls (Los Angeles, CA: The Free Press, 2014), pp. 290–291, quoted in Tuğba Sevinç, "Three Approaches to Social Unity and Solidarity" (2019) *Critical Review of International Social and Political Philosophy*, online first, 14.

This sense of meaning can, arguably, be strengthened if individuals can connect to others across the value chain (and it might get lost if they cannot). If they can take action together, this can give them a sense of agency that is the very opposite of the feeling of powerlessness vis-à-vis global economic forces that has, according to many commentators, prepared the breeding ground for right-wing populism and xenophobia. While the latter are, of course, also among the *obstacles* for transnational worker solidarity,[40] their existence provides yet more reasons for returning to the question of transnational worker solidarity, in an attempt to provide alternative narratives and social practices.[41]

What form can transnational worker solidarity take? The traditional strategy of workers showing solidarity with each other across borders – in addition to many forms of sharing ideas and helping with organizing among union networks – is the "secondary" or "sympathy" strike or boycott. While not very often making big headlines in the media, such forms of worker solidarity have a long history, and have also regularly taken place in recent years (e.g. among dock workers).[42] Many of the more recent examples, however, took place between directly neighboring countries (such as the United States and Mexico). What still seems to be largely missing are actions that would follow, say, the value chain from rare metals extracted in mines in the Global South to electronic devices assembled in South East Asia and marketed and sold in the United States or Europe, or similar value chains in areas such as textiles or food. But this seems very possible, given that materials and products are already traveling between these countries and the meaning of the work of individuals in different countries is interrelated in the way Durkheim described. Workers in the Global North could then also help push for changes within such value chains at the points where this is most urgently needed, for example, insisting on labor standards among suppliers, or putting up pressure

[40] E.g. Peter Evans, "Contribution to GTI Roundtable 'Planetizing the Labor Movement'" *Great Transition Initiative* (April 2019), available at: www.greattransition.org/roundtable/workers-world-peter-evans (last accessed September 19, 2024).

[41] See also Nastovski, "Transnational Labour Solidarity as Transformative Practice," 124–125.

[42] For examples, see Atleson, "The Voyage of the Neptune Jade," who discusses various examples from the late nineteenth century to the present; as he points out, secondary strikes are illegal in certain countries (e.g. the UK and the US,ibid., 115), but not others (e.g. in certain Scandinavian countries, pp. 161–163). But, he argues, if the company against which the actions are taken is the same, the legal situation may be different and the strike may not be illegal even in countries in which it otherwise would (p. 164). See also Herod, "The Practice of International Labor Solidarity," for an example of international solidarity with US American workers who were threatened by union-busting activities; Bacon et al., "'Your Liberation Is Linked to Ours'," for five case studies of transnational worker campaigns between the United States, Canada and Mexico, or Pernicka et al., "When Does Solidarity End?" for cases of transnational worker solidarity within Europe (among workers of GM/Opel and Volkswagen).

against "forum shopping" on the part of companies with regard to labor standards.[43]

Thus, my suggestion is that "solidarity along value chains," as a specific form of transnational labor solidarity, can play an important role in today's globalized economic system, as a counterforce to globalized corporations and as providing an alternative to right-wing narratives. It can provide focal points for action, and it can benefit from, and in turn reinforce, workers' sense of being part of larger value chains that give meaning to their work.

I hasten to add, however, that I do not defend the claim that this would be the *only* form of global solidarity that is needed; for example, the role of consumers, who might boycott companies for violating labor or environmental standards, remains crucial, not least because of the impact that a withdrawal of purchasing power can have on companies.[44] I also agree with commentators who argue that labor unions must join forces with other transnational progressive movements.[45] But this does not undermine my central point, namely that the fact that work is already organized in transnational ways provides good reasons to ask how worker solidarity could follow these structures, thereby potentially becoming an integral part of the daily experience of work and the self-understanding of employees. In Section 8.4, I discuss what role new technologies could play for this purpose – for workers who work with digital technologies, but also for those who do not but have access to a smartphone in their private lives. I also consider what changes the COVID-19 pandemic experience has brought, and what obstacles this perspective reveals.

8.4 CAN TRANSNATIONAL WORKER SOLIDARITY BENEFIT FROM NEW TECHNOLOGIES?

The organization of global value chains has massively benefitted, in recent decades, from digital technologies: communication is based on online interactions, and goods are tracked by help of QR codes and other digital tools. And yet, from the perspective of individual workers, and also for consumers, the global economy often appears opaque: one does not understand how one's

43 In the EU, there are plans for supply chain liability of companies with regard to basic labor standards and human rights. This will open up a window of opportunity for workers and unions to hold companies to account – after all, they are among the groups most "in the know" about actual practices and hence in an interesting position vis-à-vis companies.

44 E.g. Valentin Beck, "Consumer Boycotts as Instruments for Structural Change" (2019) 36 *Journal of Applied Philosophy* 543.

45 E.g. Munck, "Workers of the World Unite (At Last)."

own work is connected to those of others, with whom one is, as a matter of fact, "collaborating," but without knowing it.[46] Knowledge about the human beings who prepare intermediate products, for example, hardly travels with them along the value chain. Those who transport goods, for example, the crews on cargo ships, are equally invisible to those who process, sell, or consume these goods.

Now, it is certainly no new idea to suggest that digital technologies could help connect workers along value chains, and also to final consumers who buy products or services. Information about products could easily be made available for everyone with a smartphone to access, for example, by typing a product number into an online form or scanning a QR code.[47] Moreover, email and chat programs could be used for workers to get in touch with each other – as they often already do when there are, for example, technical problems with a delivery. As mentioned earlier, organizations such as Union Solidarity International also use social media to share information among interested followers across national boundaries. Ethnographic research shows that individuals working for platforms such as Amazon Mechanical Turk also connect via social media, to share information about their work, to trade tricks about how to get the most out of the platform, or to simply say hi to each other at the beginning of their workdays.[48]

What I would like to suggest, however, is that the experiences during the 2020–2022 COVID-19 lockdowns have brought digital collaborations, and people's proficiency at connecting with each other online, to a new level – one that could potentially be a gamechanger for transnational worker solidarity. The reason is that they allow for connections that are (a) mutual, (b) allow for genuine building of trust, and (c) thereby can increase salience and contribute to active instead of passive forms of knowledge. Before I expand on each of these points, let me acknowledge that, of course, not all workers used digital tools in such ways during the lockdowns; those whose jobs

[46] The early Polanyi had described this problem as a lack of "overview," cf. e.g. Gareth Dale, *Karl Polanyi: The Limits of the Market* (Cambridge: Polity Press, 2010), pp. 9–14.

[47] E.g. Stephanie Watts and George Wyner, "Designing and Theorizing the Adoption of Mobile Technology-mediated Ethical Consumption Tools' (2011) 24 *Information Technology & People* 257.

[48] On workers on Amazon Mechanical Turk, see Gray and Suri, *Ghost Work*; see also, on digital communication among gig workers, David Maffie, "The Role of Digital Communities in Organizing Gig Workers" (2020) 59 *Industrial Relations* 123. On the potential of social media to create new forms of solidarity, see also Heckscher and McCarthy, "Transient Solidarities." Their focus, however, is on "weak ties," while my argument rests on the idea that, within value chains, workers could also develop "strong ties."

required physical presence continued to leave their homes, often at great risks to their health. But they would also often use such digital communication in their private lives, given that, in many countries, opportunities for private encounters were minimal during the lockdown. Thus, I am interested in the broader shifts of social habits triggered by the COVID-19 lockdowns, which brought the use of digital communication tools – most importantly, videocalls – into the mainstream of social life. Developments that were already happening as technology became cheaper and younger generations grew into digital habits as "digital natives" thus saw a massive push forward.

While a lot of information was, of course, already flowing digitally before the lockdowns, many more people started using digital tools such as videocalls or group chat programs in ways that allowed for much denser forms of communication, and in which a real mutual give and take of information could take place. Participating in such forms of communication is different from being a passive recipient: it allows sharing one's perspectives no matter where one comes from, and it allows for genuine dialogue, with the opportunity to ask questions, to clarify potential misunderstandings, or to work on joint proposals. Of course, linguistic differences can still be an obstacle, but the fast improvements in automatic translation systems can help here as well (at this point, this holds mostly for written communication, but it is also getting better in oral communication, e.g. with automatic subtitling in different languages). This matters for the possibilities of transnational worker solidarity because it allows individuals from different parts of the globe to understand how the other side thinks and what they truly need or want, and thus create better conditions for consciousness raising and the forging of alliances.

The risk of, for example, solidarity actions from the Global North misfiring or being perceived as insulting or patronizing, for a lack of genuine communication, is much lower if individuals can have a few videocalls beforehand to get to know each other and their perspectives. Moreover, in such forms of communication, individuals can understand whether there are potential or real conflicts between them, or whether they might be "played out" against each other by third parties, typically employers. The transaction costs for sharing such information are much lower than if they had to write letters or travel to each other's places.

The second point I want to put forward as a hypothesis is that such forms of communication – while certainly not the same as in-person encounters – can, over longer periods of time, help to build genuine trust between different parties. As many commentators on transnational worker solidarity emphasize, solidarity needs to be built from the ground up, without relying exclusively on "technocrats and trade union administrators."[49] Some programs in the past have relied on actual visits, e.g. a program in the Philippines in which workers and labor leaders were invited for 10 days to experience the realities of Filipino workers.[50] When unionists visit each other in their respective countries, they can get a much better sense of what is at stake in their joint struggles.[51] But, of course, the costs – in terms of money, but also time and energy – for such visits are often prohibitively high. It is, however, quite well imaginable to organize transnational online encounters, for example, with a mix of group events and one-on-one encounters, including – if desired – video tours of people's living quarters, again at relatively low transaction costs.

To be sure, the hypothesis that this can lead to the building of genuine trust ultimately has to be explored empirically. "2D" communication on screens is still not the same as "3D" encounters (and while one saves time and money compared to travel, longer online events are known to be exhausting as well). Digital communication does not, per se, overcome cultural differences, the awareness of, and respect for which, are often crucial.[52] And yet, the idea that a genuine sense of collegiality can develop between individuals who are digitally connected seems much less outlandish after the experiences of the corona lockdowns, where individuals often had no chance but to try, as best they could, to connect through online tools, not only with colleagues they already knew, but also with new ones. This sense of collegiality is, arguably, much closer to the historical situation of actually working (and often living) close to each other than the forms of (typically written) digital communication that predominated before the pandemic. It seems much more plausible to think that individuals would also be willing to take certain risks for each other – because they feel they can trust each other – when they have frequently interacted in videocalls than if they have just exchanged emails.

49 Immanuel Ness, Contribution to GTI Roundtable "Planetizing the Labor Movement," *Great Transition Initiative* (April 2019), available at: www.greattransition.org/roundtable/workers-world-immanuel-ness (last accessed September 19, 2024).

50 Kim Scipes, Contribution to GTI Roundtable "Planetizing the Labor Movement," *Great Transition Initiative* (April 2019), available at: www.greattransition.org/roundtable/workers-world-kim-scipes (last accessed September 19, 2024); he notes that "As far as I can ascertain, this is the only such program like this in the world."

51 Cf. Bacon et al., "'Your Liberation Is Linked to Ours'," p. 5, citing a Canadian unionist visiting Mexican workers in their homes, who said that "They invited us to their homes and cooked for us. I can't describe my feeling in seeing the conditions of their lives."

52 On the importance of respective cultural differences see also Pernicka et al., "When Does Solidarity End?," p. 391 – concerning a case study between Germany and Poland where, arguably, the cultural differences are not as massive as between other countries in completely different regions of the world.

This leads to my third point. Arguably, the new technological possibilities, and the social practices that are developing around them, are much more suitable for leading people to *active engagement* because the fate of others is more salient for them. Knowing that there is a concrete individual at the other side, with whom one has interacted and whose family members or pets have walked through calls, makes a difference for one's psychological situation. Arguably, it leads to a greater sense of responsibility and to a feeling of being accountable to the other person for one's actions or failures to act. Rationalizing one's own passivity by claiming that "it doesn't make a difference anyway" is more difficult if there is another person who will ask one about it, and to whom one would prefer to be able to say, "at least we have tried." Thus, while certainly not creating the same kind of intense embedded social relations that prevailed in certain historical periods for certain members of the working class, digital communication can potentially lead to a greater sense of connectedness and hence make action more likely, because individuals feel more responsible for each other.

Thus, my argument in a nutshell is this: new digital technologies and the social habits that are developing around them have the potential to give a new impulse to transnational worker solidarity, because they can create levels of connectedness and trust that are closer to those experienced by certain historical worker communities, for whom social and political solidarity – in Scholz's terms – overlapped. Some individuals may already be in touch on an almost daily basis, so the step from talking about production processes to talking about working conditions seems easy to take. Some companies run "buddy programs" across continents, in which employees encounter each other through video calls; unions can easily do the same. The technical possibilities are constantly growing, as is the ability and willingness of individuals worldwide to use these tools.[53]

Here, however, another obstacle becomes clear: companies' interests and workers' interests will only, at best, overlap partially when it comes to the use of digital technology for communication across boundaries. If value chains belong to one company, there may be an interest in communication that is tied to technical or logistical functionalities – but not necessarily in communication that has to do with working conditions, let alone solidaristic action among workers. The situation gets even more complicated if value chains are

[53] One challenge, however, which I here cannot discuss for reasons of scope, is the fact that many platforms are in the hand of (Western) companies that are not very trustworthy with regard to the way in which they use data. Ideally, video call platforms would be public infrastructures that every individual worldwide could use, without having to worry about privacy.

distributed across different companies. Employees (other than those working directly in the purchasing department) may not even be able to find out which companies the raw materials or intermediate products they work on are coming from. And for reasons of "tax optimization" or the avoidance of economic risks or legal liabilities, even value chains that could theoretically be in the hand of one company are often split in today's globalized economy, increasing fragmentation.[54]

As a result, individuals often cannot make the kinds of connections that digital technology would, in principle, allow – they simply do not know, and have no right to learn, with whom to make them. This could, in principle, be changed: one could introduce a right to get to know one's "co-workers" (appropriately defined in a concrete context) and for worker representatives from different countries to meet. At the moment, however, not even solidarity actions (e.g. strikes) are legally permitted in many countries.[55] It might be a first step for unions to push for such a right, and maybe also to collect and provide information about international company structures that individual workers could draw on.[56]

Such efforts might in fact tie in with efforts on the political level to regulate markets more and to create accountability in value chains. After decades of neoliberal hegemony, the need to rein in global markets has become more and more visible, and several countries, and notably also the European Union, are taking bolder steps to hold large companies accountable for basic labor and environmental standards in their global value chains.[57] But such attempts

54 To some extent, this happens even within countries. For example, individuals might be collaborating on a project but one has a permanent, unionized contract while another one works at far worse conditions at a temporary employment agency. See also, on "fissured" workplaces, David Weil, *The Fissured Workplace* (Cambridge, MA: Harvard University Press, 2017).

55 Atleson, "The Voyage of the Neptune Jade."

56 Cf. also Herod, "The Practice of International Labor Solidarity," 356, who mentions data bases about companies maintained by international trade secretariats that could be useful for "future solidarity campaigns."

57 See European Parliament, EPRS, Ionel Zamfir, "Towards a Mandatory EU System of Due Diligence for Supply Chains," PE 659.299 (October 2020), available at: www.europarl.europa .eu/RegData/etudes/BRIE/2020/659299/EPRS_BRI(2020)659299_EN.pdf (last accessed September 19, 2024). This initiative was preceded by a "supply chain law" in Germany, and also some earlier attempts, e.g. in the context of the regulation of illegal, unreported and unregulated fishing, to ban violations of labor standards in other countries, e.g. concerning slave labor on fishing ships (Georgi Gotev, "Thai Seafood Products Could be Banned in Europe, Warns MEP" *The Guardian* (London, July 23, 2015), available at: www.theguardian .com/global-development/2015/jul/23/thai-seafood-products-banned-europe-mep-gabriel-mato (last accessed September 19, 2024).

require enforcement mechanisms[58] – and worker solidarity along supply chains might play an important role in this context. Unions can join forces across borders to push for giving workers and their representatives a voice, to make it more likely that supply chain legislation can make a real difference for the lives of workers and contribute to a path of transformation.

8.5 CONCLUSION: TECHNOLOGICAL POSSIBILITIES, BUT NO TECHNOLOGICAL DETERMINISM

In this chapter, I have discussed renewed possibilities for transnational worker solidarity through the lens of different notions of solidarity, and by comparing historical constellations of worker solidarity with today's globally fragmented value chains. I have argued that, in certain historical constellations, it was the overlap of social and political solidarity that created a fruitful social, psychological, and practical starting point for union activism and other forms of worker solidarity. Today, with value chains spreading around the globe, commentators disagree about the hopes for reviving transnational worker solidarity. I side with the optimists, arguing that new possibilities of digital communication and the normalization of their use during the lockdown periods provide reasons for cautious optimism that similar levels of psychological connectedness and even trust could grow between people connected by digital means.

Let me emphasize once more that I am fully aware that such forms of connectedness would still not hold between *all* workers worldwide. Many informal workers in the Global South, for example, form no part of transnational value chains, and yet solidarity with them would be urgently needed. Here, digital technology might still offer opportunities, but the ways in which it could be used would need to follow a different logic than that of shared value chains. For example, it could consist in sharing technical solutions that allow workers to safely report labor standard violations via apps on their private phones.

However, we should not expect technological determinism to do the work. Digital technologies can only play the role I have ascribed to them if individual workers have a chance to connect to relevant others – and, often, companies have no interest in letting them know who these others are. Here, action is needed. Governments could, ideally, grant workers the right to get to

[58] On the need to overcome power asymmetries to fight decent work deficits in value chains, see also Mark Anner, "Three Labour Governance Mechanisms for Addressing Decent Work Deficits in Global Value Chains" (2021) 160 *International Labour Review* 613.

know their colleagues along international value chains. But pushing for the introduction of such right is, in turn, something that will probably require transnational worker solidarity. As they so often are, these are chicken and egg problems that require strategic organizing, which, again, technology as such cannot deliver. It will remain to be seen how strong the forms of solidarity that are based on digital connections will be when it comes to real political action. There are some interesting signs that there can indeed be more than just warm feelings: a letter written by Amazon mechanical Turk workers to Amazon boss Jeff Bezos,[59] or the launch of an app that allows tourists to book rooms in hotels that treat their maids well, an idea that started out in a WhatsApp group.[60] Maybe – hopefully – more can grow out of such forms of solidarity and organizing, to give new momentum to forms of solidarity that are, today, urgently needed.

59 Gray and Suri, *Ghost Work*, pp. 89–90 and 135–137.
60 Stephen Burgen, "Spanish Hotel Booking App to Show Working Conditions of Staff" *The Guardian* (London, September 1, 2021), available at: www.theguardian.com/world/2021/sep/01/five-stars-for-staff-working-conditions-on-new-hotel-booking-app (last accessed September 15, 2024).

9

Populism and Trans-national Solidarity

HARIS JAMIL, RICHARD JOYCE AND SUNDHYA PAHUJA

9.1 INTRODUCTION

In the book *For a Left Populism*, Belgian political theorist Chantal Mouffe takes up the challenge posed in 1988 by the Jamaican-British political and cultural theorist Stuart Hall to theorists and political actors on the left, to 'learn from Thatcherism'.[1] Hall – influenced himself by Mouffe's work with Argentine philosopher Ernesto Laclau[2] – did so by seeking to account for the ideological formations on which former British Prime-Minister Margaret Thatcher's neoliberal revolution depended. These formations led Hall to coin the term 'authoritarian populism'. He described this as 'an exceptional form of the capitalist state, which, unlike classical fascism, has retained most (though not all) of the formal representative institutions in place, and which at the same time has been able to construct itself around an active popular consent'.[3]

The authors are grateful to Ms Caitlin Murphy for research assistance. This chapter was written with the support of an Australian Research Council Discovery Project Grant: 'International Law and the Challenge of Populism'.

1 Chantal Mouffe, *For a Left Populism* (London: Verso, 2018), chapter 2, whose title 'Learning From Thatcherism' is also the title to the concluding chapter of Stuart Hall's *The Hard Road to Renewal: Thatcherism and the Crisis of the Left* (London: Verso 1988), chapter 19.

2 See, e.g. Ernesto Laclau and Chantal Mouffe, *Hegemony and Socialist Strategy: Towards a Radical Democratic Politics*, 2nd ed (London: Verso, 2001; originally 1985).

3 Hall, *The Hard Road to Renewal*, p. 42. Hall warned that the reflex in the left to label its opponents as 'fascist' risked missing 'precisely what is specific to this exceptional form of the crisis of the capitalist state by mere name calling'. For a contemporary argument on similar lines, see Samuel Moyn, 'Allegations of Fascism Distract from the Real Danger', *The Nation*, 18 January 2021, available at: www.thenation.com/article/society/trump-fascism/ (last accessed 27 June 2023). See also Corey Robin, 'Trump and the Trapped Country', *New Yorker*, 13 March 2021, available at: www.newyorker.com/news/our-columnists/trump-and-the-

In particular, Hall was interested in the modes by which an economic programme directed at benefitting the few was made sufficiently popular to garner electoral support. Central to this, Hall argued, was the patient and determined effort to construct a new common sense which combined authoritarian political and cultural values (what Hall called 'authoritarian popular morality') with neoliberal economics. In making this argument, Hall drew on the concept of ideological hegemony from Italian political philosopher Antonio Gramsci (which was also central to Laclau and Mouffe's work).

Understanding the complementary and contradictory elements of the forces which combined to produce, in Hall and Mouffe's terms, a 'hegemonic' common sense around neoliberal values is instructive today. While anger against the economic effects of neoliberalism may be a driver of populist disaffection, the modes of political identification and action favoured by right-wing populism tend to circle back in neoliberalism's support. Indeed, as economic inequality increases, the sense of fear and social dislocation which fuels authoritarian popular morality increases along with it. Authoritarian populism does nothing to ameliorate the cultural and material maladies of neoliberalism. Instead, the forms of politics it produces involve little more than a performative rejection of some parts of the 'system' but not the still-prevailing common sense and the economic system twinned with it. So, in the common sense of authoritarian populism, the opposition to international institutions takes the form of nativism – consistent with the reactionary, fearful, racist, homophobic and transphobic elements of authoritarian popular morality. To displace the fear and insecurity engendered by the economic system, it takes aim rhetorically and juridically, primarily at the right of racialized people to move across borders, but it does not challenge the mobility of capital. This produces a highly unstable political environment, capable only of intensifying the problems it creates.

The crisis does, however, produce an opportunity. Mouffe argues that the 'current crisis of the neoliberal hegemonic formation offers the possibility of intervening to establish a different order'.[4] Two lessons from the 1980s need to be heeded, in this respect, according to Mouffe. The first is that actors on the left cannot sit back 'passively expecting the deterioration of economic

trapped-country (last accessed 27 June 2023). For a deeper engagement with the relationship between international law and fascism, see Rose Parfitt, *The Process of International Legal Reproduction: Inequality, Historiography, Resistance* (Cambridge: Cambridge University Press, 2019); Rose Parfitt, 'Fascism, Imperialism and International Law: An Arch Met a Motorway and the Rest Is History' (2018) 31 *Leiden Journal of International Law* 509–538.

4 Mouffe, *For a Left Populism*, p. 35.

conditions to work in their favour'.[5] Second, one cannot assume that an attempt to create a new order in place of neoliberalism will 'bring about significant democratic advances' and recognise that it 'might even be of an authoritarian nature'.[6] Instead, and following Hall's injunction for the left to 'Learn from Thatcherism', Mouffe argues that what is required is an organised, systematic effort to shift the prevailing 'common sense' towards a set of values supportive of left politics – a 'new hegemonic order'.[7] This is the starting point for Mouffe's call for a 'Left Populism'. The essence of this for her is that 'what is urgently needed is a left populist strategy aimed at the construction of a "people", combining the variety of democratic resistances against post-democracy in order to establish a more democratic formation'.[8]

This chapter will engage with Mouffe's call for a 'Left Populism'. It will argue that Mouffe's attempt to 'learn from Thatcherism' provides a useful updating of Hall's analysis of authoritarian populism under Thatcher in the context of contemporary populist politics in Europe. And yet, for us, Mouffe's account of Left Populism risks remaining trapped by its reification of the nation-state, betraying the anti-essentialism she invokes. Casting contemporary politics as primarily a question of competing populisms and focusing on the nation-state as the primary locus of politics, Mouffe's account may leave us unequipped to consider the international dimensions of right-wing populism and the way the nexus between the state and the global corporation figures in its rise. This may hinder the production of effective political responses to the rise of right-wing populism. Learning from the tension within Mouffe's response to populism invites us to consider whether we need to find and foster approaches to countering right-wing populism which do not locate politics as (in the first instance) a fight over control of the identity and institutions of the nation state – but rather one which begins in transnational resistance and collective action. In the search for such approaches, we turn to David Featherstone's account of trans-national solidarity. We explore this account through one current example – transnational opposition to the Adani conglomerate. We argue that activities around this opposition by a range of actors is a good illustration of what Featherstone describes, and could offer us, as scholars, some guidance in relation to both understanding and acting in solidarity with action against right-wing populism.

5 Ibid., p. 30.
6 Ibid., p. 35.
7 Ibid. See Hall, 'Learning from Thatcherism', in Hall, *The Hard Road to Renewal*, chapter 19.
8 Mouffe, *For a Left Populism*, p. 36.

9.2 A LEFT POPULISM?

Three theoretical insights underpin Mouffe's call for a 'Left Populism'. The first and overarching insight is that it forms part of an 'anti-essentialist approach' to thinking about 'the domain of the political'.[9] The second is that an anti-essentialist approach involves understanding the political domain as 'a field of conflict and antagonism'.[10] The third insight is that this conflict and antagonism occurs at the level of 'hegemonic practices', by which she means 'the practices of articulation through which a given order is created and the meaning of social institutions is fixed'.[11] In calling for a Left Populism, Mouffe seeks to take advantage of a 'double movement' she considers to be constitutive of social life. One is a 'movement of decentering which prevents the fixation of set positions' (that is, a recognition of the contingency of all social formations).[12] The second is an 'opposite movement' which is 'a result of this essential non-fixity', towards 'the institution of nodal points, partial fixations'[13] around which the contours and limits of the prevailing social order are formed. The challenge then, is to understand the hegemonic practices and discursive formations that support the current 'partial fixations' on which the prevailing social order relies and how to shift them towards a different (and in turn, ever contingent) articulation of social order.

The current social order Mouffe seeks to understand and challenge is 'neoliberalism', broadly conceived. More specifically, Mouffe's target is the consensus around so-called pragmatic policies which tacitly or explicitly concede that neoliberalism constitutes a 'post-political consensus between centre-right and centre-left'.[14] In Mouffe's account, neoliberalism has failed to live up to its own economic promises and, especially since 2008, to 'secure the allegiance of the people'.[15] More fundamentally, neoliberalism has eroded 'the two pillars of the democratic ideal: equality and popular sovereignty' through which inherent tensions within liberal democracy could be fought over.[16] For Mouffe, populism is what happens when the concepts of equality and popular sovereignty cease to structure the inevitable agonism of

9 Ibid., p. 87.
10 Ibid., p. 87, drawing on Laclau and Mouffe, *Hegemony and Socialist Strategy*.
11 Mouffe, *For a Left Populism*, p. 88.
12 Ibid., p. 89.
13 Ibid. For a similar articulation of this dynamic, see, for example, Jacques Derrida, 'Remarks on Deconstruction and Pragmatism', trans. Simon Critchley, in Chantal Mouffe (ed.), *Deconstruction and Pragmatism* (London: Routledge, 1996), pp. 79–90, pp. 83–84.
14 Mouffe, *For a Left Populism*, p. 36.
15 Ibid., p. 11.
16 Ibid., p. 13.

politics in liberal democracies. For Mouffe, Western European societies now live in a 'populist moment', in which:[17]

> [i]n the next few years … the central axis of the political conflict will be between right-wing populism and left-wing populism. And as a result, it is through the construction of a 'people', a collective will that results from the mobilisation of common affects in defence of equality and social justice, that it will be possible to combat the xenophobic policies promoted by right-wing populism.

Mouffe understands left populism as 'a discursive strategy of construction of the political frontier between "the people" and "the oligarchy"'.[18] This requires 'the construction of a people', and the recovery and deepening of the 'ideals of equality and popular sovereignty that are constitutive of a democratic politics'.[19] This approach argues that populism, of one form or another, is an essential political strategy in a political world shaped by neoliberalism and its failures.

The construction of the frontier between the people and the oligarchy demands the construction of 'the people'. In this, Mouffe argues that it is important for the left to recognise the 'democratic nucleus at the origin of many of [the] demands' of right-wing populists and attempt to 'provide a different vocabulary to orient those demands towards more egalitarian objectives'.[20] Where left populism differs from right-wing populism is that, for Mouffe, the latter conceives of 'popular sovereignty' as limited to '"national sovereignty" and reserved for those deemed to be "true nationals"'.[21] Nor does right-wing populism 'necessarily present the adversary of the people as being constituted by the forces of neoliberalism' and its 'victory could lead to nationalistic authoritarian forms of neoliberalism'.[22]

The challenge for 'Left Populism', by contrast to right-wing populism, is to establish conditions aimed at 'recovering and deepening democracy'.[23] While this will 'necessitate a far-reaching transformation of the existing relations of power and the creation of new democratic practices', Mouffe argues that 'it does not require a "revolutionary" break with the liberal-democratic regime'.[24] Indeed, one of the lessons Mouffe learns from Thatcher, is that (within the

[17] Ibid., p. 6, see also chapter 1: 'The Populist Moment'.
[18] Ibid., p. 5. This draws on Ernesto Laclau, *On Populist Reason* (London: Verso, 2005).
[19] Mouffe, *For a Left Populism*, p. 9.
[20] Ibid., p. 22.
[21] Ibid., p. 24.
[22] Ibid.
[23] Ibid.
[24] Ibid., p. 36.

Western European societies to which she directs her analysis), it is possible to 'bring about a transformation of the existing hegemonic order without destroying liberal-democratic institutions'.[25]

It is clear that Mouffe's left populism is set against neoliberalism. It is less clear, however, that it manages to avoid the nationalistic elements that right-wing populism engages in its construction of 'the people'. Mouffe recognises the danger of this, and notes that a 'frequent objection to a left populist strategy is that to bring together ... democratic demands in the creation of a "people" will produce a homogenous subject, one that negates plurality'.[26] Instead, left populism, for Mouffe, is an 'anti-essentialist approach according to which the "people" is not an empirical referent but a discursive political construction [which] does not exist previously to its performative articulation'.[27] For her, 'collective will is created through a chain of equivalence' formed through the 'designation of [a common] adversary'.[28] With the adversary being the thing held in common, the 'multiplicity of heterogenous demands' and 'internal differentiation of the group' remains intact.[29]

The difficulty arises when it comes to conceiving of the action required to achieve a 'radicalization of democracy'.[30] Here Mouffe turns to the 'citizen' as the primary 'social agent'.[31] It is '*qua* citizen that a social agent intervenes at the level of the political community'.[32] Mouffe goes on (again, aware of common objections) to argue that 'it is at the national level that the question of radicalizing democracy must first be posed' and where 'a collective will to resist the post-democratic effects of neoliberal globalization should be constructed'.[33] Once that is achieved at the national level, 'collaboration with similar movements in other countries can be productive'.[34] This is the case even as Mouffe recognises that 'the struggle against neoliberalism cannot be won at the national level alone' and must involve (in respect of Europe) alliances 'at the European level'.[35] This focus on the national and regional arises because there is, for Mouffe, a strong affective (even libidinal) investment in those forms of identification which she thinks is unwise to abandon to

[25] Ibid.
[26] Ibid., p. 62.
[27] Ibid.
[28] Ibid.
[29] Ibid., p. 63.
[30] Ibid., p. 64.
[31] Ibid., p. 65.
[32] Ibid.
[33] Ibid., p. 71.
[34] Ibid.
[35] Ibid.

right-wing populism.[36] While Mouffe argues that acting '*qua* citizen ... does not mean discarding other forms of identification' and that a 'radical democratic citizenship encourages ... a plurality of engagements',[37] her argument centres the citizen and the state. And in part this seems a consequence of her attempt to thread the line between establishing a new hegemonic formation while maintaining liberal-democratic institutions, and of her focus on (and reification of) the institutions of liberal democracy in Western Europe. There is at least a tension, if not a conflict, between her centring of the citizen and the state, and her resistance to the essentialising and homogenising affects of national identity that lie at the heart of right-wing populism.

Arguably, this tension cannot be resolved within the terms of Mouffe's analysis. At the root of this tension is the concession that we (or at least, the audience she addresses in western liberal democracies) live in a 'populist moment' within which the main fight is over the control, meaning, and purpose of the category of 'the people' or its most entrenched proxy, the nation-state. But for us it is not clear that responding to the rise of right-wing populism (within western liberal democracies and certainly not outside them) demands that we make that concession.

Of particular concern to us as scholars of international law is that Mouffe's prioritisation of the contest within the state and about who 'the people' are closes off ways of thinking about and responding to the international dimensions of right-wing populism and neoliberalism – and especially the connections between the state and global corporations. In our view, the task of responding to the rise of populism requires something other than meeting populism on its own terms. In other words, breaking out of the intensifying cycle of rising inequality, environmental catastrophe, the social dislocation of neoliberalism, and authoritarian populism, requires an asymmetrical response. It requires us to maintain a concern with radical plurality by keeping one's eye on the margins rather than at the centre.

What we do draw from Mouffe, however, is that the identification of a common adversary (or constellation of adversaries) is foundational to a collective anti-right-wing populist form of law and politics. It is this foundation which, among other things, avoids the need for collective actors to first determine their identity before engaging politically. In Mouffe's (and Laclau's) own terms, it provides a way of thinking through the operationalization of the 'chain of equivalence' between different groups and interests, and a

[36] Ibid.
[37] Ibid., p. 67.

structure for observing agonistic politics in action.[38] In the terms we will draw on here, we take it up as an invitation to think about forms and operations of solidarity. While a concern with solidarities between interest groups in view of a common adversary might seem obvious in a way, in respect of politics writ large, we think it has useful implications for thinking about the relationship between populism and international law. This is particularly true in the context of international law which gives primacy to the state as both its key subject and the source of its authority.

We turn to solidarity not because it is absent from Mouffe's work generally, nor in her thinking about populism. We don't seek to elevate solidarity as a master concept that might uniquely address the rise of populism. Instead, we seek to experiment with a particular articulation of solidarity which concentrates on the idea of collective action formed in the absence of (pre-existing) identities. It is the idea of political action in the absence of pre-existing identities (and not any magic in the word solidarity itself) that we find most helpful in trying to avoid the reifications of 'people' and 'nation' common to both right-wing populism and Mouffe's Left Populism. Though one frequently sees calls for solidarity between nations, we take up the work of David Featherstone, who argues that solidarity itself is not necessarily already trapped by the logic of nationalism, nor the need to identify and act in the name of a singular people. In Section 9.3, we will explore how Featherstone's concept of solidarity can help us to resist nationalist logics but at the same time offer potential modes of engaging with the international legal order. After setting out that conception of solidarity, we will situate that concept in the context of trans-national solidarities formed by way of opposition to the Adani conglomerate.

9.3 SOLIDARITY FROM BELOW?

Before embarking on an analysis of solidarity as a conceptual frame for responding to right-wing populism which is not trapped by logics of 'the people' and the nation state, it is important to note that we are not disputing the importance of solidaristic practices between states in contesting unjust forms of international ordering, nor of particular processes or effects of neoliberalism or right-wing populism.[39] State-based organising originating

38 See Mouffe and Laclau, *Hegemony and Socialist Strategy*, chapter 3.

39 In terms of the title of this section, we are borrowing, and not just the title, from Balakrishnan Rajagopal, *International Law from Below: Development, Social Movements and Third World Resistance* (Cambridge: Cambridge University Press, 2003).

from the Global South has been an important site of solidarity and challenge to imperialism and its legacies.[40] Recent examples of state led solidarities include Costa Rica's 'solidarity call to action' on COVID-related medical technologies[41] and perhaps the new, New International Economic Order.[42] South Africa's application instituting proceedings against Israel before the International Court of Justice concerning violation of its obligations under the 1948 Genocide Convention in relation to Palestinian people in the Gaza Strip and the support for South Africa's application from several other states (mainly, in the Global South) is another recent example of state–state solidarity.[43] South Africa's action and the support for it has been described as reactivation of the South–South state based solidarity reminiscent of Third World internationalism of the 1950s–1970s and a challenge to the Global North.[44] The solidarity action is rooted in similar historical experiences of apartheid and colonialism in the Third World states, fostering a 'collective consciousness' among these states comparing their past struggles with the right of Palestinian people to self-determination.[45] This example also shows us how

[40] See Luis Eslava, Michael Fahkri and Vasuki Nesiah (eds.), *Bandung, Global History, and International Law: Critical Pasts and Pending Futures* (Cambridge: Cambridge University Press, 2017); Adom Getachew, *Worldmaking after Empire: The Rise and Fall of Self-Determination* (Princeton: Princeton University Press, 2019); Kojo Koram, *Uncommon Wealth: Britain and the Aftermath of Empire* (London: John Murray Press, 2022); Declaration on the Establishment of a New International Economic Order, UNGA Res 3201 (S-VI) (1 May 1974).

[41] See World Health Organisation, 'Endorsements of the Solidarity Call to Action', available at: www.who.int/initiatives/covid-19-technology-access-pool/endorsements-of-the-solidarity-call-to-action (last accessed 27 June 2023).

[42] Towards a New International Economic Order, UNGA Res 73/240 (20 December 2018).

[43] *Application of the Convention on the Prevention and Punishment of the Crime of Genocide in the Gaza Strip (South Africa v. Israel)*, Application instituting proceedings and request for the indication of provisional measures (29 December 2023), available at: www.icj-cij.org/sites/default/files/case-related/192/192-20231228-app-01-00-en.pdf (last accessed 25 January 2024). Aliyu Dahiru, 'African Countries' Ringing Support for Palestine Stems from History of Violence', *HumAngle*, 17 January 2024, available at: https://humanglemedia.com/african-countries-ringing-support-for-palestine-stems-from-history-of-violence/ (last accessed 25 January 2024). Also see Christopher Gevers, 'Justice at the World Court', *Mail & Guardian*, 8 January 2024, available at: https://mg.co.za/thought-leader/opinion/2024-01-08-justice-at-the-world-court/ (last accessed 25 January 2024). Tanupriya Singh, 'Israel Scrambles as Support for South Africa's Case at the Hague Increases', *People's Dispatch*, 10 January 2024, available at: https://peoplesdispatch.org/2024/01/10/israel-scrambles-as-support-for-south-africas-case-at-the-hague-increases/ (last accessed 25 January 2024).

[44] Tricontinental, 'The Global South Takes Israel to Court: The Third Newsletter' *Tricontinental*, 18 January 2024, available at: https://thetricontinental.org/newsletterissue/south-africa-israel-international-court-of-justice/ (last accessed 25 January 2024).

[45] Dahiru, 'African Countries' Ringing Support'. Also see Gevers, 'Justice at the World Court'.

non-state solidarity activism can exert influence on state action.[46] As Erakat and Reynolds put it in relation to South Africa's support for Palestine, '[t]he consistent commitment to this position at state level is also down to the strength of Palestine solidarity activism in South Africa through the unions and social movements.'[47] The state–state and non-state pro-Palestine solidarity movements have shown how the fight against imperialist-colonialist forces need not emanate from a single political space, but rather it gains strength through collective action of all those resisting the forces of imperialism. Thus, the focus of our analysis on solidarity practice outside the state is not opposed to state–state solidarity.[48]

Instead, in this chapter we are interested in exploring forms of solidaristic trans-national organization and activity which are not centred on the primacy of the state as offering an important alternative yet simultaneous site of inquiry.[49] These modes experiment with trying to avoid the idea that, before collective action can occur, a fixed identity (state, nation or people) has first to exist or be constructed. One account of such forms of solidarity is given by David Featherstone in his *Solidarity: Hidden Histories and Geographies of Internationalism*.[50]

Solidarity, in Featherstone's account, is 'a relation forged through political struggle which seeks to challenge forms of oppression'.[51] Two elements are crucial here. First, what is being forged is not primarily identity but relation. It is only in the relation (and not in advance of it) that new forms of 'political identification' are shaped.[52] Second, that relation is formed in the process of

46 Jordyn Beazley, 'Pro-Palestine Rally Leaders Credit Public "Pressure" with Labor's Shift on Gaza', *The Guardian*, 17 December 2023, available at: www.theguardian.com/australia-news/2023/dec/17/pro-palestine-rally-leaders-credit-public-pressure-with-labors-shift-on-gaza (last accessed 25 January 2024).

47 Noura Erakat and John Reynolds, 'South Africa's Genocide Case Is a Devastating Indictment of Israel's War on Gaza', *Jacobin*, 11 January 2024, available at: https://jacobin.com/2024/01/south-africa-icj-isarel-gaza (last accessed 25 January 2024).

48 Many contributors to this collection are focused on state-to-state solidarity in different contexts. See, e.g. Chapters 3 and 4, by Okafor and Mégret, respectively. See also, UNGA, 'Report of the Independent Expert on human rights and international solidarity', UN Doc A/73/206 (20 July 2018); Eleni Karageorgiou, 'The Distribution of Asylum Responsibilities in the EU: Dublin, Partnerships with Third Countries and the Question of Solidarity' (2019) 88 *Nordic Journal of International Law* 315–358. See generally, Rüdiger Wolfrum and Chie Kojima (eds.), *Solidarity: A Structural Principle of International Law* (Heidelberg: Springer, 2010).

49 See Chapters 7 and 8, by Noll and Herzog, respectively.

50 David Featherstone, *Solidarity: Hidden Histories and Geographies of Internationalism* (New York: Zed Books, 2012).

51 Ibid., p. 5.

52 Ibid., p. 17.

struggle against oppression.[53] Solidarity, in this account, is not a form of co-operation or co-ordination between powerful actors (such as states, even if they are hierarchically less powerful than other powerful actors), but a force able to be activated by those with less power.

For Featherstone, effective solidarity constructs and cements relations between places, diverse groups and activists. He identifies a 'double sense' in which 'solidarities [are] made'. First, they are made through the creation of 'political imaginaries link[ing] different parts of the world'.[54] That creation happens in the course of 'translocal political organising'.[55] Second, they are made in the course of 'contesting particular arrangements of social and material relations'. Solidarities, for Featherstone, do not 'just produce abstracted political ideologies or identifications'. Rather, they are 'interventions in the material relations between places'.[56] Through such action 'agency … emerge[s] from below'. This kind of solidarity can be contrasted with a sense of solidarity that arises out of a given shared abstract conception, such as a 'shared sense of "humanness"'.[57] Taken as a heuristic, it also helps us to avoid the reflex to find solidarities as existing only between people who are already alike,[58] or to look for them across patterns of identification. This way of understanding solidarity also foregrounds the creative, inventive character of practices of solidarity. Transnational solidaristic action offers a distinct way of configuring spaces and political relations and, therefore, is part of the 'process of politicisation'.[59]

In other words, what we might call solidarity from below arises from the creation of political imaginaries in the course of action and through contestation over particular social and material relations. As scholars and researchers, attending to this enables us to think about forms of transnational solidarity which might be capable of challenging the existing global social, political and economic relations without having first to imagine a transformation of power within the state or to limit ourselves to looking for movements which activate existing international structures.

53 See Andrew Benjamin, 'Solidarity, Populism and Covid-19: Working Notes' (2020) 64 *Philosophy Today* 833–837, at 836. And, as Andrew Benjamin notes, this can be distinguished from what Walter Benjamin calls 'empathy with the victor'. Howard Eiland and Michael W. Jennings (eds.), *Walter Benjamin: Selected Writings 1938–1940*, 4 vols. (Cambridge, MA: Harvard University Press, 2003) vol. 4, pp. 401–411, at 406 (Paralipomena to "On the Concept of History").

54 Featherstone, *Solidarity*, p. 18.

55 Ibid..

56 Ibid., p. 15.

57 Ibid., p. 19.

58 Ibid., p. 21.

59 Ibid., pp. 5–8.

A focus on practices and oppositional struggles, rather than essences or identities, also fosters an attentiveness to the contestations around the particular political formations and dynamics of specific instances of solidaristic practices, including their problematic aspects.[60] Understanding such 'tensions and conflicts over how solidarities are constructed' is, for Featherstone, a 'necessary condition for a "politics of solidarity"'.[61] The 'crucial set of questions' which then emerges, are: (1) 'What kinds of relations do [solidarities] generate between different actors?'; (2) 'What kinds of power relations are crafted through solidarities?'; and (3) 'What kinds of political trajectories do [solidarities] shape?'[62] For the scholar interested in studying solidarity from below, or for scholar-activists interested in supporting or even practising it, these questions can be both heuristic and strategic. In the remainder of this chapter, we will consider these three questions in the context of one example: transnational solidarities which have been created through the process of challenging the operations of the Adani group of companies in India, Sri Lanka, Australia and Germany.

9.4 THE ADANI GROUP AND ITS RISE

The Adani Group is a conglomeration of companies founded in 1988 by Gautam Adani.[63] Its headquarters are in Ahmedabad, Gujarat, and it has vast and varied operations in about 50 countries, including Australia, Bangladesh, Indonesia, Israel and Sri Lanka.[64] A person living in India cannot escape Adani. It is everywhere: edible oil, electricity, housing, fruits, water, education, news channels – the list is long.[65]

Although the Adani group is vast, it has achieved its rise recently. In 2013, the group had 44 projects in India, centred on Gujarat. By 2018, the number of projects had grown to 92. In 2019, it was reported that it was present in

60 Ibid., p. 21.

61 Ibid.

62 Ibid.

63 Its businesses are spread over diverse sectors, such as: energy and utilities, transportation and logistics, defence and aerospace, airports, food, data centre, financial services, real estate, education and media.

64 John Reed and Benjamin Parkin, 'Gautam Adani's Ties with India's Narendra Modi Spur Scrutiny of Overseas Deals', *Financial Times*, 23 February 2023, available at: www.ft.com/content/38ff5ff6-aebe-46ae-bb97-c8071818b55d (last accessed 27 June 2023).

65 It took us more time to find out and visit the websites of all Adani businesses than to prepare a list of places where the protests have occurred.

more than 260 cities in India.[66] Until 2013, the Adani Group was confined mainly to sectors like energy and edible oil. It now covers significantly diversified business areas. At the start of 2014, Gautam Adani's net worth was 7.1 billion dollars; it increased by 121 percent to 15.7 billion dollars by 2019.[67] In April 2022, *Forbes* reported that Adani has become the 'richest Asian billionaire ever' and 'the world's newest centi-billionaire' joining 'an elite group of just eight other business moguls – including Elon Musk, Jeff Bezos, and Bill Gates'.[68] On 16 September 2022, Gautam Adani overtook Jeff Bezos to 'briefly become' the second richest person in the world, trailing behind only Elon Musk.[69]

The turning point for Adani came in 2014, the year when the right-wing Bhartiya Janta Party ('BJP') led by Narendra Modi came to power in India.[70] Since then, the two men have risen together. Before Modi was elected as India's Prime Minister, he was the chief minister of Gujarat, the home state of Adani. It is an open secret that Adani and Modi enjoy a close relationship.[71] When Modi was chief minister of Gujarat, Adani offered him both corporate

66 M. Rajshekhar, 'From 2014 to 2019: How the Adani Group's Footprint Expanded across India', *The Scroll*, 15 May 2019, available at: https://scroll.in/article/923095/from-2014-to-2019-how-the-adani-groups-footprint-expanded-across-india (last accessed 27 June 2023). Also see, John Hyatt and Giacomo Tognini, 'Inside Gautam and Vinod Adani's Controversial Conglomerate: And Why It May be too Politically Connected to Fail', *Forbes*, 30 March 2023, available at: www.forbes.com/sites/johnhyatt/2023/03/30/inside-gautam-and-vinod-adanis-controversial-conglomerate-and-why-it-may-be-too-politically-connected-to-fail/?sh=185bb701199d (last accessed 27 June 2023).

67 Subodh Verma, 'Under Modi Rule, Ambani, Adani Have Doubled Their Wealth', *News Click*, 13 October 2019, available at: www.newsclick.in/Under-Modi-Rule-Ambani-Adani-Have-Doubled-Their-Wealth (last accessed 27 June 2023).

68 Jemima McEvoy, 'India's Gautam Adani Is Now Richest Asian Billionaire Ever as Fortune Jumps Past $100 Billion', *Forbes*, 11 April 2022, available at: www.forbes.com/sites/jemimamcevoy/2022/04/11/indias-gautam-adani-is-now-richest-asian-billionaire-ever-as-fortune-jumps-past-100-billion/?sh=5183c35d5926 (last accessed 27 June 2023).

69 Derek Saul, 'Who Is Gautam Adani? The Indian Billionaire Briefly Became the World's no. 2 Wealthiest Person and Ranks Above Bezos and Gates', *Forbes*, 16 September 2022, available at: www.forbes.com/sites/dereksaul/2022/09/16/who-is-gautam-adani-the-indian-billionaire-briefly-became-the-worlds-no-2-wealthiest-person-and-ranks-above-bezos-and-gates/?sh=3e8c36a84431 (last accessed 27 June 2023).

70 James Crabtree, *The Billionaire Raj: A Journey through India's New Gilded Age* (London: Oneworld Publications, 2018), chapter 3.

71 Among others, Christophe Jaffrelot, 'Business-friendly Gujarat under Narendra Modi: The Implications of a New Political Economy', in Christophe Jaffrelot, Atul Kohli and Kanta Mural (eds.), *Business and Politics in India* (New York: Oxford University Press, 2019), pp. 211–233. Also see, Stephanie Findlay and Hudson Lockett, '"Modi's Rockefeller": Gautam Adani and the Concentration of Power in India', *Financial Times*, 13 November 2020, available at: www.ft.com/content/474706d6-1243-4f1e-b365-891d4c5d528b (last accessed 27 June 2023).

backing and supported his electoral campaigns.[72] Even before Modi became India's PM, there was speculation that his election would benefit the Adani group.[73] Opposition parties in India have consistently alleged that the Adani group enjoys Modi's support, and they benefit each other.[74]

Since his election, Modi's foreign policies have facilitated Adani's expansion.[75] In 2022, the chairman of Sri Lanka's Electricity Board, MMC Ferdinando, claimed before a parliamentary committee that Modi 'pressured' Sri Lankan President G Rajapaksa to award a power project to the Adani group.[76] After the controversy erupted, an official document resurfaced revealing that Ferdinando was instructed by Rajapaksa to facilitate Adani projects.[77] However, within three days of making the statement, Ferdinando

72 Jafferlot, 'Business-friendly Gujarat', 223–228. During the 2014 elections, it was credibly alleged that Modi was using the Adani group's helicopters and planes for the campaign. Akshay Deshmane, 'Lok Sabha Polls 2014: Narendra Modi Using Adani's Planes, Choppers for Campaign, says Anand Sharma', *The Economic Times*, 11 April 2014, available at: https://economictimes.indiatimes.com/news/politics-and-nation/lok-sabha-polls-2014-narendra-modi-using-adanis-planes-choppers-for-campaign-says-anand-sharma/articleshow/33616255.cms?from=mdr (last accessed 27 June 2023). Also see, Findlay and Lockett, '"Modi's Rockefeller"'.

73 Hari Mehta, 'Gautam Adani, the Baron to Watch Out for if Narendra Modi becomes King', *The Times of India*, 10 April 2014, available at: http://timesofindia.indiatimes.com/articleshow/33521536.cms?utm_source=contentofinterest&utm_medium=text&utm_campaign=cppst (last accessed 27 June 2023).

74 PTI, 'Adani Group Powering BJP's Electoral Fortunes at Expense of Indian Power Sector Consumers, Alleges Congress', *The Economic Times*, 7 March 2023, available at: https://economictimes.indiatimes.com/news/politics-and-nation/adani-group-powering-bjps-electoral-fortunes-at-expense-of-indian-power-sector-consumers-alleges-congress/articleshow/98479440.cms (last accessed 27 June 2023. Also see, Abir Dasgupta, 'Did PM Modi and BJP Disclose Election Spending on Adani Private Jet?', *AdaniWatch*, 18 January 2024, available at: www.adaniwatch.org/exclusive_did_pm_modi_and_bjp_disclose_election_spending_on_adani_private_jet_lease (last accessed 12 August 2024); Alenjith K. Johny, Sumedha Mittal and Project Electoral Bond, 'These Firms Linked to Adani Group Bought Electoral Bonds Worth Rs 55.4 cr, BJP Encashed Rs 42.4 cr', *Newslaundry*, 22 March 2024), available at: www.newslaundry.com/2024/03/21/these-firms-linked-to-adani-group-bought-electoral-bonds-worth-rs-554-cr-bjp-encashed-rs-424-cr (last accessed 12 August 2024).

75 Reed and Parkin, 'Gautam Adani's Ties with India's Narendra Modi'.

76 Scroll Staff, 'Sri Lankan Official Quits after Saying Modi 'Pressured' President to Give Power Project to Adani', *Scroll*, 13 June 2022, available at: https://scroll.in/latest/1026086/sri-lankan-official-quits-days-after-saying-modi-pressured-to-give-power-project-to-adani-group (last accessed 27 June 2023).

77 Namini Wijedasa, 'Official Letters Show CEB Chairman was Instructed to Facilitate Adani Projects', *The Sunday Times*, 19 June 2022, available at: www.sundaytimes.lk/220619/news/adani-to-expand-still-further-in-sri-lanka-through-wind-and-solar-power-projects-486419.html (last accessed 27 June 2023); A Special Correspondent, 'Explosive Allegations About Adani, Sri Lanka and the PM of India', *Adani Watch*, 5 July 2022, available at: www.adaniwatch.org/explosive_allegations_about_adani_and_the_pms_of_india_and_sri_lanka (last accessed 27 June 2023).

retracted it and quit his job.[78] Following this episode, on 17 June 2022, protests were held in Colombo against the alleged favour given to the Adani group in granting the energy project.[79]

Adani's association with right-wing populist political parties is not limited to India. Nor are its battles with indigenous peoples and destruction of environmentally sensitive lands. In 2010, Adani bought parts of the Galilee basin in Queensland in Australia. The basin contains an estimated 23 bn tonnes of coal.[80] Since then, with the support of the former Australian government, Adani developed the Carmichael coalmine and railway to the harbour. Carmichael is the largest coalmine in Australia and one of the largest in the world.[81] Despite extensive indigenous protest and NGO and direct-action campaigns against it, as well as numerous legal efforts to disrupt its progress, the mine started exporting coal at the end of 2021. Shipments take place through the environmentally vulnerable Great Barrier Reef.[82] The former government of Australia tended to a right-wing populist style. Both the then ruling Liberal Party (the conservative party in Australia) and One Nation, a significant minor party firmly in the right-wing populist camp, received extensive financial donations from the Adani group.[83] Further, Adani's operations have been called out for assisting in the acts of genocide by Israel against Palestinians and Myanmar against Rohingyas.[84] For instance, amidst

78 Sreeja MS, 'Sri Lanka Adani Row: Official Quits after Alleging Link to PM Modi', *NDTV*, 14 June 2022, available at: www.ndtv.com/india-news/sri-lanka-adani-row-energy-official-quits-after-alleging-link-to-pm-narendra-modi-3063344 (last accessed 27 June 2023).

79 Sreeja MS, '"Stop Adani": Sri Lanka Protesters Say PM Modi, President Rajapaksa Struck Deal', *NDTV*, 16 June 2022, available at: www.ndtv.com/india-news/sri-lanka-protesters-against-gautam-adani-say-pm-narendra-modi-president-rajapaksa-struck-dubious-deal-3072337 (last accessed 27 June 2023).

80 Graham Readfearn and Ben Smee, 'Adani Is Poised to Ship Its First Coal – Is this Failure for Australia's Defining Climate Campaign?', *The Guardian*, 18 December 2021, available at: www.theguardian.com/environment/2021/dec/18/adani-is-poised-to-ship-its-first-coal-is-this-failure-for-australias-defining-climate-campaign (last accessed 27 June 2023).

81 Ibid.

82 Katrina Beavan, 'Adani's First Carmichael Mine Coal Export Shipment Imminent after Years of Campaigns against It', *ABC News*, 29 December 2021, available at: www.abc.net.au/news/rural/2021-12-29/adani-ships-first-coal/100729834 (last accessed 27 June 2023).

83 Daniel Burdon, 'Adani Donated $35,000 to Liberal Party', *The Canberra Times*, 1 February 2019, available at: www.canberratimes.com.au/story/5995925/adani-donated-35000-to-liberal-party/ (last accessed 27 June 2023).

84 For details on Adani's weapons business with Israel, see #StopAdani, 'Stop Adani Weapons Business with Israel', available at: www.stopadani.com/adani_groups_business_with_israel (last accessed 13 February 2024). Also see, R. Ramachandran, 'India's Refusal to Back UN Arms Embargo on Israel May be Linked to Adani Drone Exports', *The Wire*, 17 April 2024), available at: https://thewire.in/government/indias-refusal-to-back-un-arms-embargo-on-israel-may-be-linked-to-adani-drone-exports (last accessed 12 August 2024). For details on Adani's

Israel's assault on Gaza, it was credibly reported that a joint venture between Adani Defence & Aerospace and Israel-based Elbit Systems (Adani Elbit Advanced Systems India Limited) manufactured and delivered military drones to the Israeli military.[85]

Adani's meteoric rise would have been impossible without the collaboration of governments in its respective countries of operations. Friendly governments continue to facilitate its projects, tolerate their impacts on people and the environment and quell dissent. In each of Australia, India and Sri Lanka, the governments have both granted favours to the Adani group and ignored protestors' demands. One example of this is 'the 30-year, renewable leases [received from the Gujarat government] for as little as one U.S. cent a square meter (the rate maxed out at 45 cents a square meter)'.[86] Adani has 'in turn sublet this land to other companies, including state-owned Indian Oil Co., for as much as $11 a square meter'.[87] Similarly, it was reported that, between 2005 and 2007, at least 1,200 hectares of grazing land in Gujarat was taken away from villagers and redirected to Adani concerns.[88] Modi was the chief minister of Gujarat during this period.

In Sri Lanka, Adani was able to bypass the competitive bidding process in obtaining a wind energy project.[89] Likewise, in Australia, then Prime Minister Scott Morrison granted environmental approval to Adani's Carmichael coal mine and railway infrastructure project despite widespread

business operations in Myanmar, see Rawan Arraf and Justice for Myanmar, 'Ports of Complicity: Adani Ports in Myanmar', *Australian Centre for International Justice and Justice for Myanmar*, March 2021, available at: https://acij.org.au/wp-content/uploads/2021/03/Port-of-Complicity-Report-FINAL-High-Resolution.pdf (last accessed 13 January 2024).

85 See, The Wire Staff, 'Adani JV Just Exported Lethal Drones to Israel, Same Model Being Used in Genocide-tainted Gaza War', *The Wire*, 12 February 2024, available at: https://thewire.in/business/adani-jv-just-exported-lethal-drones-to-israel-same-model-being-used-in-genocide-tainted-gaza-war (last accessed 13 February 2024); Neelam Mathews, 'Indian Sends Newly Assembled MALE UAVs to Israel', *Shepherd Media*, 2 February 2024, available at: www.shephardmedia.com/news/uv-online/india-sends-newly-assembled-male-uavs-to-israel/ (last accessed 13 February 2024).

86 Megha Bahree, 'Doing Big Business in Modi's Gujarat', *The Forbes*, 12 March 2014, available at: www.forbes.com/sites/meghabahree/2014/03/12/doing-big-business-in-modis-gujarat/?sh=620883d94df5 (last accessed 27 June 2023).

87 Ibid.

88 Ibid.

89 Meera Srinivasan, 'Adani Project Sparks Controversy in Sri Lanka Yet Again', *The Hindu*, 12 June 2022, available at: www.thehindu.com/news/international/adani-project-sparks-controversy-in-sri-lanka-yet-again/article65520090.ece (last accessed 27 June 2023). Meera Srinivasan, 'Sri Lanka Gives Nod to $442-million Wind Project of Adani Group', *The Hindu*, 23 February 2023, available at: www.thehindu.com/news/international/sri-lanka-approves-442-million-wind-power-project-of-adani-group/article66544744.ece (last accessed 27 June 2023).

opposition.[90] Similar allegations have been made in relation to Adani's power project in Bangladesh.[91]

Reflecting the symmetry of interest between the right-wing populist government of India and the Adani group, criticism of the company is often portrayed as 'anti-Indian'. This was exemplified in a recent scandal in which Hindenburg Research, a New York based investment research firm, accused the Adani group of manipulating stock and engaging in fraudulent accounting on a grand scale, with significant market ramifications for the group's value.[92] The Adani Group responded to the published report by asserting that it was 'not merely an unwarranted attack on any specific company but a calculated attack on India, the independence, integrity and quality of Indian institutions, and the growth story and ambition of India'.[93] Just as populists such as Modi, or Australia's Morrison claim that questioning their policies is 'Anti-Indian', or 'un-Australian', criticising the corporations they are intimately connected with is similarly attacked as anti-Indian, whether being unpatriotic for those within, or racist and colonial for those without. In this instance, despite facing questions from the members of Indian Parliament, activists and media, Modi remained silent on the issue.[94]

There is a bigger story to be told here about the relationship between right-wing populist governments and global corporations in many countries. For the purposes of this chapter, we are treating the anti-Adani protests as a useful site to explore the explanatory power offered by Featherstone's account. This is not to elevate that account as a transcendent measure. We take it up because of

[90] Phillip Coorey and Mark Ludlow, 'Adani Approved by Morrison Government', *Financial Review*, 9 April 2019, available at: www.afr.com/politics/federal/morrison-government-approves-adani-ends-internal-war-20190409-p51c9k (last accessed 27 June 2023).

[91] Gerry Shih, Niha Masih and Anant Gupta, 'How Political Will Often Favors a Coal Billionaire and His Dirty Fossil Fuel', *The Washington Post*, 9 December 2022, available at: www.washingtonpost.com/world/2022/12/09/india-coal-gautam-adani-godda/ (last accessed 27 June 2023).

[92] Hindenburg Research, 'Adani Group: How the World's 3rd Richest Man Is Pulling the Largest Con in Corporate History', 24 January 2023, available at: https://hindenburgresearch.com/adani/ (last accessed 27 June 2023).

[93] See Adani's response to Hindenburg's report (29 January 2023), available at: www.adani.com/-/media/Project/Adani/Invetsors/Adani-Response-to-Hindenburg-January-29-2023.pdf (last accessed 27 June 2023).

[94] The Wire Staff, '"I'll Continue to Ask, What Is PM's Relationship with Mr. Adani?": Congress Leader Rahul Gandhi', *The Wire*, 25 March 2023, available at: https://thewire.in/politics/rahul-gandhi-modi-adani-parliament (last accessed 27 June 2023). Also see, Arundhati Roy, 'Modi's Model Is at Last Revealed for What It Is: Violent Hindu Nationalism Underwritten by Big Business', *The Guardian*, 18 February 2023, available at: www.theguardian.com/commentisfree/2023/feb/18/narendra-modi-hindu-nationalism-india-gautam-adani (last accessed 27 June 2023).

the political attraction of the historical examples he provides which centre on politically anti-racist, anti-capitalist solidarity. The non-nationalist frame he provides is part of its attraction in the repertoire of forms of action we might engage in or support in the struggle against right-wing populism. But it is analytically useful too because state–state solidarity has no purchase in an example directed towards pushing back against a politics structured around an embedded state–corporate relation.

9.5 ANTI-ADANI PROTESTS AS A FORM OF SOLIDARITY FROM BELOW

Over the last decade, protests against the Adani group have been organized in several countries, including Australia, Sri Lanka, Germany and in several states of India.[95] Activists and tribal residents (Gond Adivasi) of the Hasdeo Aranya forest in Chhattisgarh have protested against the Adani group's coal mining project on their lands.[96] They argue that mining will affect the biodiversity in the region and lead to the loss of livelihood, identity, and culture of the tribal residents. Similarly, the 2020–2021 Indian farmer's protest around Delhi opposed the three farm laws passed by the Indian parliament on the basis that they put small farmers at the 'mercy of corporates'.[97] In particular, farmers believed that the Adani group would benefit from the three farm laws.[98] After more than a year of protests in 2020–2021, parliament repealed the three laws. In Sri Lanka, protests took place against the alleged pressure by Modi on then Sri Lankan President Rajapaksa for granting Adani a

[95] In India protests have taken place in several states, including the Southern states of Kerala, Goa and Gujarat, Eastern states of Jharkhand, West Bengal and Odisha, Central Indian states of Chhattisgarh and Madhya Pradesh and the Northern state of Himachal Pradesh.

[96] Rishika Singh, 'Explained: The Battle over Mining in Chhattisgarh's Hasdeo Forest', *Indian Express*, 29 May 2022, available at: https://indianexpress.com/article/explained/explained-the-battle-over-mining-in-chhattisgarhs-hasdeo-forest-7942527/ (last accessed 27 June 2023).

[97] Team Frontline, '2020: Farmers Take the Country by Storm', *Frontline*, 15 August 2022, available at: https://frontline.thehindu.com/the-nation/agriculture/india-at-75-epochal-moments-2020-farmers-protests-take-the-country-by-storm/article65722271.ece (last accessed 27 June 2023); Jeffrey Gettleman, Karan Deep Singh and Hari Kumar, 'Angry Farmers Choke India's Capital in Giant Demonstrations', *The New York Times*, 30 November 2020, available at: www.nytimes.com/2020/11/30/world/asia/india-farmers-protest.html (last accessed 27 June 2023).

[98] Echoing the farmers' concern, Hartosh Singh Bal, the political editor of the *Caravan magazine*, countered the clarification of the Adani group that it has nothing to do with farm laws. Bal explained in an essay, how the Adani group was 'well positioned to take advantage' of the new laws. Hartosh Singh Bal, 'Mandi, Market and Modi', *Caravan*, 1 March 2021, available at: https://caravanmagazine.in/essay/farm-laws-adani-reliance (last accessed 27 June 2023).

wind energy project.[99] In Australia, protests have been held against the Adani Group's Carmichael mining and rail project now for several years. Questions over Adani's projects have also been raised in other countries, including Bangladesh, Indonesia and Myanmar.[100] In the Australian case, the protest rippled outward through the German engineering firm, Siemens', decision to support the Adani coal mining project in Australia. Protestors in Germany demanded that Siemens reverse its decision.[101] Climate activists, including Thunberg, joined the fray, calling on Siemens to 'stop, delay or at least interrupt' the building of the Adani mine.[102]

A cumulative assessment of the protests against Adani does not reveal one common cause. For the Adivasis, it is a demand for '*jal* (water), *jungle* (forests) and *zameen* (land)', a popular slogan signifying the rights of tribal forest dwellers over forest resources in India. For the Indian farmers protesting against the three farm laws, it was a question of livelihood and a fight against the state and its neoliberal policies. The farmers' protest has also been seen as presenting 'an alternative vision of democracy'[103] and 'defeat of populism'.[104] Sri Lankan protesters decried the 'non-transparent and illegal' deal that

99 Sreeja MS, '"Stop Adani"'.

100 Shih, Masih and Gupta, 'How Political Will Often Favors a Coal Billionaire'; Nurliah Simmolah, 'Indonesian NGO Calls on Government to Close and Rehabilitate Adani Coal Mine', *Adani Watch*, 18 June 2021, available at: www.adaniwatch.org/indonesian_ngo_calls_on_government_to_close_and_rehabilitate_adani_coal_mine (last accessed 27 June 2023). Geoff Law, 'Adani Ports and Its Inextricable Links to Coal, Environmental Destruction and the Murderous Myanmar Military Regime', *Adani Watch*, 5 August 2021, available at: www.adaniwatch.org/adani_ports_and_its_inextricable_links_to_coal_environmental_destruction_and_the_murderous_myanmar_military_regime (last accessed 27 June 2023).

101 Christof Ruehrmir, '57,000 Germans Want Siemens to Quit Adani Mine over Climate', *The Sydney Morning Herald*, 11 January 2020, available at: www.smh.com.au/world/europe/57-000-germans-want-siemens-to-quit-adani-mine-over-climate-20200111-p53qln.html (last accessed 27 June 2023).

102 P. R. Sanjai, 'Adani, Targeted by Greta Thunberg, Undeterred by Protests for Australia', *NDTV*, 13 January 2020, available at: www.ndtv.com/india-news/adani-says-wont-stop-australia-coal-project-opposed-by-climate-activist-greta-thunberg-2163215 (last accessed 27 June 2023). In July 2022, hundreds of teachers boycotted a Science Museum exhibition in London due to a sponsorship deal with a company linked to the Adani Group. See, Matthew Taylor, 'Hundreds of Teachers Boycott Science Museum Show over Adani Sponsorship', *The Guardian*, 15 July 2022, available at: www.theguardian.com/culture/2022/jul/15/hundreds-of-teachers-boycott-science-museum-over-adani-sponsorship (last accessed 27 June 2023).

103 Natasha Behl, 'India's Farmers' Protest: An Inclusive Vision of Indian Democracy' (2022) 116 *American Political Science Review* 1141–1146.

104 Javed Iqbal Wani, 'Farmers and the Defeat of Populism', *The Indian Express*, 12 December 2021, available at: https://indianexpress.com/article/opinion/columns/farmers-protest-defeat-populism-farm-laws-7669035/ (last accessed 27 June 2023).

allowed Adani to avoid the competitive bidding process.[105] Australian protesters highlighted the way Adani's coal project would desecrate the sacred land of the traditional owners, fuel climate change, wreck water resources and destroy the Great Barrier Reef.[106]

While all these protests are directed against the activities of one corporation, at their core, they ask different questions and are concerned with diverse issues. For instance, the protests in Australia are concerned with the rights of indigenous people and the environment. In contrast, in Sri Lanka, it concerned arbitrary and non-transparent granting of a project to Adani. In India, it has involved land rights, environment protection, tribal rights and democratic deficit. Indeed, we find anti-Adani protestors conceiving their struggles differently, ranging from local and national to transnational. Thus, protests by indigenous people in India affected by the Adani projects have mainly been directed at redressing the immediate harm (such as land grabbing). In some instances, they see transnational opposition to Adani as a way to put pressure on the company to stop its activities in their region. For example, indigenous people protesting the Adani coal power plant in Godda, Jharkhand, have highlighted that the coal used for the project comes from Australia and called on people in Australia to protest against it.[107] This framing presents the call for the transnational boycott of Adani as an effective complement to their efforts to ameliorate their immediate concerns. Indeed, not in all cases do participants portray themselves as fighting against a transnational adversary or themselves as transnational actors. Following Featherstone, we want to hold on to this difference in anti-Adani protests and show how – within the limits of such difference – new forms of relationships have emerged between places, activists and diverse forms of social groups. Even though anti-Adani protests are not all alike, we show how the practices deployed in these protests (or at least in some of the protests) have forged real solidarity. Our analysis of anti-Adani protests pays attention to those 'creative practices' which have shaped new relations, linkages and connections.[108] This does not mean equating different groups, tactics or the forms of

[105] Sreeja MS, '"Stop Adani"; PTI, 'Protest Held in Sri Lankan Capital against Proposed Wind Mill Project by Adani Group', *The Indian Express*, 16 June 2022, available at: https://indianexpress.com/article/world/protest-sri-lankan-capital-wind-mill-project-adani-group-7974051/ (last accessed 27 June 2023).
[106] See, Quentin Beresford, *Adani and the War over Coal* (Sydney: UNSW Press, 2018).
[107] Watch the documentary on Adani's coal-fired power station in Godda, #Stop Adani, 'Australian Coal Is Destroying the Lives of Indigenous Peoples in Godda, India', available at: www.stopadani.com/godda (last accessed 27 June 2023).
[108] Featherstone, *Solidarity*, p. 23.

oppression they face. Rather, for us, it means paying attention to how links forged through their opposition to a common opponent 'can open up new political terrains and possibilities'.[109] Practices that forge transnational links are more discernible in protests by some groups than others. In what follows, we draw out the practices that have forged solidarity across these very different groups.

9.5.1 *Practices Producing Transnational Solidarity*

The transnational solidarity between the protests has been constructed through different practices, strategies and techniques which bring together diverse concerns emerging from Adani projects. In addition to a common strategy of protest and demonstration across different places, one of the main practices that has shaped the solidarity between groups is sharing and disseminating knowledge about the activities of Adani and the revelation of common patterns of oppression that these activities continue to generate in different countries.

Through the practice of continuous sharing of information about the effects of Adani projects, the solidarity between different groups has been crafted as a political activity bringing together the voices of oppressed and marginalized people, and activists from different parts of the world. The compendium of knowledge encapsulating diverse experiences and opinions has actively produced and shaped the solidarity movement as based on shared opposition to the government/corporation nexus. In this sense, the solidarity of anti-Adani protests is a result of creative processes based on particular practices.[110] This solidarity has deepened with increased knowledge about the actions of governments and Adani in affecting the lives of ordinary people in different parts of the world.

One example of this is AdaniWatch, established by the Australian Bob Brown Foundation. AdaniWatch reports and brings together information regarding protests and concerns against the Adani group.[111] Its website offers a rich set of resources for people worldwide to know about Adani's projects, their impacts and peoples' movement. Similarly, a grassroots environmental movement, #Stop Adani in Australia, has been instrumental in raising

[109] Ibid., p. 7.
[110] Ibid., p. 23.
[111] Adani Watch, 'About AdaniWatch – Information Is the Currency of Democracy', available at: www.adaniwatch.org/about (last accessed 27 June 2023).

concerns and organizing protests against the Adani group.[112] The activities of #Stop Adani and AdaniWatch have included collating and bringing together the concerns emerging from Adani's project in different parts of India, Myanmar, Indonesia, Sri Lanka and Australia. Information sharing has been pivotal in exposing how Adani has generated its wealth and assets, revealing Adani's close connection with governments and its associations with other companies. This has helped the solidarity movements to learn about and question the intimate state–corporation relationship.

The solidarity generated by and within anti-Adani protests is continuously strengthened by sharing knowledge about the ways in which Adani and governments are engaged in oppressing indigenous and marginalized people and causing damage to the environment. Knowledge sharing has helped understand linkages between different protest sites. One example of the way sharing information and strategies has formed more explicitly collaborative or joint activity is the 2021 global campaign by the Youth Action to Stop Adani (YAStA). YAStA brought together young people in India and Australia to protest against the Adani group. YAStA organized a week-long call to action involving more than 25 environmental youth organizations.[113] *The Caravan* magazine described the activities of various groups participating in YAStA in the following words:

> These groups mobilised the public for weeks ahead of the scheduled date, urging people to participate in the global movement through their social-media pages. The action week comprised various online events, including a video screening of statements by individuals affected by Adani project sites in India and Australia, a playlist of songs of resistance and hope curated from across the world, a masterclass on art and activism, a documentary film festival on corporate crime, and a Q&A session with the writer Amitav Ghosh on climate fiction.[114]

The solidarity fostered and expressed by YAStA involved engaging with the concerns of the people who suffered at the hands of Adani by bringing together different voices and looking at corporate oppression through the

[112] #Stop Adani, 'Who We Are', available at: www.stopadani.com/who_we_are (last accessed 27 June 2023).

[113] Nityanand Jayaraman, 'Youth Action to Stop Adani – 27 January to 2 February', *Adani Watch*, 19 January 2021, available at: www.adaniwatch.org/youth_action_to_stop_adani_27_january_to_2_february#:~:text=YAStA%20is%20a%20call%20to,environment%2C%20aggravating%20the%20climate%20crisis%2C (last accessed 27 June 2023).

[114] Tushar Dhara, 'The Young Environmental Groups Leading India's New Climate Activism', *The Caravan*, 15 March 2021, available at: https://caravanmagazine.in/environment/the-young-environmental-groups-leading-india-new-climate-activism (last accessed 27 June 2023).

prism of resistance, art and fiction. These activities represented 'passionate articulations of relations and connections'.[115] Similar forms of solidarity have been enacted from Australia.[116] For example, Australia's #Stop Adani campaign came out with a statement declaring solidarity with the protesting Indian farmers in 2020.[117] Recently, protests have taken place outside the Indian High Commission in Australia and elsewhere against Adani's project in Hasdeo forest, Chhattisgarh.[118] In addition to demonstrations, solidarity is expressed through statements, signature campaigns, online events and information sharing on websites and social media.[119] Paying attention to these practices 'through which solidarities are constructed situates such practices as transformative', in the sense that it helps ordinary people and activists make 'political connections' with those situated and struggling against government/corporation nexus in different parts of the world.[120]

Sharing information between groups provides an opportunity to understand the practical ways in which the relationship between the corporate group and the respective states in which it operates affects peoples of all kinds.[121] Such a level of organization and information sharing has helped people engage with the concerns of Adani's project worldwide, and to recognize the link between the local and transnational character of oppression. So, in the solidarity narrative, it is not an accident that indigenous peoples in Australia and India are being oppressed by the same corporation supported by the respective

[115] Featherstone, *Solidarity*, p. 64.

[116] For an account of Australian students' protest against Adani's activities, see Nicole Rogers, *Law, Fiction and Activism in a Time of Climate Change* (Abingdon: Routledge, 2020), chapter 3.

[117] Geoff Law, 'StopAdani Solidarity with Mass Protests by Indian Farmers', *Adani Watch*, 11 December 2020, available at: www.adaniwatch.org/stopadani_solidarity_with_huge (last accessed 27 June 2023).

[118] Geoff Law, 'Indian Tribal People Rally and March to Fight Adani Coal Mines', *Adani Watch*, 4 October 2021, available at: www.adaniwatch.org/indian_tribal_people_rally_and_march_to_fight_adani_coal_mines (last accessed 27 June 2023).

[119] For instance, #Stop Adani, 'Online Rally: Adani Investors #DefundClimateChaos', available at: www.stopadani.com/defundclimatechaos (last accessed 27 June 2023).

[120] Featherstone, *Solidarity*, p. 27 (citing Antonio Gramsci's, 'Some aspects of the Southern Question (September–November 1926)', in Antonio Gramsci, *Pre-Prison Writings*, edited by Richard Bellamy, trans. Virginia Cox (Cambridge: Cambridge University Press, 1994), pp. 313–337.

[121] Solidarity demonstrated through information sharing has also brought to attention the techniques and strategies employed by the corporation and state to prevent people from enjoying their rights. See, Ravi Nair, 'The Pench Conflict: A Brave Campaigner Defies Adani, Police and Assailants', *Adani Watch*, 27 May 2022, available at: www.adaniwatch.org/the_pench_conflict_those_who_oppose_handing_our_resources_to_big_corporations_are_threatened_by_the_police (last accessed 27 June 2023).

governments and state institutions. Practices of informational solidarity have brought to light the fact that the coal extracted from the Carmichael mine is planned to be used by Adani in the proposed Godda power station in Jharkhand to produce electricity.[122] The electricity produced at the Godda plant will be exported to Bangladesh.[123] Thus, Adani's operations in Queensland (Australia), Jharkhand (India) and Bangladesh are directly connected through the coal supply chain.[124]

The solidarity created amongst global anti-Adani protesters has also engendered practical and tactical techniques in fighting Adani. The activist groups in different places have urged other global and local corporations to join them in opposing Adani's projects. The Stop Adani movement in Australia demands that investors withdraw their investments from Adani projects in Australia. It maintains a webpage containing information as precise as the list of companies that have invested in Adani's Carmichael project and those that have ruled out investing.[125] Similarly, protests against Siemens in Germany, calling upon it to 'stop, delay or at least interrupt' the building of the Adani mine in Carmichael, reveal the different strategies and practices the movement has called on to subvert the Adani-State project in a transnational sense.[126]

9.5.2 *Practices Generating (Non-essentialist/Plural) Relationships*

The solidarities emerging from the anti-Adani protest offer a compendium of relationships between ordinary people and activists sensitive to environmental concerns, indigenous peoples' rights and pathologies of neoliberalism. The solidarity against Adani's activities exemplifies the idea that solidarities need not emanate from likeness between activists, places or social groups. The solidarity movement has not just attracted and brought together pre-existing communities. Instead, the protests involve(d) people divided by culture,

[122] #Stop Adani, 'Australian Coal Is Destroying the Lives of Indigenous Peoples in Godda, India'.

[123] See, Geoff Law, 'Adani Versus Local Villagers: The Battle over the Godda Power Plant in India', *News Click*, 23 April 2020, available at: www.newsclick.in/Adani-Versus-Local-Villagers-Battle-Over-Godda-Power-Plant-India (last accessed 27 June 2023).

[124] Somini Sengupta, Jacqueline Williams and Aruna Chandrasekhar, 'How One Billionaire Could Keep Three Countries Hooked on Coal for Decades', *The New York Times*, 15 August 2019, available at: www.nytimes.com/2019/08/15/climate/coal-adani-india-australia.html (last accessed 27 June 2023).

[125] Market Forces, 'Adani Coal Investors Exposed', available at: www.marketforces.org.au/campaigns/stop-adani/finance-stopadani/ (last accessed 27 June 2023); #Stop Adani, 'Investor Updates', available at: www.stopadani.com/investor_updates (last accessed 27 June 2023); #Stop Adani, 'Adani Investors: Stop Funding Adani's coal!', available at: www.stopadani.com/adani-investors (last accessed 27 June 2023).

[126] Sanjai, 'Adani, Targeted by Greta Thunberg'.

language, geography, nationality and borders. What unites them is the common opponent. Their immediate concerns and ambitions are different and yet they are united against the form of oppression effected through corporate-state relationships. The protests have provided a stimulus for activists to bring together and look at all anti-Adani protests through a similar lens – that is, as a struggle against a corporation backed by a populist government. This has helped people connect to each other's concerns and forge a transnational relationship. Thus, the civil rights network, the National Alliance of People's Movement (NAPM), extending its support to YAStA, noted that: 'YAStA made it possible to hear voices that are central to the ground resistance against Adani's excesses: people from Godda (Jharkhand), Kattupalli (Tamil Nadu), Goa, Mundra (Gujarat), Vizhinjam (Kerala), Kavalappara (Kerala), from the Farmers' Protests (Delhi), and Juru Country (Queensland, Australia), united by their struggle against corporate oppression.'[127]

The solidarity emerging from these protests has crafted a relationship based on common terms, even if the immediate demands of protestors differed across locations. First, by making central the struggle against a specific instance of the state-corporation nexus and its varied forms of adverse effects (ranging from environment degradation, indigenous peoples' rights, democratic deficit and lack of transparency and state violence). Second, by contesting existing material relations that shape that specific instance. The examples of various demonstrations across the world against Adani projects, demanding that investors not fund Adani projects, or asking governments to re-examine Adani projects (such as, recently, in Bangladesh)[128] shows how solidarity has emerged through the consistency of the challenge to the particular forms of material relations that benefit Adani and particular populist political leaders.

Slowing down these stories of resistance against Adani's activities allows us to focus on 'the generative, transformative character of solidarity and how solidaristic practices can shape new relations, new linkages, new connections' by contrast to 'accounts where the practices and identities through which solidarities are enacted are seen as primarily "given"'.[129] This introduces us to the idea of solidarity as a creative practice, rather than one based on similarities or dissimilarities of those expressing it. The relationship between anti-

[127] Counterview, 'NAPM Extends Support to Indian, Aussie Citizen Groups "Opposing" Adani Ventures', *Counterview*, 8 February 2021, available at: www.counterview.net/2021/02/napm-extends-support-to-indian-aussie.html (last accessed 27 June 2023).

[128] Staff Correspondent, 'Power Deal with Adani Only to Appease Indian Government: Speakers', *Prothom Alo*, 6 March 2023, available at: https://en.prothomalo.com/bangladesh/z3hf5x3kjw (last accessed 27 June 2023).

[129] Featherstone, *Solidarity*, pp. 18–19.

mining protesters in Australia, Adivasis and grassroots activists in India or environmentalists in Germany and elsewhere did not predate the struggle. The solidarity among anti-Adani protests has produced a new kind of relationship that did not previously exist or, rather, hasn't existed in this form – against the activities of one 'public–private partnership' or global conglomerate and its state partners. Indeed, this relationship is significantly shaped by and benefitted from the current form of organizing through social media.[130]

The new relations, linkages and connections forged through this solidarity also express non-state forms of relations. The solidarities emerging from the anti-Adani protests show that activists did not tie the identity of the participants with the state from which they come. The mere fact Adani is an Indian company and enjoys proximity with the state institutions in India has not stopped activists in Australia and elsewhere from showing solidarity with the people and groups in India which have suffered at the hands of Adani. These protests reflect transnational solidarity with the indigenous people suffering at the hands of Adani and the state.

The solidarity expressed symbolically challenges a unitary idea of the state, which treats the state as a single unified entity and as representing all identities and groups living within it. Thus, the solidarity of anti-Adani protests in India is based on the realization of plural forms of interests and relations operating within a territory and the tensions underlying them. The solidarity movement does not craft a transnational relationship based on a shared *identity*, but a shared opposition and concerns emerging from the state–corporation nexus.

These shared concerns allow people in different parts of the world to relate to plural forms of social and cultural practices. For instance, Adani Watch in Australia, in a June 2022 report on the protest by the tribal people against Adani's Godda (Jharkhand) coal-power station, described how the protest gathering began with a prayer. It described that: '[t]he gathering started with a prayer to Marang Buru, the first all-powerful ancestor, by whose grace the Santhal Adivasis of the area believe all life exists'.[131] By paying attention to the social and cultural practices of the oppressed groups, solidarities emanating from anti-Adani protests forged a relationship between them. A documentary by the Stop Adani movement on the Godda power plant shows how the tribal people (Santhal) opposing it were targeted by police officials. The documentary shows a retired teacher affected by the Adani project, stating that 'land is

[130] On digital campaigns against Adani's activities in Australia, see Beresford, *Adani and the War over Coal*, p. 291.

[131] A special correspondent, 'Indian Tribal People Join Forces to Tackle Adani's Godda Coal-power Plant', *Adani Watch*, 30 June 2022, available at: www.adaniwatch.org/indian_tribal_people_join_forces_to_tackle_adani_s_godda_coal_power_plant (last accessed 27 June 2023).

essential to the Santhal people. It is an intrinsic part of their culture'.[132] This resonates with the situation in Australia, where the Queensland government extinguished native title over 1 385 hectares of Wangan and Jagalingou country for the Adani project.[133] *The Guardian* newspaper reported that this was done without any public announcement of the decision and that the police forcibly removed protesters from their traditional lands.[134] By displacing indigenous people from their land in Queensland, Godda and elsewhere, the Adani projects attack the heart of their respective cultures. The solidarity between anti-Adani protesters brings very different people together by fashioning common linkages, political struggles and knowledges. By paying attention to stories such as these from Godda and Queensland, we can see that the solidarity movement has crafted non-state forms of relationship standing in opposition to common, conjoined, oppressors – the (populist) state and corporation.

9.5.3 *Power Relations Crafted through Solidarity*

The relation forged through the solidarity between anti-Adani protesters could also be seen as generating a form of political power against corporate oppression and state collusion. This form of power questions the idea of the state as the primary site of political power. It crafts an alternative form of solidaristic–political power that stands outside the state and challenges its actions. This form of power is shaped by the knowledge that the state is not a monolithic-unitary entity which equally furthers the interests of all classes living within it. The close association between Adani and the Modi government in particular shows, in very practical terms, how the state prioritizes the interests of the corporate class over marginalized and oppressed groups within the same state.

And so, the movement doesn't produce the state–corporation nexus as merely an abstract argument. Instead, it pays attention to the craft, techniques and idioms through which the state–corporation relationship is brought into operation. It exposes the institutional façade and 'legal' regulations that hide the intimacies between ruling power and corporate bosses. The knowledge

[132] #Stop Adani, 'Australian Coal Is Destroying the Lives of Indigenous Peoples'.

[133] Ben Doherty, 'Queensland Extinguishes Native Title over Indigenous Land to Make Way for Adani Coalmine', *The Guardian*, 31 August 2019, available at: www.theguardian.com/business/2019/aug/31/queensland-extinguishes-native-title-over-indigenous-land-to-make-way-for-adani-coalmine (accessed 27 June 2023).

[134] Dominic O'Sullivan, 'Indigenous People No Longer Have the Legal Right to Say No to the Adani Mine: Here's What It Means for Equality', *The Conversation*, 5 September 2019, available at: https://theconversation.com/indigenous-people-no-longer-have-the-legal-right-to-say-no-to-the-adani-mine-heres-what-it-means-for-equality-122788 (last accessed 27 June 2023).

about the state–corporation nexus crafted the anti-Adani solidarity movement as not being shaped by state-centric visions. It showcased the Indian state, headed by a populist leader, as an adversary of marginalized peoples rather than an ally.

This transnational form of power relations is not just shaped by the knowledge about the close nexus between the Indian state and Adani. It is also a reaction to the globalization of the corporation. The more Adani has globalized its corporate power, the more resistance to it has trans-nationalized. The activists from various places have been able to draw the connections between Adani's activities in different parts of the world and show how its operations raise similar concerns everywhere, ranging from damage to the environment to encroaching on lands of indigenous and poor people. Adani's operation in Myanmar reveals that the group had business arrangements with the Myanmar military – 'the Tatmadaw'. It has been reported that Adani's port project on the Yangon River in Myanmar involved an agreement with Myanmar Economic Cooperation (MEC), a company owned and controlled by the Myanmar military. Adani Watch notes that the project 'has drawn vehement criticism from human-rights groups and experts. The criticism arises from the Myanmar military's genocidal persecution of the Rohingya people, the illegal coup of February 2021, and the subsequent killing of hundreds of civilian protesters'.[135] The political relation generated through the solidarity with anti-Adani protest is crucial in bringing together these stories from different parts of the world and exposing how a state-centric form of political power has benefitted a corporation.

Understanding the close nexus between state and corporation also means that the political power generated through the solidarity movement strives to find solutions to local and global problems through non-state-centric forms of association. The creation of this new power relation opposing the activities of Adani and the states has tried to find the solution to environmental concerns and indigenous peoples' rights through various means and practices. Thus, during the United Nations Climate Conference in Glasgow, 'mass rallies, disruptive protests, media capturing stunts, and powerful stories told in

[135] See, Law, 'Adani Ports and Its Inextricable Links to Coal'. In May 2023, it was reported that Adani group sold its port business in Myanmar. John Reed and Chole Cornish, 'Adani Group Exits Myanmar with Sale of Port Business', *Financial Times*, 4 May 2023, available at: www.ft.com/content/9e62df75-4b01-43f7-8001-cda6c2875ffo (last accessed 27 June 2023). Also see, Josh Robertson, 'Adani Proposed Coal Ventures to Sanctioned Myanmar Military Despite Public Vow to Cut Ties, Leaked Documents Show', *ABC News*, 4 May 2023, available at: www.abc.net.au/news/2023-05-04/adani-coal-projects-myanmar-military-junta-leaked-documents/102291036 (last accessed 27 June 2023).

locations across the world from the Pacific Islands, the British Isles, throughout Asia, and North America' were planned.[136] They were 'all united with a mission to push the global investment sector to defund the fossil fuel industry'.[137] Australia's Stop Adani campaign described it as a way to push investors to stop investing in Adani's project.[138] These activities demonstrate the challenge to states and corporations as the primary actors in making and influencing laws. The solidarity forged through anti-Adani protests gives us a glimpse of how law-making can be influenced from below without attaching oneself to the state-form (irrespective of the success such solidarity practices may engender). The power relations generated through anti-Adani protests offers a potential model of resistance, based on the practices of progressive civil society groups and activists, on varied concerns emerging from the state–corporation intimacy.

9.6 CONCLUSION: POLITICAL TRAJECTORIES

We have used this chapter to explore some of the political possibilities for transnational solidarity today, and in particular as a site of action for left responses to right-wing populism. We have tried to sketch an example of the corporate–state nexus in the global political economy that produces the dislocations that populism feeds on. And we hope that the example highlights answers to the questions we posed about 'solidarity from below', and the possibilities for trans-national (and non-national) forms of solidaristic action that can accommodate many different peoples and the different roles they play, into its capacious forms of action against those economic dislocations.[139]

[136] #Stop Adani, 'Online Rally: Adani Investors #DefundClimateChaos'.

[137] Ibid.

[138] Ibid.

[139] The risks undertaken by different participants in the anti-Adani solidarity movement are not identical. Several reports indicate that protests by indigenous people immediately affected by Adani projects (such as those in Godda) or activists involved in assisting indigenous people against Adani projects (like activists and lawyers in Pench) have often faced assault, threats or intimidation by the state institutions. This is not the same for people protesting in support of them in other parts of the world. While being attentive to the differences in the risks undertaken by different participants, in this chapter, we pay attention to the relationship forged through political struggle which is not necessarily based on the *likeness* between activists, places or social relations. See Ravi Nair, 'Pench Part 1: Vicious Assaults on Opponents of Adani Coal-power Project Alleged to be the Work of "Company Goons"', *Adani Watch*, 5 July 2021, available at: www.adaniwatch.org/pench_part_1_vicious_assaults_on_opponents_of_adani_coal_power_project_alleged_to_be_the_work_of_company_goons (last accessed 14 August 2024); Chitrangada Choudhury, 'Taking over Fertile Land for Adani Group from Protesting Farmers, Jharkhand Government Manipulates New Law Meant to Protect Them', *IndiaSpend*, 1 December 2018, available at: www.indiaspend.com/taking-over-fertile-land-for-

For us, the promise of such forms exemplified by the solidarity forged through anti-Adani protests is the lack of dependence on inter-state relations. To us they seem to disrupt, or at least avoid rehearsing the boundaries created by states. National identities do not dictate the organization of the solidarity movement. A fitting example with which to close is perhaps the way coalitions of actors have organized around the activities of Adani that have endangered the indigenous rights of people 'within' different states. #Stop Adani notes that:

> Adani's coal project will violate the rights of Indigenous people along the entire chain of production. Adani are ripping the heart out of Wangan and Jagalingou country to build their coal mine. Adani's coal trains would run through Juru, Jaanga and Birri country – threatening sacred sites. Finally, Adani's coal would be burned in Godda, Jharkhand, where Adani are brutally displacing thousands of Indigenous Adivasi people to build a new coal station and burn Australian coal.[140]

Recognizing these common patterns of corporate–state violence against indigenous people in Australia and India helps us understand that a significant part of the battles for a more equal world are over rival claims to authority. The power to make and remake worlds takes place not through the exercise of raw 'power' but through practices of authorization. The #Stop Adani quote asserts that one form of authority is being asserted over rival laws and forms of authority, and that rivals are forcibly displaced.[141] The solidarity movement more broadly has brought into focus the practices and techniques through which a blended state–corporate authority is being asserted and exercised over other forms of law. In so doing, it has also created awareness about the continuing existence of those rival laws and distinct ways of relating to nature and the environment. One member of the tribal community in Chhattisgarh (India) forcefully described this link: '"Mining will be our death," he said. "It is going to devastate everything nature has given us. One-time compensation for the land is not enough – we need much more than money to survive. We need nature to be with us"'.[142]

adani-group-from-protesting-farmers-jharkhand-government-manipulates-new-law-meant-to-protect-them/ (last accessed 14 August 2024). For a discussion on 'risks undertaken' by different groups, see Chapter 2, by Scholz.

140 #Stop Adani, 'Trashes Indigenous Rights', available at: www.stopadani.com/trashes_indigenous_rights (last accessed 27 June 2023).

141 Sundhya Pahuja, 'Laws of Encounter: A Jurisdictional Account of International Law' (2013) 1 *London Review of International Law* 63–98.

142 The age of extinction, 'India's Ancient Tribes Battle to Save Their Forest Home from Mining', *The Guardian*, 10 February 2020, available at: www.theguardian.com/environment/2020/feb/10/indias-ancient-tribes-battle-to-save-their-forest-home-from-mining (last accessed 27 June 2023).

The solidarity generated through anti-Adani protests has not only recognized rival worlds and laws but in so doing constructs a rival form of association not dictated by state-centrism. This form of association and the practices involved are built on the concern of various groups affected by Adani projects and help to reveal a way of undoing the hegemony of the current political and economic order without falling back on the state and the figure of the citizen which are integral parts of that order. It suggests that the concerns relating to environmental degradation, indigenous rights, democratic deficit and institutional transparency, which are not exclusive to right-wing populist politics but are intensified by it, do not have to be, and probably will not, be solved only through the medium of state power. In a way, these practices of solidarity perform a warning against conflating state power with people's power in the course of trying to articulate a left response to right-wing populism. They show that, while the political formations of citizen and state may remain important (including as sites of solidaristic practice), they should not be understood as the sole or primary formations from which to address the transnational challenges posed or intensified by right-wing populism. But this one example does not prescribe a blueprint for action. Instead, and most usefully, it shows how solidaristic practices forge new power relations, engage different conceptions of authority and law and prefigure, imagine and enact new worlds.

10

Modern Monetary Theory and the Birth of a New Refugee Realism

PEO HANSEN

10.1 INTRODUCTION

In order to navigate the migration debate in the EU, macroeconomic knowledge is indispensable. Given the debate's strong focus on the fiscal costs of migration,[1] we must first and foremost know how the government spends, taxes and 'borrows'. In crucial relation to this, we must also be able to distinguish between the economic and political (or rules-based) constraints involved in fiscal and monetary operations. Today, the cost assumption is based on a fundamental misunderstanding of how fiscal and monetary policy actually work. This is not to say that the migration debate boils down to economic or fiscal issues – far from it. Racism and xenophobia are of course also prominent in the debate. In this context, though, we find an already large and growing scientific literature that examines and confronts these problems. But the fact that both politicians *and* researchers have long agreed that refugees coming to the EU constitute a fiscal cost has prompted very few critical research responses. Under the telling newspaper headline 'No disagreement on the costs of refugee immigration', the following can be read:

> The costs associated with refugee immigration are not a hot potato within scientific research .... On the contrary, it is correct to say that there is a scientific consensus that refugee immigration at the current employment rate

[1] P. Hansen, *A Modern Migration Theory: An Alternative Economic Approach to Failed EU Policy* (Newcastle upon Tyne: Agenda Publishing, 2021).

among refugees is a cost to public finances, says Mats Hammarstedt, Professor of Economics.[2]

As I have already indicated, there is also no conflict in politics on the question of whether it is accurate to talk about refugee reception in financial cost terms. Instead, the dividing line is between those who think we can afford it and those who think we cannot. As I will demonstrate in this chapter, the question about affordability is misplaced.

Researchers draw their conclusions about costs by way of a seemingly neutral accounting exercise: refugees pay less in taxes than they receive in welfare. Many politicians then use this accounting to justify and explain a restrictive asylum policy. Certainly, some politicians and researchers may also argue that low-skilled labour migrants may be both necessary and affordable, but only if the migrants' access to welfare is restricted. But this does not apply to refugees. It takes time for refugees to start working and paying taxes, and they may also have children. Therefore, by definition, refugees are considered burdens on public finances and welfare funding.

In this chapter, I will show that the consensual cost-perspective on migration builds on a flawed economic conception, one that works constraining on both policy options and our very thinking about migration. Much of it is due to the heavy imprint of the orthodox 'sound finance' doctrine on migration research and policy – the assumption that central governments face a budget constraint and solvency requirement much in the same way as households, municipalities and businesses. The dominant orthodox paradigm has successfully created the common sense that 'sound' fiscal policy simply reflects economic laws of gravity. 'To discuss fiscal policy', Berkley economist David Romer asserts, 'we need to know what the government can and cannot do':

> Thus we need to understand the government's budget constraint. A household's budget constraint is that the present value of its consumption must be less than or equal to its initial wealth plus the present value of its labor income. The government's budget constraint is analogous: the present value of its purchases of goods and services must be less or equal to its initial wealth plus the present value of its tax receipts.[3]

'[L]ike the household', economists Huixin Bi and Eric Leeper establish, 'the government must satisfy a budget constraint each period'.[4] The *Oxford*

[2] *Dagens Samhälle*, 'Ingen oenighet om flyktinginvandringens kostnader', 6 June 2018, available at: www.dagenssamhalle.se/chef-och-arbetsgivare/kompetensforsorjning/ingen-oenighet-om-flyktinginvandringens-kostnader/ (last accessed 15 September 2024). Author's translation.

[3] D. Romer, *Advanced Macroeconomics*, 4th ed. (New York: McGraw-Hill/Irwin, 2012), p. 586.

[4] H. Bi and E. M. Lepper, 'Sovereign Debt Risk Premia and Fiscal Policy in Sweden' (2010), *NBER Working Paper Series*, No. 15810 (National Bureau of Economic Research), p. 13.

Dictionary of Economics describes the 'budget constraint' as '[t]he limit to expenditure. For any economic agent, whether an individual, a firm, or a government, expenditure must stay within limits set by the ability to finance it'.[5] This established notion lends a kind of self-evident validity and urgency to research on the fiscal impact of migration. 'If the expansion of immigration is concentrated among the low-skilled', economists Fehr, Jokisch and Kotlikoff assert, 'the developed world's fiscal finances will deteriorate significantly'.[6]

As a corrective to the orthodox perspective, I will explain and apply Modern Monetary Theory (MMT). MMT not only provides us with tools to critique the prevailing doxa and its detrimental impact on migration policy and research. Most importantly, it also offers the tools with which we can correct and modernize migration research and migration policy, and so establish a realistic approach to both migration and the welfare state.

As will be shown, this also has fundamental consequences for our conception of human rights and solidarity, as these pertain to refugee reception and integration. This has to do with the fact that the trade-off notion just explained, by extension, also comprises the notion that there is a trade-off between solidarity/human rights and the welfare state. The more solidarity with refugees, the story goes, the less financial resources will be left for society as a whole. Human rights and solidarity here emerge as sacrifices for the receiving societies, something that manifests all too clearly in the policy vocabulary on asylum policy in the EU, where solidarity often boils down member states' 'obligations' and 'responsibilities' to 'share' or not 'share' the 'refugee burden'.[7] Equating human rights and solidarity with an 'obligation' to incur, as in this case, a 'refugee burden' speaks volumes about the success of orthodoxy's conception of a national economy as analogous with a household. In this chapter, I will flip this script, arguing that the reception of refugees in the EU is not a solidarity story about the sacrifices on the part of the receivers. Rather, a realistic approach perceives of refugees and low-earning migrants not as fiscal burdens but as the real resources they are.

Empirically, I will attend to the case of Sweden, the country that, proportionally speaking, has received the most refugees in the EU. The specific focus

5 N. Hashimzade, G. Myles and J. Black, *A Dictionary of Economics*, 5th ed. (Oxford: Oxford University Press, 2017).

6 H. Fehr, S. Jokisch and L. Kotlikoff, 'The Role of Immigration in Dealing with the Developed World's Demographic Transition' (2004), *NBER Working Paper Series*, No. 10512 (National Bureau of Economic Research), p. 26.

7 See further, E. Karageorgiou, *Rethinking Solidarity in European Asylum Law: A Critical Reading of the Key Concept in Contemporary Refugee Policy* (Lund: MediaTryck, Lund University, 2018).

is placed on the consequences of the large increase in government spending following the refugee reception in 2015. From the perspective of policy makers' certainty about the fiscal unsustainability of large numbers of refugees and the scholarly assurances concerning refugees' negative fiscal impact, the Swedish situation in 2015 should provide the ultimate worst-case scenario. Sweden, one of the most comprehensive welfare states in the EU, admitted 163 000 asylum seekers in one year. The majority of these asylum seekers were given permanent residence, which meant that they were incorporated into what orthodox economics already takes to be a bloated welfare state. In other words, all the conditions for a perfect storm were in place. By the same token, so were all the conditions for a perfect natural experiment to test the literature's assertions about fiscal burdens and trade-offs.

10.2 THE FISCAL BURDEN OF MIGRATION

Few could have failed to take note of the public debate and political manoeuvring over the fiscal impact of migration, in general, and of refugee migration, in particular. 'Objections to the perceived burden placed by immigrants on public finances', one scholar observes, 'seem to motivate much popular opposition to immigration'.[8] Under the title 'Are migrants good for the host country's economy?' another scholar observes: 'Indeed, the impact of migration on the host country's economy is possibly the most crucial question that policy-makers have to answer.'[9] In October 2021, the Danish Ministry of Finance published figures that were said to show that non-Western migrants represent a net cost of 1.4 per cent of GDP. The data fit like a glove with the Social Democratic government's goal, adopted in 2019, of 'zero asylum migration' to Denmark. According to Torben Tranæs, head of research at Denmark's National Research Centre for Welfare, it was precisely the alleged negative fiscal impact of non-Western migrants that 'changed the Social Democrats' perspective'.[10] Similarly, when the German government, in November 2023, concluded its migration deal with the Christian Democrat

[8] I. Preston, 'The Effect of Immigration on Public Finances' (2014) 124 *The Economic Journal* F569.

[9] N. Ratna, 'Are Migrants Good for the Host Country's Economy?' in A. Triandafyllidou (ed.), *Routledge Handbook of Immigration and Refugee Studies* (London: Routledge, 2016), p. 75; see also C. Vargas-Silva, 'The Fiscal Impact of Immigrants', in B. Chiswick and P. Miller (eds.), *Handbook of the Economics of International Migration* (Amsterdam: Elsevier, 2015), vol. 1B.

[10] *The Economist*, 'Denmark: No Room at the Inn' (18–31 December 2021), available at: www.economist.com/europe/2021/12/18/why-have-danes-turned-against-immigration (last accessed 18 September 2024).

opposition, extolled as 'a very historic moment' by Chancellor Olaf Scholz, much emphasis was placed on the fact that the deal 'significantly scales back social benefits for refugees'.[11]

In the news media the message concerning migrants' ostensibly negative fiscal impact is also commonplace, and during the 2015–2016 refugee crisis it was amplified even further. In September 2015, the *International Business Times* fretted: 'EU refugee crisis: how will European countries pay for the influx of thousands of people?'[12] In an equally rhetorical style, a headline in *The Atlantic* queried: 'Can the welfare state survive the refugee crisis?'[13] 'Ballooning refugee costs threaten Germany's cherished budget goals', a Reuters headline noted, while another one in *Die Welt* claimed that the 'Refugee crisis could cost [Germany] nearly one trillion euros'.[14] The sense that Germany's fiscal health was hinged on a drastic reduction in refugee numbers was growing, with the deputy finance minister, Jens Spahn, saying that '[m]oney for other things that we might want is simply not there'.[15]

Commenting on the Swedish government crisis after the 2018 elections, *The Economist* alleged that 'refugees tend to drain the public purse' and that 'this avoidable policy error has helped to poison Swedish politics'.[16] Furthermore, in its post-election analysis in 2018, *The Guardian* claimed that the '163 000 migrants' who arrived in Sweden in 2015 had been 'magnifying popular concern about a welfare system many felt was already under strain'.

[11] *Financial Times*, 'Scholz Hails "Historic" Deal to Curb Migrants' (8 November 2023), available at: www.scribd.com/document/683406444/Financial-Times-Europe-08-11-2023 (last accessed 18 September 2024).

[12] L. Tomkiw, 'EU Refugee Crisis: How Will European Countries Pay for the Influx of Thousands of People?' *International Business Times* (23 September 2015), available at: www.ibtimes.com/eu-refugee-crisis-how-will-european-countries-pay-influx-thousands-people-2110771 (last accessed 15 September 2024).

[13] H. Horn, 'Can the Welfare State Survive the Refugee Crisis?' *The Atlantic* (18 February 2016), available at: www.theatlantic.com/international/archive/2016/02/welfare-state-refugees-europe/463272/ (last accessed 15 September 2024).

[14] *Reuters*, 'Ballooning Refugee Costs Threaten Germany's Cherished Budget Goals' (17 September 2015); *Die Welt*, 'Flüchtlingskrise könnte fast eine Billion Euro kosten' (25 November 2015), available at: www.welt.de/wirtschaft/article149234485/Fluechtlingskrise-koennte-fast-eine-Billion-Euro-kosten.html (last accessed 18 September 2024). Author's translation.

[15] *Irish Times*, 'Wolfgang Schäuble Warns German Budget Surplus Must Go to Refugees' (25 February 2016), available at: www.irishtimes.com/news/world/europe/wolfgang-schauble-warns-german-budget-surplus-must-go-to-refugees-1.2548386 (last accessed 18 September 2024).

[16] *The Economist*, 'Sweden Fails to Form a Government' (17 November 2018), available at: www.economist.com/europe/2018/11/17/sweden-fails-to-form-a-government (last accessed 18 September 2024).

In particular, the article continued, Sweden is plagued by '[l]ong waits for operations, shortages of doctors and teachers'.[17]

In essence, the message was the same from Sweden's social democratic-led governments at the time. In the autumn of 2015, the finance minister, Magdalena Andersson, declared that the large refugee admission was 'financially unsustainable' and would cause fiscal deficits for the coming years. 'We will both have to reduce spending and borrow', she asserted in an interview in October 2015. 'It's about cutting migration costs as well as looking into spending cuts in other areas. But we will also have to borrow money.'[18] In November 2015, a typical headline in a major daily paper read: 'The deficit is growing: government's expenditures sharply increase due to the growing number of refugees.'[19]

During the election campaign in 2018 the Social Democrats depicted the newly arrived refugees as not being keen enough on learning the language, joining education and training programmes, finding work and thus contributing to the welfare of their new country. Whereas the prime minister, Stefan Löfven, spoke about refugees' 'duty' to make themselves 'employable' in the same breath as he promised to show organized crime the door, Magdalena Andersson said asylum seekers had better go somewhere else. Andersson, who took the most hawkish position, repeatedly declared migrant integration a failure and went as far as claiming that a restrictive asylum policy was a fiscal prerequisite for fighting child poverty in Sweden.[20] Around the same time the minister for justice and home affairs asserted that a government summer programme that subsidised bus fares for high school students had been made possible and affordable only thanks to cuts in refugee spending: 'If we had not tightened up our migration policy in 2015 there would have been no fiscal space left'.[21]

[17] *The Guardian*, 'Sweden Election: Political Uncertainty Looms after Deadlock' (10 September 2018), available at: www.theguardian.com/world/2018/sep/09/swedish-election-far-right-on-course-for-sizeable-gains-in-vote (last accessed 18 September 2024).

[18] *Dagens industri*, 'Magdalena Andersson: Flyktingsituationen inte hållbar' (22 October 2015), available at: www.di.se/artiklar/2015/10/22/magdalena-andersson-flyktingsituationen-inte-hallbar/ (last accessed 18 September 2024). Author's translation.

[19] *Svenska Dagbladet*, 'Underskottet i statens finanser växer: Statens utgifter ökar kraftigt till följd av det ökande antalet flyktingar' (23 November 2015), available at: www.svd.se/a/f82fb837-e91c-4cc3-92f0-92594171ed61/underskottet-i-statens-finanser-vaxer (last accessed 18 September 2024). Author's translation.

[20] *Dagens Nyheter*, 'Finansministern: Barnfattigdom skäl för stramare flyktingpolitik' (28 May 2018), available at: www.dn.se/ekonomi/finansministern-barnfattigdom-skal-for-stramare-flyktingpolitik/ (last accessed 18 September 2024).

[21] *Fokus*, 'Samarbetet som blev en twitterfejd' (26 May 2018), available at: www.fokus.se/veckans-brak/samarbetet-som-blev-en-twitterfejd/ (last accessed 18 September 2024). Author's translation.

10.3 THE *REAL* BENEFITS OF MIGRATION

With the change to a right-wing government in 2022, migration and refugee policy has been elevated to become the government's defining mission. With much emphasis on reducing asylum numbers and associated costs even further, the explicit aim is to implement a 'paradigm shift' in Swedish asylum and migration policy. In the autumn of 2023, the government announced that it was commissioning the National Institute of Economic Research (sorting under the Finance Department) to conduct a study on the fiscal costs of migration, focusing on the welfare costs and tax contributions of mainly refugee migrants. One the purposes is to assess from which countries the costliest migrants come.[22] To be sure, the Ukrainian refugee crisis has changed both Sweden's and the EU's tone on refugee policy. Yet, this change only applies to 'European' refugees from Ukraine. Nevertheless, Swedish governments have continued to emphasise the 'costs' of Ukrainian refugees as well.[23]

But the claim that refugees are a fiscal burden on the Swedish welfare state is guided by a fundamental misconception. Just think of *The Guardian*'s reporting just mentioned, where refugee migration is said to impact negatively on an already strained Swedish welfare state that struggles with backlogs and staff shortages in the health-care system. What the British newspaper fails to consider is the fact that, without migration, the backlogs and staff shortages would have been even more acute. As an in-depth OECD study on the matter found, the share of foreign-born medical doctors in Sweden stood at 30.5 per cent in 2015/16, up from 23 per cent in 2000/2001. Iraqi and Romanian doctors make up two of the largest groups within the cohort of foreign-born doctors in Sweden.[24] At Sweden's largest hospital, Sahlgrenska University Hospital in Gothenburg, 35 per cent of the doctors, 18 per cent of the nurses, 28 per cent of the assistant nurses and 30 per cent of the biomedical analysts

[22] *Dagens Nyheter*, 'Kritik mot nota för invandring' (7 December 2023), available at: www.dn.se/sverige/kritik-mot-nota-for-invandring-ingen-affarsverksamhet/ (last accessed 18 September 2024).

[23] *Dagens Nyheter*, 'Magdalena Andersson: Andra länder får ta ansvar för ukrainska flyktingar' (18 February 2022), available at: www.dn.se/varlden/magdalena-andersson-andra-lander-far-ta-ansvar-for-ukrainska-flyktingar/ (last accessed 18 September 2024); *Dagens industri*, 'Migrationsverket: Mellan 9 och 30 miljarder kronor att ta hand om ukrainska flyktingar' (18 March 2022), available at: www.di.se/nyheter/migrationsverket-mellan-9-och-30-miljarder-kronor-att-ta-hand-om-ukrainska-flyktingar/ (last accessed 18 September 2024).

[24] OECD, *Recent Trends in International Migration of Doctors, Nurses, and Medical Students* (Paris: OECD Publishing, 2019).

are foreign-born.[25] Moreover, close to 30 per cent nationally (and about 55 per cent in the Stockholm region) of elderly care workers in Sweden are foreign-born, of whom the overwhelming majority have a refugee background.[26] As one Swedish regional newspaper heading put it a few years ago: 'Without immigration elderly care falls apart'.[27]

The situation is similar in many other EU countries. When the pandemic hit the EU in the spring of 2020, the issue of essential workers came to the fore, and it soon became clear that low-skilled migrants were playing a key role. As a study published by the German Institute of Labour Economics summed it up:

> The overarching picture is that of a migrant workforce that acts as an integral part in keeping basic and necessary functions of European societies working amidst periods of forced closure. It is worth stressing how, among migrants, the low skilled workers are especially over-represented in a number of key occupations that are vital in the fight against COVID-19, underscoring their often neglected value within European economies.[28]

In 2018, 60 per cent of all cleaners in Sweden were foreign-born. The same was the case for 51 per cent of bus and tram drivers; 49 per cent of taxi drivers; 68 per cent of maids, nannies and related personnel; 42 per cent of restaurant and kitchen assistants; 49 per cent of machine operators in laundering; 44 of machine operators in meat and fish processing; the list goes on.[29] Although it consistently refuses to mention these facts in the public debate, in a report from 2018 even the Swedish government conceded as much: 'Without the

[25] G. Gelotte, 'När var tredje läkare är född utomlands är invandring inte en ekonomisk börda' *Dagens ETC Göteborg* (9 February 2021), available at: www.etc.se/kronika/nar-var-tredje-lakare-ar-fodd-utomlands-ar-invandring-inte-en-ekonomisk-borda (last accessed 18 September 2024).

[26] Socialstyrelsen 'Vård och omsorg om äldre: Lägesrapport 2019', p. 47, available at: www.socialstyrelsen.se/globalassets/sharepoint-dokument/artikelkatalog/ovrigt/2019-3-18.pdf (last accessed 18 September 2024).

[27] *Östgöta Correspondenten* (3 January 2015). Author's translation.

[28] F. Fasani and J. Mazza, 'Immigrant Key Workers: Their Contribution to Europe's COVID-19 Response' (2020), *IZA Policy Paper*, No. 155 (Bonn: Institute of Labour Economics, April), p. 11.

[29] Statistics Sweden, 'Pizza Makers Have Largest Share of Foreign Born Persons' (7 March 2019), available at: www.scb.se/en/finding-statistics/statistics-by-subject-area/labour-market/employment-and-working-hours/the-swedish-occupational-register-with-statistics/pong/statistical-news/the-swedish-occupational-register/ (last accessed 18 September 2024); Statistics Sweden, 'Swedish Occupational Register with Statistics 2018' (March 2020), available at: www.scb.se/contentassets/b49d7efc2653457f8179f18461d2bf38/am0208_2018a01_sm_am33sm2001.pdf (last accessed 18 September 2024).

foreign-born women and men, the elderly care would face significant problems in fulfilling its task.'[30]

10.4 THE POVERTY OF RESEARCH

The people who, proportionally, do more to maintain essential societal and welfare functions are said to burden and make those same welfare functions financially unsustainable. The task of science here must be to correct this misleading message. But that kind of science is very hard to find. At best, we find research that bases itself on the same sound finance premises as the one arriving at the trade-off conclusion, but that, instead of costs, finds fiscal benefits from migration. This conclusion rarely applies to low-earning migrants though, and never to (the initially) non-earning refugees.

When thoroughly examining the sizeable literature on the 'fiscal impact of migration', however, this lacuna is easily explained.[31] As already mentioned, when the neoclassical sound finance paradigm is applied, as it is – knowingly or unknowingly – by all the contributors to the literature, the central government is conceived of as roughly analogous to a household. This assumption applies universally, independent of the smorgasbord of different monetary regimes that any given state may adopt. This means that everyone whose tax payments fall below average is a fiscal burden. These inhabitants are said to receive more in government welfare spending than they pay in.

From the perspective of the research into the fiscal impact of migration this is just a scientific fact, and so research cannot be held accountable for being complicit in stoking the sentiment that refugee reception and low-earning migrants jeopardize the welfare state. As one expert in the field puts it: 'The lower the skills and earnings of migrants in the host country, the greater will be the strictly economic case for restricting some of their welfare rights in order to minimize the fiscal costs for existing residents.[32] The 'strictly economic' serves to indicate that the issue at hand is neither grounded nor decided within the realm of policy choices. Rather, objective economic laws of fiscal sustainability are said to constrain what is politically feasible.

[30] Swedish Government, 'Framtidens äldreomsorg – en nationell kvalitetsplan', Regeringens skrivelse (2017/18: 280, 20 June 2018), p. 16, available at www.regeringen.se/contentassets/faebe5c0bff14b9fb7cd9df7625d2e10/framtidens-aldreomsorg–en-nationell-kvalitetsplan-2017_18_280.pdf (last accessed 18 September 2024). Author's translation.

[31] For such an examination, see Hansen, *A Modern Migration Theory*.

[32] M. Ruhs, *The Price of Rights: Regulating International Labour Migration* (Princeton: Princeton University Press 2013), p. 46.

According to world-renowned economist Branko Milanovic, '[t]he arrival of migrants threatens to diminish or dilute the premium enjoyed by citizens of rich countries, which includes not only financial aspects, but also good health and education services.' Yes, you read right, migrants working in the health services are supposedly diluting 'the premium enjoyed by citizens of rich countries'. Admitting low-earning migrants therefore 'requires withholding some civic rights', Milanovic asserts. 'We can debate the sharpness of the trade-off, but cannot deny its existence.'[33] In Milanovic's quest to figure out ways to 'pay for increased migration',[34] such withholding of rights to migrants – or 'discriminatory treatment', as he terms it – are both necessary and beneficial to all. Migrants, Milanovic suggests, 'could also be made to pay higher taxes since they are the largest net beneficiaries of migration'.[35]

Finally, here's another representative scholarly view, published in the International Organization of Migration's (IOM) journal *International Migration*:

> The refugees represent a fiscal burden for the host countries at least short and medium term. Under these conditions refugee migration is unable to help to alleviate the aging related fiscal burden of the host societies, on the contrary, it contributes to its worsening. Thus, when the majority thinks that refugees represent a fiscal burden (they 'take out more from the public purse than they pay in'), they are not wrong this time. It is not possible to argue against this with solid empirical evidence. Naturally, the moral (and legal) obligation argument for accepting the refugees is still valid but it couldn't be underpinned with further economic reasoning. The moral obligations and the economic benefit are in conflict here.[36]

As asserted in the quote, the factuality of refugees constituting a 'fiscal burden' 'is not possible to argue against . . . with solid empirical evidence'. And since a fiscal burden, by definition, is synonymous with something very negative in the public debate, we should not be surprised if politicians and the public take those making up the burden – i.e. the refugees – to be undesirable too.

In response to this, the proponents of the cost perspective can simply say that to hide the truth about refugee migration goes against the scientific ethos

[33] B. Milanovic, 'There Is a Trade-off between Citizenship and Migration', *Financial Times* (20 April 2016), available at www.ft.com/content/2e3c93fa-06d2-11e6-9b51-0fb5e65703ce (last accessed 18 September 2024).

[34] B. Milanovic, *Global Inequality: A New Approach for the Age of Globalization* (Cambridge: Harvard University Press, 2016), p. 152.

[35] Milanovic, 'There Is a Trade-off between Citizenship and Migration'.

[36] Z. Gál, 'Fiscal Consequences of the Refugee Crisis' (2019), 57 *International Migration*, 341–354, at 352.

and would thus make for an even worse place to begin integration. Many would add that tampering with the truth will only aid the anti-immigration populists – a particularly common retort from mainstream politicians and scholars who want to mark their distance from the extreme right. Since so few have challenged the basic principles and maths of the cost perspective, it has gained an air of unassailable truth. But those who claim that they side with accuracy in order to avoid playing into the hands of the anti-immigration right do something even worse than allowing the cost assumption to stand unchallenged. They give it new life and credibility by insisting it be acknowledged *in advance*. It is like starting a discussion about equal pay by insisting that we first acknowledge that women are a fiscal burden on men because women pay less in taxes – and that trying to diminish or hide this 'fact' only would play into the hands of the sexists.

10.5 MODERN MONETARY THEORY

In employing the descriptive macroeconomic framework provided by Modern Monetary Theory (MMT),[37] we can explain further why the cost perspective builds on a flawed economic conception. I have already stressed that the orthodox 'sound finance' economics conceives of state spending as analogous to household spending. Here, therefore, spending amounts to little more than a cost, in the same way that a household looks at its outlays. As a consequence, the money spent on refugees would have to be made up for through tax hikes, 'risky' borrowing or by removing funds from other areas, such as welfare benefits intended for needy citizens.

For countries that issue their own fiat currencies, however, none of this applies. Since the central government is the monopoly issuer of the currency, it follows, both in logical and in concrete terms, that it necessarily has to spend or lend the currency (via the banking system) into existence before it can collect it back in taxes. If this was not the case, there would be no money to pay taxes with and the banks would have no central bank reserves to buy government bonds with. Such governments are thus the exact opposite of

[37] In explaining MMT, I draw on the following literature: D. Ehnts, *Modern Monetary Theory and European Macroeconomics* (London: Routledge, 2017); D. Ehnts, 'Modern Monetary Theory: The Right Compass for Decision-Making' (2022) 57 *Intereconomics* 128; S. Kelton, *The Deficit Myth: Modern Monetary Theory and How to Build a Better Economy* (London: John Murray Press, 2020); W. Mitchell, R. Wray and M. Watts, *Macroeconomics* (London: Red Globe Press, 2019); W. Mosler, *The 7 Deadly Innocent Frauds of Economic Policy* (US Virgin Islands: Valence Economics, 2010); R. Wray, *Modern Money Theory: A Primer on Macroeconomics for Sovereign Monetary Systems*, 2nd ed. (New York: Palgrave, 2015).

municipalities, business and households. The latter all have to collect, earn or borrow the money before they can spend; they are mere users of money, not issuers.

Consequently, as MMT explains, currency-issuing governments are not revenue-constrained in the currency they issue. This means that taxes collected by the central government are not used to fund government spending as they are when collected by countries that do not issue their own currencies or currency-using bodies such as municipalities or constituent states in federations. Central government taxes fulfil other indispensable functions and purposes. By constantly removing a large chunk of money from the private sector, taxes work as a powerful anti-inflationary measure while at the same time moving real resources (e.g. labour) from the private to the public sector. Taxes also work as an instrument regulating income and wealth distribution, and they are used to promote or discourage various industrial practices and individual behaviours. And there are, of course, other purposes that central government taxes can be made to fulfil, but revenue for spending and saving for future spending do not form part of them.

Likewise, such governments do not have to borrow their own currency in order to spend. As MMT demonstrates, the real purpose of bond sales in a sovereign currency is not fiscal (for financing purposes) but monetary. They are carried out in order for the central bank to hit its overnight interest rate target (the interest banks pay when borrowing reserves from each other overnight).[38]

[38] When a government runs a deficit, i.e. spends more than it collects in taxes, this leads to a net increase in central bank reserves in the banking system. In the system applied by most central banks until recently this, in turn, caused the overnight rate – i.e. the interest rate banks pay when they borrow reserves from each other overnight – to fall towards zero. In the banking system as a whole, the supply of bank reserves has increased, but demand has not, and this is what causes the overnight rate to fall. To keep the interest rate at the central bank's desired target level, the central bank therefore sells government bonds to reduce the reserves in the banking system ('*drain reserves*'). In other words, banks use their excess bank reserves to buy interest-bearing government bonds. The fact that banks buy government bonds when the government has a deficit makes this look like a fiscal operation to cover a deficit. But this is not the case. What is actually happening is that the central bank is conducting a monetary policy operation to control the overnight interest rate, known as 'open market operations'.

Conversely, when the government runs a budget surplus and the reserves in the banking system decrease, this creates upward pressure on the central bank's overnight rate. If the central bank wants to keep the overnight rate at the same target level, it must now instead add reserves by buying bonds. When the central bank buys government bonds from the banks, it pays with bank reserves, which means that the banking system is replenished with reserves. But if the government wishes – as advocates of modern monetary theory point out – it can also "leave excess reserves in the banking system, in which case the overnight rate would fall toward zero" (Mitchell, Wray and Watts, *Macroeconomics*, p. 326). When the interest rate is at zero, as it was

To be sure, all countries that issue their own currencies still impose unnecessary and politically invented fiscal frameworks, including balanced budget rules, debt brakes and spending ceilings. One of the most common rules stipulates that governments must 'borrow' and thus sell bonds to the private sector when it lacks the funds or deposits at the central bank to match the spending. But, again, currency-issuing governments do not need to borrow the currency whose issuing it monopolizes. In fact, as Mitchell and Fazi reveal, such governments 'could run fiscal deficits *without issuing debt at all*: the central bank could simply credit the relevant bank accounts to facilitate the spending requirements of the treasury, regardless of whether the fiscal position is deficit or surplus'.[39] Another option would be for the finance department to sell debt directly to the central bank, a procedure that is also prohibited by most countries. But, even when currency-issuing governments sell bonds to the private sector, these bonds can be 'sold' only on the premise that the government first provides the central bank reserves with which banks purchase the bonds. Again, a government 'must spend (or lend) its currency before it can receive it back either in payment of taxes or in purchase of its debt'.[40] Hence, when currency-issuing governments create fiscal frameworks that require bond sales to the private sector, or banks – instead of no sales or sales directly to the central bank – the banks pay for this by using the reserves that they have in their accounts at the central bank. And bank reserves can only be created by the central government (i.e. the treasury and the central bank); and they are created in three ways: (1) when the government spends;[41] (2) when the central bank lends bank reserves to banks; and (3) when the central bank purchases bonds.[42]

until recently in many countries, the Treasury can then choose 'to sell short-term bonds that pay a few basis points [1 basis point = 0,01%] above zero and will find willing buyers because bonds offer a better return than the alternative (zero). This drives home the point that a sovereign government with a floating currency can issue bonds at any rate it desires, normally a few basis points above the overnight interest target it has set' (Mitchell, Wray and Watts, *Macroeconomics*, p. 326). Today, most central banks have abandoned daily 'market operations'. Instead, they control the overnight interest rate by means of fixed deposit and lending rates for banks.

39 W. Mitchell and T. Fazi, *Reclaiming the State* (London: Pluto Press ,2017), p. 184, emphasis in original.

40 Mitchell, Wray and Watts, *Macroeconomics*, p. 338.

41 When the central government spends its currency, it instructs the central bank to credit the banks' central bank accounts with reserves. In turn, the banks credit the recipients' (e.g. households) bank accounts with bank deposits. This results in a net addition of reserves (in the banking system) and a net increase in *households' and businesses' bank deposits*. When the government taxes, banks debit taxpayers' deposit accounts and the central bank then debits the banks' reserve accounts.

42 Mitchell, Wray and Watts, *Macroeconomics*, p. 338.

With the onset of the pandemic in March 2020, the European Commission suspended the Stability and Growth Pact's austere fiscal rules and the ECB launched the Pandemic Emergency Purchase Programme (PEPP). In short, the PEPP involved the ECB buying all the bonds that the banks had bought from the eurozone member states – bonds the banks did not want to hold themselves. The banks thus sold on the bonds they had bought from the member states to the ECB in the secondary bond market.[43] This removed all risk for market participants as they knew they could always sell on to the ECB, and for a slightly higher price as well. As a result, eurozone countries no longer ran the risk of 'running out of money', there was no need for austerity and the ECB's actions ensured that interest rates on both short-term and long-term government bonds remained very low.[44] In fact, during the pandemic, the ECB bought all government bonds issued by the governments in the eurozone.[45]

When then ECB president Mario Draghi stated, in July 2012, that the ECB was 'ready to do whatever it takes to preserve the eurozone' – by purchasing government bonds on the secondary market – the basis for the pandemic era's unconstrained spending in the eurozone was established. But, although the 'whatever it takes' initiative demonstrated the fiat quality of the euro, it still had to co-exist with an even more rigid adherence to sound finance orthodoxy and perpetual austerity. With COVID-19 hitting in March 2020, however, this fundamentally changed; all of the fiscal austerity strings that had formerly been attached to the ECB's bond purchasing were now cut.

Many politicians, central bankers and economists criticised the ECB's actions and argued for a return to the rules and austerity policies. The critics could also argue, with good reason, that the ECB's actions ran contrary to the intentions of the EMU framework. However, what they could not claim was that the monetary union could have remained intact without the ECB's intervention as lender of last resort.

43 Ultimately, or in balance sheet terms, this procedure is equivalent to governments selling government bonds directly to the ECB in the so-called primary market (see Ehnts, 'Modern Monetary Theory'; Mitchell, Wray and Watts, *Macroeconomics*, p. 339). However, as the EU regulatory framework prohibits the latter, the ECB buys the bonds on the secondary market instead.

44 D. Ehnts, 'The Eurozone Is Fully Committed to Modern Monetary Theory (MMT)', *Brave New Europe* (4 April 2020), available at: braveneweurope.com/dirk-ehnts-the-eurozone-is-fully-committed-to-modern-monetary-theory-mmt (last accessed 18 September 2024); Ehnts, 'Modern Monetary Theory'.

45 *Financial Times*, '"Forceful for Longer": Investors Bet ECB Bond Buying Is Here to Stay' (22 July 2021), available at: www.ft.com/content/2cf6e9bd-797a-4666-a742-470c292f1fb7 (last accessed 18 September 2024).

In April 2024, these same critics finally got the best of it when the European Parliament and the Council decided to re-install the Stability and Growth Pact's austere fiscal rules, after a four-year pandemic-induced pause. A report by the European Trade Union Confederation slammed the decision, calculating that, under the new rules, a mere five countries in the EU 'would be able to meet at least minimum social and green investments needs'.[46] This will very likely spark a new round of clashes between Brussels and member states over public spending and debt levels.

In addition to this, and with the formal termination of PEPP at the end of 2022, the ECB has, for its part, created a new instrument (the Transmission Protection Instrument, TPI) that allows the ECB to intervene and, if necessary, purchase unlimited amounts of government bonds to lower bond yields in eurozone countries that run the risk of being shut out of bond markets. The TPI thus shows that the ECB will continue to act as a *lender of last resort* and as the 'quasi-fiscal arm' of the euro area.[47] To lend credibility to austerity and the fiscal rules, however, the ECB has entered the political fray, declaring, in April 2024, that, as related by the *Financial Times*, 'it could exclude countries from its new but untested bond-buying programme if they do not act on EDP [excessive deficit procedures] recommendations'.[48] Should the ECB actually decide to make good on its threat, and terminate its 'quasi-fiscal' function, then countries would not be able to fund themselves and the eurozone, as we know it, would be terminated too.

10.6 SPENDING EQUALS INCOME

As MMT also shows – and as both the unprecedented refugee and pandemic spending in Sweden and the EU confirm – the money spent by the central government always ends up *somewhere* rather than nowhere, by definition. This contrasts with the orthodox perspective, which only understands expenditure as costs, in the same negative way that a household looks at its costs. However, money cannot disappear because 'all spending must be received by

[46] European Trade Union Confederation, 'Navigating Constraints for Progress: Examining the Impact of EU Fiscal Rules on Social and Green Investments' (2024), p. 14, available at: www.etuc.org/sites/default/files/publication/file/2024-04/Publication%20-%20Fiscal%20Rules%20Report.pdf (last accessed 18 September 2024).

[47] For the quasi-fiscal role of the ECB, see W. Mitchell, 'ECB Is Running Out of Debt to Buy', Blog (7 September 2017), available at: billmitchell.org/blog/?p=36809 (last accessed 18 September 2024).

[48] *Financial Times*, 'France and Italy among 11 Countries to Fall Foul of EU Fiscal Rules' (28 April 2024), available at: www.ft.com/content/5125db1e-a0c4-4d5e-9960-59ee781ac88f (last accessed 18 September 2024).

someone, somewhere, as income'. Again, spending equals income, or, as Wray puts it, '[a]ggregate spending creates aggregate income'.[49] This means that when the state spends on refugee integration, for example, the money will show up as net income in the non-governmental sector – in municipalities, businesses and households.

MMT thus emphasises the basic accounting principle that all financial assets will, by definition, be offset by the same amount of financial liabilities. Similarly, any financial deficit will be offset by a financial surplus. Hence, it follows that 'a government deficit (or surplus) must be exactly offset by a surplus (or deficit) in the non-government sector'.[50] Understanding this, we also understand why government deficits are not something risky or bad, but just another way of expressing that there is a surplus (or net financial saving) in the non-government sector. As Tymoigne explains, 'fiscal deficits are a boost to the saving level of the domestic private sector'; they 'sustain national income by injecting more income in the economy than they remove through taxes, which improves the liquidity and solvency of other sectors'.[51] When income-dependent sectors can run surpluses, this helps to stabilize the economy as a whole. However, when budgetary rules require the government to tighten continuously, this stability is undermined, either by weakening the economy or by households and firms accumulating a risky debt burden.

10.7 REAL RESOURCES, FINANCIAL RESOURCES

Another mistake that researchers and policy makers often make is to miss the crucial distinction between *real* resources, such as labour, and *financial* resources – a distinction that constitutes one of the starting points of MMT. Therefore, they are unable to appreciate the value of the indispensable work performed by, for instance, the 60 per cent of cleaners in Sweden who are born abroad. Instead, these workers are described as fiscal burdens as they are said to receive more of the state's welfare spending than they contribute in taxes. According to this logic, Sweden would be better off without the cleaners and other people in low-wage work who came as refugees. This is a very strange logic. Because what would society look like if no one worked in cleaning or food production, or if no one took care of the elderly, drove the buses or worked as assistant nurses?

49 Wray, *Modern Money Theory*, p. 18.

50 Mitchell, Wray and Watts, *Macroeconomics*, p. 14.

51 E. Tymoigne, 'Seven Replies to the Critiques of Modern Monetary Theory' (2021), *Levy Economics Institute Working Paper* No. 996 (Levy Economics Institute of Bard College), p. 56, available at: www.levyinstitute.org/pubs/wp_996.pdf (last accessed 17 September 2024).

As already explained, the real resource contribution from the foreign-born has been substantial in Sweden.[52] The fact that Sweden is the only country in the EU (and beyond) that has not seen an increase in the median age over the last decade illustrates this.[53] With fewer Swedish-born workers joining the labour force than leaving it, the entire net addition of working age people in Sweden has, since 2008, consisted of the foreign-born. Between 2010 and 2017, the number of working age (16–64) Swedish-born people dropped by over 150 000 while the number of working age foreign-born grew by some 360 000 people.[54] This growth will pick up even more until 2025, when the foreign-born share of the working age population is set to hit 27 per cent, as compared to 18 per cent in 2010. The figures for 2017 demonstrates this well. Here, the labour market added 94 000 jobs, of which 75 000, or 80 per cent, went to foreign-born workers.[55]

Recent reports confirm this development. Over the past two years, and despite a slowing economy, unemployment amongst the foreign-born in Sweden has been dropping at a record pace. The same goes for the employment rate for the foreign-born, which now stands at 75.1 per cent. This means that the employment rate for foreign-born people in Sweden beats the overall employment rate in the EU (74.6 per cent); the overall employment rate in Sweden ranks second in the EU (82.2 per cent).[56] A recent survey from Statistics Sweden, moreover, describes the current employment situation for the unaccompanied minors (mainly from Afghanistan) who sought asylum in Sweden in 2015. The picture is striking in that it sharply contradicts the gloomy predictions made at the time concerning this particularly vulnerable and 'costly' refugee group. As Statistics Sweden reports, today 'men who came to Sweden as unaccompanied minors are employed to a higher degree than persons born in Sweden of the same age'.[57] Not only that, the proportion of

52 For a comprehensive account, see Hansen, *A Modern Migration Theory*.

53 Eurostat, 'Median Age of Population 2008–2018', available at: ec.europa.eu/eurostat/statistics-explained/index.php?title=File:Median_age_of_population,_2008–18_(years)_.png (last accessed 18 September 2024).

54 Swedish Public Employment Service (SPES), *Arbetsmarknadsutsikterna hösten 2018: Prognos för arbetsmarknaden 2018–2020*.

55 Ibid., p. 26.

56 *Dagens Nyheter*, 'Sysselsättningen ökar markant bland utrikesfödda' (10 May 2023), available at: www.dn.se/ekonomi/sysselsattningen-okar-markant-bland-utrikesfodda/ (last accessed 18 September 2024); Eurostat, 'Employment: Annual Statistics' (26 April 2023), available at: ec.europa.eu/eurostat/statistics-explained/index.php?title=Employment_-_annual_statistics#Employment_in_2022_compared_with_the_EU_target (last accessed 18 September 2024).

57 Statistics Sweden, 'Eight Out of Ten Unaccompanied Minors from 2015 Are Employed' (28 November 2023), available at: www.scb.se/en/finding-statistics/statistics-by-subject-area/

men with an income of at least three income base amounts is significantly higher among unaccompanied minors than among men born in Sweden.[58]

10.8 THE FISCAL IMPACT

To manage the reception of 163 000 refugees in 2015, the Swedish government spending increased significantly. The government made sure to inform the public that the spending was a necessary evil that would affect the fiscal health negatively. The economic expertise was even more concerned and urged the government to cut spending and introduce new austerity measures to avoid deficits and debt accumulation. The many forecasts concerning the 'negative' fiscal impact of refugees published by the government, its expert agencies and the European Commission were not presented as the uncertain forecasts they always are. Instead, the assertion that refugee spending would *cause* deficits was consistently presented as a foregone conclusion. However, it was exactly the opposite that transpired. Instead of the large and 'precarious' deficits that the experts and the government had guaranteed, the consolidated public sector ran large surpluses in all years between 2016 and 2018 – indeed, even 2015 saw a small surplus.[59]

From 2015 to 2017 Sweden paused its sound fiscal framework in order to deal with a serious situation that required a drastic increase in spending. The surplus target and the 'pay–go' rule were suspended. Despite claims to the contrary by all parties involved, the spending increases and the growth in public consumption did exactly what they often do: they stimulated demand, investment and employment. In 2016 alone, public consumption rose by 3.6 per cent,[60] a development not seen since the 1970s.[61] The economy grew and tax revenue surged so much that successive surpluses were created, which is something that may happen, albeit not necessarily. However, as modern monetary theory explains, the government budget balance is not the important thing. What matters is how the real economy is doing and how resources are

living-conditions/living-conditions/integration–analysis/pong/statistical-news/unaccompanied-minors-2015/ (last accessed 18 September 2024).

58 Statistics Sweden, 'Ensamkommande barn 2015: Boende, utbildning och sysselsättning 2022', Rapport 18, 2023, p. 27, available at: www.scb.se/contentassets/220efocac69e47aa8b44907d3fdf7714/le0105_2023a01_br_be57br2301.pdf (last accessed 18 September 2024).

59 Hansen, *A Modern Migration Theory*, pp. 141–153.

60 European Commission, 'European Economic Forecast: Autumn 2018', *Institutional Paper* 89 (DG for Economic and Financial Affairs 2018).

61 A. Nilsson and Ö. Nyström, *Flyktingkrisen och den svenska modellen* (Stockholm: Celanders förlag, 2016).

being utilised. Do the health and social care systems have enough staff and enough funds? Is private borrowing sustainable? Is investment in renewable energy growing? What about unemployment? Politicians and experts have spent a lot of precious time trying to plug the non-existent and, even if they exist, completely harmless holes in government finances that they claim refugee spending is causing. Much less thought though, has been given to the real needs and resources.

Important, too, is that, while Sweden's central government, its economic experts and the media were busy worrying about the refugee spending's negative impact on the future fiscal balance, many rural and de-populating municipalities away from Stockholm were busy welcoming this expenditure as income. Thanks to the refugee spending by the central government, 2016 ended up being one of the best fiscal years ever for Swedish local governments, with practically all of the country's 290 municipalities running surpluses.

The central government spending to the municipalities financed the reception of refugees and their initial integration. In and of itself this increased public consumption enormously; and it stimulated investment and employment, which boosted overall economic growth. But, since much more money was transferred than was needed for the immediate refugee concerns, municipalities were able to attend to other things too, such as welfare needs, schools and infrastructure. Besides impacting positively on the health of welfare services, in many municipalities refugee funds also enabled municipalities to invest, save and pay down debt.[62]

The admission of refugees – that is, *real* resources – together with the generous addition of financial resources from the central government thus proved to be a hugely virtuous combination for scores of depopulating municipalities in Sweden. With this we also see the nullification of what scholars and centrally located politicians claim to be an inescapable and indisputable trade-off between refugee spending and welfare spending. What, as Gál claims, we cannot 'argue against . . . with solid empirical evidence'[63] actually turned out to be possible to disprove. Right before our eyes, then, Sweden had built a real-world model – however reluctantly – that was capable of receiving large numbers of refugees while at the same time investing in welfare. Instead of the misconceived trade-off between migration and welfare, the Swedish case demonstrated that it is exactly the other way round. Spending on the refugees, the non-citizen newcomers, became a way of rediscovering the

62 Hansen, *A Modern Migration Theory*, chapter 7.

63 Gál, 'Fiscal Consequences of the Refugee Crisis', 352.

viability of welfare for all. But, instead of discussing its real effects and applicability as a model for the EU as a whole, the Swedish model has since been discarded and deemed fiscally unsustainable.

10.9 CONCLUSION: HUMAN RIGHTS ARE NOT AN ECONOMIC SACRIFICE

When politicians sound the alarm over refugee costs, claiming that these threaten the fiscal sustainability of the welfare state, they do so from the comfortable place of being able to cite research. Given that the cost and trade-off perspective is a product of orthodox economics, the fact that it has not been fundamentally challenged by research perspectives that do not profess themselves adherents of orthodox economics should be very puzzling. But most of all it shows both how entrenched the cost perspective is and how unknown its orthodox roots are. This means that the very concepts and worldview that set the parameters for the scholarly and public debate are hidden from view. For the most part, they are just perfunctorily assumed. Progressive scholars often end up treating the trade-off as a self-evident fact that comes with a set of equally self-evident constraints.

Political theorist Joseph Carens – who is one of the foremost academic advocates of migrants' rights – is a case in point. The trade-off advocates Ruhs and Martin refer to Carens as someone who contends that 'even if there is a trade-off between migrant numbers and rights, restricting the rights of migrants is always morally problematic'.[64] And, since Carens *does* acknowledge the trade-off as a reality, this also forces him into an intricate exposition concerning those instances where moral principles actually (albeit problematically) take a back seat to the presumed trade-off reality.[65] As an example of when it is morally justifiable to exclude migrants from welfare, Carens argues that

> the programs from which temporary workers are most likely to be excluded and the ones where the normative justification of the exclusion seems to me most plausible are programs that are financed by some general tax and that have as their primary goal the transfer of resources from better off members of the community to worse off ones. I have in mind things like income support

[64] M. Ruhs and P. Martin, 'Numbers vs. Rights: Trade-Offs and Guest Worker Programs' (2008) 42 *The International Migration Review* 249–265, at 261.

[65] J. H. Carens, 'Live-in Domestics, Seasonal Workers, and Others Hard to Locate on the Map of Democracy (2008) 16 *The Journal of Political Philosophy* 419–445, at 438–439.

programs (often called welfare in the United States) and perhaps other programs aimed at poorer members of society such as social housing.[66]

Correspondingly, Carens mentions schooling for children of irregular migrants as an example of when it is *not* morally legitimate to exclude. It is important to mention, though, that this is prefaced with an acknowledgement that 'granting irregular migrant children a right to a free public education imposes a substantial financial cost on the receiving society against its expressed will'. He admits that this and other arguments against such free public education 'have some force'; but he also believes 'that ultimately they are outweighed by the moral reasons for granting irregular migrant children a free public education'.[67]

Carens walks us through several other instances where it may or may not be morally permissible to exclude migrants from social rights. The point, however, is that this entire exercise is undertaken solely because Carens accepts the trade-off notion at face value. He, as so many other scholars, is adapting his theory to a trade-off thesis he takes to be so self-evident it needs no scrutiny.

Here, then, we can spot a general problem with much of the normative political theory around migration, citizenship and migrants' rights. It fails to examine what are presented as irrefutable economic constraints – the trade-off, the fiscal costs – and hence feels compelled to adapt and adjust to what are really *political* and *ideological* constraints dressed up as economic ones. As I have already pointed out, there is of course also the option of acknowledging the reality of the constraints but then saying that, in practice, we can still afford it because economic losses sometimes have to be accepted in exchange for moral gains and the fulfilment of human rights *obligations*. In essence, this is what Carens does when he reasons around irregular migrants' right to education. As one representative voice has it: 'There may well be a trade-off between numbers and rights, but refusing to grant immigrants a path to residency and citizenship has been argued to be fundamentally unjust and indeed inconsistent with liberal democratic ideals.'[68]

But, if politicians can cite research in support of their cost arguments against admitting asylum seekers, most of the time they do not have to. The notion that there is a trade-off between refugee migration and the welfare state is simply common sense in the public debate. The debate is not whether this

66 Ibid., 430.

67 J. H. Carens, 'The Rights of Irregular Migrants' (2008) 22 *Ethics and International Affairs* 163–186, at 169–171.

68 J. Neo, 'Riots and Rights: Law and Exclusion in Singapore's Migrant Worker regime' (2015) 2 *Asian Journal of Law and Society* 137–168, at 157.

is actually accurate; everybody agrees that refugees involve costs for taxpayers. The debate is, rather, whether these *costs* are deemed affordable or not, whether we can afford to be solidaristic or not. It is clear who is winning this debate in terms of policy outcomes; asylum policy is becoming increasingly restrictive and the residence and social rights for those refugees who still manage to enter the European Union are being curtailed. No EU member state wants to share the 'refugee burden'.

But it is a strange debate, because the losing side, or those defending refugee rights, almost always contend that human rights and solidarity never should be allowed to be subjected to cost–benefit analyses. Given that no one is questioning the assumption that refugee reception indeed constitutes a cost, this position is understandable. Under these circumstances, human rights proponents will always lose a cost–benefit debate over refugee reception. But, as I have shown here, refugee reception is *not* costly. Rather, it amounts to a beneficial addition of real resources, as illustrated in the Swedish reality above. The government spending on refugees, for its part, will do what government spending always does: it will end up as income in other sectors of the economy – that is, as income for municipalities, businesses and others involved and employed in the management of refugee reception and integration. Those advocating human rights, therefore, do not have to concede the mistaken orthodox assumption that refugees are costly. Nor do they have to think of 'the economy' as the enemy. Receiving refugees in the EU is not an economic or fiscal sacrifice.

But, let me be clear: I am not saying that Sweden or the EU should admit refugees *because* it benefits Sweden and the EU. Sweden and the EU should admit refugees to defend and uphold human rights. On the economics of it all, there is no argument. In admitting and investing in refugees – that is, *real* resources – societies in Sweden and the EU cannot but benefit.

11

Solidarity Conceptions, Neo-Liberal Economics and Law as a Public Service

BAS SCHOTEL

11.1 INTRODUCTION

This chapter examines prominent solidarity conceptions used in legal discourses in the context of unfair economic arrangements, typically associated with neo-liberalism. It looks at solidarity conceptions in legal discourses *about* and *within* law, combining an external with an internal perspective. The chapter finds that some prominent solidarity conceptions are not helpful to critically analyze neo-liberal economic arrangements, especially from a legal theory perspective. These findings echo the conceptual analyses of solidarity elsewhere in this volume.[1] The solidarity conceptions in question are circular or redundant, because they either presume solidarity to be the foundation of and thus present in every legal order (including legal orders supporting unfair economic arrangements) or they equate solidarity with cooperation. This chapter also finds that the standard policy proposals to counter and unwind neo-liberal economic arrangements, which are often informed by solidarity, are too aspirational.

These policy proposals typically involve imposing *new legal duties* on dominant economic actors and states, making their effectiveness depend on adopting new national and regional legislation and treaty law, on compliance with this legislation by dominant economic actors, and on enforcement by legal authorities. Moreover, the proposals imply that the normative resources for change lie outside the law. This suggests that the neo-liberal economic arrangements are only morally wrong, but that they cannot be questioned on the basis of existing positive law. To address this gap, this chapter explores an

[1] See Chapter 1, by Patricia Mindus.

alternative understanding of law based on existing positive law, namely law as a public service. Dominant economic actors rely on the law as a public service. They need legal authorities, especially judges, to declare their neo-liberal economic arrangements legally valid and enforceable. Positive law already offers judges the normative resources to refuse the help of the law whenever the neo-liberal economic arrangements structurally lack minimal reciprocity and fairness. This chapter's main proposition is that elite experts, namely judges sitting on the bench of Western civil and commercial courts – as opposed to or along with weaker economic actors[2] – may be the agents of change.

Section 11.2 analyzes three types of solidarity conceptions from a legal theory perspective: sociological, moral philosophical, and legal conceptions of solidarity. Section 11.3 discusses how conceptual shortcomings of solidarity are echoed in the standard critiques of neo-liberal economic arrangements and typical proposals to counter and unwind them. Section 11.4 explains the concept of law as a public service through the lens of private law. Section 11.5 concludes by exploring some practical implications and limitations of law as a public service.

11.2 SOLIDARITY CONCEPTIONS IN LEGAL DISCOURSE

11.2.1 *Sociological Conceptions of Solidarity*

Émile Durkheim's conception of solidarity is probably one of the most widely used when scholars try to explain the relationship between solidarity and law. As a sociologist Durkheim sought to identify, describe, classify, and explain social order. For him, solidarity as a form of cooperation was constitutive to social order.[3] He wanted to see how the division of labor was an essential factor in producing solidarity.[4] But "solidarity" is not an empirical phenomenon which a sociologist can simply and directly identify and measure.[5] To identify and measure solidarity as an empirical phenomenon, Durkheim needed a proxy for solidarity. To this end, he used legal systems, which can be

[2] See the contributions in this Volume, e.g. Chapter 8, by Herzog, and Chapter 7, by Noll, which explore how weaker economic actors can mobilize themselves against exploitative economic arrangements.

[3] Émile Durkheim, *De la division du travail social*, 5th ed. (Paris: Bibliothèque de philosophie contemporaine/Alcan, 1926), pp. 11–34, where Durkheim discusses the *method* for determining the social function of the division of labor.

[4] Ibid., p. 27.

[5] Ibid., p. 28.

identified, described, classified, and explained. For Durkheim, the evolution of law represented the evolution of solidarity. Each form of law represented a form of solidarity. Hence, the transformation of the well-known forms of solidarity: from the dominance of mechanical solidarity (collective economic and social relations) to the dominance of organic solidarity (division of labor, where actors operate as organs in a body with exclusive and distinctive, but interdependent functions). For Durkheim, solidarity was the explanans for social order. And, in order to identify and measure the various stages of solidarity, he used the law as empirical data. Durkheim thus used the law to explain solidarity in order to, ultimately, explain social order.

For Durkheim, solidarity has a foundational function. Solidarity constitutes the basis for any social and legal order. Thus, whenever there is a social and legal order there is solidarity. It is the task of social science to identify, describe, and characterize the type of solidarity in any given social order. And Durkheim's methodological invention was to use law as a proxy for solidarity, because law is a phenomenon that can be empirically observed.

Interestingly, in legal philosophical accounts of law and solidarity, Durkheim's sociological conceptions of solidarity, for example, mechanical and organic solidarity, remain a trope.[6] Solidarity then operates as a diagnostic concept to explain and criticize the shortcomings of positive law. Accordingly, existing arrangements of positive law (e.g. property rights, consumer rights, trade law, etc.) lack or undermine solidarity. The solution or cure is to call for more solidarity within the law, typically involving new legal duties through the adoption of new national and regional legislation and treaty law. The use of Durkheim's sociological concept of solidarity in normative legal discourses is problematic from a methodological perspective. The law cannot be critically examined through Durkheim's concept of solidarity, because for Durkheim law is already an expression of and a proxy for solidarity. In fact, it is thanks to law that one can empirically observe solidarity in any given social order. Hence, it does not make sense to speak of law "lacking or undermining" solidarity, because solidarity is the foundation of law. All law – by definition – is based on solidarity. In short, Durkheim's notion of solidarity is a foundational concept. Such a foundational concept can work for a sociological inquiry into the sources of social order. But a foundational conception of

6 Anton Zijderveld, "The Legal and Moral Dimensions of Solidarity" (2006) 35 *Netherlands Journal of Legal Philosophy* 306–330, at 312–313; Luigi Corrias, "Solidarity and Community: From the Politics of the Clan to Constituent Power" (2021) 50 *Netherlands Journal of Legal Philosophy* 129–141, at 130–131; Candida Leone, "What Is Solidarity? A Look Behind the Veil of Solidarity in 'Corona Times' Contractual Relations" (2021) 50 *Netherlands Journal of Legal Philosophy* 239–250, at 239–240.

solidarity is not helpful to critically examine the lack of solidarity within existing arrangements of positive law.[7]

11.2.2 *Philosophical Solidarity Conceptions*

Like the classical sociological conceptions, philosophical solidarity conceptions also pertain to the foundations of the social, political, and legal order. But they differ methodologically in two ways. First, philosophers are using solidarity conceptions to determine what the content of positive law *ought to be*. Second, their approach is philosophical, not sociological, because a set of uncontested *values* constitutes the starting point of their analyses. I will limit myself to two philosophical approaches: standard liberal philosophies of distributive justice and phenomenological accounts of what makes a political community. Within these broad traditions I will focus on solidarity between insiders and outsiders of a national political or legal order.

An articulated elaboration of solidarity between insiders and outsiders from a standard liberal philosophy perspective can be found in debates on so-called ethics of migration.[8] Here solidarity operates as a normative source for duties vis-à-vis outsiders that do not follow from the existing moral and legal sources for duties, for example, free will, wrongful conduct and special ties (family, friends, community, country). What do insiders owe to outsiders? There are roughly two grounds for solidarity towards outsiders. First, the predicament of the outsiders may be directly or indirectly caused by an unfair distribution of resources and public goods (e.g. an unfair global economy). The community of insiders has created this unfair distribution. The insiders keep in place and benefit from it. Helping outsiders constitutes a kind of compensation or correction for this unfair state of affairs. Insiders should reform the global economic system, introduce a global tax, give generous development aid and/or open their borders. Second, insiders may also have a duty to help out outsiders even if the former are not directly or indirectly responsible for the predicament of the latter. A case in point is the moral duty to offer asylum to those fleeing persecution or war. The classical argument for a duty to offer asylum is that the habitable places on the earth are limited and originally belonged to all humans. Nobody ought to be denied a share of the resources

7 Legal scholars could use Durkheim's solidarity conception to distinguish between different types of solidarity present in the law and then come up with a theory in order to normatively rank the various types of solidarity. But that is not how scholars are using Durkheim's solidarity concept in normative legal discourses today.

8 I draw on the discussion and the extensive literature in Bas Schotel, *On the Right of Exclusion: Law, Ethics and Immigration Policy* (London: Routledge, 2012), pp. 140–159.

needed for a life in dignity. No community has an absolute right to the resources of its territory. Since every human being has a right to a safe place on earth, insiders have a duty to offer asylum.

This standard liberal conception comes closest to a colloquial understanding of solidarity. Solidarity urges us to help others to whom we would otherwise not have a duty to offer such help. The help typically involves a positive action that is costly to the helper and involves an extra effort. Moreover, the helper does not necessarily receive anything in return for the help.[9] This liberal argument is a matter of solidarity because it appeals to a *commonality* between insiders and outsiders. The resources of the earth belonged originally to both insiders and outsiders. Both insiders and outsiders have equal moral rights to dignity and basic needs.

With respect to the law, standard liberal solidarity operates as an *aspirational* argument *de lege ferenda* based on normative resources external to law. Unlike the sociological conception of solidarity, applying this philosophical conception of solidarity to positive law does not run into methodological problems. But it does put much faith in the persuasiveness of morality. Moreover, from a legal theory perspective it is somewhat problematic if the solidarity obligations turn out to be too one-sided for the insiders. It happens to be the case that *effective* legal arrangements imposing legal duties without reciprocity, directly or indirectly, are extremely rare in law.

To many readers the idea of reciprocity as a basic feature of law may appear counterintuitive. Though some may accept that many *private* law arrangements are based on reciprocity (see discussion in Section 11.4.3), they will find it more difficult to accept this in the context of public law which often imposes duties on persons without any direct pay-off for the duty holder. One of the clearest cases is the duty to pay taxes. Some philosophers even tried to make the case that taxation amounts to forced labor.[10] Furthermore, there are arguably innumerable examples in the past and at present of rulers levying taxes for their own particular private interests. Even so, the power to levy taxes was claimed in the name of reciprocity throughout history in legal discourse.[11] This is illustrated nicely by the politico-legal justification for the absence of a

9 See also for these features, Andrea Sangiovanni and Juri Viehoff, "Solidarity in Social and Political Philosophy," in Edward N. Zalta and Uri Nodelman (eds.), *The Stanford Encyclopedia of Philosophy* (Summer 2023 edn.), available at https://plato.stanford.edu/archives/sum2023/entries/solidarity/ (last accessed 22 September 2024).

10 Edward Feser, "Taxation, Forced Labor, and Theft" (2000) 5 *The Independent Review* 219.

11 This corresponds with Joseph Raz' argument that conceptually law must claim legitimate authority and must come close to having de facto authority. See, for a discussion, Schotel, *On the Right of Exclusion*, pp. 119–138.

right to levy personal taxes on foreigners: "strangers do not enjoy the honors (honores) or the amenities of the place [of taxation], so they must not be burdened by taxes. This alone is in accordance with natural reason (naturalis ratio)."[12] This same rationale was much later captured by the so-called benefit principle: "Taxation is the equivalent for the protection which the government affords to the person and property of its citizens; and as all alike are protected, so all alike should bear the burden, in proportion to the interests secured."[13] Taxes were supposed to serve the public good, and not the private interests of the prince, as was clearly reflected in the central politico-legal concept to justify special and, later on, general taxes, namely necessity.[14]

Like the standard liberal solidarity conceptions, the phenomenological approach also starts from features that all human beings and political communities have in common. But the way solidarity operates as a source of duties is quite different. Under the standard liberal approach, the outsider is a victim of social injustice. Under the phenomenological approach the outsider is not so much a victim but an agent who is co-constitutive for the self or identity of the political community. The self or identity of a political community is always constituted in relation to the other.[15] You can only make sense of the self by acknowledging the other. As a result, if you ignore the other you ignore the self. When a community determines its inside, it must also recognize the outside. Moreover, nobody has direct knowledge of or access to what counts as the inside and outside. In effect, the inside and outside are only established by proxy, they must be re-presented. Here lies precisely the opportunity to reach out to outsiders who may have been previously excluded. Phenomenological

[12] Quote from Caspar Klock (1583–1655), according to Thier, "one of the most influential authors of tax law in his time." The quote is cited in a passage in Andreas Thier, Traditionselemente des Finanzföderalismus in der Schweiz: Zur Geschichte des interkantonalen Doppelbesteuerungsverbots (Zürich: Schulthess, 2014). I found the passage and the quote in translation by Avi-Yonah Reuven, "Nothing New Under the Sun? The Historical Origins of the Benefits Principle" (2023) 51 *Intertax* 547, p. 550.

[13] Thomas Cooley, A *Treatise on the Constitutional Limitations Which Rest upon the Legislative Power of the States of the American Union* (Boston: Little Brown & Co., 5th ed. 1883), p. 613, cited in Richard A. Epstein, "The Ubiquity of the Benefit Principle," *Coase-Sandor Institute for Law & Economics Working Paper No. 21*, 1994, p. 32. In the same paper, on p. 2, Epstein rephrases the thinking of Locke and Blackstone as follows: "the state may recover the costs of conferring benefits on its citizens, and it may recover the costs of its service by using the coercive power of taxation."

[14] E. Brown, "Cessante Causa and the Taxes of the Last Capetians: The Political Application of a Philosophical Maxim," in J. Strayer and D. Queller (eds.), *Post Scriptia: Essays on Medieval Law and the Emergence of the European State in Honor of Gaines Post. Studia Gratiana XV* (Rome: Pontifical Institute for Canon Law, 1972). Brown labels the maxim of necessity as "philosophical." The actual maxim and arguments are first of all legal.

[15] For a recent account, see Corrias, "Solidarity and Community," 132–139.

solidarity calls insiders to recognize and acknowledge an inevitable solidarity that is already there. In this respect, the phenomenological account of solidarity amounts to a kind of foundational concept similar to the sociological conception of solidarity. By not showing solidarity towards outsiders a political community misrepresents itself. In this vein, Menke argues that Germans deny their own Germanness if they do not open up to migrants.[16] While the aspirational standard liberal solidarity urges insiders to help outsiders as victims of injustice, the phenomenological account claims that insiders will become victims of their own lack of solidarity if they do not include outsiders: they will betray the experience of their own self.[17]

Compelling from a philosophical perspective, it is unclear how the phenomenological approach will ever have any practical or institutional traction. Betraying the experience of their own self does not seem to hurt the insiders that much. Their non-reciprocal self-perception does not prevent them from maintaining and exercising a dominant position over marginalized outsiders. Invoking the phenomenological conception of solidarity is like telling a bully that he is actually the weaker party and a victim of his own insecurities. This will not stop the bully. Bystanders not lending their support or acquiescence will.

The standard liberal account of solidarity amounts to an aspirational conception of solidarity. But this conception has little explanatory or diagnostic force. Solidarity is simply an antonym for the fact that insiders do not have or do not feel a duty towards outsiders. Furthermore, the aspirational conception also lacks curative force. The diagnosis and the cure fully coincide. The problem: not enough solidarity. The solution: more solidarity. The phenomenological approach does not fare better. The phenomenological and foundational conception lacks diagnostic and curative force. If it is true that solidarity is already there, and that taking into account outsiders is actually inevitable in order to constitute a meaningful community, how come this is not happening? Apparently, political communities can flourish, at least on their

[16] C. Menke, "Zurück zu Hanna Arendt. Die Flüchtlinge und die Krise der Menschenrechte" (July 2016) 806 *Merkur: Deutsche Zeitschrift für europäisches Denken* 49.

[17] Similarly, Achiume combines the liberal justice argument and the phenomenological approach to justify that political communities of the global north must grant migrants from the global south a right to admission. First, the global north has to make the global south whole for the past injustices committed by the colonial regimes. Second, the global south does not lie outside the global north. The global south is already part of the political community of the global north by virtue of being subjected to the colonial administrative and economic rule of the global north. The migrants from the global south are *already* part of the political community of the global north as subjects of former European empires. Tendayi Achiume, "Migration as Decolonization" (2019) 71 *Stanford Law Review* 1509.

own terms, while betraying the experience of their own self. While the aspirational conception has at least the benefit of clarity as to its practical implications, namely new legislation, advocates of the phenomenological approach are unclear about what more solidarity means in concrete policy and legal terms.

11.2.3 *Legal Conceptions of Solidarity*

The philosophical conceptions of solidarity have much in common with solidarity conceptions appearing in instruments of international and European law. Legal documents writ large, especially preambles and judicial argumentation, make reference to solidarity in two, often combined, forms: aspirational and foundational.[18] Aspirational are the references to solidarity in proposals to incorporate *new* legal obligations of solidarity in positive law.[19] But often these calls for solidarity are not merely aspirational. They are also declaratory: there *ought to be* new legal duties of solidarity, because solidarity *is* the basis of the *already existing* legal order. Solidarity then has a foundational meaning: it constitutes the very foundation of the legal order. Solidarity is necessary and inevitable. The new duties of solidarity merely confirm what is already there.

Here, we might raise the same objections against the aspirational and foundational nature of the philosophical conceptions of solidarity. As an aspirational conception, legal solidarity may ask too much from the law. As a foundational conception, it lacks diagnostic and curative force. If solidarity is already there, why does it not deliver? Still, these legal conceptions differ from the philosophical conceptions of solidarity in one respect. The philosophical solidarity conceptions seek to justify obligations for insiders that are one-sided: the insiders must give up economic and political

[18] For a comprehensive overview, see Alina Carrozzini and Luigi Lonardo, "The Many Faces of Solidarity and Its Role in the Jurisprudence of the Area of Freedom, Security and Justice," in Eva Kassoti and Narin Idriz (eds.), *The Principle of Solidarity. International and EU Law Perspectives* (The Hague: TMC Asser, 2023), pp. 261–279; Craig Eggett, "Solidarity as an International Legal Norm," in Eva Kassoti and Narin Idriz (eds.), *The Principle of Solidarity. International and EU Law Perspectives* (The Hague: TMC Asser, 2023), pp. 29–33; Dire Tladi, "In Search of Solidarity in International Law," in Eva Kassoti and Narin Idriz (eds.), *The Principle of Solidarity. International and EU Law Perspectives* (The Hague: TMC Asser, 2023), pp. 17–28; Eleanor Sharpston, "Thinking About Solidarity and EU Law" in Eva Kassoti and Narin Idriz (eds.), *The Principle of Solidarity. International and EU Law Perspectives* (The Hague: TMC Asser, 2023), pp. 153–162.

[19] The aspirational aspect may even turn into a messianic kind of promise. See, for this, Chapter 12, by Karageorgiou.

privileges.[20] The legal solidarity conceptions are less morally demanding. The legal solidarity conceptions do not call for strong and affluent actors to help the weak and poor. They call for cooperation and mutual support between equally strong parties. At best it is about solidarity between strong actors cooperating when helping persons in need (cf. solidarity as burden or responsibility sharing in the context of refugee protection). This conception of solidarity is neither aspirational nor foundational. But it is redundant because solidarity simply means that all strong actors will be better off if they cooperate. But, if solidarity is now equated with the need or utility to cooperate, it loses any conceptual and normative value added: all legal arrangements are about facilitating cooperation.

Moving away from international legal discourse we may ask ourselves if domestic law does not impose duties to help the weak and poor. In Section 11.2.2, I pointed out that the right to levy taxes and the duty to pay them are based on reciprocity, not solidarity. But it could be argued that in many Western countries tax revenues are used to finance welfare programs. Welfare programs may be conceived of as policies of solidarity *par excellence*. Still, we must be careful not to confuse the particular experiences of those claiming to be a net contributor to the welfare system and the self-acclaimed rationale of the system. When introducing welfare arrangements, legislators rarely present them as exclusively promoting the interests of those receiving welfare benefits. Many welfare programs have more to do with the logic of insurance, stabilizing the labor market, de-politicizing the labor movement and, more generally, promoting social stability.

Paradoxically, the legal solidarity conception doing most semantic work is the rather prosaic and neglected conception of solidarity as joint liability dating back to Roman law.[21] Solidarity is then a modality of a legal obligation, whereby a creditor has multiple debtors and the creditor can claim the entirety of the debts from each single debtor. This joint liability thus creates an additional security for the creditor, which may have motivated the creditor to enter into the transaction in the first place or offer more favorable terms to the contracting party. This solidarity conception can much better account for the (dis)connection between solidarity and law. First, solidarity is exceptional. Solidarity as joint liability is not presumed: it requires consent or special

[20] This also goes for the phenomenological account of solidarity. Though insiders re-discover their true identity when they account for others, they still may have to give up economic and political privileges.

[21] R. Monier, *Manuel élémentaire de droit romain* (Paris: Editions Domat Montchrestien, 1947, reprinted Aalen: Scientia Verlag, 1977), vol I.

legislation.[22] Second, the solidarity is between those having a duty, not between a stronger party and a person in need. Law is based on reciprocity and fairness, but not on altruism. Accordingly, the underlying rationale for the joint liability is that the debtors must have a common interest, typically a common enterprise.[23] Classical legal solidarity as joint liability is another illustration of how positive law does not normally cater to legal arrangements that impose legal duties without any direct or indirect benefits for the duty holder.

11.3 SOLIDARITY AND GLOBAL JUSTICE VERSUS THE NEO-LIBERAL ECONOMIC ORDER

The practical focus of this chapter is on neo-liberal economics. Schematically, there are two central tenets of the neo-liberal economic order.[24] First, in principle, scarce goods must be distributed through a market-based price mechanism driven by supply and demand. This mechanism relies on three pillars: freedom of contract, right to property and competition.[25] Second, the dominance of this model is beyond political and legal deliberation and discussion. Thus, political and legal institutions have no choice but to adopt and facilitate the free market.[26] According to its proponents, a neo-liberal economic order will inevitably lead to economic inequalities. But these material inequalities are not problematic. They are a precondition for a well-functioning economy and society because, in a liberal market with free competition, inequality is an incentive for today's have nots to become the haves of tomorrow. Even if in the short term the have nots will not acquire a level of personal welfare acceptable to most people, at least they have the benefit of personal liberty and thus human dignity. For they live in liberty, free from unnecessary interference by collectively organized political bodies, such as the state or trade unions.[27]

[22] Henri De Page, *Traité Élémentaire de Droit Civil Belge*, vol III, *Les Obligations* 2nd part, 3rd ed. (Bruxelles: E. Bruylant, 1967), pp. 311–312.

[23] Ibid., p. 313.

[24] See also Chapter 6, by Nanopoulos.

[25] Jessica Whyte, *The Morals of the Market: Human Rights and the Rise of Neoliberalism* (London: Verso, 2019); Thomas Biebricher, *The Political Theory of Neoliberalism* (Stanford: Stanford University Press, 2018), p. 37.

[26] Michael Wilkinson, *Authoritarian Liberalism and the Transformation of Modern Europe* (Oxford: Oxford University Press, 2021).

[27] To be sure, the neo-liberal thinkers rejected the laissez faire policies of the nineteenth century. See Biebricher, *The Political Theory of Neoliberalism*, pp. 21–25.

Many oppose the optimism of neo-liberalism.[28] Competition does not produce a fair re-distribution of wealth and resources. If there is competition between dominant economic actors, it will not lead to a significant redistribution of wealth between dominant and weaker actors. Neo-liberal arrangements mostly amount to competition among weaker actors reducing even more their bargaining power.

As a result, neo-liberal economic arrangements have catered for an on-going unequal distribution of wealth and resources giving relatively few dominant economic actors exclusive control over resources (money – cash and credit, natural resources, raw materials, minerals, metals, labor, real estate, hardware, software, data) at the expense of a large majority of weaker economic actors. The result is that large parts of the global population – in both the global south and the global north – live in economic and social precarity, in relative and absolute terms. When basic needs (e.g. work, food, housing, healthcare, education, energy, etc.) are governed by neo-liberal economic arrangements they tend to favor the particular private interests of dominant economic actors, marginalizing weaker economic actors. Weaker economic actors will find themselves in a structural unequal position with little to no bargaining power, alternatives or exit options, leading to social economic precarity and disenfranchisement for many of them. By contrast, dominant economic actors continue to accumulate wealth and expand their exclusive control over resources, reinforcing their already dominant economic position. Apart from structural economic inequality, dominance and precarity, neo-liberal economic arrangements facilitate the on-going depletion of planetary bio-diversity and sustainability. In short, on the basis of these critical observations it is clear that many neo-liberal economic arrangements lack minimal reciprocity and fairness, as they almost exclusively favor the interests of dominant economic actors at the expense of other stake holders, such as weaker economic actors and even nature.[29]

There is a huge variety of policy proposals to counter neo-liberal economics in the name of social justice and solidarity. The proposals fall roughly in one or more of the following three categories: direct redistribution of wealth, radical reform of the economic and financial system, and measures to stop

[28] See for the literature, Candida Leone, "Flexibility as Commodification and Contracts as Local Resistance" (2023) 2 *European Law Open* 467, at 468–469.

[29] To be clear I only reiterate these critical observations and do not argue for or substantiate them. The aim of this chapter is not to debunk neo-liberal theories, but to convince those opposing neo-liberal economic arrangements to not only look for solutions outside the law.

the depletion of earthly resources and bio-diversity.[30] In an obvious way these proposals can be understood as an expression of solidarity, namely solidarity between haves and have nots, present and future generations, humans and non-humans. But also in a more conceptual way the proposals show many similarities with the solidarity conceptions analyzed in Section 11.2.

First, like solidarity, the proposals often seek to impose new duties (e.g. paying taxes, paying minimum wages, negotiating fair trade deals, creating healthy working conditions, refraining from mining). Second, the duties are largely one-directional: dominant economic actors do not directly benefit from the execution of the new solidarity duties. They are a burden for which they receive nothing in return in the short term.[31] Third, dominant economic actors may consider the duties a sacrifice: they must renounce benefits to which they are normally legally entitled. Fourth, the normative source for the solidarity lies mainly *outside* the law. The duties must be imposed not in the name of already applicable law but in the name of solidarity among human beings. The solidarity duties are not laid down in positive law, but they ought to be (cf. proposals to incorporate human rights into the WTO framework). As a result, practically speaking, like solidarity, the proposals require a mass mobilization of non-legal actors to put pressure on legislators and governments to adopt new legislation and treaty law. Finally, even when incorporated into positive law, the effectiveness of the new legal duties depends on the

[30] Examples of policy proposals for the redistribution of wealth: global resources dividend, increase of inheritance tax, debt cancellation for countries of the global south, and increasing Special Drawing Rights for countries of the global south. Examples of policy proposals to reform of the economic and financial system: Tobin tax, abolition of off-shore tax schemes, reform of or withdrawal from trade agreements to favor south–south trade, abolition of the investor–state dispute settlement system, tariffs and quota for goods and services produced by dominant economic actors, abolition of subsidies for dominant economic actors and sectors of the global north, incorporate human rights in the international trade system. Examples of policy proposals for saving the planet: carbon tariffs, ban or quota for goods and services produced in an unsustainable manner, creation of funds for the development of sustainable technologies and resources. See for a recent analytical taxonomy of policy proposals to counter neo-liberal economics, Van Jackson, "A Capital Critique: Progressive Alternatives to Neo-liberal Economic Order" (2023) 78 *International Journal* 212–231, at 214–226. See also UN General Assembly, Human Rights Council, "Report of the Independent Expert on the Promotion of a Democratic and Equitable International Order" (12 July 2016), A/HRC/33/40; Thomas Piketty, *Le capital au XXIe siècle* (Paris: Seuil, 2013).

[31] Of course, this is a matter of perspective and framing. Ideally the solidarity proposals would make the economic order a more sustainable, stable, and safer place, for example, less risk of social unrest and revolution. This would then stabilize the economic position of dominant actors. Still, dominant actors do not seem to have a direct short-term interest to support the proposals, because they have the means to mitigate the adverse social and environmental effects of neo-liberal economic arrangements.

willingness of dominant actors to comply with the law and on the capacity and willingness of authorities to enforce the new laws.

In short, the dominant proposals make social justice depend on compliance by dominant economic actors, either as a result of free will or by force. But what if this logic is reversed? What if the starting point is that dominant economic actors actually depend on the law and legal authorities, instead of the other way around?

11.4 LAW AS A PUBLIC SERVICE

11.4.1 *The Point of Law as a Public Service*

Law's basic communicative structure is not so much bi-lateral in the sense of the right holder invoking law vis-à-vis an individual duty holder (as a result of a contract, tort, property right or another legal obligation). Rather the communicative structure is in essence about the right holder invoking the law vis-à-vis third parties to secure the execution of the obligation by the duty holder.[32] So, appeals to or statements of law are ultimately aimed at other members of society who are called on to help the right holder to secure his rights. The other members can be private persons (allies of the duty holder, bystanders, and so on) or public authorities. The obligations can be negative or positive. The help may comprise active physical intervention and help, or simply non-resistance. Crucially, the help is sought from other members of society and based on the law. The help is not sought from kin, friends and close neighbors. The help is based on anonymous publicness, not on special ties of blood, friendship, or proximity. From this communicative structure follow two things: (i) law must claim to be fair, and (ii) law is a public service.

The first consequence of law's communicative structure is that legal authorities must claim that legal arrangements are minimally fair and reciprocal. Legal duties deserve to be enforced against a duty holder, because the legal duty is part of a legal arrangement from which the duty holder stands to benefit directly or indirectly. For every legal duty there must be a direct or indirect counterpart, a *quid pro quo*. The reason is that ultimately other community members are supposed to help secure the performance of a legal duty. Securing, and ultimately enforcing, the execution of a legal duty can be costly and risky for those third parties. Therefore, members of society, that is,

[32] See Bas Schotel, "EU Operational Powers and Legal Protection: A Legal Theory Perspective on the Operational Powers of the European Border and Coast Guard" (2021) 22 *German Law Journal* 625–649, at 638, with reference to the literature.

the potential helpers, will only give their support to securing the execution of obligations that deserve to be secured. Executing obligations that lack any *quid pro quo*, directly or indirectly, are unreasonable and do not deserve the help from others. Even if the legal arrangements are not in reality reciprocal and fair, legal authorities certainly cannot afford to openly declare that the arrangements are not fair and reciprocal.[33] As a result, law will always make sure, at least on paper, to show that a legal arrangement is also in the interest of the duty holder.[34] Law's claim to fairness and reciprocity means that the law's own internal discourse, namely legal doctrine and legal techniques, is engrained with the logic of fairness and reciprocity. Since virtually all legal concepts are premised on the logic of fairness and reciprocity, albeit self-serving and sometimes cynical, there are opportunities for change from within the law. The second consequence of law's communicative structure is that, when a right holder invokes the law, she makes use of the law as if it were a service.[35] She calls on the law to help her secure her right. The law is a service ensured by the public at large, hence a public service. The actor invoking the law needs the service of the law, not the other way around. It also means that actors fully depend on legal authorities, more specifically judges, who decide whether or not to declare the legal arrangements valid and enforceable. Furthermore, since law is a public service, it follows that it should serve the public equally to a certain degree. So, in theory, everyone should have a more or less equal share of the public service *ceteris paribus*. It becomes problematic

[33] Cf. the sarcastic remark about law's "majestic equality" in Anatole France's *Le Lys Rouge* (Paris: Claman-Lévy, 1929), p. 113.

[34] Cf. attempts in legal doctrine to argue for reciprocal elements in slavery. When law finds it too difficult to argue that a category of persons benefits from a legal arrangement (e.g. enslaved persons), then the law can secure its internal consistency by simply denying them legal personhood. Accordingly, the law transforms a human being from a legal subject being capable of obedience into an object of coercion and discipline. Thus, colonial laws on slavery are not so much directed at enslaved persons, but at free men and foreign states. They must obey the laws on slavery and respect the private property of slave owners and not undermine the slave system. Things become schizophrenic when colonial authorities were forced to negotiate and enter into peace treaties with fugitive enslaved communities. See Chapter 7, by Noll.

[35] Law as a public service has clear commonalities with Shiffrin's idea that the state may or must refuse to lend its efforts to enforce a contract when it finds the contract is immoral. But Shiffrin's scope and approach are different. She focuses on the unconscionability doctrine, while law as a public service applies to all legal arrangements. She makes a philosophical argument to the effect that the unconscionability doctrine need not be paternalistic but can be justified on the basis of liberal egalitarianism. Law as a public service is not a philosophical justification but follows from an analysis of the law's communicative structure. Seana Shiffrin, "Paternalism, Unconscionability Doctrine, and Accommodation" (2000) 29 *Philosophy and Public Affairs* 205.

when particular actors make much more use of a public service than others without good reasons, making the use disproportionate or excessive.[36]

11.4.2 *Law and the Neo-liberal Economic Order*

Law is, thus, a public service for the members of the legal community. This is also the case for economic actors. Law makes it possible to organize economic transactions whose execution is secured by the members of the legal community. Without the law, a sophisticated and complex division of labor, means of production and credit would be impossible. In fact, the basic building blocks or code of the economic system are legal. So, in my view, the communicative code of the economic system (payment/non-payment) can be fully reduced to the communicative code of the legal system (legally valid/invalid). Similarly, quintessential economic notions such as competition and exchange value fully depend on and can be reduced to legal validity.[37] In a modern economy, virtually all economic transactions constitute legal transactions or rely on them. The economic system (even the informal economy) relies on the bulk of economic arrangements and transactions being legally valid.[38] If courts cease to sanction the legal validity and legal enforceability of property titles, contracts, mortgages, and so on, the entire modern economic order will collapse. Thanks to law, economic actors can call on the help of the members of the legal community, especially officials (both senior and rank and file), to secure and enforce the execution of economic arrangements. The upshot is that it allows economic actors to obtain and maintain exclusive control over resources *beyond their own physical span of control*.[39] Creditors no longer need to visit their debtors personally to collect and secure payments. Principals and employers can have others work for them without being physically present

[36] A good reason for a person to make more use of a public service than others is when the need to use the service is beyond her own control (e.g. health, disabilities). Or some actors may make more use of a public service because they directly contribute to the public good (e.g. transportation companies using public roads).

[37] *Contra* Niklas Luhmann, *Law as Social System*, trans. Klaus Ziegert [1993] (Oxford: Oxford University Press, 2004), p. 400.

[38] Much of the activities, assets, entities, and infrastructure that directly or indirectly contribute to criminal activities are part of the legal economy.

[39] This obviously corresponds with the features by which private law and private international law turn assets and claims into capital as identified and analyzed by Pistor, namely priority, durability, universality, and convertibility. Katharina Pistor, *The Code of Capital: How the Law Creates Inequality* (Princeton: Princeton University Press, 2019). But law as a public service helping actors to secure arrangements beyond their own physical span of control is not limited to the creation of capital. It applies to all legal arrangements: economic and non-economic; capitalist and non-capitalist.

to ensure the execution of the work. Owners can safely enjoy their property without being physically present to protect it. In short, law allows economic actors to obtain and maintain exclusive control over economic resources (e.g. money, movable assets, real estate, labor, natural resources).

Law as a public service has two crucial implications for the economic order. First, the economic arrangements which the law is expected to secure and enforce must to a certain degree be reciprocal and fair for all stakeholders involved. This applies in particular to stakeholders who have legal duties ensuing from those economic arrangements. So, when a creditor calls on the law and thus the public to secure the execution of a contract against his debtor, this contract should be more or less fair, or at least one must claim this to be the case. More importantly, the legal authorities will have to claim that the particular arrangement or particular area of law *in general* leads to reciprocal and fair arrangements. Why else would the public and thus the legal authorities help the creditor? Secondly, law as a public service also means that it is a service at the disposal of the public at large and not of only some privileged actors. There should be good reasons why we would allow some economic actors to make more use of a public service than others.

Precisely when it comes to the claim to minimal fairness and reciprocity neo-liberal economic arrangements tend to fall short, as indicated in Section 11.3. The problem is not that sometimes incidental individual neo-liberal economic arrangements lack minimal fairness and reciprocity. Whole segments of national, regional, and even global economy are governed by neo-liberal economic arrangements that structurally favor dominant economic actors at the expense of weaker actors and non-human stake holders.

Not only do neo-liberal economic arrangements lack minimal reciprocity and fairness, they also lead to an excessive appeal on the service of the law by dominant actors. Neo-liberal economic arrangements promote a massive concentration of wealth and exclusive control over resources in the hands of relatively few dominant economic actors. Obviously, these resources and wealth are beyond the dominant economic actors' *physical span of control*. It is only thanks to the law that they can secure the effective exclusive control over and monetization of their resources and wealth. The fact that the law allows actors to exercise exclusive control over resources beyond their own physical span of control is not problematic *per se*. This is simply the public service that the legal order offers to its members. However, under neo-liberal economic arrangements, dominant economic actors make excessive use of this public service, because of their massive accumulation of wealth.

There is an important difference between the public service of legally protecting massive amounts of wealth and other public services, for example, infrastructure such as public roads. The use and costs of the latter is highly regulated and subject to political decision making. How (e.g. speed, weight, freight), how much (e.g. designated lanes for trucks), and when (e.g. truck-free days, hours) the roads may be used is regulated. It is the result of an explicit balancing of interests between various users and other stakeholders (e.g. local residents, environment, other economic actors emitting N_2). The perceived utility and costs of transportation companies making more use of the roads than individual citizens are weighted, balanced, argued, and decided in a process of explicit political decision making. The same goes for how much and how transportation companies must pay for the public service. Similar regulations and political decision making are lacking when it comes to the legal protection of massive wealth accumulation.

11.4.3 *Reciprocity and Fairness within Private Law*

In Section 11.3, I indicated that proponents of a neo-liberal economic order believe that economic inequalities will lead to a more efficient redistribution of wealth and resources thanks to competition based on an almost unfettered freedom of contract and right to property. Advocates of global justice do not share this belief. They see the almost unfettered freedom of contract and right to property as the root cause of the problem. Therefore, they want to get rid of it. Yet, both camps seem to agree on two things. First, the neo-liberal economic arrangements are made possible thanks to positive law, especially contract, property, and company law. Second, the neo-liberal logic is engrained in positive law, especially private law (including company law). Accordingly, both camps believe that there are no normative resources within positive law to resist and counter neo-liberal economic arrangements.[40] As a result, proponents of a neo-liberal order confidently adopt what they believe is a kind of originalist interpretation of private law. Since it will automatically lead to an almost unfettered individual autonomy and free will. By contrast, opponents of neo-liberal economic arrangements have recourse to instruments outside existing private law. As mentioned,, they call for legal reforms imposing *new* legal *duties* on dominant economic actors. They urge for radical changes in existing positive law through adopting new legislation and treaty law.

[40] Neo-liberal thinkers advocated state intervention in order to create and maintain "truly competitive conditions." For example, minimal wage to avoid workers to sell their labor at any price. See Biebricher, *The Political Theory of Neoliberalism*, pp, 41–42. But, crucially, these corrections were to come through legislative interventions. Apparently, existing positive private law arrangements did not have the normative resources to correct the market.

I am not sure why advocates of social justice concede so easily to the neo-liberal interpretation of law. Critical scholars have showed aptly how law and lawyers have been complicit in shaping exploitative colonial and, later on, neo-liberal economic arrangements.[41] But they have not considered that these legal interpretations may be contrary to the law itself. They rarely explore the possibility that the law itself may point to better interpretations. In a similar vein, when legal scholars criticize private law and propose more just arrangements, they often seek recourse to normative sources outside positive law and rely on political philosophy.[42]

I am not contesting here the value of the external perspectives on law. But there is a risk of giving up too easily on the law, as if neo-liberal economic arrangements are only unsound from a philosophical perspective but perfectly fine from the perspective of positive law. It may make judges complacent: as if they do not have the resources from within existing positive law to refuse lending legal support to neo-liberal economic arrangements.

A powerful example of such resources from within the law is revealed by the work of Robé. He makes a basic but incredibly important observation that shareholders do not own the company, legally speaking. It means that the neo-liberal mantra of shareholder value and the individual autonomy of shareholders allowing them to do with a company as they deem fit as if it was their property simply has no basis in law. The firm has a purpose, interests, assets, debts, and prerogatives of its own that do not coincide with those from the shareholders.[43] In the remainder of this section I will superficially glance over

[41] E.g. Pistor, *The Code of Capital*; Andrew Fitzmaurice, *Sovereignty, Property and Empire, 1500–2000* (Cambridge: Cambridge University Press, 2019); Carmen Gonzalez, "Racial Capitalism, Climate Justice, and Climate Displacement" (2021) 11 *Oñati Socio-Legal Series* 108.

[42] E.g. Martijn Hesselink, *Justifying Contract in Europe. Political Philosophies of European Contract Law* (Oxford: Oxford University Press, 2021); Lyn Tjon Soei Len, "The Effects of Contracts Beyond Frontiers: A Capabilities Perspective on Externalities and Contract Law in Europe", PhD Thesis, University of Amsterdam, 2013. For Pistor, the resources for change also lie outside the law: "re-politicization of social economic life" (Pistor, *The Code of Capital*, pp. 231–232). To be clear, Hesselink and Len do make excellent legal doctrinal analyses.

[43] Jean-Philippe Robé, *The Legal Structure of the Firm* (2011) 1 *Accounting, Economics, and Law* 1. My approach also fits the project of Larissa Katz which proposes an alternative understanding of property from within positive law, namely property as an office. Larissa Katz, "Governing through Owners: How and Why Formal Private Property Rights Enhance State Power" (2012) 16 *University of Pennsylvania Law Review* 2029. Yet the important difference is that she seeks to impose constraints and duties on the property owner, albeit from within his "mandate" as a property owner. Law as a public service does not put any constraints directly on right holders, it simply refuses them the service of the law if the legal arrangement lacks structurally minimal reciprocity and fairness. Furthermore, law as a public service is not limited to holders of property rights but extends to any claim in the name of the law.

some legal concepts and legal materials of private law to show how much reciprocity and fairness are engrained in the logic of private law. Unlike Robé, I am not an expert on company law and private law. But this is precisely the point. Any jurist having some familiarity with private law could come up with these and surely many other examples of how the basic legal institutions of private law are premised on minimal reciprocity and fairness.[44]

The definition of the right to property in the French civil code tradition asserts that the right to property gives the owner "the most absolute right over a thing." This also includes the *jus abutendi*. The notions absolute right and the *jus abutendi* have led to the belief that the modern right to property constitutes the basis for the neo-liberal doctrine of unfettered individual autonomy of the property owner. The property owner should be completely free to use his property as he deems fit. If he decides to use his property in an inefficient way, he will be ultimately sanctioned by the market. Yet, this interpretation is simply not correct. "Absolute" simply means the "fullest" right one can have over a thing *compared to other rights* over a thing. Property right is, thus, fuller than the right to use and the so-called naked property right.[45] Moreover, the owner's so-called *jus abutendi* associated with property does not mean a right to abuse, but simply means that the owner had the ultimate say in when and how *to dispose of* – as in transfer – the property.[46] Furthermore, the very provision that establishes the right to property immediately allows the legislator to limit the right to property. At a more functional level, the general rationale behind the extensive right of property under modern law was to promote the free circulation and utilization of assets, especially land, that was often very much restricted under the laws of the *ancien régime* leading to unproductive asset utilization.[47] The point was that society at large was to benefit from this circulation of goods. This also explains that the owner cannot stipulate that his good can never be transferred except by inheritance (e.g. clauses d'inaliénabilité perpétuelles).[48] By the same token, easements on property, thus limiting the exclusive use of the land by the owner, were still

44 I draw on French, Belgian, and Dutch legal materials. I expect to find similar results in other European jurisdictions.

45 Henri De Page, *Traité Élémentaire de Droit Civil Belge*, vol V, Des biens et des différentes modifications de la propriété, 1st part (Bruxelles: E. Bruylant, 1975), p. 795.

46 Ibid.

47 Jean-Étienne-Marie Portalis, "Discours préliminaire du Code Civil," in *Portalis, Discours, rapports et travaux inédits sur le Code civil* (Paris: Joubert, 1844), pp. 55–56, available at http://catalogue.bnf.fr/ark:/12148/cb311381564 (last accessed 22 September 2024).

48 E.g. Art. 900-1 French Civil Code.

possible precisely because in the interest of third parties.[49] In other words, the owner has been granted the prerogatives of the right to property on the premise that it would lead to the common good.[50]

Inheritance law is arguably the regime that is most complicit in increasing the discrepancy between the haves and have nots in terms of wealth accumulation.[51] But even the underlying rationale of modern inheritance law in the civil law tradition is based on fairness. After the reform of inheritance law under the Napoleon civil code it was no longer possible for a property owner to transfer by will his entire estate to his oldest son only. The new civil code ensured that a large part of the estate was reserved to all his children in equal parts. It was felt that this distribution was fairer and more productive than the accumulation of wealth in the hands of one person, often the eldest son.[52] Similar concerns of fairness informed the possibility to still allow the testator to legate a part of his estate to non-family members. This would allow illegitimate children and persons working for the testator who structurally contributed to his wealth (e.g. household personnel, laborers, artisans, overseers) to get some fair compensation for their efforts.[53]

The fairness is probably most clearly reflected in the basic legal structure of contract law, namely reciprocity. Most contractual arrangements must have a cause or consideration. It means that contractual obligations must have a *quid pro quo* character: for each duty there must be counterpart. To be sure there are one-sided contracts but they are the exception and in a way suspect. This is precisely why, under the law of gifts, the donor receives a preferred treatment allowing him to escape from his duty to transfer ownership which would not be possible under normal reciprocal contracts.[54] Similarly, it is telling that the one-sided contract of a loan of a thing (for free, if not it would be a lease) presumably originated as a special favor for friends and neighbors.[55] It, thus, escapes the normal logic of contract law as a way to organize cooperation among parties without a special tie (e.g. blood, friendship, proximity). Interestingly, it has become a rather common contract because the lender often has a direct (economic) interest in lending the thing to the borrower

49 Jean-Étienne-Marie Portalis, "Exposé des motifs de titre sur la propriété," in *Portalis, Discours, rapports et travaux inédits sur le Code civil* (Paris: Joubert, 1844), p. 222.

50 Ibid., p. 223: "Dans toutes les occurrences, il faut soumettre toutes les affectations, toutes les volontés partiuclières à la grande pensée de bien public."

51 Piketty, *Le capital au XXIe siècle*, p. 575.

52 Portalis, *Discours préliminaire*, p. 60.

53 Ibid.

54 E.g. Art. 7:176 and 7:178 Dutch Civil Code.

55 Art. 7A:1777 Dutch Civil Code. A. W. Jongbloed, "Commentaar op Burgerlijk Wetboek Boek 7A art. 1777 t/m 1780" (Sdu Uitgevers, 13 November 2016).

(e.g. replacement vehicle, shopping carts, bottles and glasses with deposit). The logic of reciprocity is clearly reflected in the *exceptio non adempleti contractus*: the duty to perform your part of the deal is suspended because of lack of reciprocity in the execution of the contract.[56] Fairness and reciprocity are equally prominent in the possibility to have a contract nullified if a contracting party abused circumstances of dependence, putting the other party in a weak position.[57] Also, the reciprocal character of the law when organizing cooperation follows clearly from the prohibition on the leonine clause: a contract that attributes all the profit to one partner is null.[58] Precisely, when confronted with a lack of reciprocity in economic arrangements, the essentially reciprocal character of contract law becomes evident. This is powerfully captured by the explanatory memorandum of the legislative proposal of 1901 introducing the regulated labor contract in Dutch law in 1907:

> It is indeed true: in other [normal] contracts one can see that sometimes one party is stronger, sometimes the other. But the roles change. For example, in the context of sales contracts, at one moment the buyer has the upper hand, at another it is the seller who dictates. On the contrary, when it comes to [labor contracts] it happens that the same party is almost always the weaker one, namely the laborer.[59]

In short, already a quick glance at basic legal institutions and materials of private law shows that the law enabling economic arrangements is premised on a logic of reciprocity and fairness. If so, it means that positive law already has the normative and technical resources to counter structurally unfair and non-reciprocal arrangements. There is no need to seek recourse to solidarity conceptions in legal discourse to criticize and even unwind unfair and non-reciprocal neo-liberal economic arrangements. For the dominant solidarity conceptions are either foundational, circular and redundant, simply equating solidarity with cooperation. Or they are too aspirational, requiring massive changes in legislation and treaty law, inspired by moral resources located outside existing positive law. Too much reliance on solidarity conceptions may distract us from what can be done already in the name of existing positive law.

56 E.g. Art. 6:262 Dutch Civil Code.
57 E.g. 5.37 Belgian Civil Code.
58 E.g. Art. 32 Belgian Company Code.
59 A. E. Bles, *De wet op de arbeidsovereenkomst: geschiedenis der wet van den 13den juli 1907 (Staatsblad no. 193)*, Part 1 (The Hague: Boekhandel vh Gebr. Belinfante, 1907), p. 2. Author's translation.

11.5 PRACTICAL IMPLICATIONS AND LIMITATIONS OF LAW AS A PUBLIC SERVICE

If indeed law is a public service and legal arrangements must display minimal reciprocity and fairness, then legal authorities have a powerful instrument in their hands. In this respect, law as a public service points directly at the main agents for change, namely judges and strategic litigators.[60] Whenever dominant economic actors seek to secure and enforce economic arrangements through law, judges may refuse to validate or enforce them in part or whole, if they lead to a structural lack of reciprocity and fairness. The most obvious cases are those where weaker and adversely affected actors are parties to these agreements. But one could also imagine third parties bringing cases. The legal possibility has already been convincingly explored in the context consumer–retailer contracts for garments produced in sweatshops. The contracts may be declared null because they are against public order and good morals.[61] One could envision a similar exercise in the context of the contractual arrangements facilitating the depletion of planetary resources (e.g. engineer contracts, mining contracts, sales of minerals, etc.). In the latter case it is clear that the contracting parties do not have an interest in seeking invalidation or non-enforcement of the economic arrangements. But some third parties clearly have an interest. The interests of third parties are identical to those who brought successful climate cases before national courts and even the ECtHR.[62] Still, there is of course a crucial legal difference. These climate cases are based on non-contractual liability and human rights violations, the remedies being compensation and a binding order to take measures. In these cases, the remedies are not declaring the economic arrangements legally invalid and not enforceable. Still, it may be legally possible and conceivable for a third party to request a court to order a contracting party to refrain from executing a contract or particular aspects thereof. It is not the same as an invalidation of the contract or a court refusing to enforce the contract. But it may have similar effects. For what really matters is that the wider economic

[60] Such clear identification of the agents of change is missing in Pistor's account. See, for this point, Matthias Thiemann, "The Political Economy of Private Law: Comment on 'The Code of Capital – How the Law Creates Wealth and Inequality'" (2021) 11 *Accounting, Economics, and Law* 37–51, at 49.

[61] See Len, "The Effects of Contracts Beyond Frontiers," pp. 109–140.

[62] HR December 20, 2019, ECLI:NL:HR:2019:2006 (case before the Dutch Supreme Court between the environmental NGO Urgenda and the Dutch State); Rb. Den Haag May 26, 2021, ECLI:NL:2021:5337 (case against Shell before the District Court of The Hague); *Verein Klimaseniorinnen Schweiz and Others v.* Switzerland, ECtHR April 9, 2024, no 53600/20.

and financial community (e.g. investors, banks, suppliers, clients, traders, governments issuing licenses, credit rating companies) knows that the contracts are legally tainted. This will directly impact the economic and financial attractiveness of a dominant economic actor (e.g. share prices, credit rating). For most dominant economic actors rely for credit and equity on financial institutions and capital markets. Moreover, casting legal doubt on contractual arrangements in a single case is likely to have an impact on the wider economic sector.

To be sure, the law as a public service has clear limitations. The obvious one is jurisdiction. If the dominant economic actors make use of legal arrangements outside the jurisdiction of European judges, then there is not much for the judges to declare invalid or non-enforceable. For the dominant actors simply do not need the help of Western law. As a result, in these cases judges cannot counter or unwind neo-liberal economic arrangements by refusing dominant actors the help of the law. This is not a minor limitation as the majority of natural resources and a large part of the human resources are sourced from the global south under arrangements not governed necessarily by Western law. By the same token, it is also a fact that the monetization of the proceeds from these extra-territorial arrangements often take place in Western jurisdictions. It remains to be explored how invalidation or non-enforcements of the legal titles pertaining to this monetization may be operationalized.

Another limitation may be the attitudes of Western judges. If, as I claim, private law in Europe already has the resources to deny the legal validity and enforceability of neo-liberal economic arrangements, how come judges failed to do so? Probably, the principles of private law, such as minimal reciprocity, are not enough. According to some observers, judges may need more explicit legal rules to counter neo-liberal economic arrangements.[63] Also judges may think that these are matters that go beyond points of law and solely belong to political decision making. A lot depends on how individual judges will conceive of and do their job. Interestingly, even when securing structurally unfair economic arrangements, courts typically do not conceive of themselves

[63] Cf Candida Leone, "Coding for the 99 per cent? Principles and the Preconditions of Capital Minting" (2022) 1 *European Law Open* 351–362, at 360–362. Elsewhere, Leone notices that "a rather plain application of contractual principles represents what seems to be the *only* counterbalance to corporate profit-seeking offered in the system of 'supply security' rules." Leone, "Flexibility as Commodification," p. 474. But the applicable contractual principle was that a party, including an energy company after a unilateral transfer of a portfolio of contracts, may not unilaterally change a contract, by replacing it with its own terms. This contractual principle offers little protection to neo-liberal economic arrangements that are already exploitative from the outset.

as merely serving the private interests of dominant actors. A case in point is the notorious Argentine sovereign debt case in which a court in New York ruled in favor of so-called "vulture funds" (the plaintiffs) against Argentina.[64] The court secured an economic arrangement which, according to most observers (including major financial institutions, financial newspapers and even the US government), was not reciprocal and fair towards the debtor, that is, Argentina, other creditors and other stakeholders and interests (e.g. the Argentine people and economy). Still, the court made clear it was not merely serving the particular interests of a single private party, but the public interest, the rule of law, and the financial markets.[65] Furthermore, the court explicitly balanced the various public interests at stake when enforcing the duty to pay the debt. The court found that enforcement would not have adverse consequences for Argentina as a debtor, the Argentine economy and the other external debt creditors.[66] The court also found that bringing the case to court was the only way for the plaintiffs to secure payment, suggesting that the plaintiffs made a fair use of the US court system.[67]

To be sure, the Argentine sovereign debt case, like most judgements today, is in terms of its actual legally binding decision, clearly not an example of judges refusing to lend support to structurally unfair economic arrangements. But the objective of this chapter was not to show that judges today only secure economic arrangements when they find them to be sufficiently fair and reciprocal. The point of this chapter has been to show that judges could potentially do so. Judges could refuse to offer the help of the law to dominant actors if an economic arrangement structurally lacks fairness and direct or indirect reciprocity. Judges may refuse the help of the law, not out of solidarity or other moral reasons located outside positive law but simply because law is a public service.

64 *NML Capital, Ltd. v. Republic of Argentina*, 144 F. Supp. 3d 513 (S.D.N.Y. 2015). For the discussion of the legal and factual background of the case I relied on Pablo J. López and Cecilia Nahón, "The Growth of Debt and the Debt of Growth: Lessons from the Case of Argentina" (2017) 44 *Journal of Law and Society* 99.

65 "Finally, an order of specific performance serves the public interest of enforcing contracts, maintaining confidence in debt markets, and upholding the rule of law. As the Court of Appeals held back in 2013, 'the interest – one widely shared in the financial community – in maintaining New York's status as one of the foremost commercial centers is advanced by requiring debtors, including foreign debtors, to pay their debts.' *Id.* at 248. The same holds true today." *NML Capital, Ltd. v. Republic of Argentina*, p. 521.

66 *NML Capital, Ltd. v. Republic of Argentina*, p. 522.

67 "Ordering specific performance therefore ensures basic fairness by placing these plaintiffs on equal footing with the Lead Plaintiffs." *NML Capital, Ltd. v. Republic of Argentina*, p. 522.

12

International Law and the Messianic Promise of Solidarity

ELENI KARAGEORGIOU

12.1 SOLIDARITY, RELIGION, AND INTERNATIONAL LAW

Solidarity has a long history within sociology, political science and philosophy, serving different purposes and objectives.[1] Throughout history it was drawn on for both good and ill and expressed itself in both nationalist and internationalist variants. It has offered a vocabulary of class struggle for political radicals, but

Thanks to commentators and participants of the Gothenburg Workshop 'Solidarity: We Know It When We See It', on 25 March 2022 for our constructive discussions and invaluable comments on earlier drafts.

[1] Emile Durkheim, *The Division of Labour in Society* (New York: Macmillan, 1893); Georg Simmel, *Soziologie: Untersuchungen über die Formen der Vergesellschaftung* (Leipzig: Verlag von Duncker & Humblot, 1908); Célestin Bouglé, *Le Solidarisme* (Paris: Giard, 1924); Ernesto Laclau, *Politics and Ideology in Marxist Theory* (New York: Verso, 1977); Jürgen Habermas, *Autonomy and Solidarity: Interviews with Jürgen Habermas*, edietd by Peter Dews (New York: Verso, 1992); Kurt Bayertz, *Solidarity, Philosophical Studies in Contemporary Culture*, vol 5 (Dordrecht: Kluwer Academic Publishers, 1999); Chandra Talpade Mohanty, *Feminism without Borders: Decolonizing Theory, Practicing Solidarity* (Durham, NC: Duke University 2003); Hauke Brunkhorst, *Solidarity: From civic friendship to a global legal community*, trans. Jeffrey Flynn (Cambridge, MA: MIT Press, 2005); Tommie Shelby, *We Who Are Dark: The Philosophical Foundations of Black Solidarity* (Cambridge, MA: Belknap, 2005); Steinar Stjernø, *Solidarity in Europe: The History of an Idea* (Cambridge: Cambridge University Press, 2005); Lawrence Wilde, 'The Concept of Solidarity: Emerging from the Theoretical Shadows?' (2007) 9 *British Journal of Politics and International Relations* 171; Sally Scholz, *Political Solidarity* (University Park: Pennsylvania State University Press, 2008); Carol Gould, 'Varieties of Global Responsibility, Social Connection, Human Rights and Transnational Solidarity', in Ann Ferguson and Mechthild Nagel (eds.), *Dancing with Iris: The Philosophy of Iris Marion Young* (New York: Oxford University Press, 2009), pp. 199–212.

also provided a language for the bourgeoise's weariness in the face of what is perceived as disorder.[2]

Solidarity's place in religious accounts, especially in the age-old Christian notions of love and care, has been prominent. Christians had to find a way to engage themselves in this world without forsaking the world to come, and the way to bridge these two worlds had to include formulations legitimating collective action, and engagement in the living conditions of a suffering humanity in order to do God's will on earth.[3]

As suggested in a growing body of literature on the relation between international law and religion,[4] international law is deeply embedded in the Christian tradition, its structure, dogmas and hierarchies. It's also been argued that fundamental concepts of international law are 'secularized theological concepts'[5] with human rights considered as 'a kind of world-wide secular religion'.[6] This is the starting point for the present chapter, which invites the reader to look at modern international law and central concepts within it drawing upon theological modes of analysis.

Following the severance of early international law from its religious roots, attempts to transform it into a value-based international system were reflected in the role of solidarity as the guiding principle of the new legal order following decolonization and the emergence of newly independent states on the world stage associated with a promotion of a 'new morality' in

2 For more details see Eleni Karageorgiou, 'Rethinking Solidarity in European Asylum Law: A Critical Reading of the Key Concept in Contemporary Refugee Policy', PhD Thesis, Lund University Media-Tryck, 2018. On unwanted and unwelcome solidarities, see Chapter 4, by Mégret.

3 Stjernø, *Solidarity in Europe*, p. 84. See also Gerald J. Beyer, 'The Meaning of Solidarity in Catholic Social Teaching' (2014) 15 *Political Theology* 7.

4 See e.g., Mark Janis and Carolyn Evans (eds.), *Religion and International Law* (The Hague: Martinus Nijhoff, 1999); Samuel Moyn, *Christianity and Human Rights* (Princeton: Princeton University Press, 2016); and Martti Koskenniemi, Mónica García-Salmones Rovira and Paolo Amorosa (eds.), *International Law and Religion: Historical and Contemporary Perspectives* (Oxford: Oxford University Press, 2017).

5 Carl Schmitt, *Political Theology: Four Chapters on the Concept of Sovereignty*, trans. George Schwab (Chicago: University of Chicago Press, 2005), p. 35.

6 Among others, Elie Wiesel, 'A Tribute to Human Rights', in Danieli Yael, Elsa Stamatopoulou and Clarence J. Dias (eds.), *The Universal Declaration of Human Rights: Fifty Years and Beyond* (Amityville, NY: Baywood, 2009), p. 3. Cf Michael Ignatieff, *Human Rights as Politics and Idolatry* (Princeton: Princeton University Press, 2003). See also, John Witte, Jr. and Frank S. Alexander (eds.), *Christianity and Human Rights: An Introduction* (Cambridge: Cambridge University Press, 2010) on how religion has been infused into human rights. Finally, see Susan Marks' account on how the story of human rights can be told and on the 'cliché' of human rights as 'a secular religion'. Susan Marks, 'Human Rights in Disastrous Times', in James Crawford and Martti Koskenniemi (eds.), *The Cambridge Companion to International Law* (Cambridge: Cambridge University Press, 2012), p. 313.

international law.[7] Solidarity was presented as part of the 'new principle of global equity whereby those nations that have the necessary means are expected to assist those that do not'.[8] As Tallgren puts it, 'international institutions and rules are seen as a way of achieving the goals uniting human beings and nations as they follow their instincts of sociability and solidarity'.[9]

Apart from providing a framework for cooperation and joint action to address common challenges, international law is required to ameliorate inequalities of opportunity and structural disadvantage.[10] Thus, solidarity became a counterweight to reliance on state discretion. Yet, instead of a means to tackle the root causes of asymmetries and power structures, in the different legal domains in which solidarity operates, for instance environmental law,[11] UN peace and security law,[12] and refugee protection,[13] solidarity has been an emergency driven concept. It has been invoked to deal with 'hot' situations, that is, complex interrelationships between a wide range of parties, and to manage the likely future effects of crises that have not yet materialized.[14] As discussed in detail in Section 12.2.2, in all these domains, solidarity cohabits uneasily with law, as decisions about how to tackle environmental

[7] Agnès Hurwitz, *The Collective Responsibility of States to Protect Refugees*, Oxford Monographs in International Law (New York: Oxford University Press, 2009), p. 139.

[8] Jean-Pierre L. Fonteyne, 'Burden-Sharing: An Analysis of the Nature and Function of International Solidarity in Cases of Mass Influx of Refugees' (1983) 8 *Australian Yearbook of International Law* 162–188, at 179.

[9] Immi Tallgren, 'The Faith in Humanity and International Criminal Law', in Martti Koskenniemi, Mónica García-Salmones Rovira and Paolo Amorosa (eds.), *International Law and Religion: Historical and Contemporary Perspectives* (Oxford: Oxford University Press, 2017), p. 337.

[10] The 2005 General Assembly Resolution 59/193 on the 'Promotion of a democratic and equitable international order', under 4 lit. f describes 'solidarity' as 'a fundamental value, by virtue of which global challenges must be managed in a way that distributes costs and burdens fairly, in accordance with basic principles of equity and social justice, and ensures that those who suffer or benefit the least receive help from those who benefit the most'.

[11] Convention to Combat Desertification in those Countries Experiencing Serious Drought and/or Desertification, Particularly in Africa, Paris, 14 October 1994, in force 26 December 1996, 33 ILM 3 (1994); art 3 lit. b states that parties should improve cooperation and coordination 'in a spirit of international solidarity and partnership'.

[12] Charter of the United Nations, San Francisco, 26 June 1945, in force 24 October 1945, 1 UNTS XVI, art 49 states: 'The Members of the United Nations shall join in affording mutual assistance in carrying out the measures decided upon by the Security Council'.

[13] See e.g. UNHCR ExCom Conclusion No. 89 (LI) (2000) which refers to 'international solidarity, burden-sharing and international cooperation to share responsibilities' and No. 100 (LV) on International Cooperation and Burden and Responsibility Sharing in Mass Influx Situations (2004).

[14] The concept of 'hot law' has been developed by Fisher in relation to environmental law in Elizabeth Fisher, 'Environmental Law as "Hot" Law' (2013) 25 *Journal of Environmental Law* 347. Fisher is building on the work of the sociologist Michel Callon who describes 'hot'

disasters, confront security issues and deal with humanitarian emergencies cannot be disentangled from assumptions about how the world is understood and organized and about what constitutes a 'problem' and a 'solution' at any given situation.

The present chapter seeks to offer insights on the Volume's focal question 'what does it mean to pose the solidarity question today', locating it in the context of the operation of international law and of global governance. It asks what happens to solidarity when employed in international discourse and how this may reveal a legacy of Christian messianism. The chapter departs from the commonly held position that solidarity in international legal discourse is primarily a conceptual outcome of the decolonization era. Instead, it positions the genealogy of solidarity within early Christian writings in which the western theological concepts of suffering, love and salvation are detailed. Linking the Pauline doctrine and writings of early theologians, such as Augustine, to the processes of modernity – of which notions such as the West, the Global South, good neighbourliness and human rights are a part – the concept of solidarity is thus traced to a particularly Christian dynamic. As such, the promise of solidarity in international legal discourse, human rights discourse and migration/refugee discourse, the argument goes, is analogous to the way in which forms of messianism manifest themselves through a Christian logic of love, sacrifice and debt.

The analysis in the coming paragraphs proceeds as follows: Section 12.2 draws attention to the messianic logic underpinning the routine operation of international law zooming into the way in which human rights defers fulfilment in a manner resembling this logic. Section 12.3 goes deeper into Christian theology and the way solidarity plays out in the writings of Paul and other early theologians. Against this background, Section 12.4 explores the temporal elements of the 'messianic' in the Pauline doctrine and contrasts it with the 'messianism' of international law which significantly informs the function of solidarity within it. Finally, Section 12.5 offers an alternative thinking of solidarity in international law whereby the messianic is not denounced but rather embraced.

situations as those situations in which 'everything becomes controversial: the identification of intermediaries and overflows, the distribution of source and target agents, the way effects are measured. These controversies which indicate the absence of a stabilized knowledge base, usually involve a wide variety of actors. The actual list of actors, as well as their identities will fluctuate in the course of a controversy itself and they will put forward mutually incompatible descriptions of future world states.' Michel Callon, 'An Essay on Framing and Overflowing: Economic Externalities Revisited by Sociology', in Michel Callon (ed.), *The Laws of the Markets* (Oxford: Blackwell, 1998), p. 260.

12.2 INTERNATIONAL LAW, HUMAN RIGHTS AND THE EVER EMERGING 'UNIVERSALITY'

12.2.1 *Establishing the Messianic in International Law*

To say that key international law concepts have a theological origin is not new.[15] Take, for example, sovereignty. Hobbes calls God 'the Soveraign of all Soveraigns', despite attributing anthropocentric character to the state.[16] For this reason, Derrida suggests that 'This humanistic or anthropologistic modernity of the institution of sovereignty and the state retains a profound and fundamental theological and religious basis'.[17] Here, I trace a particular aspect of this theological basis, namely the messianic, with the view to exploring how this influences the way in which international law routinely operates and what this entails for the function of solidarity as an international law concept.

Messianic expectations have been discussed as a core element of international law,[18] with the discipline being portrayed as holding the promise of a saviour. International law has been perceived as including the 'announcement of something that remains eternally postponed'[19] and, therefore, seen as a temporary error-prone solution that allows individuals to live in a state of everlasting 'emergence'[20] until the promise of cooperation, development

[15] See, among others, Paul W. Kahn, *Political Theology: Four New Chapters on the Concept of Sovereignty* (New York: Columbia University Press, 2011), p. 3.

[16] Thomas Hobbes, *Leviathan*, edited by Richard Tuck (New York: Cambridge University Press, 1991), p. 260.

[17] Jacques Derrida, *The Beast and the Sovereign*, trans. Geoffrey Bennington (Chicago: University of Chicago Press, 2009), vol. I, p. 54.

[18] Central components in Christian tradition, such as dominion, interference, freedom and public/private, surface in the logic of international law, not surprisingly perhaps as sixteenth to early nineteenth centuries jurists were directly influenced by theological considerations (e.g. Suarez, Vitoria, Grotius). On this, see David Kennedy, 'Primitive Legal Scholarship' (1986) 27 *Harvard International Law Journal* 1. Legal scholarship has presented a rich body of research for understanding modern practices, including economic development, international trade law, human rights through the lens of Christian narratives of salvation, suffering and sacrifice. See, among others, Judith Grbich, 'Secrets of the Fetish in International Law's Messianism', in Anne Orford (ed.), *International Law and Its Others* (Cambridge: Cambridge University Press, 2006), pp. 197–220; Jean-Luc Nancy, 'Deconstruction of Monotheism' (2003) 6 *Postcolonial Studies* 37; Jennifer L. Beard, 'Understanding International Development Programs as a Modern Phenomenon of Early and Medieval Christian Theology' (2003) 18 *Australian Feminist Law Journal* 27.

[19] Martti Koskenniemi, 'What Is International Law For?', in Malcolm D. Evans (ed.), *International Law* (Oxford: Oxford University Press, 2003), p. 111.

[20] Thomas M. Franck, *Fairness in International Law and Institutions* (Oxford: Oxford University Press/Clarendon Press, 1995); Martti Koskenniemi, 'Legal Cosmopolitanism: Tom Franck's Messianic World' (2003) 35 *New York University Journal of International Law and Politics* 471.

and rights is fulfilled. Modernity as understood in international law and governance 'always seeks an escape, promising a world that is more universally egalitarian, if not lovely'.[21]

This resembles the messianic vision reflected in Judaism (waiting for the Messiah, a figure of salvation arising in the end of times) and in Christianity (waiting for the return of Jesus of Nazareth, the Messiah who already came to earth and whose return is expected in the final days, i.e. the Parousia). To be 'born again' in Christian tradition is to do away with a previous mode of existence. In the Pauline doctrine, one can live under the regime of the law, which is death, or one can live according to the spirit, which is life in Christ: to be born again, as a new man.[22]

The messianic manifests itself within the human rights realm as well. Müllerson has described human rights as a language 'expressed not in terms of being but of becoming'.[23] A closer look at the Universal Declaration of Human Rights (UDHR) reveals a specific type of *pledge*: to leave behind and not repeat the wrongs and inequalities that led to two world wars and immense human suffering. To be 'born again' in human rights, as in Christian tradition, is thus to do away with a previous state of being. It's been argued that the countries signing the UDHR had been driven by 'faith as trust in the meaning of history, in man's ability to make history different from what it has been in the past'.[24] This points to a hope for justice translated into rights for everyone, whose full realization is deferred[25] heavily reliant on a 'common understanding of these rights and freedoms'.[26]

In human rights law and practice, the promise of emancipation focuses on how governments treat individuals, on participatory issues and on legal remedies. Kennedy and Koskenniemi have stressed that linking law with human

[21] John D. Haskell, 'The Traditions of Modernity within International Law and Governance: Christianity, Liberalism and Marxism' (2016) 6 *Human Rights and Globalization Law Review* 29–50, at 49.

[22] See Alain Badiou, *Saint Paul: The Foundation of Universalism*, Series: Cultural Memory in the Present, trans. Ray Brassier (Stanford: Stanford University Press, 2003), pp. 75–85.

[23] Rein Müllerson, 'Human Rights Are Neither Universal Nor Natural', (2018) 17 *Chinese Journal of International Law* 925–942, at 928.

[24] George Grima, 'Human Rights in a Theological Perspective' (1987) 38 *Melita Theologica* 33–52, at 36.

[25] Pursuant to its Preamble, the Universal Declaration of human rights is proclaimed 'as a common standard of achievement for all peoples and all nations, to the end that every individual and every organ of society, keeping this Declaration in mind, shall strive by teaching and education to promote respect for these rights and freedoms and by progressive measures, national and international …' UN General Assembly, Universal Declaration of Human Rights, 217 A (III), 10 December 1948.

[26] Ibid.

rights or development, for example, was bringing with it great promise. However, the more squarely these vocabularies became part of governments' programs, entangled in struggles over the setting of political agendas, the more significant decisions of social distribution escaped into an opaque private sphere and 'out of the reformers' reach'.[27] Formalism, bureaucratization, professionalization and human rights mainstreaming has been questioned as depriving the project of any revolutionary ambitions its conception may have generated.

Mutua has captured the purported universality and cultural neutrality of the human rights project through the metaphor of 'Savages' (the evil state), 'Victims' (the powerless individuals) and 'Saviours' (UN, Western countries, INGOs)[28] which, essentially, points to the triptych of sin, suffering and the Messiah.[29] The universal vocabulary of human rights has been criticized for promising the existence of an 'international community' that is unavailable and for acting 'as if it knows what justice means, always and for everyone'.[30] Justice is defined as 'a relationship to the state rather than simply a condition in society',[31] hence distracting attention from background politics and economic conditions and the way they inform what justice is.

Critical legal studies have pointed to the fact that the language of human rights has obscured other languages (e.g. religious vocabularies, local traditions, economics) that could bring about meaningful change. Social solidarity, in particular, has been referred to as an emancipatory vocabulary crowded out by human rights.[32] Kennedy critiques the human rights movement for encouraging an elitist solidarity based on a false sense of unity of experience, 'making it hard to articulate differences in the projects of male and female

27 See Martti Koskenniemi, 'Law, Teleology and International Relations: An Essay in Counter disciplinarity' (2012) 26 *International Relations*, 3–34, at 14; and David Kennedy, 'The "Rule of Law", Political Choices, and Development Common Sense', in David M. Trubek and Alvaro Santos (eds.), *The New Law and Economic Development: A Critical Appraisal* (Cambridge: Cambridge University Press, 2006), especially pp. 158–173.

28 Makau Mutua, 'Savages, Victims, and Saviors: The Metaphor of Human Rights' (2001) 42 *Harvard International Law Journal* 201.

29 See the wording in the Preamble to the United Nations Charter, 'WE THE PEOPLES OF THE UNITED NATIONS DETERMINED to save succeeding generations from the scourge of war, which twice in our lifetime has brought untold sorrow to mankind', United Nations, Charter of the United Nations, 1 UNTS XVI, 24 October 1945.

30 David Kennedy, 'Reassessing International Humanitarianism: The Dark Sides', in Anne Orford (ed.), *International Law and its Others* (Cambridge: Cambridge University Press, 2006), p. 134. For further analysis see Rob Dickinson, Elena Katselli, Collin Murray and Ole W. Pedersen (eds.), *Examining Critical Perspective on Human Rights* (Cambridge: Cambridge University Press, 2012).

31 Kennedy, 'Reassessing International Humanitarianism', p. 134.

32 Ibid., p. 133.

Palestinian human rights lawyers, Americans and Nigerians'.[33] Nevertheless, there has been no further elaboration on how a social solidarity vocabulary is meant to function.

12.2.2 *Solidarity and Its Complicity with International and Human Rights Law*

In Section 12.2.1 it was established that Christianity remains in conversation with modernity, especially considering how ostensibly secular texts, concepts and institutions are shaped by a religious heritage. The question then becomes: how does this inform the meaning and function of solidarity in international law? To address this question, one should pose a more basic one: given that international law's basis is organized around sovereignty and the state, is there any room for solidarity whatsoever? According to von Mohl's thesis, state sovereignty and the international community are the two main pillars and interrelated goals of international law.[34] In this constellation, it is not hard to imagine how solidarity comes into the picture. Mohl's understanding of the principle of international community is not limited to a 'consciousness of collectivity'[35] at the international level. Rather, a sense of collectivity and community goes hand in hand with individual freedom, with their combination leading to what has been described as 'responsible independence'.[36]

Following this line of reasoning, one could argue that solidarity which lies at the bottom of an international community is not oppositional but rather complementary to sovereignty in that it preserves the element of authority and independence, adding to the picture the need for the protection of common interests. The problem thus lies in how these interests and thereafter their protection have been envisaged and actualized through international law.

33 David Kennedy, 'The International Human Rights Movement: Part of the Problem?' (2002) 15 *Harvard Human Rights Journal* 101–125, at 120.

34 See Robert von Mohl, 'Die Pflege der internationalen Gemeinschaft als Aufgabe des Völkerrechts', in Robert von Mohl (ed.), *Staatsrecht, Völkerrecht und Politik, vol. I: Staatsrecht und Völkerrecht* (Tübingen: Laupp & Siebeck, 1860).

35 See Stefan Kroll, 'Community, Enforcement and Justification: The International Law of Intervention in World-Societal Perspective', Osgoode Hall Law School, Toronto: Osgoode CLPE Research Paper No. 12/2012, p. 12.

36 Stefan Kroll, 'The Justification of International Intervention: Theories of Community and Admissibility', in Fabian Klose (ed.), *The Emergence of Humanitarian Intervention: Ideas and Practice from the Nineteenth Century to the Present* (Cambridge: Cambridge University Press, 2016), p. 77.

International economic law is symptomatic of how the dynamic of solidarity should and should not be understood. Although, following decolonization the principle was conceived as a duty 'owed' by the global north to the global south, there has been no indication that this dept will ever be paid. As MacDonald[37] points out:

> State practice and the practices of international organizations have recognized 'solidarity rights' only in situations where there are obligations on *both* sides, including, for example, the duty of developing countries to supply natural resources, to use financial assistance efficiently and to realize specific development projects. The kind of reciprocity involved here does not always imply 'equal' obligations; rather, the relationship is understood in a broader sense of displaying *a balance of long-term interests* between developed countries, who give assistance, and developing countries, who receive it.

To be in solidarity, therefore, means that 'no one wins unless everyone wins'. At the heart of this thinking lies the idea of an order based on formal equality which requires there being *future* gain for everyone involved and which obscures any consideration of responsibility in the present moment for past and ongoing losses.

International environmental law is yet another field where the transition from an international law of 'co-existence' to that of 'co-operation', to use Friedmann's typology,[38] has been seen as necessary. However, despite having initiated ways of concerted action with a view to achieving common goals,[39] the role of solidarity as promoting justice-oriented solutions has been debated and, at any rate, limited to a managerialism focusing on 'common but differentiated responsibilities'[40] based on capacity and resources calculations. There has been, in other words, a focus on the present time as the basis for

[37] Ronald St. J. MacDonald, 'Solidarity in the Practice and Discourse of Public International Law' (1996) 8 *Pace International Law Review* 259–302, at 280. MacDonald recalls Vattel's view that solidarity involves a mutuality of obligation so that all states' general situation is improved, as expressed in Emer de Vattel, *Le Droit des Gens ou Principes de la Souveraineté* (1758, Reprint Geneva, 1958), Préliminaires ss. 1–16, at 2.

[38] Wolfgang Friedmann, *The Changing Structure of International Law* (New York: Columbia University Press, 1964).

[39] See e.g. Organisation for Economic Co-operation and Development (OECD), Recommendation of the Council on Principles concerning Transfrontier Pollution, 14 November 1974, OECD/LEGAL/0133.

[40] On the functioning of the principle of common but differentiated responsibilities in a variety of subdisciplines of international law see Maarten den Heijer and Harmen van der Wilt (eds), *Netherlands Yearbook of International Law 2020: Global Solidarity and Common but Differentiated Responsibilities* (The Hague: T. M. C. Asser Press, 2022), vol 51.

advancing 'quick fixes', deferring questions of distribution of wealth and power to an unknown future time.

Within the mainstream human rights tradition, solidarity has been reflected in the concern of states for the protection of human rights of all people. However, state practice confirms that an impoverished and narrow conception of solidarity has materialized so far. In the manner that Christianity is grounded on the relation between humans and their suffering, human rights are invoked as a response and solution to human suffering stemming from natural disasters, climate change as well as man-made calamities including armed conflicts, extreme poverty and inequality. Violent conflicts around the world, from Vietnam to Ukraine, resulting in large-scale human suffering, have generated much discussion at the UN level as to how external support could alleviate the increasing number of humanitarian crises. High levels of inequality fuel tensions between the haves and the have-nots and, according to the 2022 Emergency Watchlist compiled by the International Rescue Committee (IRC), more than a quarter of a billion people today need humanitarian assistance, an increase of 63 per cent within two years. David Miliband, President of the IRC, speaks of a 'near-permanent crisis' that amounts to a 'system failure'.[41] 'When reality departs from rhetoric, we must have the courage to call it out. Without genuine solidarity, there can never be real trust. This is very much the sentiment of the Global South', as per Subrahmanyam Jaishankar, Indian External Affairs Minister,[42] inequality, solidarity and crises are put together.[43] In the face of a constant sense of crisis, genuine solidarity is referred to as the only way out of 'collective helplessness'.

It is precisely this vocabulary of solidarity as a response to and protection during 'crisis' that creates expectations of peace and stability, yet what the world is faced with, instead, is an illusion of peace; peace is conceived in terms of war, see for instance the war against terrorism, against migration, against

[41] International Rescue Committee, '2022 Emergency Watchlist', New York: International Rescue Committee, December 2021, pp. 3–4.

[42] UN General Assembly, 26 September 2023, 78th Session.

[43] See the Political Declaration adopted at the High-level Political Forum on Sustainable Development (HLPF), under the auspices of the General Assembly in September 2023 (Sustainable Development Goals Summit). A/RES/78/1, paras 8–10. Para 8 states 'The achievement of the SDGs is in peril . . . Our world is currently facing numerous crises. Years of sustainable development gains are being reversed. Millions of people have fallen into poverty, hunger and malnutrition are becoming more prevalent, humanitarian needs are rising, and the impacts of climate change more pronounced. This has led to increased inequality exacerbated by weakened international solidarity and a shortfall of trust to jointly overcome these crises.' Para 9 continues 'We commit to bold, ambitious, accelerated, just and transformative actions, anchored in international solidarity and effective cooperation at all levels'.

COVID-19. Otto suggests that, instead of more militarization, which delivers a perpetual condition of insecurity and anarchy, a resistance to this and reconceptualization of peace as solidarity might be more constructive.[44] In the same vein, critical security studies scholars have been cautioning that it is crucial to be aware of the politics one legitimizes by subscribing to a securitized, militarized and confrontational mindset[45]. But also, I would add, a messianic mindset. For instance, one might point to recent and past invocations of solidarity with Afghani women, narrated as helpless, subordinated to non-Western masculinities and as therefore in need of rescue by heroic Western men.[46] Along the same lines, solidarity has been at play in the 'responsibility to protect' doctrine, used to justify what is presented as a life-saving intervention 'when the interests of humanity were being infringed by the excess of a barbarous or despotic government'.[47]

Drawing on thinkers such as Foucault, Agamben and Butler, a rich body of research has examined the ways in which representations of concepts associated with security, such as protection, have been constructed as 'truths' in a manner that underpins and reproduces dominant power relations. For feminists, the purportedly apolitical notion of protection/aid or assistance is problematic as masking the reality, namely that for many people it is the one who claims to be providing protection that is their primary source of danger (the patriarch, the employer, the state, the liberal international community).[48] Arguably, the way in which solidarity has been narrated in contemporary discourses (e.g. the refugee crisis and the need for solidarity between states to avert the threat) qualifies it for being included in those concepts. The emergency rhetoric focuses on temporary solutions to counter the threat of migrant mobilization.[49] In fact, migration emergencies are generally portrayed

44 Dianne Otto, Lecture on 'Rethinking International Law's "Peace": A Queer Feminist Perspective', organized by the University of Essex, 24 May 2021, online.

45 Among others, Claudia Aradau, 'Security and the Democratic Scene: Desecuritization and Emancipation' (2004) 7 *Journal of International Relations and Development* 388–413, at 399.

46 See e.g. Laura J. Shepherd, 'Veiled References: Constructions of Gender in the Bush Administration Discourse on the Attacks on Afghanistan Post-9/11' (2006) 8 *International Feminist Journal of Politics* 19.

47 Martti Koskenniemi, *The Gentle Civilizer of Nations: The Rise and Fall of International Law, 1870–1960* (New York: Cambridge University Press, 2001), p. 95.

48 Chris Rossdale, 'Anarchism and Critical Security Studies', in Carl Levy and Saul Newman (eds.), *The Anarchist Imagination: Anarchism Encounters the Humanities and the Social Sciences* (Abingdon: Routledge, 2019), p. 66.

49 On this, see Eleni Karageorgiou and Gregor Noll, 'What Is Wrong with Solidarity in EU Asylum and Migration Law?' (2022) 4 *Jus Cogens* 131.

as unexpected and unmoored from structural causes[50], obscuring the complex and long-term institutional causes[51].

As a result, although one may expect solidarity to potentially disrupt the formalism of expectation in international law, the analysis in this section speaks for the opposite. A human rights approach to solidarity has focused on accountability based on specific norms agreed upon as enforceable rights of individuals and groups rather than on a commitment to social justice which calls for structural reform of societies. Solidarity has been 'bureaucratized' and mainstreamed, oftentimes in a manner that has furthered suppression and exclusion.[52]

12.2.3 *Could Solidarity's Radical Potential be Redeemed?*

Based on the analysis in Section 12.2.2, any kind of radical potential solidarity may bear, this has been reduced to questions of charitable assistance, voluntary pledges or immediate (*ad-hoc*) reactions to emergencies to the extent they do not disturb the *status quo*. Perhaps this does not come as a surprise considering the limitations and structural flaws of the international system, including human rights law. Does this mean that solidarity must be dismissed altogether?

Drawing on responses to the critique of human rights, especially those establishing a basis for defending human rights from within the Marxist tradition,[53] O'Connell suggests that rights must be understood as 'struggle concepts', 'a terrain in which the interests of different groups are fought over'.[54] Understood this way, human rights can and should be deployed in emancipatory political projects today 'beyond narrow formalistic, and overly

[50] For an extensive analysis of migration emergencies, see Jaya Ramji-Nogales, 'Migration Emergencies' (2017) 68 *Hastings Law Journal* 609.

[51] Benjamin Authers and Hilary Charlesworth, 'International Human Rights Law and the Language of Crisis' (2013) RegNet Research Paper No. 2013/18, p. 22.

[52] See, among others, Obiora Chinedu Okafor, 'The Future of International Solidarity in Global Refugee Protection' (2020) 22 *Human Rights Review* 1; and Eleni Karageorgiou, 'The Distribution of Asylum Responsibilities in the EU: Dublin, Partnerships with Third Countries and the Question of Solidarity' (2019) 88 *Nordic Journal of International Law* 315.

[53] See e.g. Robin Blackburn, 'Reclaiming Human Rights' (2011) 69 *New Left Review* 126; and Prabhat Patnaik, 'A Left Approach to Development' (2010) 45 *Economic and Political Weekly* 33.

[54] Paul O'Connell, 'On the Human Rights Question' (2018) 40 *Human Rights Quarterly* 962–988, at 984.

juridical concepts of what human rights are, and stress the centrality of social and political struggle in the formulation and defense of human rights'.[55]

Following this line of reasoning, solidarity's potential in putting the social question,[56] namely the material limits of the system, squarely on the table becomes clearer. It may give (human rights) law the flexibility it needs beyond a strict international obligations and national discretion distinction to promote decentralization and diversity. What remains unanswered, though, is whether and how human rights can break free of the attachment to the nation-state and the prescriptions of neoliberal economics;[57] and to what extent solidarity 'defended' by human rights can 'de-centre the nation-state, the market and international human rights law as the arbiters of freedom'.[58]

In a journal article from 2001, Koskenniemi begins with the following:

> Human rights are like love, both necessary and impossible. We cannot live without them, but we cannot have them, either. As soon as we are safely installed in a social order that promises to guarantee our rights, that order starts to appear oppressively totalitarian. We need new rights, or new interpretations of old rights. Routine kills love, as it does to rights-regimes.[59]

In the Foreword to this Volume he argues that solidarity may be 'a little like love' – due to its capricious, susceptible to constant change character – or perhaps 'like the Event in Alain Badiou's sense', responding 'to the implicit appeal of the other, within or outside a religious frame'.[60] This begs the question, could solidarity be a means to resist this 'routine' function of

55 Ibid., p. 964. See also Ed Sparer, 'Fundamental Human Rights, Legal Entitlements, and the Social Struggle: A Friendly Critique of the Critical Legal Studies Movement' (1984) 36 *Stanford Law Review* 509–574, at 560.

56 Orford argues 'This social question is a question of how human life can escape the demands of the market. You could pose that in a minimal way: who is going to look after the poor? But you could also pose it in a much more ambitious form: how do we limit the capacity of the market to demand that everything be sacrificed to its logic?' See 'I Want to Put the Social Question Back on the Table' – An Interview with Anne Orford, OpinioJuris, 27 November 2019, available at: https://opiniojuris.org/2019/11/27/i-want-to-put-the-social-question-back-on-the-table-an-interview-with-anne-orford/ (last accessed 14 September 2024). See also Anne Orford, *International Law and the Politics of History* (Cambridge: Cambridge University Press, 2021).

57 On an analysis of the neoliberal character of solidarity see Chapter 6, by Nanopoulos.

58 For an account of how human solidarities and loyalties developed in communities based on queer kinship ties can offer hope, see Dianne Otto, 'The Politics of Legibility: "The Family" in International Human Rights Law', in Shane Chalmers and Sundhya Pahuja (eds.), *Routledge Handbook of International Law and the Humanities* (Abingdon: Routledge, 2021), pp. 329–340.

59 Martti Koskenniemi,' Human Rights, Politics and Love' (2001) 19 *Nordic Journal of Human Rights* 33–45, at 33.

60 See the Foreword, by Koskenniemi.

international law providing 'the vehicle for a virtual summoning of all'?[61] And, if yes, what kind of 'love' would this transformation require?

Like solidarity, the notion of love has different meanings for different speakers in different contexts. Essentially, its meaning is constantly performed and reperformed depending on who is using it and on which occasion. There have also been several terms used to accommodate different conceptualizations of love, including the Greek 'agape' and the Latin 'caritas', both central concepts in Christian tradition. This tradition is centred in a conceptualization of love which, unlike in the quote by Koskenniemi, can be both necessary and possible. In Section 12.3, I turn to early Christian theology and explore the relevance of the notion of *agape* (*love*) to contemporary discussions on solidarity as a core concept and emerging principle in international law.[62]

12.3 SOLIDARITY AS CHRISTIAN LOVE: AN IMPOSSIBLE PROMISE

The notion of *agape* (God's love for humankind and the love that one should have for God and for one's fellow human beings)[63] is deemed as the precursor of the Christian idea of solidarity, manifested in the unselfish love of *thy neighbour*.[64]

The revolutionary potential of *agape* is described in the Pauline political theology.[65] Paul's Letter to the Romans reads:

> Let no debt remain outstanding, except the continuing debt to love one another, for whoever loves others has fulfilled the law. The commandments,

61 Alain Badiou, *Metapolitics*, trans. Jason Barker (New York: Verso, 2005), p. 141.

62 On the relationship between *agape* and law from a wide range of perspectives, see by Robert F. Cochran Jr. and Zachary R. Calo (eds.), *Agape, Justice, and Law: How Might Christian Love Shape Law?* (Cambridge: Cambridge University Press, 2017). For a culture and humanities perspective, see Wystan H. Auden, 'Law, Say the Gardeners Is the Sun', in *Collective Shorter Poems, 1927–1957* (London: Faber and Faber, 1969).

63 See e.g., Prov. 17:9, 17; 18:24; 19:7; 27:5–6. See also 1 John 4:8 'But anyone who does not love does not know God, for God is love' and 1 John 4:16 'We know how much God loves us, and we have put our trust in his love. God is love, and all who live in love live in God, and God lives in them.'

64 Matt. 22:39; Mark 12:30; Luke 10:25.

65 Schmitt considers Paul as an early representative of a healthy political realism and 'historical consciousness' within the Christian tradition. See Walter Rech, 'Eschatology and Existentialism: Carl Schmitt's Historical Understanding of International Law and Politics', in Matilda Arvidsson, Leila Brännström and Panu Minkkinen (eds.), *The Contemporary Relevance of Carl Schmitt: Law, Politics, Theology* (Abingdon, Oxon: Routledge, 2015), p. 154, citing Carl Schmitt 'Three Possibilities for a Christian Interpretation of History' (2009) 147 *Telos: Critical Theory of the Contemporary* 167–170, at 169.

> 'You shall not commit adultery', 'You shall not murder', 'You shall not steal', 'You shall not covet', and whatever other command there may be, are summed up in this one command: 'Love your neighbor as yourself.' Love does no harm to a neighbor. Therefore love is the fulfillment of the law.[66]

Agape, here, is the greatest of commandments or else the essence of the law (*nomos*)[67], while any other commandments are ways in which love can be put into practice. In Paul's account, *agape* is more than an internal concern or feeling. It becomes a duty that has to be externalized in order to be fulfilled. Taubes underscores the revolutionary potential of *agape* in the context of Pauline political theology, arguing that Paul side-lines *nomos* (the Jewish law) in favour of the Christian command of *agape*.[68] In a similar way, Singer considers *agape* to be 'the bond that establishes a fellowship between what is divine and what is human'.[69] According to her, *agape* (God's love of man) precedes and takes precedence over *nomos*, which represents a submissive form of love (to God's will).[70] Here an analogy with solidarity is visible: Christian *agape* is to love what solidarity is to law.

Love is also a key feature for Augustine (Saint Augustine of Hippo). In his writings, Augustine reveals the entanglement of love, the law and sin. More specifically, Augustine says that sin is 'acting contrary to the commandment of love'.[71] From John's 'God is love'[72], Augustine expands to 'God is love and love is God'.[73] Augustine's political theology is deeply concerned with love. Engaging with questions of coercion and domination grounded on self-love as opposed to justice grounded on common love/love of others, Augustine advocates for a social life preoccupied with loving service, seeking justice, and the dispensation of that justice to individuals and parties that have been wronged.[74] In this sense, Augustine's new society

66 Romans 13:8–10.

67 Jacob Taubes, *The Political Theology of Paul*, trans. Lana Hollander (Stanford: Stanford University Press, 2003).

68 Ibid., pp. 23–28.

69 Irving Singer, *The Nature of Love: Plato to Luther* (MIT Press Scholarship Online: August 2013), vol I, p. 269, doi.org/10.7551/mitpress/9780262512725.002.0012 (last accessed 8 September 2025).

70 Ibid.

71 Homilies on 1 John.

72 1 Jn. 4:8.

73 Homilies on the First Epistle of John. On this see e.g. Lewis Ayres, 'Augustine on God as Love and Love as God' (1996) 5 *Pro Ecclesia* 470.

74 Amongst his numerous written works, see *Confessions* (c. 400) and *The City of God* (c. 413–426). According to his commentators, the city of God should not be confused with Heaven. Instead, it is the city in which living persons exhibit the love of others, and, as such, it has roots in this world transiting into the next. The relations of love in this world prefigure the

is grounded on a sense of solidarity bound by a re-forming (Rom. 12:2) power of love.[75]

In early Christian teachings, *agape* embodies the elements of asymmetry, struggle and heterogeneity, while its revolutionary side is reflected in its appeal to an ever-expanding community that ultimately includes the entire human race.[76] The inclusion into the group of *agape*'s addressees of the concept of the enemy could be seen, in Schmittian terms, as indicating that *agape* has a genuinely political aspect (an expression of the agonistic relations between different social groups such as Jews, Jewish Christians, non-Jewish Christians, pagan Romans). This, however, has been seen as its weakness. Christian *agape* has been criticized for imposing an overly ambitious universal duty to love everyone, including one's enemies, which one is bound to fail to fulfil; *agape* as a promise of a payment of self-sacrificing de-nationalized friendship, impossible to discharge.[77]

City of Love to come, which Paul says is the true hope of Christians and the only hope for the world. See, inter alia, Ernest L. Fortin, 'Augustine's "City of God" and the Modern Historical Consciousness' (1979) 41 *The Review of Politics* 323; Lieven Boeve, Mathijs Lamberigts and Maarten Wisse, (eds.), *Augustine and Postmodern Thought: A New Alliance Against Modernity* (Leuven: Peeters, 2009); John M. Rist, *Augustine Deformed: Love, Sin and Freedom in the Western Moral Tradition* (Cambridge: Cambridge University Press, 2014); Gillian Clark, 'Caritas: Augustine on Love and Fellow Feeling', in Ruth R. Caston and Robert A. Kaster (eds.), *Hope, Joy, and Affection in the Classical World, Emotions of the Past* (New York, 2016; online edn, Oxford Academic, 23 June 2016) and Anthony Dupont, Bernard Bruning and Kristiaan Venken, 'The Relationship between Augustine's Anthropological Duality and His Doctrine of the Two Cities' (2023) 14 *Religions* 791.

75 On Augustinian solidarity as the result of a process of 're-formation' and as the antidote to empire, see John Cavadini, 'Ideology and Solidarity in Augustine's City of God', in James Wetzel (ed.), *Augustine's City of God: A Critical Guide* (Cambridge: Cambridge University Press, 2012).

76 Along the same lines, in recent Catholic social teaching, solidarity is seen not merely as a diffuse feeling of compassion but a firm and lasting commitment to the best for all and for the other. See John Paul II, 'On Social Concern. Sollecitudo Rei Socialis', in Gregory Baum and Robert Ellsberg (eds.), *The Logic of Solidarity: Commentaries on Pope John Paul II's Encyclical on Social Concern* (Maryknoll, NY: Orbis Books,1990). and John Paul II, *Sollicitudo Rei Socialis*, Encyclical given in Rome, at St. Peter's, on December 30, 1987. Pope John Paul II refers to Adam's recognition of Eve as 'bone of my bone and flesh of my flesh' (Gen. 2:18–21) to support his contention that 'solidarity helps us to see the "other" – whether a person, people or nation – not just as some kind of instrument' but as an equal partner sent by God to share in the 'banquet of life' and stewardship of God's creation. On this, see Meghan J. Clark, *The Vision of Catholic Social Thought: The Virtue of Solidarity and the Praxis of Human Rights* (Minneapolis, MN: Fortress Press, 2014). See also Chapter 1, by Mindus.

77 See Cornelius Castoriadis, *Ce qui fait la Grèce. 2, La cité et les lois: séminaires 1983–1984* (Paris: Éditions du Seuil, 2008).

More minimalist readings of *agape* are not uncommon amongst commentators. The parable of the Good Samaritan[78] has been seen as setting a standard of universal love towards needy people one encounters 'by chance'. Within this context, Christian love is primarily a response to immediate needs and specific situations: feeding the hungry, clothing the naked, caring for and healing the sick and so on. Along these lines, Sangiovanni has expressed scepticism for the concept of love in the Christian tradition – with focus on the Catholic teaching – which, charitably construed, is not grounded primarily in the shared experience of human suffering as a result of original sin, but 'in the injunction to universal love', as a means of 'alleviating suffering wherever it is found'.[79] Thus, on his reading, it is action '*on behalf of* another rather than *with* another' (emphasis in the original).[80]

In addition, there are instances in early Christian texts where kinship becomes key to describe the special bond among the faithful. The teaching of the Letter to the Galatians is emphatic: 'So then, as we have opportunity, let us do good to all, and especially to those who are of the household of faith'.[81] Here, the importance of supporting those within the family of believers is underscored. The quasi-theological Durkheimian notion of 'mechanical' solidarity[82] harks back to this homogeneity of a society of believers and rests on an idea of an undifferentiated whole to be distinguished from the outside. On the other hand, advocating for a supportive Christian community as a powerful testimony to the love of God does not have to be seen as antithetical to a broader vision of *agape*. Augustine states that, to love enemies is 'to love them in order that they may be at one with us, *that they also may love*'.[83]

78 Luke 10:25–37.

79 See Andrea Sangiovanni, 'Solidarity as Joint Action' (2015) 32 *Journal of Applied Philosophy* 340–359, at 350. Sangiovanni argues that 'it is no coincidence that in Christian texts, it is often very difficult to discern a distinction between the use of the term *solidarity* and *caritas*, often translated as love, compassion, or charity'.

80 Ibid.

81 Galatians 6:10. See also John 13:34–35, where the command to love one another as a defining characteristic of discipleship is emphasized.

82 Durkheim, *The Division of Labour*. See Chapter 11, by Schotel.

83 Ayres, 'Augustine on God as Love and Love as God', 480. According to Ayres, Augustine's interpretation of loving one's enemies is christological namely, seen through Christ's prays for the absolute forgiveness of the thieves crucified with him. For further analysis on forgiveness and sin, see Greg Jones, *Embodying Forgiveness: A Theological Analysis* (Grand Rapids, MI: Eerdmans, 1995).

This points to a process of active participation and a complex dynamic of mutuality,[84] while at the same time naming a goal experienced as an obligation for community members to realize.

According to Paul, the possibility of executing the command to love your neighbour arises from an awareness of the kairos (Rom. 13:11). Despite the controversy among commentators around the Pauline meaning of kairos[85] and the way it shapes an understanding of the messianic time, there are indications that Paul is not referring to a future event but rather focuses on the present moment as such, 'now'.[86] In his reading of Paul, Welborn suggests that

> the 'critical time' (kairos) of Romans 13:11 does not refer to a future Judgment Day in which Christians must prove themselves, but designates the 'time of the now,' in cognizance of which one can fulfill the commandment to love the neighbor.[87]

84 Ayres, 'Augustine on God as Love and Love as God', 481. Ayres' understanding of love is inspired by Rowan D. Williams, 'Sapientia and the Trinity: Reflections on the De trinitate', in Bernard Bruning, Mathijs Lamberigts and Jan Van Houtem (eds.), *Collectanea Augustiniana: Mélanges T. J. Van Bavel* (Leuven: Leuven University Press, 1990) [=Augustiniana 40–41 (1990–91)], vol. 1, pp. 317–332. See further, Max Pensky, *The Ends of Solidarity Discourse Theory in Ethics and Politics* (Albany: SUNY Press, 2008).

85 On this, see inter alios Fréderic Godet, *Commentary on St. Paul's Epistle to the Romans* (Grand Rapids, MI: Kregel, 1977); James D. G. Dunn, *Word Biblical Commentary 38b Romans 9–16* (Dallas: Word, 1988); Friedrich Blass and Albert Debrunner, *A Greek Grammar of the New Testament and Other Early Christian Literature*, trans. and rev. Robert W. Funk (Chicago: University of Chicago Press, 1961).

86 Kairos is qualified by the temporal adverb 'nun', which draws attention on the present moment as such, 'now'. See Walter Bauer, *A Greek–English Lexicon of the New Testament and Other Early Christian Literature*, 3rd ed, edited by Frederick William Danker (Chicago: University of Chicago Press, 2000), p. 681.

87 Larry L. Welborn, *Paul's Summons to Messianic Life Political Theology and the Coming Awakening* (New York: Columbia University Press, 2015), p. 13. Agamben is of the view that 'what interests the apostle is not the last day, not the instant in which time ends, but the time ... that remains between time and its end'. Giorgio Agamben, *The Time That Remains: A Commentary on the Letter to the Romans*, trans. Patricia Daley (Stanford: Stanford University Press, 2005) 62; See also the discussion in Ryan L. Hansen, 'Messianic or Apocalyptic? Engaging Agamben on Paul and Politics', in Douglas Harink (ed.), *Paul, Philosophy, and the Theopolitical Vision: Critical Engagements with Agamben, Badiou, Žižek, and Others* (Eugene, OR: Cascade Books, 2010), pp. 198–223. For a critique of Agamben's interpretation of kairos which 'never arrives', see Welborn, *Paul's Summons to Messianic Life*, pp. 15–17. Welborn contends that it is a 'paradoxical tension between an *already* and a *not yet* that defines Paul's conception of salvation' according to Agamben. Welborn highlights the difference between chronos (the law of time) and kairos. The latter 'arrests and suspends chronos' says Welborn, referring to (Rom. 3:21); (Rom. 3:26) and (Rom. 8:18): Welborn, *Paul's Summons to Messianic Life*, p. 16.

In other words, although the approaching judgement, the future heavenly kingdom and the period of waiting under the direction of the Spirit are central elements of messianism in the Pauline teaching and practice[88], there is also a duty to be realized in the present time, as a precursor or a presupposition of what is to come. With this in mind, the problem of solidarity in international law and human rights is that it is imagined in a future redemption moment (second coming, thought in popular terms as a future event) and not as a dimension of the present (the kairos *behind* the present chronos). In this process of discharging the duty to love, suffering has a particular function. It is part of divine providence; Jesus was sent in human form specifically in order to suffer death on behalf of mankind. Hebrews 2:5–18 explains why the Messiah, Jesus Christ, had to experience human suffering and temptation to become the 'Captain' of salvation (from Greek 'archēgon tēs sōtērias autōn'). As Jesus went to the Father through suffering and death, so the Way of Perfection is through suffering. In other words, *agape* as love and loyalty of God's loving kindness is displayed primarily in its ability to persevere through all sorts of obstacles and trials.[89] Augustine emphasizes the link between the form and purpose of God's love[90], stressing that 'God has loved us in order that we might love, and has offered himself as sacrifice'.[91] The legal analogon of Christ's suffering would be rights violations which have to occur so that the duty of solidarity can be triggered.

There is tension at play here that needs to be highlighted. *Agape* in early Christian theology has a powerful socio-political character and a radical potential guided by an intention to engage in an empathetic process of transformation, of 'becoming one' with the other. At the same time, this 'radicalism' at the heart of *agape* does create concern in that it may be seen as overpromising by imposing an obligation of universal scope which is bound to fail. To resolve this tension and to respond to the need for a realistic account of what can be achieved in the 'here and now', more minimalist approaches to understanding *agape* as brotherhood or as acts of charity and tolerance have been suggested. The risk, though, of reducing *agape* to sentiments of mercy and philanthropy, similar to solidarity, would be to distort the concept somewhat, stripping it from its political core.

88 Shailer Mathews, 'The Social Teaching of Paul. IV: The Messianism of Paul' (1902) 19 *The Biblical World* 370–377, at 372.

89 The ultimate expression of God's loyal love is expressed in Paul's teaching in Romans 8 'For Your sake we are killed all day long; We are accounted as sheep for the slaughter.' Romans 8:36.

90 Homily 7 on the First Epistle of John.

91 Ayres, 'Augustine on God as Love and Love as God', 483.

12.4 CAN SOLIDARITY ESCAPE INTERNATIONAL LAW'S DIVINE MESSIANISM?

A pertinent insight from the discussion on the notion of *agape* in early Christian theology concerns the questions *when* and *how* the duty to love is to be fulfilled. The call to love the other must be understood in relation to the notion of *kairos*, which lies at the heart of the Pauline eschatological orientation. While many conceive of *kairos* in Rom 13 to denote the future-oriented, in-between time, awaiting the return of Christ, a focus on the present time and its relationship to the past might be more fruitful. According to Paul, the experience of the messianic event of death and resurrection shapes the present moment in the life of believers and generates 'an awakening'. Holmes suggests that this awakening responds 'to a higher ethical purpose, an active struggle against hypnotizing forces, and a collective consciousness bound by love'.[92] I would argue that this purpose is better imagined as an active struggle against *aphasia*.[93] An understanding of the messianic as a mechanism of awakening and collective consciousness of the past instead of an eternal postponement to a totally unknown future time has implications on the function of international law and of solidarity within it. To put it simply, the potential of the 'now time' coupled with past awareness might have more to offer than the potential of the 'to come'.

Such an understanding is not far from Derrida's conception of the 'messianic'[94] – as opposed to messianisms – namely of a mode of thinking that 'historicizes time by disallowing any recourse to an ultimate extra-temporal instance',[95] and 'a structure of experience' of an opening to the future or of the

92 For more detail, see Christopher T. Holmes, 'Review of L. L. Welborn, *Paul's Summons to Messianic Life: Political Theology and the Coming Awakening*. Insurrections: Critical Studies in Religion, Politics, and Culture. Columbia University Press, 2013. P. 152. Pbk. $28.00. ISBN: 9780231171311' (2017) 39 *Horizons in Biblical Theology* 97–100, at 99.

93 I take my cue here from Debra Thompson who has used the term in relation to race to denote an unwillingness to confront how race operates in an imperial and neocolonial manner in today's society. In our case it is used to refer to an unwillingness to confront past injustices and how they persist/intrude upon the present. Thompson notes that, unlike amnesia 'which indicates some unfortunate series of events that led to an unintentional forgetting of how the modern world system was founded on, and continues as, a hierarchical racial order', aphasia indicates 'a calculated forgetting, an obstruction of discourse, language and speech'. See Debra Thompson, 'Through, against and beyond the Racial State: The Transnational Stratum of Race' (2013) 26 *Cambridge Review of International Law Affairs* 133–151, at 135. See also Tendayi Achiume, 'Racial Borders' (2022) 110 *Georgetown Law Journal* 445–508, at 447.

94 See Jacques Derrida, *Specters of Marx: The State of the Debt, the Work of Mourning and the New International*, trans. Peggy Kamuf (New York: Routledge, 1994), pp. 59, 167–168.

95 Andrea Cassatella, '"Normativity without Telos": The Messianic in the Thought of Jacques Derrida' (2012) 4 *Bamidbar: Journal of Jewish Thought and Philosophy* 24–43, at 37.

future as openness to 'the other'.[96] This understanding of the messianic inherited by Marx's legacy has been contemplated by several commentators, including Benjamin, Bloch and others.[97] Although an in-depth analysis of the various conceptions of 'messianic' goes beyond the scope of this chapter, it should be noted that a waiting for the future is not to be conceived as a paralysing passivity but rather as a sense of imminence and action that affirms the promise to a future.[98] This waiting is the Derridean messianic: a universal structure directly tied to a concern for justice.[99] A concern that is not infinitely deferred as part of a resolving eschatology. Rather, the messianic energizes the struggle for transformation,[100] urgently affirming that one is to act responsibly and to decide in the present time, as opposed to awaiting a future to be actualized.

To be sure, unlike Christianity, in Derrida's conception of the messianic, the messiah is never to come because if the messiah were to actually arrive, it would cease to have a messianic characteristic, the characteristic of the to come. And then justice would become 'calculable, related to a program, a

[96] Derrida, *Specters of Marx*, p. 168. See also Jacques Derrida, 'The Villanova Roundtable A Conversation with Jacques Derrida', in John D. Caputo (ed.), *Deconstruction in a Nutshell: A Conversation with Jacques Derrida* (New York: Fordham University Press, 2020), p. 22; John D. Caputo 'The Messianic: Waiting for the Future', in John D. Caputo (ed.), *Deconstruction in a Nutshell: A Conversation with Jacques Derrida* (New York: Fordham University Press, 2020), p. 162; P. Fitzpatrick, *Modernism and the Grounds of Law* (Cambridge: Cambridge University Press, 2001); Peter Fitzpatrick with Sundhya Pahuja, Richard Joyce, Kathleen Birrell and Ben Golder, 'A Training in Conduct', in Shane Chalmers and Sundhya Pahuja (eds.), *Routledge Handbook of International Law and the Humanities* (Abingdon: Routledge, 2021), p. 83; Joseph Nietlong, 'Derrida and the Structure of the 'Messianic' in the Specter of Marx' (2019) 12 *Predestinasi* 102.

[97] See, among others, the concept of the 'weak messianism' in Walter Benjamin's work including his 'Theses on the Concept of History' (1940). On this, see Roger K. Green, 'Benjamin, Method, and Weak Messianism' (2020) 19 *Journal for Cultural and Religious Theory* 413 and Alexander Gelley, *Benjamin's Passages: Dreaming, Awakening* (New York: Fordham University Press, 2014). See also Ernst Bloch, *Atheism in Christianity: The Religion of the Exodus and the Kingdom*, intr. Peter Thompson, trans. J. T. Swann (London: Verso, 2009); For a more comprehensive analysis, see Benjamin Steele-Fisher, 'Messianic Illusions: Taubes, Bloch, Benjamin and the Necessity of Interiority' (2021) 9 *Critical Research on Religion* 249; Sami Khatib, 'Derrida & Sons: Marx, Benjamin, and the Specter of the Messianic' (2013) *Anthropological Materialism*, available at https://anthropologicalmaterialism.hypotheses.org/1810 (last accessed 8 September 2025); and Tarik Kochi, 'Anticipation, Critique and the Problem of Intervention: Understanding the Messianic: Derrida through Ernst Bloch' (2002) 13 *Law and Critique* 29.

[98] Derrida, *Specters of Marx*, p. 211.

[99] Nietlong, 'Derrida and the Structure of the "Messianic"', 105.

[100] David Newheiser, 'Derrida and the Danger of Religion' (2018) 86 *Journal of the American Academy of Religion* 42–61, at 44.

law, and a foreseeable outcome'.[101] The key takeaway, however, is that the lack of a fully present messiah (like with the absence of Christ in Pauline's doctrine) is not an issue, but rather the very condition of a future and a catalyst to continue to hope and work towards the future.

To put it differently, there is a 'structurally conditioned mismatch' between the expectations created by the use of solidarity terminology and the reality of international law and human rights law in particular.[102] The heritage of solidarity as it plays out in Christianity creates the expectation for an everyday life supporting that realization of the essence of the law, namely *agape*. International law maintains the argument for 'emergence',[103] yet, within its structures, solidarity as the means for transformative action is eternally postponed to a future moment. Rather than encouraging the creation of permanent institutions that can support movements for social change which would pre-empt future crises, solidarity functions to sustain certain institutional ideals from radical adaptation.

Along the same lines, the distinction between believers and non-believers, inherent in religious thinking, manifests itself in contemporary international legal thought and in human rights vocabulary through binaries such as, nationals/non-nationals, migrants/refugees, economically active/non economically active EU citizens, civilized/un-civilized nations, developed/undeveloped, and so on, one side denoting the 'fulfilled' and the other the unfulfilled.

If *agape* in early Christian texts is understood as a means of working 'against the premises of the culture it was intended to transform'[104], then in today's highly competitive and monetized culture, it could be seen as inviting individuals to resist 'cost-benefit' solutions to social issues, as well as to resist divisions which mean to perpetuate unequal distribution of power and opportunity.

To go back to the discussion on solidarity and legal rights, advocating for a right to solidarity or for 'solidarity rights', such as the right to peace, to development and so on is not sufficient for solidarity's radical potential to emerge. In fact, when understood as a right, solidarity is confronted with all

[101] Elijah Prewitt-Davis, 'Liberating Deconstructions: The Messianic in James Cone and Jacques Derrida' (2013) 64 *Union Seminary Quarterly Review*, 101–107, at 107.

[102] Karageorgiou and Noll, 'What Is Wrong with Solidarity', 152.

[103] See Anne Orford, 'Human Rights after Faith – An Introduction to the "Cultures of Human Rights" Symposium' (2006) 7 *Melbourne Journal of International Law* 1.

[104] James Boyd White, 'Afterword: Agape and Reframing', in Robert F. Cochran Jr. and Zachary R. Calo (eds.), *Agape, Justice, and Law: How Might Christian Love Shape Law?* (Cambridge: Cambridge University Press, 2017), p. 316.

the structural limitations of international law referred to earlier, making it likely to legitimize oppression.[105] As Sparer puts it

> This contradictory relationship of legal rights to human freedom and community serves only to demonstrate that legal rights, by themselves, are insufficient for their announced purposes. It is the relationship of social movement and struggle to the use of legal rights which is determinative.[106]

The above considered, the messianicity implied in the narration and actualization of the principle of solidarity resembles more a divine messianism and less the messianic in Paul's theology or Derrida's political philosophy. Solidarity seems trapped in the impossibility of *agape*'s promise (universalism) and prone to the risk of its infinite postponement that is solidarity is to come when (and if) those in need will 'put their house in order', with no memory of how this house came to be in disorder in the first place (history) and no translation of what this entails (responsibility). This leads us to conclude that, if solidarity is conceptualized as futurity, the past of injustice is forgotten as irrelevant. If, on the other hand, solidarity is the now of the kairos, injustice becomes a lived experience, and no memory of the past is necessary.

12.5 SOLIDARITY AS THE DISCIPLINE OF LIVING TOGETHER?

Is an alternative thinking of solidarity in international law possible? What does it take for solidarity to become the vocabulary of the periphery against the centre, offering an offset for the overblown claims of human rights? What kind of economic or distributive considerations is solidarity expected to bring to the fore and which social, religious or other remedies is it supposed to promote? Could emancipating people as solidarity 'beneficiaries' – as opposed to right holders, potentially stress collective claims, shift the focus to the relationship among different groups and between groups and the state and enable cross-alliances, flexibility and sharing solutions?

Loizidou suggests that 'law is not imagined as the space where radical ideas and practices can be accommodated, but rather a space where the status quo is preserved'.[107] As discussed in Section 12.4, emphasizing solidarity not as a response to crisis but through the lens of *agape* in Paul's theology, namely as

[105] On this, see Paolo G. Carozza and Luigi Crema, 'On Solidarity in International Law' (2003) *Caritas in Veritate Foundation*, pp. 11–12, https://ssrn.com/abstract=294996.

[106] Sparer, 'Fundamental Human Rights', 514.

[107] Elena Loizidou, 'What Is Law?', in Carl Levy and Saul Newman (eds.), *The Anarchist Imagination: Anarchism Encounters the Humanities and the Social Sciences* (Abingdon: Routledge, 2019), p. 187. See also Peter Goodrich, *Languages of Law: From Logics of Memory to Nomadic Masks* (London: Weidenfeld and Nicolson, 1990).

struggle for transformation and antidote to aphasia, might allow for re-imagining the world order. A similar account can be traced in loving politics (politics as relationship)[108], which, like politics in Badiou's account,[109], refers to a space of collectivity.

Unger argues that 'solidarity does not differ in kind from love'; it is in fact the social (or collective) manifestation of love, where love is 'neither an act nor an emotion, but a gift of self, an opening up to another person ...'.[110] Drawing on this, Banakar claims that

> solidarity is a particular form of concern about, and understanding of, the other, where the other is not simply treated as the bearer of formal equal rights, or the object of respect, but as a person whose life, fate and ultimately welfare touches our own. Once solidarity is turned into legal rules and principles and implemented by legal authorities in a formal exercise of power, it becomes reified, thus losing its special love-like social quality, which transcends formal rights and entitlements.[111]

Following this line of thought, Cotterrell holds that 'there is a limit to the amount of progress in practical regulation that can be achieved by elaborating a concept of solidarity as a value in general terms'.[112] The point being that excessive formalism incapacitates solidarity.

The wise crafting of law is a crucial means of allowing solidarity in international law as the discipline of living together flourish. As Pahuja puts it, following Fitzpatrick's thought,[113]

> ... law, like love,[114] responds to the world, in both its fixity and change ... 'We must be vigilant against the tendency of law to declare itself just, of justice to declare itself Rights, and of community to become colony. Our

108 Vishwam J. Heckert, 'Loving Politics: On the Art of Living Together', in Carl Levy and Saul Newman (eds.), *The Anarchist Imagination: Anarchism Encounters the Humanities and the Social Sciences* (Abingdon: Routledge, 2019), p. 134. On the question of love, politics and truth, see Alain Badiou and Nicolas Truong, *In Praise of Love* (London: Profile Books Ltd, 2012).

109 See Badiou, *Metapolitics*, and Alain Badiou, *Being and Event*, trans. Oliver Fetham (New York: Continuum, 2005).

110 Roberto Mangabeira Unger, *Law in Modern Society* (New York: Free Press, 1976), p. 207.

111 Reza Banakar, 'Law, Love and Responsibility: A Note on Solidarity in EU Law', in Reza Banakar, Karl Dahlstrand and Lotti Ryberg Welander (eds.), *Festskrift till Håkan Hydén* (Lund: Juristförlaget, 2018).

112 Roger Cotterrell, *Sociological Jurisprudence* (London: Routledge, 2018), p. 220.

113 See Peter Fitzpatrick, 'Law Like Poetry: Burnt Norton' (2001) 23 *Liverpool Law Review: A Journal of Contemporary Legal and Social Policy* 285.

114 See Wystan H. Auden, 'Law Like Love', in David Kader and Michael Stanford (eds.), *Poetry of the Law: From Chaucer to the Present* (Iowa City: University of Iowa Press, 2010), pp. 108–109.

> duty is not to save the Other with (our) law, or (our) knowledge, but to meet lawfully with those who live by other laws'.[115]

Along the same vein, Lilla Watson, an aboriginal activist and artist, argues: 'if you have come here to help me, then you are wasting your time. But if you come up because your liberation is bound up with mine, then let us work together'.[116] Put simply, the focus of international law should be to train its objects towards solidarity as a mutual partnership in the pursuit of freedom as opposed to *ad hoc* charity.

From a critical political-theological perspective, if one subscribes to Horkheimer's claim that Marxism is nothing else than secularized Christianity, concerned with the liberation of the oppressed, the exploited, the marginalized, a solidary society is that grounded on a secularized duty of a de-nationalized, neighbourly love, whose promise – free from messianisms – relates precisely to a 'potentiality in the present'.[117]

12.6 SOLIDARITY AS A RADICALLY PRESENTIST PROMISE

Religious patterns of thought and practice remain operative within modern international law order. A testimony to that is the strategic role of solidarity in international legal discourse which, despite the absence of a theocratic authority, it oscillates between a programmatic secularism and a religious sociability. In this chapter, I have taken issue with the transcendental and oftentimes opportunistic reference to 'solidarity' by situating it within the broader discussions on international law's purpose and architecture. In the search for continuities and contingencies, I propose to put today's discussions on solidarity in international law in front of the mirror of early Christian theology. Solidarity belongs to a vocabulary rooted in the notion of 'love' as a post-theological strategy and in the idea that law, as an empirical matter is an expression of normative relations between interdependent individuals. Like religion itself, solidarity does have a social purpose, which imparts a dynamic enthusiasm capable of overriding reverses, yet it simultaneously reflects a vanity of attempting to provide immediate solutions to long standing structural problems.

[115] Fitzpatrick with Pahuja, Joyce, Birrell and Golder, 'A Training in Conduct', pp. 80, 82.

[116] Lilla Watson, 'Recognition of Indigenous Terms of Reference', Keynote Address at 'A Contribution to Change: Cooperation Out of Conflict Conference: Celebrating Difference, Embracing Equality', Hobart, Tasmania (21–24 September 2004).

[117] (Rom. 13:11–12) and Welborn, *Paul's Summons to Messianic Life*, p. 16.

To the question 'what is international law like with solidarity as one of its foundational components?', this chapter responds that, in the current structures, international law is directly or indirectly marked by a prevailing canonical model of solidarity, notably one tied to the state, territory and sovereignty. This model features linear time, in which solidarity's fulfilment lies in the future crystallizing aspects of Christian *agape* concerned with emergency help and philanthropy, that do not essentially address injustice but rather tend to perpetuate it.

Solidarity lives in an uneasy cohabitation with international law. Seen against the backdrop of a 'crisis', it seems to be normalizing a coercive system as well as to enhancing faith to institutions which have created asymmetry in the first place. Making solidarity a principle in international law has allowed the law to solidarity being infiltrated by the vocabulary of technocracy (or securitization), blending it smoothly with human rights. Its exercise through the means of modern law has brought solidarity farther from its nature, bringing it close to defining obligations and less to opening space for social movements and collective action to tackle structural injustices.

The chapter goes on to ask whether 'an alternative thinking of solidarity and of international law is at all possible?' Here the response is that, for international law to be organized around a conceptualization of solidarity as Christian love, means to rethink solidarity as the more radical aspects of *agape* and to embrace its messianic openness to something beyond immanent calculation as politically indispensable. As I have shown, early Christian theology offers an understanding of the salience of the present moment as an awakening that presses forward; that endures uncertainty for the sake of the future but builds on a past consciousness and decides responsibly. Responsibly, here, is to be imagined as taking different meanings depending on the circumstances. Precisely like the messianic in the Pauline doctrine, the messianic in the promise of solidarity could be seen as preserving the possibility of solidarity action that transcends any formal understanding of what solidarity is and how it can be operationalized.

It is, indeed, tempting to assume that concepts and values in international law have a single correct meaning and a particular function. However, this chapter emphasizes a legacy of Christian thought in international law that points to an imminent moment that cannot be envisioned in advance, similar with the circumstances under which solidarity is to be demanded and offered. Instead of considering this as a drawback and a barrier for solidarity to work in the present time, it can be embraced as the basis for an openness to the unknowable and for a flexibility of action. What is not disputed is that, this openness to the 'not yet' should be followed by an awareness of an 'already', that is of past experience with winners and losers and with persisting consequences in need of evaluation and re-evaluation.

Index

For EU product safety concerns, contact us at Calle de José Abascal, 56–1°,
28003 Madrid, Spain or eugpsr@cambridge.org.

www.ingramcontent.com/pod-product-compliance
Ingram Content Group UK Ltd.
Pitfield, Milton Keynes, MK11 3LW, UK
UKHW020839290926
15470UKWH00004B/1442

* 9 7 8 1 0 0 9 5 8 0 5 4 0 *